AFFORDABLE HOUSING AND PUBLIC POLICY

CHICAGO ASSEMBLY BOOKS

Creating Jobs, Creating Workers: Economic Development and Employment in Metropolitan Chicago (1990)

Paying for Health Care: Public Policy Choices for Illinois (1992)

Affordable Housing and Public Policy: Strategies for Metropolitan Chicago (1993)

Crime, Communities, and Public Policy (forthcoming)

The Chicago Assembly is a collaborative project of the Center for Urban Research and Policy Studies at the University of Chicago and the Metropolitan Planning Council of Chicago.

Affordable Housing and Public Policy

Strategies for Metropolitan Chicago

Edited by

Lawrence B. Joseph

A Chicago Assembly Book

Center for Urban Research and Policy Studies
The University of Chicago

Distributed by University of Illinois Press

ISBN 0-9626755-2-0 (paper)

Published by:

>   The University of Chicago
>   Center for Urban Research and Policy Studies
>   969 E. 60th Street
>   Chicago, IL 60637

Distributed by:

>   University of Illinois Press
>   54 E. Gregory Drive
>   Champaign, IL 61820

CONTENTS

LIST OF TABLES

PREFACE:
THE CHICAGO ASSEMBLY

The Chicago Assembly is designed to illuminate important public policy issues facing Chicago and the broader metropolitan region of northeastern Illinois. The project is a collaborative endeavor of the Center for Urban Research and Policy Studies at the University of Chicago and the Metropolitan Planning Council. The major objectives of the Chicago Assembly are to focus attention and stimulate informed discussion on critical policy issues in the Chicago region; to educate government officials, community and civic leadership, and the general citizenry regarding the factual background and the range of policy options in each issue area; to facilitate more effective communication among decision-makers from the public and private sectors, as well as from city, suburban, and statewide entities; and to raise the level and quality of public policy discourse in metropolitan Chicago on a continuing basis.

Each year the Chicago Assembly considers a public policy issue that has critical importance for the Chicago area, as well as broader national implications. In preparation for each annual assembly, the project commissions a set of background papers and commentaries written by leading public policy experts. The background material is distributed to participants in advance of the assembly itself, which includes prominent representatives from government, business, labor, civic groups, community-based organizations, relevant professional groups, and academia. The Chicago Assembly is a working, participatory enterprise, where regional leaders gather for an intensive two-day period to deliberate about fundamental issues *and* to reach some conclusions. Each Chicago Assembly produces a written report, containing findings and recommendations, that is endorsed by participants at a concluding plenary session. The final report is an integrated document reflecting major points of agreement and disagreement among participants. Shortly after the assembly, the report is released for general distribution throughout the Chicago metropolitan area. Subsequently, the Chicago Assembly publishes a book containing the background papers, commentaries, and final report. Finally, the project facilitates various follow-up activities that emerge from each assembly.

This book is a product of the third annual Chicago Assembly, "Affordable Housing in Metropolitan Chicago," which was held November 4-5, 1991, in St. Charles, Illinois. The assembly on housing was made possible by grants from the M. R. Bauer Foundation and the John D. and Catherine T. MacArthur Foundation. Continental Bank provided in-kind support for the reproduction of background papers and the Chicago Assembly Report, as well as funding for printing of this book.

Laurence E. Lynn, Jr.   Deborah C. Stone

Director, Center for Urban   Executive Director
   Research and Policy Studies   Metropolitan Planning Council
University of Chicago

ACKNOWLEDGMENTS

The Chicago Assembly is a joint endeavor of the Center for Urban Research and Policy Studies at the University of Chicago and the Metropolitan Planning Council. Susan Smith and Amy Keller of the University's School of Social Service Administration (SSA) served as project assistants for the Chicago Assembly during 1991 and 1992.

The Chicago Assembly Report on "Affordable Housing in Metropolitan Chicago" was developed with the help of a drafting committee consisting of discussion leaders, recorders, and other assembly participants: Eduardo Camacho, Pat Dowell-Cerasoli, Thomas Fuechtmann, Douglas Gills, Kathleen Gilmer, Elizabeth Hollander, Thomas Lenz, Jennifer Miller, Lynn Montei, Philip Nyden, Michael Roche, Paul Roldan, Don Samuelson, Barbara Shaw, Donna Smithey, Nikolas Theodore, Wim Wiewel, and Timothy Wright. Patrick Barry wrote the initial draft of the report.

Barbara Ray, managing editor of *Social Service Review*, once again did an outstanding job as copy editor for this volume. Michele Tully, a graduate student at SSA, assisted in the final preparation of tables for the introduction and several other chapters. Jeff Hall of University of Chicago Printing Services designed the cover.

L.J.

INTRODUCTION

Lawrence B. Joseph and Laurence E. Lynn, Jr.

Housing policy activism at the national level began in the 1930s, when the federal government became involved in regulation and support of the housing finance system through the establishment of the Federal Home Loan Bank (1932), the Federal Housing Administration (1934), and the Federal National Mortgage Association (1938). In addition, the U.S. Housing Act of 1937 initiated direct assistance for low-income households through the public housing program, with the federal government providing funds for capital costs and local housing authorities building and managing the projects. In the decades that followed, federal policies and programs included tax incentives and other financial support for homeownership, subsidies for the construction and rehabilitation of private rental housing, rent supplements for low-income households, operating subsidies for public housing projects, and fair housing legislation (Struyk, Turner, and Ueno, 1988, pp. 55-70; Weicher, 1980, pp. 31-52).

The Housing Act of 1949 declared a goal of "a decent home and suitable living environment for every American family," but progress toward that goal has been halting and haphazard. Federal housing assistance for lower-income individuals and families has never been established as an entitlement that is made available to all eligible households. For example, among more than 200,000 Illinois families receiving public assistance under AFDC (Aid to Families with Dependent Children), only about 20 percent live in subsidized housing (State of Illinois, 1991, p. 28).[1] There has never been a national consensus on the definition of housing needs, the public sector's role in producing and maintaining an

---

[1] By contrast, subsidies for homeowners through the federal income tax code operate much like an entitlement program. Anyone who owns a home is entitled to claim deductions for mortgage interest payments and property taxes (Keyes and DiPasquale, 1990, p. 5).

adequate housing stock, and when and how to provide housing assistance to individuals and families (Orlebeke, 1988, p. 2).

The federal government's role in housing policy expanded in the 1960s, when the Department of Housing and Urban Development (HUD) was established, and in the 1970s, with the legislative high point being the Housing and Community Development Act of 1974. During the 1980s, however, federal activism diminished considerably. The Reagan administration viewed most forms of direct federal intervention in the housing sector as wasteful and counterproductive. In fiscal year 1982 (the first Reagan budget year), budget authority for housing assistance administered by HUD was reduced from $26 billion to less than $15 billion, a 43 percent cut. New budget authority continued to decline throughout most of the 1980s, reaching a low point (under $8.6 billion) in 1988 (see Table 1).[2] In addition, the Reagan administration virtually eliminated support for new construction of subsidized private housing for low-income households, preferring instead to focus on "demand-side" approaches such as housing certificates and vouchers.[3]

State and local governments have not typically been leaders or innovators in housing policy. Both states and localities have served as funding conduits for various federal housing programs. The principal impact of local governments on housing has been through their traditional regulatory functions in areas such as land use, building construction, and housing occupancy. In many communities, these regulatory powers have resulted in higher housing costs and have been used to exclude lower-income households (Turner, 1989; Nenno, 1987; Nenno, Brophy, et al., 1982).

---

[2] Because of previous long-term funding commitments (which are typical for housing programs), annual federal outlays continued to rise. In addition, there was an anomalous increase in outlays for housing assistance in fiscal year 1985. This reflected a change in the method of financing public housing, which generated about $14 billion in one-time expenditures (U.S. House of Representatives, 1992, p. 1681).

[3] Under the Section 8 program, housing certificates make up the difference between "fair market rent" as established by HUD and 30 percent of the tenant's monthly adjusted income. Vouchers allow for more flexibility and can be used for housing with rents higher than the HUD guidelines, provided that the tenant pays the difference (U.S. House of Representatives, 1992, pp. 1674-1675).

TABLE 1:　Federal Budget Authority and Outlays for Housing Assistance
Administered by HUD, 1977-1991

Fiscal Year	Net Budget Authority ($ millions)	Outlays ($ millions)
1977	$28,579	$ 2,928
1978	32,169	3,592
1979	25,123	4,189
1980	27,435	5,364
1981	26,022	6,733
1982	14,766	7,846
1983	10,001	9,419
1984	11,425	11,000
1985	11,071	25,064
1986	10,032	12,179
1987	8,979	12,509
1988	8,592	13,684
1989	8,879	14,466
1990	10,557	15,690
1991	19,239	16,917

Source:　U.S. House of Representatives, Committee on Ways and Means,
Overview of Entitlement Programs: 1992 Green Book (Washington, D.C.: U.S.
Government Printing Office, 1992), pp. 1680-1681.

During the 1980s, some state and local governments responded to changing federal priorities by taking a more activist
stance on housing issues.　California, Connecticut, Maryland,
Massachusetts, and New Jersey were among the states that made
the strongest commitments in that direction.　Many of the new
state initiatives were small-scale variants of federal programs—for
example, assistance for first-time homebuyers and subsidized financing of rental housing for low- or moderate-income households
and for groups with special needs (e.g., the elderly, the disabled,
the homeless).　In addition, some states and localities adopted
regulatory approaches to the housing affordability problem—for
example, through "inclusionary zoning" schemes, which involve
incentives and mandates to promote the development of low- and

moderate-income housing. A handful of cities (e.g., Boston and San Francisco) also established "linkage" policies, which imposed fees on major commercial development projects in order to fund affordable housing programs (Turner, 1989; Stegman and Holden, 1987a, 1987b; Terner and Cook, 1990; Nenno, 1987). Finally, some cities made extensive use of Community Development Block Grant (CDBG) funds for housing activities, although this source of federal assistance was also cut back significantly. Between 1981 (the last fiscal year of the Carter administration) and 1989 (the last fiscal year of the Reagan administration), CDBG expenditures declined by 27 percent in nominal dollars and by 46 percent in inflation-adjusted dollars (Joseph, 1991, p. 30).

Community development corporations (CDCs) and other nonprofit organizations committed to the production of low-income housing also became more visible actors in the 1980s. Their efforts were limited, however, by changing federal priorities, including cutbacks in community development funds and other resources that could be used for operational support and capacity-building. In the face of shrinking federal subsidies, some private foundations (most notably the Ford Foundation) expanded their support for CDCs (Mayer, 1990, pp. 374-376; Ford Foundation, 1989, pp. 31-34). In a number of cities (including Chicago), community-based housing organizations became involved in public-private partnerships that included local government agencies, financial institutions, major corporations, and nonprofit intermediary organizations such as Local Initiatives Support Corporation (LISC). These partnerships were designed to mobilize public and private resources for the development of low-income housing without large, direct federal subsidies (Stegman and Holden, 1987a, pp. 97-139).

By the latter part of the 1980s, there was a growing perception of a crisis of housing affordability in the United States. Between 1975 and 1988, inflation-adjusted incomes of renter households nationwide declined by about 4 percent, while inflation-adjusted rent levels increased 17 percent. Moreover, the rate of homeownership declined in the 1980s after rising steadily for three decades (Turner and Reed, 1990, p. 2). The National Housing Task Force, a privately initiated and privately funded effort undertaken with the encouragement of congressional leaders, issued a report calling for a new housing policy agenda (National Housing Task Force, 1988; Keyes and DiPasquale, 1990). Some of the report's major recommendations were incorporated into the

National Affordable Housing Act of 1990, which marked a new wave of housing policy activism.

The first major federal housing legislation since 1974, the National Affordable Housing Act involved both a new infusion of funds and a reorientation of federal housing policy, with the roles of state and local governments, as well as community-based organizations, significantly enhanced. The cornerstone of the legislation was the HOME Investment Partnerships program, which established housing block grants for states and eligible localities. HOME funds can be used for a wide range of affordable housing efforts, including new construction, moderate or substantial rehabilitation, tenant-based rental assistance, and subsidies for first-time homebuyers and existing low-income homeowners. Participating jurisdictions must set aside at least 15 percent of their funds for nonprofit, community-based housing development organizations. In addition, each recipient of HOME funds is required to formulate a five-year Comprehensive Affordable Housing Strategy (CHAS), with annual updates, and to establish a process for citizen participation and input in formulating the CHAS (Zuckman, 1990).

According to HUD, the HOME program is intended to empower state and local governments to design affordable housing strategies to address local needs and housing conditions. The goals of HOME include both increasing the availability of affordable housing for low-income and very low-income households and building partnerships between state and local governments, on the one hand, and private and nonprofit organizations, on the other (U.S. Department of Housing and Urban Development, 1992, p. 3).[4] States and localities must identify and assess relevant housing needs, establish priorities for meeting those needs, and provide their own funds to match the federal grants.[5] The new federal housing agenda thus presents both new opportunities and new challenges for state and local governments—including the

---

[4] Under the HUD standards for determining eligibility for housing assistance, "low-income" is defined as 80 percent or less of the local-area median income (adjusted for household size), and "very low-income" is defined as 50 percent or less of the median.

[5] Matching requirements were waived for the first year of the HOME program (FY 1992). For FY 1993, the matching requirements were 30 percent for new construction and 25 percent for other uses of HOME funds.

State of Illinois, the City of Chicago, and other local governments
in the Chicago metropolitan area—in developing policy strategies
for affordable housing in the 1990s.[6]

SOCIAL, ECONOMIC, AND HOUSING TRENDS
IN METROPOLITAN CHICAGO

The Chicago metropolitan area, encompassing the six counties of
northeastern Illinois (Cook, DuPage, Kane, Lake, McHenry, and
Will), has nearly 7.3 million residents, or about 63 percent of the
state's population.[7] Over the past several decades, the city of
Chicago has experienced a declining share of the region's population—from 57 percent in 1960 to 38 percent in 1990. According
to the 1990 U.S. Census, Chicago's population had fallen to less
than 2.8 million. This represented a loss of about 221,000 (7.4%)
during the 1980s, which was somewhat smaller than the loss of
364,000 (10.8%) during the 1970s. By contrast, the five collar
counties gained a total of more than 300,000 residents in both the
1970s and 1980s (see Table 2).

The region's Black population, after increasing by about one-
third in 1960s and by 17 percent in the 1970s, remained relatively
stable during the 1980s. Black residents comprised 19 percent of
the metro area in 1990, about the same proportion as in 1980.
The White population declined from 70 percent in 1980 to about
65 percent in 1990, while region's Hispanic population increased
from 8 percent to more than 11 percent. In the city of Chicago,

---

[6] For a list of HOME fund allocations in metropolitan Chicago, see
Table 1 of Charles Orlebeke's chapter in this volume (Orlebeke, 1993).

[7] For the most part, this book will use the six-county definition of
the Chicago metro area, which is equivalent to the Chicago SMSA
(Standard Metropolitan Statistical Area) formerly used by the U.S. Bureau of the Census. The American Housing Survey has used an eight-
county definition of metropolitan Chicago, which includes two additional
Illinois counties (Grundy and Kendall). The 1990 U.S. Census uses two
distinct definitions of the metro area: The Chicago PMSA (Primary
Metropolitan Statistical Area) consists of Cook, DuPage, and McHenry
counties. The Chicago-Gary-Lake County CMSA (Consolidated Metropolitan Statistical Area) encompasses the eight Illinois counties plus parts
of northwest Indiana (Gary-Hammond PMSA) and southeast Wisconsin
(Kenosha PMSA).

TABLE 2: Population by County, Chicago Metropolitan Area, 1960-1990 (in 1,000s)

	1960	Pct. Distr.	1970	Pct. Distr.	1980	Pct. Distr.	1990	Pct. Distr.
Cook	5,130	82.5%	5,494	78.7%	5,254	74.0%	5,105	70.3%
Chicago	3,550	57.1	3,369	48.3	3,005	42.3	2,784	38.3
Suburbs	1,579	25.4	2,124	30.4	2,249	31.7	2,321	32.0
DuPage	313	5.0	490	7.0	659	9.3	782	10.8
Kane	208	3.3	251	3.6	278	3.9	317	4.4
Lake	294	4.7	383	5.5	440	6.2	516	7.1
McHenry	84	1.4	112	1.6	148	2.1	183	2.5
Will	192	3.1	248	3.6	324	4.6	357	4.9
Total	6,221	100.0	6,977	100.0	7,104	100.0	7,261	100.0

Sources: U.S. Bureau of the Census, *County and City Data Book*, 1962, 1972, and 1983 editions; Northeastern Illinois Planning Commission, based on data from the 1990 U.S. Census.

the Black population actually declined by 112,000 (a 9.5% loss), while increasing by more than 104,000 (a 46% increase) in the rest of the metro area. Nonetheless, the region remained highly segregated, with more than three-fourths (76%) of the Black population living in the city of Chicago (compared to 84% in 1980). In the Cook County suburbs, more than half of the Black population is concentrated in just eight municipalities. In DuPage County, the Black population nearly doubled between 1980 and 1990, but it was still less than 2 percent of the county total.[8]

Just as population in metropolitan Chicago has been shifting from the central city to the suburbs over the past several decades, so has employment. In 1972, the city of Chicago accounted for 56 percent of all private employment in the six-county region. Its share declined to 48 percent in 1979 and 39 percent in 1990.

[8] For more detailed data by county, see Table 2 of Doris Holleb's chapter in this volume (Holleb, 1993).

During the recessionary 1979-83 period, when Chicago was losing more than 100,000 jobs, employment actually expanded in some other parts of the region—in northwestern Cook County, DuPage County, and Lake County. Between 1983 (a low point) and 1990 (a high point), private sector employment showed a net gain of only 7 percent in the city of Chicago while increasing 29 percent in suburban Cook and more than 60 percent in the five collar counties. The areas of highest employment growth (e.g., DuPage County, northwest suburban Cook County) have typically been areas that remain largely inaccessible to the region's racial minorities (see Table 3).

TABLE 3:   Private Employment by County, Chicago Metropolitan Area, 1972-1990 (in 1000s)

	1972	Pct. Distr.	1979	Pct. Distr.	1983	Pct. Distr.	1990	Pct. Distr.
Cook	2,044	84.7%	2,097	81.0%	1,944	79.4%	2,247	73.4%
Chicago	1,347	55.8	1,246	48.2	1,124	45.9	1,201	39.3
Suburbs	668	27.7	818	31.6	789	32.2	1,015	33.2
North	124	5.2	152	5.9	152	6.2	187	6.1
Northwest	158	6.6	238	9.2	248	10.1	380	12.4
West	142	5.9	148	5.7	131	5.4	140	4.6
Southwest	154	6.4	162	6.3	149	6.1	164	5.3
South	89	3.7	118	4.6	109	4.4	144	4.7
DuPage	117	4.9	184	7.1	215	8.8	380	12.4
Kane	78	3.3	95	3.7	87	3.6	120	3.9
Lake	91	3.8	112	4.3	114	4.7	184	6.0
McHenry	27	1.1	34	1.3	34	1.4	53	1.7
Will	54	2.2	66	2.5	56	2.3	75	2.5
Metro Area	2,413	100.0	2,588	100.0	2,450	100.0	3,060	100.0

Note: Totals for Cook County include unclassified areas not identified with any specific sub-area.

Source: Illinois Department of Employment Security, *Where Workers Work: Chicago Metropolitan Area, 1990.* A Summary of Employment Covered under the Illinois Unemployment Insurance Act (Chicago: Illinois Department of Employment Security, 1990).

TABLE 4: Changes in Median Household Income by County, Chicago
Metropolitan Area, 1979-1989

	In nominal dollars			In constant (1982-84) dollars		
	1979	1989	Pct. Chg.	1979	1989	Pct. Chg.
Cook	$19,187	$32,673	70.3%	$25,928	$26,349	1.6%
Chicago	15,301	26,301	71.9	20,677	21,210	2.6
Suburbs	24,542	41,128	67.6	33,165	33,168	0.0
DuPage	27,509	48,876	77.7	37,174	39,416	6.0
Kane	22,102	40,080	81.3	29,868	32,323	8.2
Lake	25,210	46,047	82.7	34,068	37,135	9.0
McHenry	23,473	43,471	85.2	31,720	35,057	10.5
Will	23,329	41,195	76.6	31,526	33,222	5.4
Metro area	20,728	36,327	75.3	28,011	29,296	4.6

Source: Northeastern Illinois Planning Commission, based on data from the
U.S. Census, 1980 and 1990.

Another critical economic trend of the 1980s involved the incomes of Chicago-area households. Median household income for the metro area as a whole increased 75 percent during the decade, but in inflation-adjusted dollars, the gain was less than 5 percent. Real income growth was actually smaller in the Cook County suburbs than in the city of Chicago, while each of the collar counties showed gains of 5 to 10 percent (see Table 4).[9] Even more striking are the figures for the eighteen municipalities in the region that are eligible for CDBG funds. Median household income in eight of these communities declined in real dollars between 1979 and 1989. Only two gained more than 10 percent (see Table 5).

[9] Inflation adjustments in the Tables 4-6 are based on the U.S. Department of Labor's revised Consumer Price Index for all urban consumers (CPI-U-X-1), which uses a rental equivalence measure of homeowner costs (U.S. Bureau of the Census, 1992a, pp. A1-B2).

TABLE 5:   Changes in Median Household Income for CDBG-Eligible
Municipalities in Metropolitan Chicago, 1979-1989

	In nominal dollars			In constant (1982-84) dollars		
	1979	1989	Pct. Chg.	1979	1989	Pct. Chg.
Arlington Heights	$30,205	$51,331	69.9%	$40,818	$41,396	1.4%
Aurora	20,193	35,039	73.5	27,288	28,257	3.6
Berwyn	17,992	31,326	74.1	24,314	25,263	3.9
Chicago	15,301	26,301	71.9	20,677	21,210	2.6
Chicago Heights	18,585	27,551	48.2	25,115	22,219	-11.5
Cicero	16,730	27,170	62.4	22,608	21,911	-3.1
Des Plaines	25,470	42,176	65.6	34,419	34,013	-1.2
Elgin	19,747	35,554	80.0	26,685	28,673	7.4
Evanston	21,715	41,115	89.3	29,345	33,157	13.0
Joliet	18,966	30,967	63.3	25,630	24,973	-2.6
Mount Prospect	27,093	46,508	71.7	36,612	37,506	2.4
Naperville	34,147	60,979	78.6	46,145	49,177	6.6
North Chicago	15,853	25,500	60.9	21,423	20,565	-4.0
Oak Lawn	24,202	38,665	59.8	32,705	31,181	-4.7
Oak Park	20,601	40,453	96.4	27,839	32,623	17.2
Schaumburg	26,273	47,029	79.0	35,504	37,927	6.8
Skokie	27,402	42,276	54.3	37,030	34,094	-7.9
Waukegan	19,091	31,315	64.0	25,799	25,254	-2.1

Source: Northeastern Illinois Planning Commission, based on data from the
U.S. Census, 1980 and 1990.

In addition, the economic gap between the poorest and wealthiest communities in the metropolitan area grew markedly during
the 1980s (see Table 6).   The ten wealthiest municipalities (as
measured by household income in 1989) all showed substantial increases in inflation-adjusted median household income from 1979
to 1989.   Some registered real income gains of 40 percent or
more.   All of these communities are overwhelming White.   By
contrast, in all but one of the ten poorest municipalities (the
exception being Chicago), inflation-adjusted median household

TABLE 6: Changes in Median Household Income for Wealthiest and Poorest Municipalities (over 1,000 population) in Chicago Metropolitan Area

	In nominal dollars			In constant (1982-84) dollars		
	1979	1989	Pct. Chg.	1979	1989	Pct. Chg.
Riverwoods	$50,000	$125,074	150.1%	$67,568	$100,866	49.3%
Kenilworth	64,150	123,705	92.8	86,689	99,762	15.1
South Barrington	50,165	122,487	144.2	67,791	98,780	45.7
Winnetka	48,872	118,456	142.4	66,043	95,529	44.6
Inverness	52,277	113,799	117.7	70,645	91,773	29.9
Glencoe	51,354	112,321	118.7	69,397	90,581	30.5
Oak Brook	55,667	110,331	98.2	75,226	88,977	18.3
Long Grove	46,713	107,596	130.3	63,126	86,771	37.5
Kildeer	52,126	105,060	101.6	70,441	84,726	20.3
Barrington Hills	51,019	104,002	103.8	68,945	83,873	21.7
Summit	18,007	27,126	50.6	24,334	21,876	-10.1
Chicago	15,301	26,301	71.9	20,677	21,210	2.6
North Chicago	15,853	25,500	60.9	21,423	20,565	-4.0
Merrionette Park	17,222	25,128	45.9	23,273	20,265	-12.9
Hodgkins	15,810	23,802	50.6	21,365	19,195	-10.2
Harvey	18,033	23,201	28.7	24,369	18,710	-23.2
Phoenix	13,445	21,853	62.5	18,169	17,623	-3.0
Dixmoor	15,893	20,357	28.1	21,477	16,417	23.6
Robbins	14,826	17,194	16.0	20,035	13,866	-30.8
Ford Heights	10,727	14,032	30.8	14,496	11,316	-21.9

Source: Northeastern Illinois Planning Commission, based on data from the U.S. Census, 1980 and 1990.

income declined—in several cases, by 20 percent or more. Most of these less affluent communities have substantial numbers of Black residents, and five of them have Black majorities.[10]

---

[10] The only ones without substantial Black populations are Merrionette Park (96% White) and Hodgkins (69% White, 30% Hispanic).

TABLE 7:   Changes in Monthly Housing Costs by County, Chicago
Metropolitan Area, 1980-1990

	Gross Rent			Selected Owner Costs (With Mortgage)		
	Median 1980	Median 1990	Pct. Chg.	Median 1980	Median 1990	Pct. Chg.
Cook	$246	$478	94.3%	$415	$840	102.4%
Chicago	231	445	92.6	371	734	97.8
Suburbs	300	557	85.7	442	887	100.7
DuPage	322	625	94.1	529	1,067	101.7
Kane	275	508	84.7	456	876	92.1
Lake	285	558	95.8	537	1,067	98.7
McHenry	289	537	85.8	478	935	95.6
Will	259	453	74.9	445	831	86.7
Metro area	255	493	93.3	444	897	102.0

Note: Gross rent includes contract rent, utilities, and fuel.   Selected owner
costs include mortgage payments, property taxes, insurance, utilities, and fuel.

Source: Northeastern Illinois Planning Commission, based on data from the
U.S. Census, 1980 and 1990.

In a period when median household incomes, especially in
less affluent communities, were lagging, housing costs in metropolitan Chicago were spiraling upward. During the 1980s, rising housing costs for both owners and renters typically outpaced
increases in both household incomes and the overall cost of living.
Between 1980 and 1990, median gross rent for the metro area increased 93 percent in nominal dollars, while median monthly costs
for homeowners with mortgages more than doubled (see Table 7).[11]   As noted earlier, over roughly the same period (1979-

---

[11] Gross rent includes contract rent, utilities, and fuel.   Monthly
owner costs include mortgage payments, property taxes, insurance, utilities, and fuel.

1989), median household income in the region increased only 75 percent. Similarly, in nearly all of the region's CDBG-eligible municipalities, increases in median housing costs outstripped gains in median household income (see Table 8).[12]

According to HUD guidelines, a household faces an excessive cost burden if its gross housing costs exceed 30 percent of its gross income. In 1980, 29 percent of Chicago-area renters had a gross rent burden of *35 percent* or more. In 1990, nearly a third of the region's renters (more than 300,000 households) had a similar cost burden. In the city of Chicago, 36 percent of renter households had a cost burden of 35 percent or more in 1990 (see Table 9). The growing housing cost burden has been heaviest for low-income households. In 1990, more than 80 percent of the region's poor renters (those with household incomes under $10,000) had housing costs that consumed 35 percent or more of their incomes. A majority of renters in the next income bracket ($10,000-19,999) had a similar cost burden (see Table 10).

Among the poorest of the poor, the problem of housing affordability can turn into homelessness. The extent of homelessness is inherently difficult to measure, although it does seem clear that the problem became dramatically worse during the 1980s. National estimates have varied widely, ranging from 300,000 in a HUD study to 3 million claimed by some advocacy groups (Ford Foundation, 1989, p. 19). In a 1990 report, the Illinois Coalition for the Homeless estimated that there were 60,000 to 80,000 homeless persons in the state over the course of a year. During the year ending June 30, 1990, the Chicago Department of Human Services counted nearly 22,000 homeless individuals in shelters funded by the City. More than half were members of families, and more than a third were under the age of sixteen (State of Illinois, 1991, pp. 24-27). The causes of homelessness are complex. For some individuals and families, homelessness is a straightforward housing affordability issue. Others are forced onto the streets by intolerable home situations (e.g., domestic violence). For the chronic homeless, financial difficulties are often intertwined with substance abuse or mental illness (Keyes, 1990, pp. 405-406).

---

[12] There were three exceptions. In Evanston and Oak Park, both relatively affluent communities, household income kept up with gross rent, although not with owner costs. In North Chicago, a relatively poor community, median household income lagged behind inflation and rising renter costs but still managed to keep ahead of owner costs.

TABLE 8:   Changes in Monthly Housing Costs for CDBG-Eligible
Municipalities in Metropolitan Chicago, 1980-1990

	Gross Rent			Selected Owner Costs (With Mortgage)		
	Median 1980	Median 1990	Pct. Chg.	Median 1980	Median 1990	Pct. Chg.
Arlington Heights	$347	$711	104.9%	$507	$1,050	107.1%
Aurora	261	499	91.2	414	772	86.5
Berwyn	235	448	90.6	375	785	109.3
Chicago	230	445	93.5	371	734	97.8
Chicago Heights	239	402	68.2	372	643	72.8
Cicero	222	415	86.9	356	732	105.6
Des Plaines	312	577	84.9	403	837	107.7
Elgin	268	501	86.9	444	862	94.1
Evanston	336	636	89.3	572	1,203	110.3
Joliet	225	403	79.1	400	667	66.8
Mount Prospect	338	615	82.0	459	930	102.6
Naperville	334	698	109.0	655	1,356	107.0
North Chicago	238	485	103.8	428	668	56.1
Oak Lawn	306	534	74.5	396	796	101.0
Oak Park	274	535	95.3	462	1,039	124.9
Schaumburg	370	739	99.7	505	947	87.5
Skokie	343	645	88.0	475	963	102.7
Waukegan	260	490	88.5	412	747	81.3

Note: Gross rent includes contract rent, utilities, and fuel.   Selected owner
costs include mortgage payments, property taxes, insurance, utilities, and fuel.

Sources: U.S. Bureau of the Census, *1980 Census of Housing: Volume 2, Metropolitan Housing Characteristics—Chicago, Ill., Standard Metropolitan Statistical Area* (Washington, D.C.: U.S. Government Printing Office, 1983);
U.S. Bureau of the Census, *1990 Census of Population and Housing: Summary
Social, Economic, and Housing Characteristics—Illinois* (Washington, D.C.:
U.S. Government Printing Office, 1992); Northeastern Illinois Planning Commission.

TABLE 9: Households with Cost Burden of 35% or More of Household
Income (in previous year), Chicago Metropolitan Area, 1980-1990

Renters:

	1980		1990	
	Households	Pct.	Households	Pct.
Cook	258,309	30.1%	271,644	33.8%
Chicago	203,954	32.1	206,046	35.8
Suburbs	54,355	24.6	65,598	28.7
DuPage	11,467	20.9	17,325	24.9
Kane	6,779	23.7	8,505	27.5
Lake	8,156	24.2	11,991	29.2
McHenry	2,350	26.8	3,111	27.2
Will	5,725	23.9	6,728	27.3
Metro area	292,786	29.1	319,304	32.5

Homeowners with Mortgage:

	1980		1990	
	Households	Pct.	Households	Pct.
Cook	72,625	10.7%	94,669	12.6%
Chicago	29,275	12.6	37,752	15.5
Suburbs	43,350	9.8	56,917	11.3
DuPage	13,990	10.0	23,269	12.8
Kane	5,976	10.9	7,294	11.1
Lake	11,125	13.1	15,525	13.8
McHenry	4,078	12.3	5,656	12.7
Will	6,479	9.9	9,454	11.8
Metro area	114,273	10.8	155,867	12.6

Note: Renter costs include contract rent, utilities, and fuel. Owner costs include mortgage payments, property taxes, insurance, utilities, and fuel.

Source: Northeastern Illinois Planning Commission, based on data from the U.S. Census, 1980 and 1990.

TABLE 10:   Renter Housing Costs as Percentage of Household Income, Chicago Metropolitan Area

Gross Rent (1990) as Pct. of Household Income (1989)
(Number of Households)

Household Income	0-19%	20-24%	25-29%	30-34%	35%+	Total
< $10,000	9,175	7,913	11,954	10,955	175,215	215,212
$10,000-19,999	12,503	16,483	29,073	34,126	112,487	204,672
$20,000-34,999	79,044	79,879	60,335	32,053	28,931	280,242
$35,000-49,999	108,076	31,332	11,734	4,383	2,581	158,106
$50,000+	109,348	10,007	2,658	1,244	90	123,347
Total	318,146	145,614	115,754	82,761	319,304	981,579

Gross Rent (1990) as Pct. of Household Income (1989)
(Percentage Distribution)

Household Income	0-19%	20-24%	25-29%	30-34%	35%+	Total
< $10,000	4.3%	3.7%	5.6%	5.1%	81.4%	100.0%
$10,000-19,999	6.1	8.1	14.2	16.7	55.0	100.0
$20,000-34,999	28.2	28.5	21.5	11.4	10.3	100.0
$35,000-49,999	68.4	19.8	7.4	2.8	1.6	100.0
$50,000+	88.7	8.1	2.2	1.0	0.1	100.0
Total	32.4	14.8	11.8	8.4	32.5	100.0

Note: Gross rent includes contract rent, utilities, and fuel.

Source: Northeastern Illinois Planning Commission, based on data from the U.S. Census, 1990.

POLICY STRATEGIES FOR METROPOLITAN CHICAGO

The chapters in this book address different aspects of the crisis of housing affordability, the implications of the National Affordable Housing Act of 1990, and the roles of state and local governments, community-based organizations, and other nongovernmental actors in policy strategies for affordable housing. In the lead chapter, Doris Holleb presents a broad overview of housing trends in metropolitan Chicago during the 1980s. She documents rising costs for both renters and homeowners and examines contrasts in the housing stock and neighborhood conditions in both the city of Chicago and the suburbs. Looking at the demand side of the affordable housing problem, she highlights lagging income growth, growing economic disparities, and increases in the number and proportion of persons living in poverty, especially in inner-city neighborhoods. The chapter concludes with specific policy recommendations for the City of Chicago, the region's suburban municipalities, the State of Illinois, and the federal government.

Charles Orlebeke's chapter outlines the evolution of federal housing policies from the 1930s to the present. Orlebeke contends that the instability of the federal government's role in housing is related to the complexity of housing policy objectives and the diverse constituencies attempting to influence housing policy. Federal housing programs have often had multiple objectives beyond the provision of shelter—for example, economic growth, income redistribution, encouragement of homeownership, and community development. At the same time, housing policies have been shaped by broader debates over fiscal policy and intergovernmental relations. Orlebeke concludes with a discussion of the National Affordable Housing Act of 1990, the most recent "synthesis" of federal housing policy, and its implications for the Chicago area.

Thomas Lenz and Barbara Shaw examine state and local housing policy initiatives in Illinois. They identify several critical policy issues affecting affordable housing development in Chicago and elsewhere in the state: the lack of top-level planning and coordination of housing policies, programs, and resources; the failure of both the State of Illinois and the City of Chicago to provide adequate funding to address the scope of the housing affordability problem; and the programmatic shift away from targeting the very poor and toward serving households on the high end of the low- and moderate-income spectrum. Lenz and Shaw conclude with a discussion of trends that are likely to shape affordable housing policies in Chicago and Illinois in the 1990s.

Community-based housing initiatives in Chicago are the focus of the chapter by Teresa Córdova, who contends that the community approach to affordable housing is based on a philosophy of neighborhood empowerment. She describes national lobbying efforts that resulted in the Community Reinvestment Act and Neighborhood Housing Services; the importance of technical assistance, cost-cutting measures, and grants for start-up costs; creative financing through public-private partnerships; innovative management and ownership structures; and the significance of ongoing advocacy efforts by community-based organizations. Córdova concludes by criticizing an economic system that does not provide enough affordable housing and by endorsing the notion of "decommodification" of housing based on values of social ownership, public financing, and equitable resource allocation.

Alexander Polikoff offers a critical examination of public housing in Chicago—in particular, high-rise projects that house large concentrations of poor, Black families. He shows how the development of huge public housing high-rises in the 1950s and 1960s contributed to the creation of Chicago's "second ghetto." Several decades later, these projects continue to exacerbate the problems of the urban underclass. Public housing high-rises are now deteriorating, and Polikoff argues that instead of rebuilding or modernizing these structures, we should seize the opportunity to dismantle them, provided there is an effective, adequately funded plan for replacement housing. This strategy would require both a new attitude toward demolition of existing public housing projects and more flexibility in regard to the form of replacement housing, which should include scattered-site public housing as well as rent subsidy programs that enable former high-rise residents to move to private housing in non-ghetto communities.

James Rosenbaum's chapter focuses on the Gautreaux program, which was the result of an anti-discrimination lawsuit brought against the Chicago Housing Authority and HUD. The Gautreaux program provides housing vouchers to former public housing residents, enabling them to move either to middle-income, White suburbs or to neighborhoods within the city. Rosenbaum summarizes a series of studies comparing suburban movers with city movers in terms of social integration and employment of adults, education of their children, and employment experiences of youth. The findings suggest that residential integration can indeed reduce the education and employment gaps between low-income Blacks and middle-income Whites. Rosenbaum contends that the experience of the Gautreax program supports the basic premises of housing voucher strategies: that the poor are willing to move to middle-income communities that offer better opportunities and that the poor will gain economic and educational benefits from such moves.

The problem of homelessness in Chicago is the subject of Charles Hoch's chapter. Hoch argues that the housing affordability squeeze affecting the poor has been intensified by a number of political and economic changes, including erosion in the real value of public aid benefits, diminishing employment opportunities, and the dwindling supply of low-rent housing, especially SRO (single-room-occupancy) hotels. He contends that public initiatives to help the homeless, which have emphasized emergency shelter and services, promote stigma and social isolation. In addition, these well-intentioned efforts are based on a misleading "mobility model" that places unrealistic expectations on the individual poor and offers false hopes for obtaining permanent housing. Hoch believes that the homeless would benefit most from redistributive policies—for example, raising welfare benefits and expanding subsidized housing. Among the available "remedial" (as opposed to redistributive) options, shelter programs are the least desirable. Instead, there should be more emphasis on eviction-prevention measures and on support for various forms of shared housing.

The final two chapters offer perspectives on affordable housing outside the state of Illinois. Rachel Bratt presents a wide-ranging discussion of nonprofit housing development in Boston. She summarizes the national record of nonprofit housing development, surveys the unusually broad array of state and local programs to support the development of affordable housing in Boston, and identifies critical resource needs and organizational dilemmas of nonprofit housing developers. Bratt see two major challenges for the future of nonprofits: their capacity to maintain and manage housing projects over the long run and their ability to go beyond housing production and contribute to neighborhood revitalization by providing other social benefits for their communities. The Boston experience offers lessons regarding what a city and state can accomplish by working together and how the public sector can best support nonprofit housing initiatives. At the same time, the Boston case illustrates the limits of state and local support systems, as well as the complexity of nonprofit housing development using current tools and programs.

Roland Anglin's chapter examines fair housing policies in New Jersey. The *Mount Laurel* decisions of the New Jersey Supreme Court overturned exclusionary zoning policies that restricted the development of low- and moderate-income housing in the growing suburbs. The state's Fair Housing Act was designed to respond to the court's intervention (and to avoid further litigation) by determining municipal "fair shares" in the distribution of obligations to provide affordable housing. Anglin argues that a complex set of political forces substantially diluted the intent of the original court decision, which was to increase the residential mobility of low-income, urban households. One distinctive component of the New Jersey Fair Housing Act is the provision for "regional contribution agreements" (RCAs), under which some suburban municipalities can meet part of their affordable housing obligations by paying for housing development in other communities (usually cities). Anglin contends that RCAs, if reconstituted, could serve as an indirect tax on exclusion by class and race, with the revenue earmarked to fund low-income housing in central cities. Such a policy would also, however, entail explicit abandonment of the goal of residential desegregation.

Each chapter is accompanied by one or more critical commentaries. These short essays—by John Weicher, Phillip Clay, Robert Katz, George Tolley, Douglas Gills, Richard Taub, Deborah Stone, Paul Fischer, Susan Grossman, Kristin Faust, and William Peterman—provide some additional perspectives on affordable housing issues from both policy analysts and policy advocates.

Earlier versions of the essays in this book were originally prepared for the third annual Chicago Assembly, "Affordable Housing in Metropolitan Chicago," held in November 1991. Participants included more than 90 state and regional leaders from the public sector, the business community, labor unions, community and civic organizations, advocacy groups, private foundations, and universities. The essays are preceded by the Chicago Assembly Report on affordable housing, which calls for a broad, multi-tiered, regional housing strategy. Major priorities identified by participants include a concerted effort to rebuild the housing stock of older, deteriorating neighborhoods, especially in the city of Chicago; the creation of more affordable housing in high-growth suburban areas that are accessible to jobs; and confronting the problem of homelessness, the most extreme consequence of the problem of housing affordability. Movement toward a regional housing agenda should involve linking housing opportunities with employment opportunities and other social resources, eliciting stronger leadership from state and local governments, fostering regional cooperation and coordination on housing issues, and building a broad-based constituency for affordable housing in metropolitan Chicago.

REFERENCES

Ford Foundation (1989). *Affordable Housing: The Years Ahead.* New York: Ford Foundation.

Holleb, Doris B. (1993). "Disparities and Opportunities in Chicago-Area Housing." In this volume.

Illinois Department of Employment Security (1990). *Where Workers Work: Chicago Metropolitan Area, 1990.* A Summary of Employment Covered under the Illinois Unemployment Insurance Act. Chicago: Illinois Department of Employment Security.

Joseph, Lawrence B. (1991). *Fiscal Federalism in Metropolitan Chicago: Federal and State Aid to Local Governments in the 1980s.* Prepared for the Regional Revenue and Spending Project, sponsored by the Chicago Regional Partnership. Chicago: Center for Urban Research and Policy Studies, University of Chicago.

Keyes, Langley C. (1990). "Housing and the Homeless." In Denise DiPasquale and Langley C. Keyes, eds., *Building Foundations: Housing and Federal Policy.* Philadelphia: University of Pennsylvania Press.

Keyes, Langley C., and Denise DiPasquale (1990). "Housing Policy for the 1990s." In Denise DiPasquale and Langley C. Keyes, eds., *Building Foundations: Housing and Federal Policy.* Philadelphia: University of Pennsylvania Press.

Mayer, Neil S. (1990). "The Role of Nonprofits in Renewed Federal Housing Efforts." In Denise DiPasquale and Langley C. Keyes, eds., *Building Foundations: Housing and Federal Policy.* Philadelphia: University of Pennsylvania Press.

National Housing Task Force (1988). *A Decent Place to Live.* Washington, D.C.: National Housing Task Force, March 1988.

Nenno, Mary K. (1987). "States Respond to Changing Housing Needs," *Journal of State Government*, vol. 60, no. 3 (May/June 1987), pp. 122-127.

Nenno, Mary K., Paul C. Brophy, et al. (1982). *Housing and Local Government.* Washington, D.C.: International City Management Association.

Orlebeke, Charles J. (1988). "Housing in the Chicago Region." In *State of the Region: Background Papers.* Sponsored by the Regional Partnership. Chicago: Metropolitan Planning Council.

_____ (1993). "Federal Housing Policies." In this volume.

State of Illinois (1991). *Comprehensive Housing Affordability Strategy (CHAS), FY 1992 - FY 1996.* Chicago: Illinois Housing Development Authority.

Stegman, Michael A., and J. David Holden (1987a). *Nonfederal Housing Programs: How States and Localities Are Responding to Federal Cutbacks in Low-Income Housing.* Washington, D.C.: Urban Land Institute.

_____ (1987b). "States, Localities Respond to Federal Housing Cutbacks," *Journal of State Government,* vol. 60, no. 3 (May/June 1987), pp. 110-116.

Struyk, Raymond J., Margery A. Turner, and Makiko Ueno (1988). *Future U.S. Housing Policy: Meeting the Demographic Challenge.* Washington, D.C.: Urban Institute Press.

Terner, Ian Donald, and Thomas B. Cook (1990). "New Directions for Federal Housing Policy: The Role of the States." In Denise DiPasquale and Langley C. Keyes, eds., *Building Foundations: Housing and Federal Policy.* Philadelphia: University of Pennsylvania Press.

Turner, Margaret Austin, with Veronica M. Reed (1989). *The State Role in U.S. Housing Policy: Recent Trends and Challenges for the Future.* Washington, D.C.: The Urban Institute.

Turner, Margaret Austin, and Veronica M. Reed (1990). *Housing America: Learning from the Past, Planning for the Future.* Washington, D.C.: The Urban Institute.

U.S. Bureau of the Census (1983). *1980 Census of Housing: Volume 2, Metropolitan Housing Characteristics—Chicago, Ill., Standard Metropolitan Statistical Area.* Washington, D.C.: U.S. Government Printing Office.

_____ (1992a). *Money Income of Households, Families, and Persons in the United States: 1991.* Current Population Reports, Series P-60, No. 180. Washington, D.C.: U.S. Government Printing Office.

_____ (1992b). *1990 Census of Population and Housing: Summary Social, Economic, and Housing Characteristics—Illinois.* Washington, D.C.: U.S. Government Printing Office.

U.S. Department of Housing and Urban Development (1992). *The HOME Program—HOME Investment Partnerships: Program Guide.* Washington, D.C.: U.S. Department of Housing and Urban Development, Office of Community Planning and Development.

U.S. House of Representatives, Committee on Ways and Means (1992). *Overview of Entitlement Programs: 1992 Green Book.* Washington, D.C.: U.S. Government Printing Office.

Weicher, John C. (1980). *Housing: Federal Policies and Programs.* Washington, D.C.: American Enterprise Institute.

Zuckman, Jill (1990). "Housing Authorizations," *Congressional Quarterly*, December 8, 1990, pp. 4091-4104.

AFFORDABLE HOUSING IN METROPOLITAN CHICAGO

Report of the Chicago Assembly

The Chicago Assembly on "Affordable Housing in Metropolitan Chicago," which was held November 4-5, 1991, was attended by more than 90 regional leaders. Participants included representatives from state and local governments, the business community, labor unions, community-based organizations, civic organizations, advocacy groups, private foundations, and universities. Chicago Assembly participants engaged in two days of intensive discussion and deliberation about the crisis of housing affordability, the implications of the National Affordable Housing Act of 1990, and the roles of state and local governments, community-based organizations, and the private business sector in developing affordable housing strategies for metropolitan Chicago. Affordable housing has long been considered a strictly urban problem, but in the past decade, it has graduated to a suburban and regional concern. While the greatest need remains in the city of Chicago, there has been a growing realization in the region's suburbs and smaller cities that more affordable housing is needed in those communities as well. This shift in perception—that affordable housing is a *regional* problem—creates opportunities for new constituencies, alliances, and resources that can benefit the entire metropolitan area.

BACKGROUND

The critical importance of housing stems not only from the fact that shelter is a basic human need, but also from the recognition that housing is closely linked with access to other key social resources, such as schools and jobs. Over the past fifteen years, affordability has become the major housing problem in the United States; large sectors of the population cannot afford to rent a decent apartment, buy a new home, or maintain an existing home. Housing costs for low-income households have risen faster than for any other group, while their real incomes have declined. Between 1974 and 1985, median rents nationwide increased 11 percent in inflation-adjusted dollars; for the poor, the increase was 30 percent. In the early 1970s, poor families spent an average of about 30 percent of their incomes on housing; this cost burden had increased to 58 percent by 1985 (Ford Foundation, 1989, pp. 12-13). The spiraling inflation of the 1970s and the severe recession of the early 1980s also created housing affordability problems for the middle class. The average after-tax cash burden for first-time homebuyers was 23 percent in 1970 and 45 percent in 1982. By 1988, this housing cost burden had declined to 33 percent, but it was still far above the levels of the 1960s and early 1970s (Apgar, 1990, pp. 42-43).

Housing Trends in Metropolitan Chicago

Data from the U.S. Census indicate that the total housing stock in the six-county Chicago metropolitan area increased 6 percent (about 157,000 units) from 1980 to 1990. Changes were not uniform across the region, however. There was especially strong growth in DuPage County (25%), Lake County (22%), and McHenry County (25%), while the number of housing units in the city of Chicago *declined* 3.5 percent, including a net loss of more than 66,000 occupied rental units—a 10 percent loss (Holleb, 1993).[1]

Housing costs for the region's homeowners and renters grew substantially during the 1980s. Median home values increased 64 percent in Cook County, 75 percent in DuPage County, and 86 percent in Lake County, while the consumer price index for metropolitan Chicago increased only 60 percent. Housing costs for renter households grew even more. Median contract rents increased 99 percent in Cook County, 93 percent in DuPage, 89 percent in Kane, 96 percent in Lake, 94 percent in McHenry, and 78 percent in Will (Holleb, 1993). Over roughly the same time period (1979-1987), per capita income in the metropolitan area as a whole barely kept pace with inflation. In real, inflation-adjusted dollars, per capita money income actually declined in the city of Chicago (by 0.4%), in suburban Cook County (by 1.2%),

---

[1] The six-county Chicago metropolitan area encompasses Cook, DuPage, Kane, Lake, McHenry, and Will counties.

in Kane County (by 1.2%), and in Will County (by 5.6%) (Joseph and Lynn, 1990, p. 7).

There is a stark contrast in metropolitan Chicago between the expanding private housing market for the relatively affluent and the lack of decent, affordable housing for low- and moderate-income families and individuals. The poor, in particular, have been hardest hit by the region's changing housing market. In 1987, 87 percent of poor renter households in the eight-county Chicago metropolitan area spent 30 percent or more of their income for housing (including rent and utilities), while more than two-thirds of poor renter households had a housing cost burden of at least 50 percent. Similarly, 86 percent of poor homeowners spent 30 percent or more of their income on housing, and 61 percent spent 50 percent or more (Sheft, 1991, pp. 2-4).[2]

The Chicago metropolitan area is also characterized by widespread racial disparities and segregated housing patterns. According to the 1990 census, the population of the six-county metropolitan area is 19.4 percent Black and 11.5 percent Latino. But relatively few minorities live in those areas that have been experiencing the greatest employment growth—for example, northwest suburban Cook County (1.3% Black, 5.3% Latino) and Du-Page County (1.9% Black, 4.4% Latino) (see Leadership Council, 1991). Minority households are also much more likely to be facing serious housing affordability problems. In 1987, 29 percent of White households, 49 percent of Black households, and 47 percent of Latino households in metropolitan Chicago spent 30 percent or more of their income on housing (Sheft, 1991, p. 47).

Current Housing Programs and Policies

The federal government has been involved in housing policy in numerous ways over the past five decades. Major federal programs and policies have included:

- funds for the construction and operation of public housing by local housing authorities;

---

[2] The eight-county metropolitan area also includes Grundy and Kendall counties, as well as Cook, DuPage, Kane, Lake, McHenry, and Will.

- mortgage insurance and mortgage interest subsidy programs for homebuyers;
- direct loans and mortgage interest subsidies for private and nonprofit developers of rental housing;
- tax credits for investors in low-income housing;
- rental assistance and voucher programs for low-income households;
- subsidies for homeowners (at all income levels) through income tax policies that allow deductions for mortgage interest payments and real estate taxes.[3]

During the 1980s, there were major changes in federal housing programs that resulted in significant reductions in funding for new subsidized housing units. There were also changes in federal tax law that greatly reduced private incentives for developing low- and moderate-income housing.[4]

In response to changing federal policies and the growing problem of housing affordability, states, localities, and not-for-profit organizations have become increasingly involved in housing issues. Most state programs have represented variations on the traditional federal approach of subsidized financing, either in the development of multi-family housing for low- and moderate-income households or in support of first-time homebuyers. Examples of recent state and local housing initiatives in the Chicago region include the following:

- The Illinois Affordable Housing Trust Fund (1989), administered by the Illinois Housing Development Authority, uses revenue from the state real estate transfer tax to provide low-interest loans and grants to develop housing for low-income and very low-income households.
- The Cook County Tax Reactivation Program (1983), a co-operative effort between the City of Chicago and Cook

---

[3] For a more detailed discussion, see Orlebeke, 1993.

[4] The federal government's definition of a low-income household is one whose income is 80 percent or less of the median for a given area (with adjustments for family size). A subset of low-income households is very low-income households, whose incomes are no greater than 50 percent of the median. Moderate-income households range from 81 to 95 percent of the median, while middle-income households range from 96 to 120 percent of the median.

County, transfers tax-delinquent multi-family residential properties to developers who agree to rehabilitate the properties for low- and moderate-income families.
• The Chicago Low-Income Housing Trust Fund (1989) provides operating and rental assistance to housing for very low-income individuals and families.
• New Homes for Chicago (1990), a program initiated by the Chicago Department of Housing, offers city-owned land and other subsidies to developers of single-family homes for low- and moderate-income first-time homebuyers.[5]

Key non-governmental actors in Chicago's affordable housing arena have included community development corporations, advocacy groups such as the Chicago Rehab Network and the State-wide Housing Action Coalition, and intermediary organizations such as Local Initiatives Support Corporation (LISC), the Chicago Equity Fund (CEF), Community Investment Corporation, and Neighborhood Housing Services. Local public-private partnerships have also helped fill the void in federal housing leadership. A prime example of this approach is the Chicago Housing Partnership, which brings together representatives from city and state government, financial institutions, CEF, LISC, community organizations, and private developers. The partnership has served as a coordinating, planning, and problem-solving vehicle for affordable housing efforts in Chicago (see Lenz and Shaw, 1993; Córdova, 1993).

A new set of federal initiatives has been instituted in the National Affordable Housing Act of 1990, which broadens the roles of state and local governments, as well as community-based organizations, in housing policies and programs. The HOME Investment Partnerships program offers federal block grants to states and localities and requires them to provide matching funds.[6] At least 15 percent of HOME funds must be used for housing to be developed, sponsored, or owned by community housing develop-

---

[5] For a more detailed discussion, see Lenz and Shaw, 1993.

[6] The original matching requirements—25 percent for rental assistance and moderate rehabilitation, 33 percent for substantial rehabilitation, and 50 percent for new construction—were waived for the first year of the HOME program (FY 1992). For FY 1993, the matching requirements were 30 percent for new construction and 25 percent for all other uses of HOME funds.

ment organizations.   In addition, each jurisdiction receiving
HOME funds must formulate a five-year comprehensive housing
affordability strategy (CHAS), to be approved by the Department
of Housing and Urban Development (HUD) and to be updated on
an annual basis.

Other major provisions of the National Affordable Housing
Act include the following:

• The National Homeownership Trust is designed to help
first-time homebuyers through interest-rate subsidies and
down-payment assistance.

• Homeownership and Opportunity for People Everywhere
(HOPE) programs involve efforts to help public housing residents to buy public housing (HOPE I), help tenants of multi-
family buildings owned or subsidized by HUD to buy the
buildings in which they live (HOPE II), and help low-income
families to buy single-family homes (HOPE III).

• Under certain HUD programs of the 1960s and 1970s—Section 221(d)(3) and Section 236—owners of private, subsidized
rental housing were allowed to convert the units to market-
rate housing when their contracts expired or by prepaying
their mortgages. The National Affordable Housing Act contains provisions to encourage the preservation of these units
for low- and moderate-income households.

• The National Affordable Housing Act encompasses a number of programs involving housing and supportive services for
populations with special needs, including the elderly, people
with disabilities, the homeless, and persons with acquired
immune deficiency syndrome (AIDS).[7]

Policy Challenges for Metropolitan Chicago

The problem of affordable housing is broad and complex. The
most critical housing problems are those of the region's low-
income population, including the working poor, families on public
assistance, elderly persons living on fixed incomes, and people
who are homeless or at risk of becoming homeless. For many
households, one consequence of the housing affordability squeeze

[7] For a more detailed discussion, see Orlebeke, 1993; Zuckman,
1990, pp. 4091-4104.

has been severe overcrowding. In some cases, this involves large families living in small apartments; in other cases, it involves several different families sharing inadequate living space. The housing affordability problem is not confined to low-income households, however. Growing numbers of moderate-income and middle-income households are paying larger and larger shares of their incomes in order to have a place to live.

The National Affordable Housing Act offers new resources and opportunities for state and local governments, not-for-profit agencies, and other key actors in the regional housing arena. It also presents challenges—formulating housing affordability strategies and setting priorities for spending new federal funds. Difficult decisions must be made regarding which population groups are in greatest need, what types of housing stock should be developed, where to target resources geographically, and how to coordinate policies and programs throughout the region.

MAJOR PRIORITIES

Chicago Assembly participants endorse the objective, stated in the federal Housing Act of 1949 and affirmed in the National Affordable Housing Act of 1990, of "a decent home and a suitable living environment for every American family." The pursuit of this goal in metropolitan Chicago requires a broad, coordinated, multi-tiered approach. High priorities for a regional housing strategy should include rebuilding older low-income communities in both the city of Chicago and some suburbs, creating more affordable housing in high-growth suburban areas, and eliminating the problem of homelessness.

Rebuilding Older Low-Income Communities

A concerted effort must be made to rebuild the housing stock of older, deteriorating neighborhoods in the city of Chicago, as well as in some suburban areas. These communities have suffered from disinvestment and segregration and from the subsequent loss of services and amenities. A wide range of housing types should be included in the rebuilding effort, depending on the community's needs. Expansion of the supply of affordable housing should be complemented by job-creation efforts, better social services, and improved education and job training, as well as better coordination of all these programs. Affordable housing is but one key element for community revitalization throughout the region.

Affordable Housing in High-Growth Suburban Areas

A crucial step in developing a regional housing strategy is the creation of more affordable housing in the suburbs, especially in areas that have been experiencing population and employment growth. Affordable housing in high-growth suburban areas is needed on several different levels: rental housing for entry-level and lower-wage workers; owner-occupied housing for moderate-income families buying their first homes; and affordable housing to meet the growing needs of current suburban residents, including young adults seeking entry-level housing in their home communities, divorced or widowed households, and elderly residents who want to remain in the communities in which they have lived, worked, and raised their families.

Eliminating Homelessness

The most extreme consequence of the problem of housing afford-ability has been the increasingly visible population of homeless persons, especially in urban areas. It is inherently difficult to obtain accurate estimates of the homeless population. The 1990 U.S. Census recorded 6,800 homeless persons in Chicago, while the Chicago Department of Human Services received more than 28,000 requests for emergency shelter during that same year (City of Chicago, 1991, p. 6). The Chicago Coalition for the Homeless estimates that the city had more than 50,000 persons who were homeless at one time or another during 1990. While there have been some efforts by the federal government, local governments, and nonprofit agencies to increase the availability of emergency shelters and related services, there must be much more attention paid to the long-term housing needs of homeless individuals and families (see Hoch, 1993).

KEY ISSUES AND RECOMMENDATIONS

Community Building

Providing affordable housing is much more than the production of shelter; it is also a community-building process. Affordable housing is a key to stable, viable communities, and the maintenance of viable communities is central to the development of human resources. Housing policies must respond to local needs and desires while also fitting into a larger set of regional objectives. By rebuilding social and economic structures in addition to the housing stock, the areas will become more desirable, more people will stay or move in, and community life can be revitalized. As communities are energized, opportunities for human resource development are enhanced.

For many communities in both the city of Chicago and some suburban areas, the most appropriate affordable housing strategy can be termed "preservation plus." Such a strategy would begin with the priority of identifying and preserving the existing stock of affordable housing. When appropriate, additional elements can be added to this initial emphasis on preservation. In some cases, housing preservation efforts can be complemented by rehabilitation, which is often preferable to demolition of old buildings, and by new construction, which can help provide diversity within a community and improve its image.

Promoting social and economic diversity: Housing policies and programs should help balance a community when possible. Racial, ethnic, and economic diversity can be fostered in a number of different ways—for example, by building scattered-site, low-income housing in middle-class and upper-middle-class areas. Homeownership programs can be used to provide step-up housing for residents of low-income neighborhoods and to attract and retain middle-income families. There should also be efforts to preserve diversity in communities that are currently racially and economically integrated.

Including residents in planning and implementation: Successful housing strategies will require the cooperation and involvement of local citizens, whether the issue is gentrification, low-income housing, or neighborhood revitalization. Involving community residents in planning and implementation makes good political sense. Likewise, tenant participation and empowerment can be crucial elements in strengthening communities.

Community-based organizations: Community-based organizations such as community development corporations (CDCs) have played significant roles in rebuilding urban communities and bridging the gaps between the supply of affordable housing and the demand. The efforts of these organizations have included facilitating community-based planning, maintaining accountability of private and public players in the community development process, and advocacy of resources for balancing central-business-district development with the need to maintain viable neighborhoods. More resources are needed for CDCs—from both the public and private sectors. Linkages between private housing developers and CDCs should be encouraged in an effort to create effective partnerships that result in both additional affordable housing development and strengthening the technical capacity of CDCs. In addition, both established and fledgling community-based organizations can learn from the experiences of those CDCs and private-sector entities that have been most successful in the development of affordable housing.

Training and technical assistance: There is significant support among Chicago Assembly participants for the development and promotion of training and technical assistance programs that enhance the capabilities of those involved in affordable housing activities. Beneficiaries of such programs could include community organizations (both in the city of Chicago and elsewhere in the metropolitan area), emerging private-sector owners and managers, people involved in resident management or cooperative ownership arrangements, and smaller municipalities that are receiving federal HOME grants. Some of these training and technical assistance efforts could be implemented through professional organizations and through curriculum development in both community colleges and four-year colleges.

Fair Housing Opportunities

All housing policies should strive to break down barriers and expand housing choices. Racial barriers in particular still exist on a large scale in much of the Chicago metropolitan area. The continued existence of segregated housing patterns is a major contributor to the affordability problem because it limits choices for thousands of families and because it creates pressure in integrated areas to resegregate. Current fair housing laws and human rights ordinances are not uniformly observed or enforced, and some government policies reinforce existing patterns of segregation and discrimination.

More effective enforcement: Chicago Assembly participants recommend more effective enforcement of fair housing laws throughout the region, as well as an aggressive policy of affirmative marketing for both housing industries and government programs. There should also be more aggressive use of fines and monetary penalties against real estate agents who engage in racial steering, as well as effective enforcement of existing laws that prohibit racial discrimination in mortgage lending practices.

Fair housing centers: An important role is played by fair housing centers, which help to train real estate agents, conduct affirmative marketing campaigns, and perform spot-testing for housing discrimination. There are currently only six such agencies in the six-county Chicago metropolitan area. Many suburbs, as well as large tracts of the city of Chicago, remain essentially closed to Blacks, Latinos, and other disadvantaged minorities. Families with children often face additional discriminatory barriers. Expansion of fair housing programs should emphasize choice for residents and should be sensitive to the desires of those residents who do not want to move to other areas.

Other approaches to removing barriers: Various Chicago Assembly participants suggested other ideas regarding fair housing:

- expanded use of housing vouchers;
- incentives to encourage municipalities to embrace diversity and discourage them from remaining segregated;
- making affirmative marketing a requirement for all housing with any public subsidy of any kind;
- policies designed to preserve communities that are currently racially and economically integrated;
- a stronger, proactive state role in fair housing enforcement.

*The "Supply Side": Preserving and Expanding
the Stock of Affordable Housing*

Supply-side approaches to the affordability problem in the private
housing market may involve subsidies for the development of low-
and moderate-income housing, as well as policies designed to preserve the existing stock of both subsidized and non-subsidized
housing. These approaches include loan subsidies, tax incentives,
and various methods for reducing the costs of housing construction
and rehabilitation.

Low-Income Housing Tax Credit: The Low-Income Housing
Tax Credit (LIHTC) is currently the major federal tool enabling
the corporate sector and the community-based sector to produce
and deliver housing that is affordable for low- and moderate-income families. The LIHTC legislation was scheduled to expire
at the end of 1991 but was extended through June 1992. Any in-
terruption in the flow of LIHTCs will have a devastating impact
on the provision of affordable housing. Chicago Assembly participants strongly support permanent extension of the Low-Income
Housing Tax Credit legislation.[8]

Streamlined financing: There is a need to streamline financing procedures for the development of affordable housing. Multi-
layer financing packages, invented out of necessity, have become
ever more elaborate and cumbersome. Many packages require
five or more different sets of papers, lawyers, and government
sign-offs. Finding ways to consolidate and expedite financing
procedures would speed up the process and reduce transaction
costs.

Preservation of existing HUD-subsidized buildings: The National Affordable Housing Act of 1990 contains provisions to
encourage the preservation of Section 221(d)(3) and Section 236
subsidized housing units for low- and moderate-income households. HUD is required to provide current owners with incentives
to continue renting to low-income tenants or to provide fair-market
value to owners who sell the properties to others who are committed to keeping the units affordable to low-income households.

---

[8] *Editor's note:* The LIHTC expired in June 1992 and had not been
renewed as of early 1993.

There should be a systematic effort to publicize and promote the immediate potential for extending the life of Section 221(d)(3) and Section 236 apartment projects in both the city of Chicago and the suburbs.

Regulatory reforms: Many Chicago Assembly participants argue for closer examination of zoning restrictions and other exclusionary aspects of the local public approval process. In many municipalities, affordable housing is impeded by mandates for large lot sizes, prohibitions against multi-family development and townhouse construction, and excessive infrastructure requirements.

There is also concern that building codes are often unnecessarily complex and require "more house" than needed (although some believe that building codes have a relatively minor impact compared to zoning and land-use regulations). Some participants contend that use of modular components, factory-built housing, plastic pipe, and flexible wiring can help reduce housing costs. Others advocate consideration of a uniform, clear, basic building code, such as the model code developed by the Building Officials and Code Administrators International (BOCA).

The role of unions: Most housing construction that receives federal funding must comply with the Davis-Bacon Act, which requires workers to be paid locally prevailing union wage rates, thereby increasing housing costs. Some Chicago Assembly participants note the importance of unions in assuring good wages, skills training, and worker safety, while others express concern that construction jobs and apprenticeship programs have not been accessible to racial minorities and women. Some participants urge cooperative efforts between affordable housing activists and construction trade unions in developing programs to expand the stock of affordable housing, provide jobs for both current construction trade members and young community residents who need jobs and training, and extend to minority communities entrance into the skilled, mainstream, union labor market.

Other supply-side ideas: Various Chicago Assembly participants suggested other ideas regarding the supply-side aspects of the affordable housing problem:

   • reinstating federal project-based rent subsidies, which have provided important financial support in the past for the development of affordable housing;

- providing rehabilitation financing for troubled suburban apartment projects that could add to the stock of affordable housing, thereby converting community problems into assets;
- expanding Cook County's Class 9 property tax incentives for the rehabilitation of multi-family housing;
- reducing the assessment level for those Cook County Class 3 properties (mostly multi-family structures with seven or more dwelling units) that provide affordable housing.

The "Demand Side": Targeting Households

Demand-side approaches are based on the premise that the key to the problem of housing affordability is inadequate household income. Demand-side subsidies are typically tied to individuals and households rather than to housing projects or housing units. Many Chicago Assembly participants maintain that the most efficient way to generate affordable housing is to increase the purchasing power of residents. This allows the market to respond to individual preferences and, if used within a fair-housing environment, can help promote economic and racial diversity.

Economic and human resource development: There is broad agreement that the strongest way to boost the ability of residents to afford housing is to build up the region's base of well-paying jobs. This is a long-term proposition that will require meshing housing policy with economic development, education, and job training efforts. Some participants also maintain that a resolution of the current housing crisis must pursue the goal of moving more households above the poverty level. This goal can be pursued through community-building efforts as well as through coordinated linkages of economic development, education, and vocational skills training with employment opportunities available in the metropolitan area.

Rent subsidies: Many Chicago Assembly participants strongly endorse the expansion of rent subsidy programs such as Section 8 rent certificates and housing vouchers, which allow people to seek apartments throughout the metropolitan area. Supporters of voucher programs emphasize the importance of giving people more options in seeking housing; they contend that vouchers can be viewed as a human resource investment. Studies of former Chicago Housing Authority residents who use vouchers as part of the *Gautreaux* desegregation decree found that, with appropriate counseling and support, people chose to locate in communities throughout the region. The new environments often had more demanding and effective schools for children and better job opportunities for parents (Rosenbaum, 1993).

Other Chicago Assembly participants, however, are very skeptical about the long-term value of vouchers for low-income households and question whether scarce resources should be used for such an approach. They contend that higher priority should be given to revitalizing existing communities and strengthening community support structures than to dispersing individuals and households to different areas. Another objection is that the widespread use of vouchers, in the absence of an expanded housing stock, can result in higher rents in certain communities, thereby exacerbating the housing affordability problem. Finally, there is concern about equitable distribution of vouchers among communities and groups in the Chicago area.

Homeownership: Mortgage insurance programs, mortgage revenue bonds, and other subsidies for first-time homebuyers provide essential assistance for low- and moderate-income families seeking homeownership. In addition, access to homeownership can be enhanced by encouraging community and financial institution partnerships that reduce barriers to obtaining financing for homeownership.

Federal income tax deductions for mortgage interest payments, though crucial to most homebuyers, also represent a large government subsidy to the upper class and to others who own two or more homes. Some Chicago Assembly participants suggested ideas for creating a more equitable deduction and possibly raising funds for other housing programs. These ideas include eliminating the deduction for second homes, capping deductions above a certain level (e.g., $150,000), and replacing all deductions with a flat-rate tax credit.

The National Affordable Housing Act includes several new homeownership initiatives (HOPE programs) for low-income people—including public housing residents (HOPE I), tenants of multi-family buildings owned or subsidized by HUD (HOPE II), and low-income households seeking to buy single-family homes (HOPE III). While some Chicago Assembly participants are especially supportive of the idea of tenant ownership, there is also considerable skepticism about the HOPE programs. Many believe that HOPE I and II, in particular, are badly conceived and that homeownership for low-income families is not viable if they lack the resources for debt service and for both routine and major maintenance.

Reverse mortgages: Some participants suggest consideration of "reverse mortgage" (or home equity conversion) programs that allow senior citizens and others who are "house-rich but income-poor" to remain in their homes and meet housing expenses such as property taxes and utilities. In September 1991, the state legislature amended the Illinois Banking Act to facilitate the use of reverse mortgage loans for homeowners aged 62 or older.

Public Housing

Public housing projects, especially those managed by the Chicago Housing Authority (CHA), have been plagued both by serious problems and by negative stereotypes that are unfairly applied to the majority of residents. It is important to recognize that each public housing development is different and requires a variety of approaches for success. To be effective, public housing must include effective building maintenance, adequate security, and supportive services for residents with special needs.

CHA high-rise buildings: Chicago Assembly participants believe that replacement housing is especially worth pursuing for those aged, deteriorated CHA high-rises that do not merit rebuilding. Although federal regulations currently appear to prohibit the use of "modernization" funds for one-for-one replacement housing, this policy should be changed. Rebuilding the high-rises risks reinforcing existing concentrations of poverty. In recognition of that fact, the CHA has begun a demonstration program under which two rehabilitated high-rise buildings are being populated with a mixed-income tenant profile. However, low-rise, scattered-site housing and other forms of replacement housing could better serve residents while supporting affordable housing goals for both the city and the region. Some assembly participants also believe that housing vouchers should be given serious consideration, but others are skeptical of that approach.

Federal operating subsidies: Federal subsidies for local housing authorities are generally not adequate to assure proper maintenance of public housing projects. These operating subsidies are currently based on number of managed units. Many Chicago Assembly participants contend that this should be changed to number of occupied units, which would give management greater incentive to make public housing units habitable.

Populations with Special Needs

The homeless: The National Affordable Housing Act requires state and local governments to periodically report to HUD on their strategies for addressing homelessness and their use of federal funds under the McKinney Homeless Assistance Act. Long-term solutions to the problem of homelessness must go beyond providing emergency shelter and transitional housing and should include preservation and expansion of single-room-occupancy (SRO) buildings, shared housing services, and mutual housing. Attention should also be paid to the adequacy of benefits for people receiving public assistance; recent severe cutbacks in Illinois's General Assistance program are likely to exacerbate the problem of homelessness. As a short-term homeless prevention measure, many Chicago Assembly participants advocate a program of emergency financial assistance for low-income households to remain in their homes during periods of crisis (such as illness or loss of a job).

Other groups with special needs: In addition to the homeless, there are other population groups that often require both affordable housing and supportive services. These groups with special needs include large families, single-parent households, persons with disabilities, the elderly, and persons with AIDS. Examples of crucial supportive services include:

- congregate housing services for the elderly and disabled;
- nutritional, housekeeping, transportation, health care, and other services that enable individuals to continue to live independently;
- social services for those who are mentally ill or who have chronic alcohol or drug abuse problems;
- day care for families with children (especially single-parent families);
- job training and placement services.

TOWARD A REGIONAL HOUSING AGENDA

In the diverse Chicago region, affordable housing means different things in different communities, and no single program can solve all the problems. More resources are urgently needed, and new and creative policies for the region are essential. Furthermore, housing policies must include links to employment, job training, education, transportation planning, and larger political realities.

Linking Housing with Other Social Resources

Stronger connections must be made between housing opportunities and employment opportunities. Many Chicago Assembly participants believe that any business attraction and relocation efforts must address the creation of nearby affordable housing as part of the package. For instance, some participants contend that state financing should not be made available to municipalities or companies that do not develop an affordable housing plan. The move of Sears Roebuck headquarters from Chicago to suburban Hoffman Estates, far from most affordable housing and public transit, was mentioned often as an example of a failure to coordinate employment and housing needs.

In some cases, location of housing in relation to transportation can help solve problems of affordability. Building on less expensive land, near public transit, may be preferable to building on more expensive land closer to job locations. Better public transportation overall is needed, although it should be considered a complement to, not a substitute for, affordable housing development near suburban job locations. Some Chicago Assembly participants express concern that transportation programs could simply become a way to provide employers with inexpensive labor without addressing the needs for housing and supportive services in the home communities of workers who will be burdened with long commuting times.

In addition to housing-employment linkages, housing policies should be related to job training, education, and social services. There must be better coordination of housing programs with supportive services for the populations with special needs, including the very poor, large families, single-parent households, persons with disabilities, the frail elderly, and persons with AIDS.

Stronger Leadership Roles for State and Local Governments

Chicago Assembly participants believe that there must be a stronger and more aggressive role by state government in formulating a housing agenda for Illinois and in coordinating policies and programs that affect housing affordability. Some maintain that this should take the form of a new cabinet-level department; others are willing to consider a new agency within the Department of Commerce and Community Affairs or a significantly enhanced policymaking role for the Illinois Housing Development Authority.

Some Chicago Assembly participants proposed specific tasks for a state housing agency:

- establishing production targets for various types of affordable housing, with public funds leveraged to the greatest possible extent to meet those targets;
- developing laws that could override or amend local exclusionary zoning provisions that impede housing affordability;
- mandating that local governments go through the process of planning for the provision of affordable housing;
- coordinating policies and programs in the various state agencies that deal directly or indirectly with housing issues.

Many participants also express support for stronger policy leadership and more effective policy coordination within the city of Chicago. Suggestions include strengthening the Chicago Department of Housing and granting more authority to the commissioner, streamlining department programs, and improving the CHAS process.

Regional Cooperation

Chicago Assembly participants agree on the necessity of going beyond the local level and fostering regional cooperation and coordination on affordable housing issues. Some participants advocate voluntary cooperation through a regional housing entity that would formulate the equivalent of a comprehensive housing affordability strategy (CHAS) for metropolitan Chicago. Others contend that regional coordination would not be possible unless mandated by the state. Regardless of the process, such an effort should bring together mayors and city managers, housing agencies, intergov-

ernmental groups, planning agencies, community organizations,
and others involved in housing and economic development policy.
A regional housing entity could:

• conduct or sponsor badly needed research on the scope and
details of the affordability problem, including a comprehensive assessment of the availability and condition of the existing stock of affordable housing in the region;
• bring together people with different housing agendas (e.g.,
government officials, community leaders, builders, bankers)
to resolve some of the key conflicts over housing policy;
• create a forum for developing demonstration projects for
mixed-income housing and mixed-income communities;
• provide a vehicle for pooling resources across municipal and
county boundaries—for example, by creating consortiums of
smaller municipalities that receive federal HOME grants;
• collect and disseminate information on the financing and
operating programs available to those interested in preserving
and expanding the stock of affordable housing;
• serve as a "Super CHAS Council" that would coordinate the
various housing affordability strategies formulated by municipal and county governments.

Building a Constituency for Affordable Housing

Implementation of the policies recommended by the Chicago Assembly will require building a broad-based constituency for affordable housing in the region.   Mobilizing the larger resources
needed, targeting resources to individuals and communities with
the greatest needs, and increasing the availability of affordable
housing in the suburbs will be impossible unless a broad constituency supports those goals.   Education of the general public and
elected officials on regional interdependence will help to open up
exclusionary areas and lessen pressure to resist housing affordability strategies.   In addition, support from the business community
is crucial in developing linkages between housing opportunities
and employment opportunities.   More corporate leaders need to be
educated about the value of creating affordable housing near the
workplace, as well as about the importance of employment training opportunities.
Building support for a regional affordable housing strategy
will require drawing a sharp contrast between the costs of "doing

nothing" and the benefits of "doing something." The dangers of not addressing the problem include further segregation between rich and poor, continued decline of low-income neighborhoods, and higher long-term costs of infrastructure decay and social problems. Potential benefits for the region include less traffic congestion, a broader tax base, enhanced labor supply in the suburbs, greater racial and economic diversity within communities, and reduced social ills in poor communities.

CONCLUSION

Both policy coordination and constituency-building for affordable housing issues will be complicated in the diverse Chicago metropolitan area. The city of Chicago already has a large number of community-based organizations, resource and advocacy groups, and intermediary organizations involved in affordable housing activities. A key policy challenge for the city is to adapt programs for a variety of neighborhoods across a vast geographic area. By contrast, in suburban communities, where local governments make policy for small geographic areas, the challenge involves overcoming immense political fragmentation in order to facilitate cooperation among different municipalities and other units of local government.

Given the diversity of the metropolitan area and the complexity of the issues, Chicago Assembly participants sometimes held divergent views on how best to tackle the region's affordable housing problems. There were disagreements, for example, over targeting resources to different population groups and geographic areas. Many participants strongly maintained that any housing affordability policy must first address households and communities with the greatest needs. They decried the current waste of human potential, argued strongly for expanding the choices and opportunities available to low-income people, and called for "deep subsidies" to serve the housing needs of this population. Others participants, however, maintained that, given limited resources, more households could be assisted and more affordable housing units could be created by using "shallow subsidies" with a lower cost per unit. These participants believed that housing policies are likely to garner broader political support (in both socioeconomic and geographic terms) if subsidies are used to create a larger number of new units of housing for both low- and moderate-income households—both in the suburbs where affordable housing is not available and in urban neighborhoods where it could contribute to revitalization.

Despite these disagreements, Chicago Assembly participants were understanding of the needs of communities different from their own and are willing to pursue a regional housing strategy that would involve a central theme of sharing benefits and sharing responsibilities. Such a strategy would recognize *affordable housing as a regional resource* and would consider its development and preservation for the benefit of the metropolitan area as a whole.

REFERENCES

Apgar, William C., Jr. (1990). "The Nation's Housing: A Review of Past Trends and Future Prospects for Housing in America." In Denise DiPasquale and Langley C. Keyes, eds., *Building Foundations: Housing and Federal Policy.* Philadelphia: University of Pennsylvania Press.

City of Chicago (1991). *Comprehensive Housing Affordability Strategy (CHAS), FY 1992 to FY 1996.* Chicago: Chicago Department of Housing.

Córdova, Teresa (1993). "Community-Based Initiatives to Provide Affordable Housing in Chicago." In this volume.

Ford Foundation (1989). *Affordable Housing: The Years Ahead.* New York: The Ford Foundation.

Hoch, Charles (1993). "The Homeless in Chicago." In this volume.

Holleb, Doris B. (1993). "Disparities and Opportunities in Chicago-Area Housing." In this volume.

Joseph, Lawrence B., and Laurence E. Lynn, Jr. (1990). "Introduction." In Lawrence B. Joseph, ed., *Creating Jobs, Creating Workers: Economic Development and Employment in Metropolitan Chicago.* Chicago: Center for Urban Research and Policy Studies, University of Chicago; distributed by University of Illinois Press.

Leadership Council for Metropolitan Open Communities (1991). *Jobs, Housing, and Race in the Chicago Metropolitan Area: A Geographic Imbalance.* Chicago: Leadership Council, April 1991.

Lenz, Thomas J., and Barbara A. Shaw (1993). "State and Local Policies Affecting Affordable Housing in Illinois." In this volume.

Orlebeke, Charles J. (1993). "Federal Housing Policies." In this volume.

Rosenbaum, James E. (1993). "Closing the Gap: Does Residential Integration Improve the Employment and Education of Low-Income Blacks?" In this volume.

Sheft, Mark (1991). *Chicago, Illinois—A Place to Call Home: The Crisis in Housing for the Poor.* Washington, D.C.: Center on Budget and Policy Priorities.

Zuckman, Jill (1990). "Housing Authorizations," *Congressional Quarterly*, December 8, 1990, pp. 4091-4104.

DISPARITIES AND OPPORTUNITIES IN CHICAGO-AREA HOUSING

Doris B. Holleb[*]

In the economic doldrums of the early 1990s, affordable housing had become a frontline issue. Much had gone awry on the home finance front, running the gamut from multiple foreclosures to massive failures of savings and loan institutions to a credit crunch for any new building. Construction of multi-family rental units had dipped to its lowest point since the 1950s. Symptoms of personal financial distress abounded, from middle-class families deferring hopes for homeownership to low-income renters trapped in derelict dwellings in dangerous neighborhoods.

The high cost of housing had become a burden to more people in more places in metropolitan Chicago than in any recent time. Once a problem limited largely to the poor, rising rents and receding prospects for homeownership troubled many middle-income families as well. Young two-earner couples, elderly pensioners, large families, and steadily employed Black and Hispanic breadwinners all found themselves priced out of standard dwellings in satisfactory neighborhoods of city and suburb.

To quote Jack Kemp, former secretary of the U.S. Department of Housing and Urban Development (HUD):

> A widely reported study by the U.S. Census Bureau recently revealed that 57 percent of American families are unable to buy a median-priced home in their community. Just 9 percent of all renters have the financial wherewithal to become home-owners, and the figures are even worse for black and Hispanic renters, 98 percent of whom cannot afford to buy a median-priced home (*Wall Street Journal*, 1991).

For these and other reasons, housing issues were once again on the front burner—across the nation and the Chicago region.

To understand the extent, nature, and sources of cost pressures in Chicago's diverse housing markets, three broad lines of inquiry will be followed. First, national housing trends are briefly outlined to provide a context for observing local changes. Chicago-area trends, typical of those in the nation's industrial heartland, are emphasized in the balance of the chapter.[1] Changes in the supply of local housing units are summarized, spotlighting both the upward spiral in home values and rents and the vivid contrasts in the housing stock and neighborhoods of city and suburb. Turning next to the demand side of local housing markets, lagging income growth and expanding poverty are highlighted as seminal sources of excessive housing burdens. The chapter concludes with a discussion of policy objectives and with specific recommendations for city, suburban, state, and federal governments.

NATIONAL HOUSING TRENDS

The scarcity of affordable housing is neither a new nor the only serious housing problem confronting the nation, but it has surely become the most widespread (Holleb, 1981). During the 1980s, shelter costs shot up, and many renters and new homeowners found themselves burdened with heavy payments. Numerous independent observers have reached this conclusion using varied standards of "affordability" and techniques of analysis (Apgar et al., 1990; Dolbeare, 1990; Sheft, 1991; Stone, 1990).

Four trends of the 1980s converged to aggravate the problem in the early 1990s:

• The cost of rental housing rose most rapidly, outstripping inflation and increases in home prices. Lower-income renters bore the brunt of excessive housing costs.

----

[1] The geographic boundaries of the Chicago metropolitan area are defined for analytic and policy purposes to include the six Illinois counties that composed the 1980 Standard Metropolitan Statistical Area (SMSA); namely, Cook, DuPage, Kane, Lake, McHenry, and Will counties.

- The distribution of personal income in the United States was more unequal than in any previous period since World War II. Households with the lowest incomes were caught in a pincers of rising housing expenditures and lagging income growth.
- Metropolitan areas continued to expand geographically, and socioeconomic, racial, and fiscal disparities widened among neighboring residential communities. Rapid population and job growth in peripheral locations reduced access of inner-city minority workers to outlying employment opportunities.
- The supply of subsidized housing lagged further behind mounting demand. Federal subsidies and tax incentives for the construction of lower-income housing units were systematically phased out or restricted, and new commitments for other forms of local housing assistance were limited.

CHICAGO-AREA HOUSING TRENDS

During the 1980s, changes in Chicago-area housing costs echoed national trends quite closely, including both favorable and unfavorable patterns, but several significant differences emerged. In contrast to the roller-coaster price swings found in coastal metropolises, Chicago-area home prices and rents were much less volatile. In fact, prices in the many sub-markets of the area mostly responded in classical ways to local shifts in supply and demand. Thus, home prices tended to soar in hot markets of population and job growth and to lag in built-up areas that were growing slowly or declining. Rents, however, shot up across the region, even in declining areas.

On the one hand, by national standards, the Chicago region seemed to offer an ample supply of homes and apartments in diverse community areas of city and suburb. Costs, though elevated somewhat, remained well within the budgets of most middle- and upper-income families. For example, the 1990 median value of a home in the city of Chicago ($78,700) was roughly the same as the nationwide median ($79,100), although comparable home values in Chicago's suburbs were significantly higher. In fact, the region's moderately priced housing market may be viewed as an attractive, comparative advantage in the context of competing for new industrial and commercial investment and for stimulating future job growth.

On the other hand, four very unfavorable, interrelated trends also emerged starkly during the decade. First, for households in the lower half of the income spectrum, housing burdens rose dramatically for the poorest households least able to sustain them. Concurrent changes in the supply and demand for low-priced rental units boosted relative costs sharply.

Second, disparities among communities within both city and suburbs were greatly accentuated during the 1980s. Socioeconomic, ethnic, and racial differences among residential areas widened over the course of the decade. Rich areas grew richer, and poor areas lagged behind or grew even poorer. Home prices and rents reflected these growing polarities, not just among city neighborhoods, not just between city and suburbs, but among suburban residential areas as well.

Third, the geographic mismatch between the location of housing for lower-income workers and emerging job opportunities was further aggravated. Job growth remained vigorous in green-grass, suburban sites, in contrast to the shuttering of factories and shops near historically working-class neighborhoods.

Fourth, neighborhood conditions in ghetto poverty areas deteriorated badly. Guns, drugs, gangs, and more continued to drive out stable, wage-earning families. Both the number and proportion of Black residents in the city declined for the first time in the 20th century. Older dwellings in the worst areas were often left in disrepair, dilapidated, abandoned, and then demolished. This process decimated the supply of low-cost, private-market, rental housing. Foreclosures on low-cost bungalows and owner-occupied two-flats also soared in poverty areas.

To provide a framework for understanding complex shifts in the region's housing supply, let us look at data on three dimensions of change: (1) Chicago-area housing costs in a comparative national context, (2) two decades of rising home values and rents, and (3) contrasts in the housing stock of city and suburbs with regard to tenure, age, vacancy rates, and neighborhoods.

Comparative Costs Nationwide

Inflationary pressures during the 1980s in Chicago-area housing markets were moderate compared with skyrocketing costs in such East Coast areas as New York, Boston, and Washington, D.C., or in West Coast metropolitan areas. A comparative analysis of housing costs across major metropolitan regions from 1980 to 1989 (based on data from the American Housing Survey) found that Chicago-area home prices had actually declined slightly when measured in constant 1989 dollars. Gross rents, however, continued to increase during those years by some 16.7 percent. This rise in rents, though significant, was found to be relatively moderate compared with increases in other major urban regions (Apgar et al., 1990, p. 31).

Looking at the first wave of housing data from the 1990 census and comparing them with earlier censuses, I reached somewhat different conclusions about local home prices. During the 1980s, there was a modest, but nonetheless significant, rise in median home values in each of the six Illinois counties of metropolitan Chicago and in the city as well. These increases tracked a nationwide rise in median home values quite closely, a rise of about 68 percent over the decade. Nonetheless, increases in the values of Chicago-area homes surpassed the local rate of inflation, which was 60.2 percent between 1980 and 1990. In addition, the high interest rates of the 1980s plus increased local property taxes boosted the monthly costs of homeownership. Although home values advanced throughout the region, homes in Lake and DuPage counties led the pack with strong upward surges of 86.2 percent and 74.6 percent respectively (see Table 1).

Comparing changes in the city of Chicago alone with those in the nation's ten largest central cities, the 1990 median home value of $78,700 in Chicago fell squarely in the middle. Comparable median home values in the other cities ranged from highs of $244,500 in Los Angeles and $189,600 in New York City to lows of $58,000 in Houston and $25,600 in Detroit. In calculating rates of increase among the ten largest cities during the 1980s, the 66.7 percent rise in Chicago also fell right into the middle, midway between cities with heated-up housing markets and those in distress. For example, increases in home values ranged from sharp rises of 263 percent in New York City and 154 percent in Los Angeles to sluggish rises of only 22 percent in Houston and 18 percent in Detroit. The very low increases in home values in the latter cities reflected local economic distress and, in Texas, much overbuilding as well (*Chicago Sun-Times*, 1991).

TABLE 1: Median Home Values and Contract Rents, Chicago Metropolitan Area, 1970, 1980, 1990

	Median Home Value			Pct. Change 1970-80	Pct. Change 1980-90
	1970	1980	1990		
Cook County	$24,400	$62,100	$102,100	154.5%	64.4%
City of Chicago	21,200	47,200	78,700	122.6	66.7
DuPage County	28,300	78,500	137,100	177.4	74.6
Kane County	20,700	60,500	102,500	192.3	69.4
Lake County	24,500	73,400	136,700	199.6	86.2
McHenry County	20,900	66,200	111,000	216.7	67.7
Will County	18,800	55,500	89,900	195.2	62.0
CPI (base=1983)*	38.9	82.2	131.7	111.3	60.2

	Median Contract Rent			Pct. Change 1970-80	Pct. Change 1980-90
	1970	1980	1990		
Cook County	$114	$207	$411	81.6%	98.6%
City of Chicago	108	188	377	74.1	100.5
DuPage County	168	294	568	75.0	93.2
Kane County	124	232	439	87.1	89.2
Lake County	128	248	487	93.8	96.4
McHenry County	113	237	461	109.7	94.5
Will County	103	212	377	105.8	77.8
CPI (base=1983)*	38.9	82.2	131.7	111.3	60.2

* Consumer Price Index: price level changes in metropolitan Chicago.

Sources: For 1970 and 1980, U.S. Bureau of the Census, *Characteristics of the Population: General Housing Characteristics, Part 15 - Illinois*. For 1990, Northeastern Illinois Planning Commission, based on data from the 1990 U.S. Census.

Rising Home Values and Rents

Looking back to 1970, how much have Chicago-area home values and rents actually risen? Data from the decennial censuses of 1970, 1980, and 1990 provide a good overview of broad-gauged changes; they are presented in Table 1. Changes in the Chicago-area consumer price index have also been incorporated into these tables to provide yardsticks for comparing real increases in home values and rents with nominal price increases over the course of 20 years of monetary inflation.

Before analyzing the contents of the tables, a few words of caution about interpreting census data might be helpful. First, "home values" in Table 1 differ somewhat from "home prices" based on actual market sales. The former are derived from estimates of householders who fill out the census forms. They may be near, but are not identical to, current selling prices.

Second, comparisons of average changes, in this case median changes at ten-year intervals, offer a good way to delineate the general direction of trends. Conclusions based exclusively on medians, however, can sometimes be misleading, particularly if deviations from the median happen to be large. In the city and suburbs of Chicago, variations in housing costs, what I call "disparities," are enormous. In fact, the extent of these disparities, in itself, constitutes a serious problem.

Finally, the City of Chicago formally rejected the official 1990 census results because of a widely acknowledged population undercount, common to major central cities. Earlier censuses had also undercounted residents of central cities, particularly Black males and illegal aliens. Therefore, Chicago joined with other cities in a suit against the U.S. Department of Commerce. That court action is still pending. Nonetheless, if used with understanding, the census provides the best, and often the only, data for reasonably valid comparisons over long stretches of time, among distant places, and for small geographic areas.

Home values: Turning now to Chicago-area data specifically, what actually happened to housing values and rents? Looking again at Table 1, the rise in median home values outpaced inflation considerably during the 1980s, with values in Lake and DuPage counties appreciating most rapidly. Yet, these increases were found to be relatively moderate when compared with those elsewhere. Furthermore, they were noticeably slower than the soaring increases in home values that took place

in the Chicago area during the 1970s. During the 1970s, with
the coming of age of the baby boom generation, home values
throughout the region had appreciated more than twice as fast
as those in the 1980s.

During both decades, however, not all residential areas
were swept along in the inflationary tide. A fine-grained,
spatial analysis, beyond the scope of this chapter, would reveal
that inflation aggravated differences in home values between
those in growing suburbs in the northern and western sectors of
the region, such as Naperville in DuPage County, and in lagging suburban areas toward the south, such as University Park
in Will County. Widening differences also emerged among residential areas within city limits. Home values moved in opposite directions, for example, in Lincoln Park, an affluent, predominantly White community on the north side, and in Woodlawn, a low-income, predominantly Black community on the
south side, even though much of the housing stock in each
neighborhood is similar in age and had been similar in quality
when originally built early in the century.

To understand why the explosive surges and slumps in
housing costs found elsewhere had been dampened in the Chicago-area market, one must look beyond the housing sector.
The principal reasons were twofold: economic and demographic.

The first reason was rooted in the dismal performance of
the local economy during the early 1980s. The economic recession of 1980-1982 took a particularly heavy toll in the industrial
Midwest. Lagging recovery and high unemployment in a period of historically high interest rates together limited the effective market demand for homes. Even though rents rose steeply
during those years, which would normally spur the demand for
homeownership, renters with stagnant or declining real incomes
could not afford to purchase homes.

The second reason grows out of two decades of sluggish local population growth. Although the net population growth in
the Chicago area has been almost stagnant, increases were un-
evenly distributed. The city of Chicago sustained particularly
heavy losses as residents continued the outward trek (see Table 2). Furthermore, population losses would have been far
steeper had not a new large wave of foreign immigration, principally from Latin America and Asia, hit the region during the
1980s. The new immigrants often settled into declining city

and suburban neighborhoods, partially offsetting the out-migration or, as in Cicero, actually increasing the local population.

In short, a foundering local economy, sluggish or negative net population growth, and an aging baby boom generation together reduced the rapid rate of new household formation that had prevailed during the 1970s. These combined changes tempered the effective market demand for homeownership.

Rents: Turning to the rental sector, median contract rents moved in very different patterns during those years.[2] In the 1980s, rents soared in the city of Chicago and in each of the suburban counties, even in areas of declining population and household growth. Between 1980 and 1990, median contract rents increased far faster than consumer prices, both regionwide and nationwide (Table 1).

When contrasted with the sagging rents of the 1970s, this sharp rise in rents during the 1980s seemed even more dramatic. Between 1970 and 1980, changes in median contract rents had lagged much behind rates of regional and national inflation everywhere in the area, including in the city and each of the counties. In fact, during the 1970s, real rents, adjusted to eliminate monetary inflation, had actually declined throughout the Chicago region as well as nationwide (Mills and Kaiser, 1990). The most dramatic drop in real rents had occurred in the city of Chicago and in DuPage County (Table 1). Consequently, the turnabout and the explosive rent increases of the 1980s hit tenants in both places with special force.

What drove up rents during the 1980s? To oversimplify somewhat, on the one hand, more high-priced units came onto the market, principally from new construction, remodeling, and other improvements in quality. On the other hand, the supply of lower-cost, lower-quality units was greatly diminished. As in the 1970s, condominium conversions continued to absorb the best of the existing rental units, and neglect, abandonment, and demolition leveled the worst. Interest and local property tax rates also soared so that the cost of maintaining and operating older apartments often outstripped inflation and rents. Land-

---

[2] Contract rent is the monthly monetary rent specified in a lease agreement. Gross rent includes not only the contract rent but also the estimated average monthly cost of utilities and fuel if paid for by the tenant.

lords, caught in this fiscal squeeze, walked away in droves from marginal buildings in neighborhoods with uncertain prospects.

Altogether, the net loss of rental units at the bottom end of the cost spectrum was precipitous. Privately owned, small-scale, pre-World-War-II apartment buildings that had historically comprised the bulk of the low-cost housing supply in the region were fast disappearing. Such dwellings became rapidly dwindling resources not only in the city, but in older, suburban poverty areas as well.

Contrasts in City and Suburban Housing Stock

Turning from costs to the physical housing stock itself, the supply of homes and apartments in the city of Chicago contrasts dramatically with that in the suburbs. Differences in such things as density, architectural style, tenure, age, vacancies, and abandonments are easily recognized by the casual observer. These visible, tangible differences have widened in the past quarter century as large-scale suburban subdivisions and ex-urban development picked up steam, siphoning growth from old city neighborhoods.

Changes in the housing stock usually reflect geographic patterns of population growth and decline. In the past 20 years, trends toward deconcentrated patterns of settlement have quickened in the Chicago area and throughout the nation. Thus, between 1970 and 1990, for example, the population of the six-county region grew by only 4.1 percent, rising from 6.98 million persons to 7.26 million. This small net gain lagged far behind the comparable rise of 22 percent in the total U.S. population. It also obscured heavy losses in the city's population. In fact, since 1970, all net growth in the region has taken place exclusively in suburban counties, where rates of population increase have mostly kept pace with those in the nation as a whole. But even in the suburbs, the population of built-up, older towns, where poor and minority families had settled, often stagnated or declined.

During both decades, the population of the city of Chicago plummeted. Altogether, over half a million inhabitants were lost. By 1990, the city's population totaled only 2.78 million persons, a drop back to the level of 1920. So steep was the decline that Chicago suffered an unprecedented net loss of Black residents during the 1980s (see Table 2).

TABLE 2:   Population by Race/Ethnicity, Chicago Metropolitan Area, 1980
and 1990

	Pop. 1980	Pct. Distr.	Pop. 1990	Pct. Distr.	Pop. Change 1980-90	Pct. Change 1980-90
Metro Area						
Total	7,103,624	100.0%	7,261,176	100.0%	157,552	2.2%
White	4,943,208	69.6	4,757,986	65.5	-185,222	-3.7
Black	1,414,814	19.9	1,406,443	19.4	-8,371	-0.6
Hispanic	579,914	8.2	836,905	11.5	256,991	44.3
Other	165,688	2.3	259,842	3.6	94,154	56.8
Cook County						
Total	5,253,655	100.0	5,105,067	100.0	-148,588	-2.8
White	3,288,841	62.6	2,915,634	57.1	-373,207	-11.3
Black	1,334,956	25.4	1,301,196	25.5	-33,760	-2.5
Hispanic	499,538	9.5	694,194	13.6	194,656	39.0
Other	130,320	2.5	194,043	3.8	63,723	48.9
City of Chicago						
Total	3,005,078	100.0	2,783,726	100.0	-221,352	-7.4
White	1,311,808	43.7	1,056,048	37.9	-255,760	-19.5
Black	1,187,168	39.5	1,074,471	38.6	-112,697	-9.5
Hispanic	423,357	14.1	545,852	19.6	122,495	28.9
Other	82,745	2.8	107,355	3.9	24,610	29.7
Suburban Cook						
Total	2,248,577	100.0	2,321,341	100.0	72,764	3.2
White	1,977,033	87.9	1,859,586	80.1	-117,447	-5.9
Black	147,788	6.6	226,725	9.8	78,937	53.4
Hispanic	76,181	3.4	148,342	6.4	72,161	94.7
Other	47,575	2.1	86,688	3.7	39,113	82.2
DuPage County						
Total	658,835	100.0	781,666	100.0	122,831	18.6
White	613,928	93.2	691,833	88.5	77,905	12.7
Black	7,610	1.2	15,119	1.9	7,509	98.7
Hispanic	16,796	2.5	34,567	4.4	17,771	105.8
Other	20,501	3.1	40,147	5.1	19,646	95.8

TABLE 2 (continued)

	Pop. 1980	Pct. Distr.	Pop. 1990	Pct. Distr.	Pop. Change 1980-90	Pct. Change 1980-90
Kane County						
Total	278,405	100.0%	317,471	100.0%	39,066	14.0%
White	236,333	84.9	250,551	78.9	14,218	6.0
Black	13,119	4.7	18,353	5.8	5,234	39.9
Hispanic	26,217	9.4	43,535	13.7	17,318	66.1
Other	2,736	1.0	5,032	1.6	2,296	83.9
Lake County						
Total	440,372	100.0	516,418	100.0	76,046	17.3
White	384,635	87.3	430,566	83.4	45,931	11.9
Black	27,968	6.4	33,736	6.5	5,768	20.6
Hispanic	20,468	4.6	38,570	7.5	18,102	88.4
Other	7,301	1.7	13,546	2.6	6,245	85.5
McHenry County						
Total	147,897	100.0	183,241	100.0	35,344	23.9
White	144,041	97.4	175,299	95.7	31,258	21.7
Black	81	0.1	287	0.2	206	254.3
Hispanic	2,835	1.9	6,066	3.3	3,231	114.0
Other	940	0.6	1,589	0.9	649	69.0
Will County						
Total	324,460	100.0	357,313	100.0	32,853	10.1
White	275,430	84.9	294,103	82.3	18,673	6.8
Black	31,080	9.6	37,752	10.6	6,672	21.5
Hispanic	14,060	4.3	19,973	5.6	5,913	42.1
Other	3,890	1.2	5,485	1.5	1,595	41.0

Note: White, Black, and Other include non-Hispanics only. Persons of Hispanic origin may be of any race.

Source: 1990 and 1980 U.S. Census Public Law 94-171 File Tapes as reported in Northeastern Illinois Planning Commission Data Bulletin 91-1, February 1991.

Changes that matched these population shifts had been taking place in the area's housing supply. Contrasts in city and suburban trends were evident with regard to such factors as tenure, age of housing stock, and gains or losses of housing units.

Tenure: Looking first at tenure (at renting versus owning), the city has long provided the lion's share of rental housing in the region. It has ranged in quality from luxurious and expensive to squalid and cheap. Nonetheless, the bulk of low- and moderate-income rentals in the region was still to be found in the city. In 1990, two out of five, just over 40.5 percent, of the 2.8 million total housing units in the six-county region were located within city limits. But the predominant proportion of rental units, nearly three out of five, or 58.5 percent, of the region's one million total rental units were located within the city (calculations based on Table 3).

In contrast, of the region's 1.6 million owner-occupied units, little more than a quarter, or 26.6 percent, were to be found in the city. This might seem a disproportionately low number of homeowners in a nation where nearly two-thirds of the total population, or 64.2 percent in 1990, lived in dwellings that they owned. But multi-family, rental dwellings have been centered, historically, in the largest, mature central cities, often in neighborhoods that reflect the life-styles of earlier times. Homeowners, of course, predominated in the suburbs, and moderate- and low-cost rentals were scarce or nonexistent in many suburbs. In 1990, of all owner-occupied housing units in the Chicago area, nearly three out of four, or 73.3 percent, were located in the suburban ring (Table 3).

Age of housing stock: Looking next at the age of housing structures, contrasts were equally striking. The suburban housing stock was, on average, much newer than that in the city. For example, the median year of construction of all residential structures in the city in 1990 was 1944. The comparable median in suburban counties ranged from 1962 in Kane and suburban Cook, to 1968 in Lake and Will, to 1969 in McHenry, to 1972 in DuPage (Northeastern Illinois Planning Commission, 1992).

TABLE 3:   Housing Units (in 1,000s) by Tenure and Vacancy, Chicago
Metropolitan Area, 1970, 1980, 1990

	No. of Units			Pct. Distr. 1990	Change, 1970-80		Change, 1980-90	
	1970	1980	1990	1990	Units	Pct.	Units	Pct.
Metro Area								
Total	2,294.8	2,640.8	2,798.0	100.0	346.0	15.1	157.2	6.0
Owner-occup.	1,155.1	1,425.4	1,595.2	57.0	270.3	23.4	169.8	11.9
Renter-occup.	1,028.5	1,061.3	1,024.7	36.6	32.8	3.2	-36.6	-3.5
Vacant	111.2	154.1	178.2	6.4	42.9	38.6	24.1	15.6
Cook County								
Total	1,854.9	1,994.2	2,021.8	100.0	139.3	7.5	27.6	1.4
Owner-occup.	847.6	979.8	1,042.9	51.6	132.2	15.6	63.1	6.4
Renter-occup.	918.4	899.3	836.6	41.4	-19.1	-2.1	-62.7	-7.0
Vacant	88.9	115.1	142.3	7.0	26.2	29.5	27.2	23.7
City of Chicago								
Total	1,208.8	1,174.7	1,133.0	100.0	-34.1	-2.8	-41.7	-3.5
Owner-occup.	396.4	425.9	425.3	37.5	29.5	7.4	-0.6	-0.1
Renter-occup.	741.5	667.5	599.9	52.9	-74.0	-10.0	-67.6	-10.1
Vacant	70.9	81.3	107.9	9.5	10.4	14.6	26.6	32.7
Suburban Cook								
Total	646.1	819.5	888.8	100.0	173.4	26.8	69.3	8.5
Owner-occup.	451.3	554.0	617.6	69.5	102.7	22.8	63.7	11.5
Renter-occup.	176.9	231.8	236.7	26.6	54.8	31.0	4.9	2.1
Vacant	17.9	33.8	34.5	3.9	15.9	88.4	0.7	2.0
DuPage County								
Total	142.4	234.8	292.5	100.0	92.4	64.9	57.7	24.6
Owner-occup.	108.4	164.7	208.0	71.1	56.3	51.9	43.3	26.3
Renter-occup.	27.8	57.3	71.44	24.4	29.5	105.9	14.1	24.5
Vacant	6.2	12.8	13.2	4.5	6.6	107.4	0.4	3.1

TABLE 3 (continued)

	No. of Units			Pct. Distr. 1990	Change, 1970-80		Change, 1980-90	
	1970	1980	1990		Units	Pct.	Units	Pct.
Kane County								
Total	77.1	98.5	111.5	100.0	21.5	27.8	12.9	13.1
Owner-occup.	49.8	63.1	74.5	66.8	13.3	26.7	11.4	18.0
Renter-occup.	24.8	30.6	32.7	29.3	5.8	23.3	2.1	6.7
Vacant	2.4	4.8	4.3	3.9	2.4	97.0	-0.5	-10.3
Lake County								
Total	110.4	150.5	183.3	100.0	40.0	36.3	32.8	21.8
Owner-occup.	72.7	102.4	129.0	70.4	29.7	40.9	26.6	26.0
Renter-occup.	30.3	37.3	44.9	24.5	7.0	23.3	7.6	20.5
Vacant	7.5	10.8	9.3	5.1	3.3	43.7	-1.5	-13.6
McHenry County								
Total	36.3	53.0	66.0	100.0	16.7	46.0	13.0	24.6
Owner-occup.	25.1	38.8	50.3	76.2	13.6	54.3	11.5	29.7
Renter-occup.	8.0	10.3	12.7	19.2	2.4	29.5	2.3	22.7
Vacant	3.2	3.9	3.0	4.6	0.7	21.6	-0.9	-21.9
Will County								
Total	73.7	109.8	122.9	100.0	36.0	48.9	13.1	12.0
Owner-occup.	51.4	76.6	90.5	73.6	25.2	48.9	13.9	18.1
Renter-occup.	19.2	26.5	26.4	21.5	7.2	37.5	-0.0	-0.1
Vacant	3.0	6.7	5.9	4.8	3.7	121.1	-0.7	-11.2

Sources: For 1970 and 1980, U.S. Bureau of the Census, *Characteristics of the Population: General Housing Characteristics, Part 15 - Illinois* (1970 and 1980). For 1990, Northeastern Illinois Planning Commission, based on data from the 1990 U.S. Census.

Many moderately priced subdivisions had been built in the suburbs after World War II for veterans with low-cost mortgages. Since then, as highways reached into open country, other new developments have mushroomed. Only a few century-old mansions and farmsteads have remained in use, dotting the area, mostly in historic river towns and railroad-age suburban cities. But housing conditions greatly resembling those in the city can be found on a smaller scale in such older industrial satellite cities as Joliet or Waukegan and in a few corners of such close-in towns as Oak Park or Evanston. These small, historic centers formed the core of dispersed suburban mini-ghettos. During the 1980s, however, racially segregated neighborhoods expanded elsewhere in the suburbs, particularly in such southern Cook County towns as Harvey, Chicago Heights, Markham, and Riverdale, along a corridor where low-income, Black families with federal rental assistance (Section 8 certificates) had concentrated (Clements, 1992, p. 20).

In the city of Chicago, half the dwellings were built before the end of World War II and many before World War I. In 1990, for example, the mean age of all occupied residential buildings in Chicago, a total of 426,000 structures, was 66 years. Single-family homes were somewhat newer, with a mean age of 58 years for the city's total of 278,000 homes. However, the mean age of Chicago's 96,000 two-flats still in use was 80 years. Roughly half of them were built before 1910 in an era of gaslights and streetcars (Chicago Department of Housing, 1990). These diverse, sturdy edifices, survivors of a technology long since supplanted, have provided shelters to countless successive waves of inhabitants. With timely maintenance and minimum upgrading, much of this old, low-cost, low-rise stock can remain in use. Similar units still do yeoman duty in most European cities. New "low-income" units are much more costly to build and are typically beyond the means of low-wage workers (Fisher, 1991). For such workers, for women with large families, or for foreign immigrants clustering near their compatriots, the city's aging, walk-up apartments and modest row-houses continue to offer "decent" shelter at relatively low cost. Since housing subsidies reach only a fraction of the area's working poor and near poor, the shelter that is found in the private market has been this "old stock," the "affordable" housing of the area.

Gains and losses of housing units: Much of the older housing stock in the city stood vacant in 1990, awaiting an uncertain
future of renovation or destruction.   Vacant homes, vacant
apartments, vacant shops, vacant lots, and vacant land are the
last stops on a long trail of disinvestment in housing and neighborhood enterprises.   High vacancy rates also herald the continuing hemorrhaging of homes and apartments in future years.
City and suburban housing trends diverged sharply with regard to both net gains or losses of housing units and vacancy
rates.   Both are the harbingers of future housing losses or addi-
tions.   Housing trends did converge in city and suburbs, however, in one significant aspect of change.   New construction and
rehabilitation were most vigorous in prosperous White residential areas, and losses were most acute in Black poverty areas.
During the 1980s, the city sustained huge losses of rental
units, almost comparable to the vast devastation of the 1970s
(see Table 3).   Between 1980 and 1990 alone, more than
67,000 occupied rental units were lost from a total city rental
stock of about 667,000 units.   This decline amounted to 10 percent of the total stock, but it came on the heels of a comparable
decline of 10 percent during the 1970s.   Beyond the enormous
cumulative devastation of the past 20 years, further losses are
threatened in the coming decade because of a large overhang of
rental units that have remained unoccupied.
Furthermore, in 1990, about 9.5 percent of the city's total
housing stock of 1.1 million units stood vacant.   This proportion even surpassed the vacancy rate of 6.9 percent in 1980
(Table 3).   Coincidentally, this high proportion of empty units
was roughly comparable to the nationwide vacancy rate of
10 percent, which had also reached a historically unprecedented
peak by 1990.
Poverty areas have been emptying out (see Table 4).   With
low expectations about future property values, with limited access to credit and insurance, and with deteriorating neighborhood conditions, housing disinvestment has quickened.   Abandoned buildings are prime sites for fires and crimes.   After
years of neglect, the end of the line is the empty lot.   By 1990,
in a city that had been virtually all built up decades ago, vacant
lots dominated the scarred landscape of concentrated poverty
areas.   For example, in Woodlawn and Kenwood-Oakland, declining neighborhoods abutting Hyde Park, the prospering University of Chicago enclave, fully 70 percent of the land stood

vacant in 1992, and half of it was owned by the City (*Chicago Tribune*, 1993).

TABLE 4:   Community Areas in City of Chicago with Greatest Loss of Housing Units and Population, 1980-1990

Community Area	Poverty Rate 1989	Housing Units 1980	Housing Units 1990	Change, 1980-90 No.	Change, 1980-90 Pct.
Washington Park	58.4%	12,091	9,124	-2,967	-24.5%
East Garfield Park	48.1	10,945	8,531	-2,414	-22.1
Grand Boulevard	64.7	20,868	16,409	-4,459	-21.4
West Garfield Park	40.8	9,583	7,934	-1,649	-17.2
Woodlawn	37.0	15,824	13,109	-2,715	-17.2
Oakland	72.3	5,210	4,335	-875	-16.8
North Lawndale	48.4	18,595	15,686	-2,909	-15.6
Austin	25.7	44,771	38,030	-6,741	-15.1
Citywide total	21.6	1,174,703	1,133,039	-41,664	-3.5

Community Area	Poverty Rate 1989	Population 1980	Population 1990	Change, 1980-90 No.	Change, 1980-90 Pct.
Oakland	72.3%	16,748	8,197	-8,551	-51.1%
Washington Park	58.4	31,935	19,425	-12,510	-39.2
Grand Boulevard	64.7	53,741	35,897	-17,844	-33.2
West Garfield Park	40.8	33,865	24,095	-9,770	-28.8
Fuller Park	49.2	5,832	4,364	-1,468	-25.2
Woodlawn	37.0	36,323	27,473	-8,850	-24.4
East Garfield Park	48.1	31,580	24,030	-7,550	-23.9
North Lawndale	48.4	61,534	47,296	-14,238	-23.1
Citywide total	21.6	3,005,078	2,783,726	-221,352	-7.4

Source: Northeastern Illinois Planning Commission, based on data from the 1990 U.S. Census.

These many vacated lots—scattered, untended, and un-kempt—represent a valuable potential resource, ripe for future renewal.   When assembled, they can be reused, for example, for modern industrial sites, for low-rise in-fill housing, for schoolyard expansions, or simply held as green space, as much needed mini-parks, for countless, unforeseen future uses.[3]   Cur-rently, these lots are often given away piecemeal and not always to the highest bidder.

In the suburbs, diametrically opposite trends have prevailed. Suburban housing markets were much tighter than those in the city, and few units stood vacant.   Land on the fringes has been gobbled up for new development, feeding a strong demand for homes and apartments.   In 1990, vacancies amounted only to about 4.2 percent of the total suburban housing stock, reflecting a slightly tighter market than in 1980.   During the 1980s, the net addition of 200,000 units to the housing supply had been quickly absorbed, and the number and proportion of empty units dropped in each of the suburban counties (Table 3).

Paradoxically, one common troublesome trend emerged in both city and suburbs during those years.   The geographic pat-tern of housing loss or gain was quite similar: The greatest net gains were found in prosperous, predominantly White residen-tial areas.   The grand champion of growth in DuPage County, for example, was Naperville, where the number of housing units more than doubled in the 1980s, rising from about 14,000 to more than 30,000 dwelling units.   In the city, significant in-creases in housing units, running counter to the dominant trend of losses, occurred in the Near North Side, the Loop, Lincoln Park, other contiguous neighborhoods, as well as in scattered northwest and southwest sites bordering the suburbs.   Net housing losses, however, were mostly found in lower income, predominantly Black areas—in such southern suburbs as Har-vey, Oak Lawn, or Chicago Heights and in the poorest Chicago neighborhoods on the west and south sides (see Table 4).

These twin trends of the 1980s heightened disparities among residential communities throughout the region.   Despite a small, but significant, rise in the number of Black, Asian-American, and Hispanic suburban residents, these divergent housing trends suggest that local barriers of income, ethnicity, and race were

---

[3] "In-fill" housing involves new construction on scattered, vacant sites in neighborhoods that are otherwise fully built-up.

mostly maintained during the 1980s. As will be seen later, the changes in per capita income between 1979 and 1989 confirm widening disparities between rich and poor residential areas within each suburban county as well.

Neighborhoods

Running against the tide of losses, the process of upgrading derelict housing and of reclaiming neighborhoods has actually been underway in a few city and suburban areas, and not just in the expensive ones. A mini-renaissance has been taking place in such multi-ethnic city neighborhoods as Albany Park, West Rogers Park, and Bucktown, as well as within specific sectors of suburban cities dispersed throughout the area, running from Aurora to Elgin, from Cicero to Waukegan. Immigrants of many tongues and colors have sparked this small-scale renewal. Fixing up old homes and shopping strips, they have clustered together, staking out for restoration a few community areas. The balance of the low-cost stock, however, has mostly been left to age, gracelessly, until boarded up and demolished.

What factors determine the life or death of the affordable old clunkers that remain mostly in the housing supply of the city, the seeming bargains awaiting renewal? As every real estate agent knows, beyond the inherent quality, characteristics, and condition of the dwelling itself, much depends on location and, most of all, on market expectations. To illustrate with an extreme example, compare the current price of a turn-of-the-century, single-family, limestone townhouse near the lake in Lincoln Park with a similar one on the boulevard in Oakland. Both would have cost upwards of $15,000 in 1960. But by 1990, the house in Lincoln Park, modernized and restored, might sell for more than half a million dollars, while that in Oakland might well have been abandoned. During those decades, Lincoln Park homes were gradually reclaimed, block by block, by young professional families, mostly White and employed downtown. By 1990, the neighborhood had become the fifth richest in the city. Although Oakland was equally convenient to downtown jobs and lakefront amenities, the concentration of poor, Black residents intensified after 1965. In 1990, it was the poorest city neighborhood, with 72 percent of its residents below the poverty line (*Chicago Reporter*, 1992).

To summarize a vast body of social research, three inter-related factors seem to determine the fate of older housing and neighborhoods.   The first factor in housing choice has always been location, including proximity to employment.   The second determinant rests on a set of perceptions that influence expecta-tions about future neighborhood conditions and services (Goetze, 1976).   Significant factors usually include the quality of schools, safety, transportation, amenities, and even architec-tural style.   Finally, racial, ethnic, and class considerations permeate most decisions about reinvestments in declining areas.

Supportive public policies, neighborhood by neighborhood, tailored to specific needs, will be critical if the best of the old stock is to be salvaged and improved.   Rehabilitation costs and even basic maintenance costs are often too expensive for fami-lies with very low incomes.   Furthermore, middle-income fami-lies are usually reluctant to invest effort and savings into mod-ernizing housing in a neighborhood whose future is perceived as problematic (Taub, Taylor, and Dunham, 1984).   These and other observations provide the rationale for policy recommenda-tions in the concluding section.

LAGGING INCOMES, RISING POVERTY

Adverse trends in the distribution of personal income have played havoc with the housing budgets of middle- and low-in-come families.   Over the course of the 1980s, families with incomes near or below average were caught in a nasty pincers, pinioned between rising home prices or rocketing rents and stagnating or declining real incomes.

The affordability of housing rests on two legs, on the per-sonal incomes of its occupants as much as on its costs.   What-ever the specific standard adopted, "affordability" is always a relative concept, customarily measured as a ratio of housing costs to household incomes.   Consequently, a change in either would make a difference.   Even without a significant rise in housing costs, a decline or a slow rate of increase in personal incomes would produce "excessive" housing expenditures.   The latter is what actually happened after the 1975 recession to many poor, near poor, and moderate-income families in the Chicago area.

The difficulty of making ends meet was further com-pounded, as we have seen, by significant increases in the real costs of rental housing. A recent study of poverty and housing, based on data from the 1987 American Housing Survey, found that between 1975 and 1987, the median income of renter households, adjusted for inflation, fell by 17 percent in the eight-county Chicago region, while housing costs for the typical renter household rose more than 14 percent in real dollars during those years (Sheft, 1991, p. 19).[4]

Three interrelated income trends can be distinguished: a relative decline in the earnings of middle- and lower-income workers; widening income differences among the region's residential areas; and changes in the scale, social composition, and concentration of poverty. As for the first, the roots of housing cost problems in working-class neighborhoods can be traced to rising inequality in the distribution of personal incomes, nationwide and regionwide. The earnings of low-skilled, full-time workers, particularly men, have actually declined in real dollars since 1979 (Levy and Michael, 1991; Blank, 1993).

Second, dramatic contrasts in income levels, both between and within Chicago's city and suburban areas, illuminate a spatial pattern of growing income inequalities. These sharp geopolitical disparities have compounded the difficulties of providing affordable housing near growing employment centers.

Third, regarding poverty, budgetary pressures from housing costs have been most acute for low-wage workers and families subsisting on fixed pensions or welfare payments. In 1990, for example, the earnings of a full-time, year-round worker, holding a minimum-wage job and supporting a family of three, fell below the official poverty line. By the end of economic expansion of the 1980s, the number and proportion of persons with poverty level incomes had scarcely budged. Subsequently, in the recession of the early 1990s, unemployment and poverty both shot up (*New York Times*, 1992). In August 1991, for example, almost one in ten of all U.S. families, more than 23.6 million persons, relied on food stamps to supplement their skimpy budgets, a record high for the program (*New York Times*, 1991b).

---

[4] The eight-county Chicago metropolitan region includes Grundy and Kendall counties as well as Cook, DuPage, Kane, Lake, McHenry, and Will.

Bipolar Income Trends

The 1980s was a decade of widening income disparities. No matter what the method of measurement, nor whether data are analyzed by income classes, between city and suburb, among city neighborhoods, or among suburban areas, divergent trends in the distribution of incomes emerged. Differences in the findings of various analysts have related chiefly to the size of the gaps and their causes, but rarely to the trends.

Looking first at broad national trends, changes in the distribution of personal income have been much studied by observers from across the political spectrum (Phillips, 1991; Levy and Michael, 1991; U.S. House of Representatives, 1991; Burtless, 1990). All agree that the extremes, both the high and low ends of the income distribution spectrum, have increased at the expense of the middle.

A common way of tracing these changes is to divide all families in the United States into quintiles, based on incomes received in a specific year, and then to observe shifts over the years in total U.S. income distributed to each quintile. Specific techniques used in analyzing these changes have varied, but all reveal similar trends.

In Table 5, I have chosen to compare income shares in 1973, 1979, and 1989 because all were peak years of economic activity. Focusing on changes between 1979 and 1989 alone, the total share for families with incomes in the top quintile rose significantly, from 44.4 percent to 47.1 percent. As for changes in the three middle quintiles, the lower the income share, the greater the proportionate decline or slowdown. For the lowest quintile, the proportionate fall in income was most significant. During the so-called prosperous 1980s, families in the lowest quintile suffered most, caught in both an income and a housing cost squeeze. The bottom fifth of all U.S. families include not only the poorest of the poor, but working-class families as well. Most of them receive no housing subsidies, and rarely do they benefit from income-tax deductions for homeownership.

To summarize the patterns of the past fifteen years: the rich became relatively richer, the poor became poorer, and the incomes of most Americans, ranging in the middle of the spectrum, either stagnated or dropped somewhat when adjusted for inflation. The chief source of shrinking family incomes at the

TABLE 5:   U.S. Family Cash Income by Quintiles, 1973, 1979, 1989

Quintile	Mean Family Income in Constant (1989) Dollars			Pct. Change 1973-89	Pct. Change 1979-89
	1973	1979	1989		
Lowest	$ 6,061	$ 5,994	$ 5,866	-3.2%	-2.1%
Second	15,416	15,306	15,107	-2.0	-1.3
Middle	25,909	25,609	25,823	-0.3	0.8
Fourth	37,946	38,680	40,374	6.4	4.4
Highest	66,364	68,230	77,716	17.1	13.9
Overall	30,341	30,764	32,978	8.7	7.2

Quintile	Percentage Shares		
	1973	1979	1989
Lowest	4.0%	3.9%	3.6%
Second	10.2	10.0	9.2
Middle	17.1	16.6	15.7
Fourth	25.0	25.1	24.5
Highest	43.7	44.4	47.1
	100.0	100.0	100.0

Source: U.S. House of Representatives, Committee on Ways and Means, *Overview of Entitlement Programs: 1991 Green Book* (Washington, D.C.: U.S. Government Printing Office, 1991).

bottom end was a relative decline in the earnings of low-skilled workers, particularly males (U.S. Bureau of the Census, 1992, pp. 1-8).[5]

Income differences have also typically diverged by race and ethnicity. To illustrate the range in 1990, the median income of all households in the United States was $30,056. Among ethnic groups, the highest median income, at $36,784, was received by Asian-American households.[6] This compared with $31,435 for non-Hispanic Whites, $24,156 for Hispanics, $20,908 for Native Americans, and $19,758 for African-Americans (U.S. Bureau of the Census, 1992). During the 1980s, the longstanding measured gap in median household income between Blacks and Whites narrowed slightly but remained very wide. In 1989, for example, the median income of Black households represented 63 percent that of Whites, compared with 62 percent in 1979. Since residential areas in metropolitan Chicago are highly segregated by race and ethnicity, these differences typically magnify disparate income patterns among communities.

Geographic Disparities

Great difference in average income levels can be found among the many communities that together compose the socioeconomic mosaic of metropolitan Chicago. Geographically specific decennial census data about personal incomes provide good measuring rods for comparing the extent of these differences in 1989. They also provide snapshots of changes that transpired between the beginning and the end of the decade.

A crosscutting view of sharply contrasting income levels within the region is revealed in median household income data from the 1990 census. Persisting differences are found on three fronts: between Chicago and its suburbs, among city neighborhoods, and among suburban municipalities. The comparisons that follow were chosen to illustrate some of the contrasts.

---

[5] In the Chicago area, bipolar trends in the distribution of personal income have also been underway, paralleling national trends, but comparable detailed analyses are not yet available.

[6] The per capita income figures for Asian-Americans are lower than those for Whites mostly because their households are larger.

First, median household income in 1989 in Chicago was
$26,301, well below that in the nation as a whole at $30,056.
In the region's suburban counties, however, comparable median
household incomes were higher than those in the nation and
much higher than those in Chicago. They ranged from a low of
$40,080 in Kane County to $48,876 in DuPage County.

Second, on a smaller geographic scale, income disparities
were even more clear-cut. Among the city's 77 officially designated community areas, median household incomes diverged
sharply, ranging from $51,225 in Forest Glen, the richest com-
munity, located near the northern outskirts of the city, to
$5,068 in Oakland, the poorest community, located along the
south lakefront.

Third, suburban counties also contained both very rich and
very poor municipalities. They ranged from the highest 1989
median household income of $125,074 in Riverwoods to the
lowest of $14,032 in Ford Heights. However, even in poor
suburban municipalities, incomes were usually more than two or
three times greater than those in city poverty areas. Among top
earning suburban municipalities, median household incomes
were also double or triple those in the wealthiest city areas.

Turning next to data on per capita incomes, unmistakable
trends toward greater disparities are revealed in Tables 6 and 7.
Note particularly the widening gaps in per capita personal incomes between 1979 and 1989 for selected pairs of municipalities within each of the suburban counties (Table 7). Although
very rich or very poor residential enclaves in suburban counties
may be physically proximate, they have remained socially distant. Far more critical, however, are the consequences of political fragmentation in neighboring towns and the fiscal autonomy
of multiple local governments. Fragmentation has fostered
competitive development policies and perpetuated exclusionary
housing practices.

Poverty Patterns

An upward drift in the scale of poverty has swelled the ranks of
households with burdensome housing costs. Four significant
changes have been underway:

> • Poverty has been more widespread, both nationwide and
> regionwide.

- Poverty has persisted during prosperity, with lingering unemployment and lower labor-force participation.
- The incidence of poverty has risen most rapidly among women and children, particularly among Black and Hispanic families.
- Poverty has been more concentrated spatially as well as racially.

TABLE 6: Per Capita Money Income by County, Chicago Metropolitan Area, 1979, 1989

| | Per Capita Income | | |
	1979	1989	Pct. Change 1979-89
Cook County	$ 8,229	$15,697	90.8%
City of Chicago	6,933	12,899	86.1
Suburban Cook	9,961	19,052	91.3
DuPage County	10,464	21,155	102.2
Kane County	8,467	15,890	87.7
Lake County	10,103	21,765	115.4
McHenry County	8,641	17,271	99.9
Will County	7,993	15,186	90.0
Metro Area	8,560	16,739	95.6
U.S.	7,295	14,420	97.7
CPI (base=1983)*	71.8	125.0	74.1

Sources: For 1979, U.S. Bureau of the Census, *Current Population Reports*, Series P-26, No. 88-ENC-SC (March 1990); for 1989, Northeastern Illinois Planning Commission (based on data from the 1990 U.S. Census).

* Consumer Price Index: price level changes in metropolitan Chicago.

TABLE 7:   Changes in Per Capita Money Income for Selected
Municipalities in Chicago Metropolitan Area, 1979 to 1989

	Per Capita Income		Pct. Chg. 1979-89	Pop. 1980	Pop. 1990
	1979	1989			
City of Chicago	$ 6,933	$12,899	86.1%	3,005,078	2,783,726
Suburban Cook					
Winnetka	22,482	62,482	177.9	12,772	12,174
Harvey	5,946	8,690	46.1	35,810	29,771
DuPage County					
Oak Brook	22,349	60,347	170.0	7,245	9,178
West Chicago	7,489	13,241	76.8	12,550	14,796
Kane County					
Geneva	10,987	21,232	93.2	9,881	12,617
Carpentersville	7,055	11,803	67.3	23,272	23,049
Lake County					
Lake Forest	19,800	47,200	138.4	15,245	17,836
North Chicago	5,606	9,165	63.5	38,774	34,978
McHenry County					
Lakewood	11,736	29,950	155.2	1,254	1,609
Harvard	7,978	13,337	67.2	5,126	5,975
Will County					
Frankfort	8,785	23,817	171.1	5,390	7,180
Romeoville	6,797	12,323	81.3	15,519	14,074
Metro Area	8,560	16,739	95.5	7,103,624	7,261,176
U.S.	7,295	14,420	97.7		
CPI (base=1983)*	71.8	125.0	74.1		

* Consumer Price Index: price level changes in metropolitan Chicago.

Sources: For 1979, U.S. Bureau of the Census, *Current Population Reports*
Series P-26, No. 88-ENC-SC (March 1990); for 1989, Northeastern Illinois
Planning Commission (based on data from the 1990 U.S. Census).

First, poverty was more extensive at the outset of the 1990s than at any time since 1983, nationwide and regionwide. Both the absolute number of persons with incomes below the poverty line and the percentage of poor persons in the total population, the "poverty rate," was significantly higher in 1991 than in 1989, 1979, or even 1973 (U.S. House of Representatives, 1992, pp. 1274-1275).[7] Looking back to 1973, poverty had receded to its lowest point in the previous 30 years; the poverty rate had dropped to 11.1 percent or to a total of 22.9 million persons with incomes below the poverty line. But in 1979 and 1989, despite economic prosperity, poverty had remained widespread and more extensive than in 1973.

In short, high levels of poverty persisted throughout the 1980s and into the early 1990s, oscillating with the business cycle, but never retreating to the low points of the early 1970s. To illustrate the direction of change, consider comparable poverty data for 1979, 1989, and 1991, the latest available year. The total number of poor persons nationwide, for example, rose from 26 million in 1979 to 31.5 million in 1989, and poverty rates rose accordingly from 11.7 percent to 12.8 percent (U.S. House of Representatives, 1992, pp. 1274-1275). In 1991, during a recession, the poverty rate jumped to 14.2 percent, and the number of persons with incomes below the poverty line soared to 35.7 million, the highest number since 1964, just before the War on Poverty (*New York Times*, 1992). This high 1991 rate nonetheless remained somewhat below the 1983 nationwide rate of 15.2 percent, the worst year of the last decade, a year in which the incomes of over 35.2 million persons had sunk below the poverty line. Data for 1992, a year of lingering recession and high unemployment, will undoubtedly reveal further increases.

Beyond the enlarged scale of poverty, a second set of critical trends relating to the social incidence of poverty also pre-

---

[7] The poverty line is determined annually by the Social Security Administration. It is based on an estimate of the minimum pre-tax, cash income needed to provide necessities, such as food, shelter, and clothing, either for an individual or for families of differing sizes. For example, a family of four was classified as poor if it had a cash income of less than $12,675 in 1989, or of $13,942 in 1991. The poverty level is updated each year to reflect changes in the Consumer Price Index. Non-cash benefits, such as Food Stamps and Medicaid, are not counted as income.

vailed in the 1980s. Specifically, poverty continued to recede among the elderly and to widen among women and children, multiplying most rapidly among minority families. The poverty rate among elderly persons, for example, was 12.2 percent in 1990, a significant drop from 15.7 percent in 1980 and from 29.5 percent in 1967, a generation ago. Nonetheless, many older persons, especially women, continued to have low incomes, clustered barely above the poverty line.

Women heading households and their children comprised an accelerating proportion of the poor. The growing incidence of poverty among children is ominous for the nation's future. The poverty rate for all U.S. children reached 20.6 percent in 1990, compared with 18.3 percent in 1980, and 15.1 percent in 1970. Thus, one in five children was growing up in a financially disadvantaged household. For children living in Black or Hispanic households, the proportions were much higher, and their numbers have been accelerating for decades. By 1990, 31.9 percent of all Black children and 28.1 percent of all Hispanic children, compared with 10.7 percent of all non-Hispanic White children, were living in poverty (U.S. House of Representatives, 1992, p. 1275). As will be seen later, the comparable proportions are even higher in large cities such as Chicago.

Turning to the Chicago metropolitan area, dominant national trends in poverty patterns prevailed there as well. What specific changes occurred in the extent, the social composition, and the location of poverty in the region? First, the sheer number of persons living in the region with incomes below the poverty line was enormous. The total in the six counties together has ranged from lows of roughly 800,000 persons in years of peak economic activity, as in 1989 and 1979, to highs of more than one million persons in years of recession, as in 1983 (see Table 8). Whether in good times or bad, however, about three-fourths of all poor persons in the region lived within the boundaries of the city of Chicago.[8]

---

[8] The ebb and flow of poverty fluctuates with the vicissitudes of the economy. Consequently, census data on changes in the poverty population between 1979 and 1989 are singularly unrevealing because these happened to be years of low unemployment. In addition, neither countywide nor citywide totals illuminate the intense spatial concentrations of poverty because the geographic aggregations are too gross. Despite these caveats, Table 8 does provide a rough overview of minimum levels and approximate locations of the region's poor.

Second, the nationwide shift in the incidence of poverty from the elderly to the young has also prevailed in the Chicago area. A recent study by the Children's Defense Fund, analyzing 1990 census data, confirmed this change in the city of Chicago. Although more than one-fourth (26.2%) of children living in all large U.S. cities (with populations of over 100,000 persons) were impoverished in 1989, the comparable proportion in Chicago was much higher (*Chicago Sun-Times*, 1992b). Nearly 250,000 children, representing fully one-third (33.9%) of all the city's children, were living in poverty-level households, typically headed by single women. Among minority households, an even larger proportion of children were growing up poor and living mostly in concentrated, often segregated, poverty areas. In 1989, 17 percent of Chicago's non-Hispanic White children under 18 years of age were living in households with incomes below the poverty line. In Black households, the comparable proportions were much higher. Almost half (47%) of all Black children were growing up in poor households. As for Hispanic and Native-American children, the proportion had reached 31 percent; for Asian-American children, it was 20 percent (*Chicago Sun-Times*, 1992b).

Third, the region's poverty population is largely concentrated within the city of Chicago. A scan of city and county poverty rates in 1989 highlights the gross differences that prevail and, as expected, confirms the disparate income patterns observed earlier (Table 8). In the city of Chicago, for example, the poverty rate in 1989 reached 21.6 percent, compared to a nationwide rate of the 13.5 percent. Thus, even before the impact of recession, more than one in five of all Chicago residents was subsisting on an income below the poverty line, a proportion little changed from a decade earlier. In contrast, comparable rates in the collar counties were much lower than those in either the city or the nation. Countywide rates were from 2.7 percent in DuPage, 3.5 percent in McHenry, 5.2 percent in Lake, 5.3 percent in suburban Cook, 6.0 percent in Will, and 6.8 percent in Kane.

In both suburbs and city, however, comparisons of average rates alone may obscure specific geographic concentrations of poverty. Even within prosperous suburban counties, high concentrations of poverty can be found, albeit in a limited number of places. In 1989, for example, only 24 of the 263 suburban municipalities had poverty rates of more than 10 percent. And these were virtually the same areas that had sheltered the poor

in 1979.   The concentration of poverty in low-income, Black
suburbs in particular was often as intense as in poor city areas.
In 1989, almost half the population (49.2%) of Ford Heights,
the poorest municipality in Cook County, had incomes below
the poverty line.

TABLE 8: Poverty Population in Metropolitan Chicago, 1979, 1983, 1989

	Poverty Pop. 1979 (1,000s)	Rate	Poverty Pop. 1983 (1,000s)	Rate	Poverty Pop. 1989 (1,000s)	Rate
Cook County	705.7	13.6%	NA	NA	713.3	14.2%
Chicago	601.4	20.3	754.0	27.2%	592.3	21.6
Suburban Cook	104.3	4.7	NA	NA	121.0	5.3
DuPage County	19.8	3.0	NA	NA	20.9	2.7
Kane County	16.7	6.1	NA	NA	21.3	6.9
Lake County	21.9	5.3	NA	NA	25.6	5.2
McHenry County	6.2	4.2	NA	NA	6.3	3.5
Will County	20.3	6.4	NA	NA	21.0	6.0
Metro Area	790.6	11.3	1,020.0	14.4	808.4	11.3
U.S.	26,072.0	11.7	35,303.0	15.2	31,534.0	12.8

NA = Not available.

Sources: For 1979 and 1989, Northeastern Illinois Planning Commission
(based on data from the U.S. Census, 1980 and 1990). For 1983, U.S. Bureau of the Census, *Characteristics of Population Below the Poverty Line:
Current Population Reports*, P-60, No. 147 (Washington, D.C., 1983). For
nationwide figures, U.S. House of Representatives, Committee on Ways and
Means, *Overview of Entitlement Programs: 1992 Green Book* (Washington,
D.C.: U.S. Government Printing Office, 1992).

Detailed comparisons of poverty, beyond the scope of this chapter, in Chicago's 77 designated community areas also provide stark testimony to persisting geographic differences. According to a study in *The Chicago Reporter*, the ten poorest city neighborhoods identified in the 1990 census were the very same ten poorest that were found in the 1980 census. In declining, segregated, Black neighborhoods, the exodus of middle- and working-class families has left poverty ever more concentrated. The poorest city neighborhood, Oakland, for example, has sustained enormous population and housing losses since 1965. And its poverty rate has risen accordingly from 42.7 percent in 1969 to 65.6 percent in 1979 to 72.3 percent in 1989 (*Chicago Reporter*, 1992).

To summarize the area trends of three decades, pockets of poverty have deepened profoundly while affluent enclaves have flourished. The difficulty of building regional cooperation on common problems, particularly housing, is obviously compounded by these gaping contrasts in poverty and plenty, within both city and suburbs.

Policy Guidelines

In what ways do these trends toward income inequality and sustained poverty bear on housing policies? Here are a few guidelines for assessing local housing priorities.

First, since the "affordability" problem is as rooted in low incomes as in high costs, its resolution requires policies that transcend housing alone. Over the long run, the best way to close the affordability gap would be to raise the incomes of low-wage earners to cover expenditures for at least maintaining low-cost housing. Without spelling out specific ways of incorporating housing and neighborhood development into a larger framework of economic development, two commonly used strategies can be identified, namely "jobs-to-people" and "people-to-jobs" (Joseph, 1990; Gottlieb, 1991). Both ways of raising incomes by promoting local development are currently conceivable. The "jobs-to-people" strategy became feasible in the 1990s mostly because large swaths of previously built-up city lands were emptied out over the course of three decades. At this juncture, derelict sites could be assembled on a scale sufficient to transform dying, dangerous neighborhoods into viable modern industrial parks with affordable housing nearby. Regarding the "people-to-jobs" strategy, for city workers cut off from employment opportunities in costly suburban areas, programs that would expedite access to distant job sites should supplement the direct provision of low-income housing near outlying centers. Programs, for example, to bridge the mismatches in job locations, job-market information, and job skills would include improvements in public transit, employment training, job searches, health care, and more. Otherwise, upwardly mobile families of all races and ethnic origins will be outward bound and bequeath older city neighborhoods exclusively to the hardcore unemployed.

Second, the upward trajectory of poverty—in good times as well as bad, in suburb as well as city—indicates that poverty and housing problems will persist even in the face of vigorous economic activity. Poverty has become less responsive to economic growth because many more low-income groups remain outside the job market and because of secular, structural shifts in labor demand (Cutler and Katz, 1991). Women supporting children alone and young men with rudimentary work skills comprise rising proportions of the poor. Caught in a conundrum of interrelated problems, housing often has a low priority in their personal scale of needs. Thus, programs that focus on building strong communities, on raising economic self-sufficiency and educational quality, from pre-school through job training, are critical to improving conditions in concentrated poverty neighborhoods. If these efforts are successful, low-cost housing may be salvaged as well.

Third, the prospects appear dim for raising the earning capacity of the poorest of the poor enough to pay for the minimum costs of maintaining rental housing. Hobbled with multiple problems in the job market, the incomes of destitute persons in Chicago have fallen well below the official poverty line. Barely subsisting at standards of living found in third-world nations, their incomes have nearly sunk to "absolute poverty" levels, defined by the World Bank as the income level required to support a minimum daily caloric intake. Some Chicago Housing Authority (CHA) residents have been subsisting at that marginal standard of living. Less than 10 percent of CHA residents are employed. Three-fourths of them receive some form of governmental support, and most have incomes below $5,000 a year (Bjorklund, 1991; *Chicago Sun-Times*, 1992a). For persons with such low incomes, *no* shelter costs would seem to be "affordable" because public assistance payments barely pay for food, clothing, and transportation (Stone, 1990).

Fourth, the sheer scale of poverty, particularly in the city, is daunting. The number of poor persons needing housing assistance is totally incommensurate with the scale of current programs. By 1990, after more than a quarter of a century of varied public and private housing programs, the total volume of assisted units available in the city of Chicago amounted to well under 80,000 units.[9] Persons with poverty incomes, however, must be reckoned in the hundreds of thousands, ranging somewhere between 600,000 to 750,000 persons during the 1980s (see Table 8). Well-designed, well-intentioned public-private programs have been able to assist no more than several thousand households annually, even with the best of "creative financing" and enormous efforts by community groups. For example, under the exemplary Gautreaux rent subsidy program, only 4,700 families have been assisted over the course of 25 years (*Chicago Sun-Times*, 1993).[10] Despite declining population, local leaders appear to be running a treadmill, losing sound, affordable units faster than they can be replaced.

Fifth, the rising concentration of poverty, both spatially and racially, is a self-reinforcing trend that will worsen without direct intervention. Selective out-migration of successful Blacks and Latinos from declining city neighborhoods has isolated the poor and heightened the intensity of "underclass" behavior. Social scientists agree that so-called "neighborhood effects" greatly influence child-rearing and adolescent behavior (Wilson, 1991). Neighborhood conditions and institutions can influence for good or ill such basic personal traits as self-esteem, values, discipline, and perception of opportunity. Although the social dynamics are still murky, different groups are clearly affected differently.

There is much less agreement, however, about ways to counteract the unrelenting dangers of "mean streets." Small-scale, individually tailored, comprehensive demonstration programs that combine housing, education, health care, employment, and other social services have often been successful

---

[9] Estimated from City of Chicago, 1991, p. 29.

[10] The Gautreaux program is discussed elsewhere in this volume (Rosenbaum, 1993; Polikoff, 1993).

(Schorr, 1988).   The challenge is to find ways to replicate them
on a scale commensurate with the vast pool of need.   The challenge is to move from individually focused "retail" programs to
group-based, self-help, "wholesale" programs that will reverber-
ate on at least a neighborhood scale.

POLICY CHOICES

In a period of fiscal austerity and scarce resources for housing,
policy choices are limited.   Since the problem of excessive
housing costs has multiple roots, a multi-pronged strategy is
most likely to be effective.   Several policy paths seem most
promising at this juncture.   Each level of government can contribute in different ways to alleviating the problem of affordable
housing and, in concert, support an effective, coordinated set of
strategies.   Starting with the City of Chicago and moving up the
governmental ladder, a brief summary of what I view as central
issues and objectives precedes a list of recommendations for
achieving them.

City of Chicago

An adequate supply of low- and moderate-cost housing can be
found in many city neighborhoods if it can be preserved and
modernized in cost-effective ways.   The rehabilitation of sound
existing buildings should be a prime housing objective.   The
crushing burden of providing costly services to growing numbers of virtually destitute families, however, suggests other vital
supporting objectives.   Housing development programs must be
complemented by a palette of policies that will promote economic opportunities.   Working-class and middle-income families
of all races and nationalities must be encouraged to remain in
the city.   Their investments and efforts as active participants are
vital to the success of most housing and neighborhood improvement programs.   The critical common link to achieving these simultaneous objectives would be a strategy that targets the improvement of neighborhoods instead of individual housing structures.   Priorities in public services should be tailored to the
varied needs of particular kinds of neighborhoods and groups.
A few specific recommendations are listed here.

• First, to preserve the existing low-cost housing stock, intervene earlier, while structures are still habitable, to prevent foreclosures, vandalism, and ultimate abandonment.
• Second, revise building and zoning codes to permit modern, low-cost rehabilitation techniques suited to the architecture of older, low-rise, multi-family apartments and homes.
• Third, encourage partnerships with community and affinity groups, such as immigrant societies or unions, to restore multi-family rental buildings and to construct new, mixed-income, in-fill apartments.
• Fourth, combat redlining in mortgages and insurance and monitor the enforcement of the Community Reinvestment Act.
• Fifth, widen access to credit by reserving scarce public funds for low-interest rehabilitation loans to small-scale, owner-occupied rental buildings and to community groups that might wish to build limited-equity ownership cooperatives.
• Sixth, create tax-exempt land trusts to assemble and hold vacant lands for planned future development, whether for economic, residential, or recreational re-use.
• Seventh, coordinate comprehensive planning for capital improvements, education, and the delivery of public services in each residential area in order to reflect differing local priorities.

Suburban Counties and Municipalities

In contrast to the city of Chicago, low- and moderate-income housing is scarce in most suburban areas, particularly in growth sectors of the region. Therefore, the central policy objective should be to increase the supply of low- and moderate-income homes and apartments that are accessible to jobs in growth areas.

The provision of affordable rental units near job centers and transit hubs can bring many benefits. First, by cutting the distance and time spent commuting, traffic gridlock, tailpipe emissions, and energy consumption are likely to be reduced. Second, labor shortages in expanding job centers would be relieved. Finally, provision of reasonably priced rentals would permit lower-income residents, such as municipal employees,

young people raised in the community, and the elderly, to remain in the area.

By 1990, about three-fifths of all jobs, housing units, and
persons living in the six-county area were located outside the
city. Continued population growth in the suburbs is foreseen.
Yet the Chicago region remains the nation's grand champion of
political fragmentation. More than 1,200 units of local government can be found in the six-county metropolitan area alone.
These include over 260 municipalities and many special dis-
tricts, but exclude countless local governments in adjacent Wisconsin and Indiana counties that, altogether, compose the integrated economic region.

The political barriers to areawide cooperation in the Chicago region are formidable, particularly on socially sensitive issues such as housing. Consequently, a combination of state fiscal incentives in conjunction with administrative requirements
may be necessary to help suburban community leaders perceive
their long-term self-interest in moving toward socioeconomic
diversity. The following policies are suggested:

- First, a formal regionwide process of cooperation should
be instituted to coordinate planning for balancing job
growth with affordable housing and transit. Its purposes
would be to bridge the spatial mismatches of workers and
jobs and to assure that a fair share of low-income units be
distributed throughout the region. In the past, the Northeastern Illinois Planning Commission (NIPC) provided leadership for a voluntary process of cooperation, but statutory
powers to implement plans and to enforce policies reside
with local governments.
- Second, to bridge enormous socioeconomic disparities
within each of the collar counties, county boards and mayors of large municipalities should undertake plans for developing scattered-site, small-scale, low- and moderate-income
housing near transportation and shopping hubs. The cooperation of major local employers could be enlisted in financing such joint housing ventures.
- Third, to contain rising housing prices, local governments
should be required to review building codes, land-use regulations, and subdivision regulations and to modify those that
raise costs excessively. Prohibitions against accessory
apartments and modular building techniques, imposition of
impact fees, and extended delays in the permitting process

are common-place examples. Such regulations far exceed health and safety standards, their primary objectives. They boost housing prices, often deliberately, in order to exclude low- and moderate-income families (U.S. Department of Housing and Urban Development, 1991).

• Fourth, to provide equal opportunity in housing and job markets, laws against discrimination must be enforced, and steering or other disguised discriminatory practices must be prohibited.

State of Illinois

The State has a unique role in the provision of affordable housing, one that transcends the financing or construction of housing units per se. Only state government has regionwide authority in metropolitan Chicago. Leadership in a regional development process that envisions socially balanced residential communities as essential components of long-range economic growth is ultimately a state responsibility, even though some state officials would acknowledge this reluctantly.

However jealously localities in the Chicago area may guard their land-use and regulatory powers, these powers are derived, constitutionally, from state government. To overcome local resistance to balanced growth, state officials need not resort to the politically explosive expedient of pre-empting land-use powers, as has been done in a few states. Illinois, instead, should be the catalyst to the bottom-up, cooperative endeavors recommended in the previous section. Its leadership in promoting regional, fair-share, affordable housing programs is critical since local elected officials will often encounter opposition from narrow interest groups. Potent carrots and sticks rest in the hands of state government. Direct financial incentives are most effective. Even though state budgets are extremely tight at this juncture, current expenditures can often be redirected and targeted to elicit local compliance. Listed below are options designed to engender cooperation among multiple, competitive municipalities.

• First, strengthen and extend the mission of existing regional and county planning agencies by committing funds expressly to planning for mixed-income, affordable housing in the context of economic development.

• Second, target portions of federal and state housing funds, administered by the Illinois Housing and Development Authority, to job-rich communities that lack affordable rental housing.
• Third, direct major new state investments in infrastructure exclusively to areas with mixed-income housing plans.
• Fourth, withhold state-administered grants for sewer, water, or road improvements to areas that adhere to exclusionary zoning practices and excessive subdivision regulations or that impose unreasonable extractions and impact fees.
• Fifth, set aside a percentage of transportation funds allocated to the Chicago area specifically for public transit to job centers from low-income suburban and city areas. In the short term, before route and travel patterns are firmly established, small buses, mini-vans, and other forms of paratransit should be used for reverse commuting and cross-suburban transit.
• Sixth, explore regional revenue-sharing options to reduce reliance on local property taxes. The rationale for exclusionary housing practices and "fiscal zoning" is often rooted in efforts to enhance local revenues. These, in turn, rely heavily on property tax assessments. The wide variations in taxing capacities among the region's many jurisdictions are often perverse. Since fiscal disparities usually reflect socioeconomic disparities, the poorest municipalities may paradoxically have to pay the highest property tax rates (Rafuse, 1991).[11]

---

[11] For example, in 1992, Ford Heights, the poorest municipality in Cook County, with a 1989 per capita income of only $4,660, had a property tax rate of more than $18 per $100 of assessed valuation. By contrast, in South Barrington, a rich Cook County municipality with a 1989 per capita income of $47,248, the rate was less than $7 per $100 of assessed valuation (*Chicago Tribune*, 1992b). Assessed valuation of property is not the same as market value. In Cook County, different classes of real estate are assessed at different levels for tax purposes. For example, single-family homes are assessed at 16 percent of market value, while commercial properties are assessed at 38 percent.

Federal Government

Since the Great Depression of the 1930s, the federal government has played a strategic role in local housing markets. Despite shifting program priorities and funding cutbacks during the
Reagan years, it has ostensibly maintained the commitment to
the 1949 goal of providing "a decent home and suitable living
environment for every American family."

As recently as 1990, Congress reaffirmed this commitment
in the National Affordable Housing Act. Six specific objectives
of federal policy were spelled out that together articulated the
distillation of half a century of national housing goals.[12] All
were time-honored, significant objectives, but the second one
restated the purpose of this chapter directly: "to increase the
nation's supply of decent housing that is affordable to low-
income and moderate-income families and accessible to job opportunities."

How best can this forthright objective be achieved? The
first obvious way would be to appropriate funds sufficient to
implement the recently enacted 1990 housing programs. The
second would be to restore cutbacks in other viable programs,
such as Community Development Block Grants, targeted principally to cities that provide shelter for millions of the nation's
poor.

In the immediate future, however, prospects seem dim for
boosting direct housing expenditures in amounts anywhere near
the scale of need. Fiscal austerity will undoubtedly prevail
deep into the 1990s because of the ballooning federal deficit and
gloomy short-term economic prospects. On the one hand, the
Congressional Budget Office has forecast lower tax collections
because of slower economic growth and lower personal incomes. On the other hand, higher outlays are also foreseen for
expanded entitlement programs and for interest payments on the
huge federal debt (*New York Times*, 1991a). Little room is left
for increasing discretionary appropriations such as housing.

Furthermore, despite the ringing rhetoric of venerable housing goals, housing assistance has never been an entitlement program, granted automatically to any who might qualify. Nor
have housing subsidies ever been formally incorporated into the
"safety net." In 1987, for example, housing assistance, from

---

[12] These objectives are listed in the appendix to this chapter.

any government source, was extended to only one-third of all poor renter households in the Chicago metropolitan area (Sheft, 1991, p. 22). The chief entitlements to be found in the conundrum of federal programs built up over the years, conceivably, may be the homeowner benefits, granted automatically through the income tax code. But the impact of these tax preferences is regressive, benefiting wealthy households more than poor ones.

At this juncture, tenant-based rental subsidies, the currently favored cost-effective form of extending federal assistance to low-income households, reach only a fraction of those who qualify for them. To illustrate, a recent HUD study found that in 1989, as many as 13.8 million renter households, comprising 41 percent of the total of 33.8 million renter households in the nation, would be eligible for housing assistance according to current income criteria. Of course, not all of these "very low-income" households, to borrow HUD terminology, will seek or need housing assistance. But those with household incomes amounting to less than half the local median are conceivably eligible. In 1989, rental assistance was actually extended to roughly 4 million households, representing about 12 percent of total renters and 29 percent of the income-eligible pool. Many more needy households were reached in this way than in the previous decade (Casey, 1992, p. 4).

The number and proportion of tenant-based subsidies have gradually increased during the past fifteen years.[13] This rise reflects a major shift in federal housing priorities. A systematic withdrawal from construction and project-based subsidies, inherited from previous administrations, has been underway, and growing emphasis was placed instead on tenant-based assistance. During those years, budget authority and new commitments for housing production declined accordingly (U.S. House of Representatives, 1992, p. 1677).

For these and other reasons, state and local housing initiatives have become more critical. The recommendations set forth here reflect these views. Mostly they emphasize parsimonious ways of realigning federal housing priorities and tax

---

[13] In 1992, according to the Congressional Budget Office, over 4.6 million households received rental subsidies, more than double the 2.1 million households in 1977 (U.S. House of Representatives, 1992, p. 1679).

code benefits.   Four changes in the tax code head the list of cost-effective ways of addressing housing needs.

First, the frequently extended Low-Income Housing Tax Credit should be permanently incorporated into the tax code. Created in the 1986 Tax Reform legislation, it encouraged corporations and, to a limited extent, individuals, to finance low-income housing through tax credits.   As the principal vehicle for harnessing public-private cooperation in building new units for working-class families, it has helped to finance more than 325,000 rental units nationwide and 3,300 regionwide since its inception (*Chicago Tribune*, 1991).[14]

Second, in order to limit that conversion of older, federally subsidized rental units to market-rate housing, recently enacted preservation incentives should be fully implemented.   These economic incentives were designed to preserve the low-income rental stock, built decades ago by private developers under a variety of federal assistance programs.   After 20 years, developers have had the right to pre-pay mortgages on certain federally subsidized units.   During the 1990s, many will surely exercise that right, particularly if the housing is well maintained and located in good neighborhoods.   As many as 1.2 million housing units, representing over 25 percent of the nation's total assisted stock, may be lost in the coming years (*Chicago Tribune*, 1989).   If possible, local not-for-profit organizations should be helped to acquire these properties when they are refinanced by private developers.

Third, first-time homebuyers should be permitted to use retirement savings in IRA accounts, without penalties, for equity payments on the purchase of a home.   This change will not only facilitate homeownership but also encourage savings by young workers for tangible near-term as well as long-term goals.

Fourth, the homeowner income tax deductions for mortgage interest and local property tax payments should be limited, restructured, and ultimately phased out.   These tax-code ben-

---

[14] Locally, the Chicago Equity Fund was the first fund to be established in the nation for the purpose of pooling corporate capital for investments in affordable housing.   The cumulative sum amassed since 1975 had surpassed $59 million by 1991 (*Chicago Tribune*, 1992a).   Beyond the 3,300 units of affordable housing completed by 1992, another 2,404 units were in development, according to reliable sources at Local Initiatives Support Corporation in Chicago.

efits for homeowners are the only housing "entitlement" program extant. Yet as currently structured, they offer the most benefits to those who least need help.

A process of gradual reduction is foreseen, one that would disturb real estate markets the least and benefit lower-income homeowners the most. To illustrate some of the options, a systematic phase-out might begin, for example, by eliminating deductions for second homes, or by capping the upper limit of total monetary deductions, or by transforming the deduction into a flat housing tax credit, unrelated to the value of the house. However popular current benefits may be, there are three good reasons to revise them. They are costly, unfair, and probably unnecessary to promote homeownership.

Regarding cost, homeowner-related tax benefits constitute the largest housing subsidy program of the federal government, albeit indirectly. This drain on tax revenues is expected to total more than $55 billion by 1992 (U.S. House of Representatives, 1991, p. 869). Looking back at the last decade, these so-called "tax expenditures" (in essence, revenues lost to the federal government) have more than doubled in only ten years. The drain in revenues from housing deductions rose from $22 billion in 1980 to $47 billion in 1990.

Regarding equity, these benefits are very regressive because they tend to be inversely correlated with income. Wealthy homeowners receive the largest shares, and low-income homeowners receive lesser benefits. Renters receive none at all, except in the unlikely event that landlords might choose to pass the benefits along to tenants in the form of lower rents.

The preference for homeownership is so widely shared that costly incentives to promote it are unnecessary. Other nations, such as Canada and Australia, with comparably high rates of homeownership, offer few special tax incentives. Furthermore, because households with the lowest earnings also have the lowest income taxes, they benefit least from this form of assistance when purchasing a home. In short, if even a fraction of the projected $55 billion in "tax expenditures" for housing could be recouped and partially sequestered, other more equitable housing programs could be supported.

Fifth, there should be full funding for the HOME provisions of 1990 National Affordable Housing Act. As the first major piece of housing legislation since 1974, the act offers three principal initiatives. These include the HOME Investment Partnerships program, the Homeownership Opportunity for Peo-

ple Everywhere (HOPE) program, and the National Homeownership Trust.   The HOME program provides block grants to
state and local governments for affordable housing initiatives
and is a valuable addition to the federal urban policy arsenal.

Sixth, if sluggish economic growth persists, the construction
of low-income housing would be a time-honored way to stimulate economic activity.   In the past, the housing sector has been
a balance wheel in the economy, often leading the recovery.
During the Great Depression, the first public housing legislation
was enacted as much to prime the pump as to clear the slums.

Conclusion

To summarize, these many policy recommendations are all directed toward opening opportunities for affordable housing,
toward closing disparities within the region, and toward facilitating access to employment.   In fulfilling these mutually supportive goals, there are three priorities.   The provision of low-
and moderate-income housing in suburban areas of high job
growth heads the list of critical needs.   No less vital is the
preservation of the dwindling stock of sound, older dwellings,
both publicly and privately owned, mostly located in the city
and nearby suburbs.   Finally, the thinning out and emptying out
of vast swathes of industrial and residential land on the west
and south sides of Chicago offer an unprecedented opportunity
for comprehensive redevelopment.   With little displacement,
these abandoned, dangerous combat zones can be transformed
into more than "enterprise zones."   These wasted acres can be
reclaimed as green acres, as the sites of modern industrial parks
surrounded by diversified, mixed-income housing, with model
schools and multiple supportive services.   In the closing years
of the century, we must seek new ways to turn bleak, pock-
marked streets into strong communities, into healthy neighborhoods with renewed vitality, civility, and hope.

94   *Doris B. Holleb*

APPENDIX: OBJECTIVES OF THE NATIONAL
AFFORDABLE HOUSING ACT OF 1990

The stated objectives of the 1990 National Affordable Housing
Act read well, namely:

- to ensure that every resident of the United States has access to decent shelter or assistance in avoiding homelessness;
- to increase the Nation's supply of decent housing that is
affordable to low-income and moderate-income families and
accessible to job opportunities;
- to improve housing opportunities for all residents of the
United States, particularly members of disadvantaged minorities, on a nondiscriminatory basis;
- to help make neighborhoods safe and livable;
- to provide every American community with a reliable,
readily available supply of mortgage financing at the lowest
possible interest rates;
- to encourage tenant empowerment and reduce generational
poverty in federally assisted and public housing by improving the means by which self-sufficiency may be achieved.

REFERENCES

Apgar, William C., Jr., Denise DiPasquale, Jean Cummings,
    and Nancy McArdle (1990). *The State of the Nation's
    Housing, 1990.* Cambridge, Mass.: Joint Center for Hous-
    ing Studies, Harvard University.
Bjorklund, Richard (1991). "Seven Viewpoints on Rehab Pro-
    posals," *One City*, vol. 4, no. 4 (July/August 1991), p. 3.
    Chicago: Chicago Council on Urban Affairs.
Blank, Rebecca M. (1993). "The Employment Strategy: Pub-
    lic Policies to Increase Work and Earnings." In Sheldon
    Danziger, Gary Sandefur, and Daniel Weinberg, eds., *Pov-
    erty and Public Policy.* Cambridge, Mass.: Harvard Uni-
    versity Press, forthcoming.
Burtless, Gary, ed. (1990). *A Future of Lousy Jobs? The
    Changing Structure of U.S. Wages.* Washington, D.C.:
    The Brookings Institution.
Casey, Connie H. (1992). *Characteristics of HUD-Assisted
    Renters and Their Units in 1989.* Washington, D.C.: U.S.

Department of Housing and Urban Development, Office of Policy Development and Research, March 1992.

Chicago Department of Housing (1990). Harris File.

Chicago Reporter (1992). Vol. 21, no. 7 (July 1992), p. A-9.

Chicago Sun-Times (1991). August 4, 1991, pp. 1, 5.

_____ (1992a). August 11, 1992, p. 5.

_____ (1992b). August 12, 1992, pp. 1, 24.

_____ (1993). January 20, 1993, p. 58.

Chicago Tribune (1989). May 10, 1989, sec. 1, p. 8.

_____ (1991). August 11, 1991, sec. 2, p. 3.

_____ (1992a). July 29, 1992, sec. 2, p. 3.

_____ (1992b). September 5, 1992, sec. 1, p. 1.

_____ (1993). February 7, 1993, sec. 1, p. 10.

City of Chicago (1991). *Comprehensive Housing Affordability Strategy (CHAS), FY 1992 to FY 1996.* Chicago: Chicago Department of Housing.

Clements, Bill (1992). "Is Section 8 Housing Spurring Segregation in the Suburbs?" *Chicago Enterprise*, vol. 7, no. 2 (September 1992), pp. 18-28.

Cutler, David N., and Lawrence F. Katz (1991). "Untouched By The Rising Tide," *Brookings Review*, Winter 1991, pp. 41-45.

Dolbeare, Cushing N. (1990). *Out of Reach: Why Everyday People Can't Find Affordable Housing.* Washington, D.C.: Low Income Housing Information Service.

Fisher, Thomas, ed. (1991). "Affordable Housing: An American Birthright?" *Progressive Architecture*, Special Issue (June 1991), pp. 87-100.

Goetze, Rolf (1976). *Building Neighborhood Confidence: A Humanistic Strategy for Urban Housing.* Cambridge, Mass.: Ballinger.

Gottlieb, Harry N. (1991). *Jobs, Housing, and Race in the Chicago Metropolitan Area.* Chicago: Leadership Council for Metropolitan Open Communities.

Holleb, Doris B. (1981). "Housing and the Environment: Shooting at Moving Targets," *Annals of the American Academy of Political and Social Science*, vol. 453 (January 1981), pp. 180-221.

Joseph, Lawrence B., ed. (1990). *Creating Jobs, Creating Workers: Economic Development and Employment in Metropolitan Chicago.* Chicago: Center for Urban Research and Policy Studies, University of Chicago; distributed by University of Illinois Press.

Levy, Frank, and Richard C. Michael (1991). *The Economic Future of American Families: Income and Wealth Trends*. Washington, D.C.: Urban Institute Press.

Mills, Edwin S., and Kevin Kaiser (1990). "Low Income Housing in the 1980s." In Mark Alan Hughes and Therese A. McGuire, eds., *National Trends and Local Policies in Urban Housing*. *Research in Urban Economics*, vol. 8. Greenwich, Conn.: JAI Press.

New York Times (1991a). August 16, 1991, p. A8.

———— (1991b). October 31, 1991, p. A1.

———— (1992). September 4, 1992, p. A1.

Northeastern Illinois Planning Commission (1992). 1990 Census of Population and Housing, Summary Tape File 3, Profile Report.

Phillips, Kevin (1991). *The Politics of Rich and Poor: Wealth and the American Electorate in the Reagan Aftermath*. New York: Harper.

Polikoff, Alexander (1993). "'Chicago Is Not About to Give Up on a Bad Idea': The Future of Public Housing High-Rises." In this volume.

Rafuse, Robert W., Jr. (1991). "Fiscal Disparities in Chicagoland," *Intergovernmental Perspective*, vol. 17, no. 3 (Summer 1991), pp. 14-19. Washington, D.C.: Advisory Commission on Intergovernmental Relations.

Rosenbaum, James E. (1993). "Closing the Gap: Does Residential Integration Improve the Employment and Education of Low-Income Blacks?" In this volume.

Schorr, Lisbeth B. (1988). *Within Our Reach: Breaking the Cycle of Disadvantage*. New York: Doubleday.

Sheft, Mark (1991). *Chicago, Illinois—A Place to Call Home: The Crisis in Housing for the Poor*. Washington, D.C.: Center on Budget and Policy Priorities.

Stone, Michael E. (1990). *One-Third of a Nation: A New Look at Housing Affordability in America*. Washington, D.C.: Economic Policy Institute.

Taub, Richard P., D. Garth Taylor, and Jan D. Dunham (1984). *Paths of Neighborhood Change: Race and Crime in Urban America*. Chicago: University of Chicago Press.

U.S. Bureau of the Census (1992). *Workers With Low Earnings: 1964 to 1990*. Current Population Reports, Series P-60, No. 178. Washington, D.C.: U.S. Government Printing Office.

U.S. Department of Housing and Urban Development (1991). *"Not In My Back Yard": Removing Barriers to Affordable Housing.* Report of the Advisory Commission on Regulatory Barriers to Affordable Housing. Washington, D.C.: U.S. Department of Housing and Urban Development.

U.S. House of Representatives, Committee on Ways and Means (1991). *Overview of Entitlement Programs: 1991 Green Book.* Washington, D.C.: U.S. Government Printing Office.

――――― (1992). *Overview of Entitlement Programs: 1992 Green Book.* Washington, D.C.: U.S. Government Printing Office.

Wall Street Journal (1991). July 8, 1991, p. A11.

Wilson, William Julius (1991). "Poverty, Joblessness, and Family Structure in the Inner City: A Comparative Perspective." Conference paper, University of Chicago, October 1991.

COMMENTS

John C. Weicher[*]

Doris Holleb makes two main points: housing is becoming an increasing burden for low-income families because of rising costs and declining real incomes, and needed housing is being lost, especially in some city neighborhoods. In my judgment, her analysis is unfortunately limited by reliance on the decennial census, which at present is only partially available for 1990. My comments serve first to supplement and, I believe, correct her discussion; then I turn to some of the policy issues that she raises.

Affordability is indeed the most serious housing problem facing the poor—in the Chicago area as well as in the nation as a whole. Fully 70 percent of the low-income families in the United States with severe housing problems live in physically adequate housing but pay more than half their income to do so; fewer than 15 percent live in seriously inadequate housing (U.S. Department of Housing and Urban Development, 1991). The Chicago metropolitan area shows a similar, but even more pronounced, pattern: as of 1987 (the latest available data), 81 percent of the low-income families with severe housing problems lived in physically adequate housing but had a rent burden of more than 50 percent of their income, while only 6 percent lived in seriously inadequate housing (U.S. Department of Housing and Urban Development, 1993).[1]

---

[*] The opinions expressed in this commentary are the author's and not necessarily those of the U.S. Department of Housing and Urban Development or the U.S. General Accounting Office.

[1] I use the term "severe housing problems" as synonymous with "worst case need," the term used by Congress to describe those households whose housing is regarded as being of special concern and who should receive priority for housing assistance. Such households are very low-income renters (with incomes below 50% of the area median) that either pay 50 percent of their income for rent, live in seriously inadequate housing as defined in the American Housing Survey (AHS), or are homeless. In practice, the homeless are not counted in the AHS.

Nevertheless, Professor Holleb's discussion of affordability is overly negative. First, she is not correct in reporting a fall in real income since 1979 for the lowest three quintiles of the U.S. income distribution. Real incomes have risen across the distribution. This is not widely recognized because the official income statistics do not take account of a change in the method of calculating the cost of homeownership in the Consumer Price Index (CPI). Before 1983, the CPI used home purchase prices and mortgage rates. Since then, it has used the annual rental value of owner-occupied homes. As a result, the CPI was driven up during the 1970s and early 1980s by rising mortgage rates, but did not reflect their subsequent decline. When either the old or new method is used consistently, real incomes have risen more since 1969 or 1979 than the official series shows (Weicher, 1987). The Census Bureau has calculated income data by the new method, and these data show that all quintiles of households and all but the bottom quintile of families enjoyed higher mean real incomes in 1989 than in 1979. All show an improvement since 1980 (U.S. Bureau of the Census, 1990, p. 107). Similarly, the poverty rate, measured consistently, was lower in 1989 than in 1980.[2]

Second, the affordability picture has improved since the early 1980s; during the economic recovery of the latter part of the decade, incomes rose faster than rents in the United States (Apgar et al., 1991). This is also true for low-income renters (U.S. Department of Housing and Urban Development, 1991), and for the Chicago metropolitan area as a whole.[3] Comparison of 1980 and 1990 overlooks this improvement.

The loss of housing in some city neighborhoods needs to be put in perspective. American Housing Survey (AHS) data for the Chicago area show that the quality of the housing inventory has improved every four years. Part of the reason is that the least desirable housing has been dropping out of the inventory—the

---

[2] I have not updated the income data for the years since 1989 because the decennial census data on housing and other attributes used by Professor Holleb refer to the decade of the 1980s.

[3] The Chicago-area statements are based on comparison of rent and income data from the American Housing Survey for the Chicago metropolitan area between 1983 and 1987, as well as the residential rent component of the CPI for Chicago.

oldest, smallest, least well-equipped, in the worst condition.[4] This housing is mainly located in the city; fully three-quarters of the units removed from the inventory were in Chicago. As Professor Holleb's data indicate, the largest proportional losses of housing units were in old, poor neighborhoods.

Professor Holleb regards the loss of this housing as a problem, and it undoubtedly is for the communities where the housing was located. But from a housing market perspective, the loss appears to result more from demand than supply considerations. The rental vacancy rate in metropolitan Chicago rose from about 5 percent in 1970 to over 8 percent by 1990, while the rate in the city of Chicago rose from about 6 percent to about 9.5 percent. At the same time, crowding within occupied units has declined. The units lost from the inventory are not creating a housing shortage, even for the poor.

I agree with many of Professor Holleb's policy recommendations, although certainly not all of them. Rather than try to discuss them all, I want to focus on one recommendation she makes and one she does not.

Holleb favors eliminating homeowner tax deductions for mortgage interest and property taxes. These deductions are a popular target, and few scholars of tax policy support them. In my judgment, however, they should be retained for several reasons (Woodward and Weicher, 1989). The most relevant to Professor Holleb's concern about vertical equity is the need for consistent treatment of owner-occupied and rental housing. The homeowner should be viewed as a landlord renting to him- or herself. Landlords also receive the mortgage interest and property tax deductions, but these are not considered to be tax expenditures and, therefore, are not included in the data used by Professor Holleb. Given that rental units constitute one-third of the housing stock and all landlords can claim the deductions as business expenses,

---

[4] Space limitations do not permit presentation of detailed data to support the argument in the text. Detailed data are available on request. Also, fully consistent information is not available for many variables over the last 20 years. The AHS questionnaire was changed after 1983, for example, so that comparable information on units lacking complete plumbing is not available for 1987. Nonetheless, nearly all the available data support the broad statement in the text: Housing quality has improved in the Chicago metropolitan area, and the housing that has been removed from the inventory is generally much less desirable than the housing that remains.

their value is surely large. Further, since rental housing markets are competitive, the deductions are passed on in the form of reduced rents to tenants, most of whom are in the lower half of the income distribution.[5] Eliminating the mortgage interest and property tax deductions for homeowners does not achieve equity between owners and renters, owners and landlords, or owners and assisted housing residents.

Even if the deduction were eliminated, the political realities and vagaries of policymaking strongly imply that the tax revenue would not be used for housing. The congressional committees that control tax policy do not have jurisdiction over low-income housing programs. They would probably use the revenue for programs they do control. If somehow the revenue were made available to the appropriations committees, housing would still not be likely to benefit. When the FHA mortgage limits were raised in 1989 in an appropriations bill, the higher mortgage insurance premiums (which are counted as offsetting receipts) were, in effect, spent for the space station.

Finally, I am puzzled that in Professor Holleb's long list of policy recommendations, she leaves out the most cost-effective programs and the only ones that have not been plagued by scandals: housing vouchers and certificates, which now help over one million families to live in decent, privately owned housing of their own choosing. A large body of research indicates that vouchers and certificates reach poor people who live in bad housing—and place them in decent housing—about as effectively as new construction programs. Vouchers and certificates also serve poor people who already live in decent housing but who incur great expense relative to their incomes. This group includes the vast majority of low-income renters with housing problems in the Chicago area, as discussed above. Vouchers and certificates solve their rent-burden problem, helping them to continue living in their homes and their neighborhoods (Weicher 1990). In addition, although housing vouchers and certificates are not often regarded as neighborhood stabilization or revitalization programs, there is a study of neighborhood housing markets in Chicago that con-

---

[5] The major differences in tax treatment between owner-occupied and rental housing are that homeowners are not taxed on the imputed rental value of their home, and they do not pay capital gains taxes in most cases and cannot claim deductions for maintenance and depreciation as they occur. Landlords do pay capital gains taxes in most cases and can claim such deductions.

cludes that older neighborhoods are better served by vouchers or certificates than by new subsidized construction. Housing vouchers encourage the occupancy and maintenance of the better, older stock in the neighborhood, whereas new construction programs may weaken the neighborhood by reducing the demand for existing housing (Taub, Taylor, and Dunham, 1984, p. 192).

If affordability is indeed the serious problem that Professor Holleb and I both think it is, the appropriate policy would seem to be one that addresses it directly by bringing down the cost of adequate housing that is already available and, in many cases, already occupied by low-income households, rather than building more subsidized housing at much greater expense.

REFERENCES

Apgar, William C., Jr., Denise DiPasquale, Jean Cummings, and Nancy McArdle (1991). *The State of the Nation's Housing, 1991.* Cambridge, Mass.: Joint Center for Housing Studies, Harvard University.

Taub, Richard P., D. Garth Taylor, and Jan D. Dunham (1984). *Paths of Neighborhood Change: Race and Crime in Urban America.* Chicago: University of Chicago Press, 1984.

U.S. Bureau of the Census (1990). *Money Income and Poverty Status in the United States: 1989.* Current Population Reports, Series P-60, No. 168 (September 1990). Washington, D.C.: U.S. Government Printing Office.

U.S. Department of Housing and Urban Development (1991). *Priority Housing Problems and "Worst Case" Needs in 1989: A Report to Congress.* Washington, D.C.: U.S. Department of Housing and Urban Development, June 1991.

_____ (1993). *The Location of "Worst Case" Needs in the Late 1980s: A Report to Congress.* Washington, D.C.: U.S. Department of Housing and Urban Development, January 1993.

Weicher, John C. (1987). "Mismeasuring Poverty and Progress," *CATO Journal,* vol. 6, no. 3 (Winter 1987), pp. 715-730.

_____ (1990). "The Voucher/Production Debate." In Denise DiPasquale and Langley C. Keyes, eds., *Building Foundations: Housing and Federal Policy.* Philadelphia: University of Pennsylvania Press.

Woodward, Susan E., and John C. Weicher (1989). "Goring the Wrong Ox: A Defense of the Mortgage Interest Deduction,"

National Tax Journal, vol. 42, no. 3 (September 1989), pp. 301-313.

FEDERAL HOUSING POLICIES

Charles J. Orlebeke

The Reagan years were tough for housing advocates. In a decade of general retrenchment in federal domestic programs, housing seemed to have been hit hardest of all—most accounts putting the housing cut in the 70-to-80-percent range. In the 1960s and 1970s, the housing lobby—a formidable alliance of those who seek to do good and those in the homebuilding and real estate industry who seek simply to do well—had successfully pushed for a large federal commitment to housing. But in the Reagan era, housing groups were mainly at the barricades, struggling to hold a corner here and there of the old territory and resisting the Reagan administration's effort to install housing vouchers as the central instrument of federal housing assistance. As in most areas of domestic policy, President Reagan did not get everything he wanted, but he did get quite a bit. And while the battle was going on in Washington, state and local governments were fashioning a multitude of homegrown housing assistance programs that were tailored to local constituencies and less dependent on federal funds.

The purpose of this chapter is to outline how the nation got to this point in housing policy, culminating in the National Affordable Housing Act of 1990—the most ambitious and comprehensive housing legislation since 1974. In this chapter, I sketch the evolution of federal housing programs and pull out for analysis some of the major themes and issues that have marked housing policy debates. I then review the major components of the 1990 housing act and comment briefly on implications for Chicago.

A grand design for "national housing policy," an idea popular in the 1960s, is unfortunately nowhere in sight. The main action in housing—as in other areas of major domestic programming—is shifting to states and cities. Chicago's challenge will be to use the tools available from the federal government and combine them with other resources to fashion an affordable housing strategy.

THE EVOLUTION OF FEDERAL HOUSING PROGRAMS

For well over half a century, the federal government has inter-
vened in the nation's housing market more or less directly. It has
insured mortgages for homes and apartments, created a "secondary
market" for mortgages, provided financing at subsidized interest
rates for eligible homebuyers and apartment developers, given
local governments money to build and operate public housing,
given low-income persons vouchers of various kinds to shop the
private rental market, provided funding for homeless shelters, and
given local governments community development block grants that
may be used for housing rehabilitation. The federal government
has also tinkered with the tax system in a variety of ways and for
various purposes: for example, to encourage homeownership
through the deductibility of mortgage interest and property taxes,
to stimulate apartment construction by offering accelerated depreciation rates, to provide tax incentives for preserving historic
structures, and, more recently, to offer tax credits for investors in
low-income housing.
    The search for a policy underpinning these variegated initia-
tives—many of which have been started, stopped, re-started, and
adjusted in arcane ways over the years—leads typically to the
much-quoted goal declared in the 1949 housing act: "a decent
home and a suitable living environment for every American family." There had been housing programs before 1949, chief among
them the resoundingly successful Federal Housing Administration
(FHA) home mortgage insurance mechanism created in 1934, and
the more controversial and modestly scaled public housing program launched in 1937, but in 1949, the U.S. Congress authorized
a new $1.5 billion program of grants and loans for slum clearance
(later called "urban renewal") and authorized 800,000 units of
public housing to be built by local housing authorities such as the
Chicago Housing Authority. Although the public housing target
would not be realized for over two decades, the 1949 legislation
began the period when "the housing problem" became a permanent
part of the political landscape, and its declaration of the national
housing goal has been a durable rallying point for housing advocates.
    In the 1960s, federal housing programs branched out into new
subsidy techniques, especially direct federal loans to rental housing developers (both private and nonprofit) at below-market interest rates, producing housing targeted to the income group just
above that of public housing tenants. But prior to the milestone

1968 housing act, all subsidized housing starts were little more than a footnote to total housing production; not until 1966 did subsidized starts ever make up more than 5 percent of total starts.

During the 1960s, the groundwork was laid for an unprecedented surge in subsidized housing production in the 1970s. Several forces came together to build a national consensus: an activist president, Lyndon B. Johnson; a new cabinet-level Department of Housing and Urban Development (HUD, established in 1965); a President's Committee on Urban Housing chaired by a distinguished industrialist, Edgar Kaiser; the civil rights movement with its focus on the profound needs of the poor and minorities; and a deep slump in housing production in 1966 and 1967. Despite the frustration of Vietnam and the outbreak of urban riots across the land, the 1960s were also a time of new confidence in the federal government's capacity to analyze complex problems and design solutions with some degree of precision.

Housing experts in the 1960s looked at census data and foresaw a crisis on the horizon for the 1970s. The 1960 census had identified one out of six units as either dilapidated or deteriorating, and one out of eight as overcrowded; furthermore, as postwar babies matured and would form families of their own, market demand was expected to overwhelm the limited housing stock unless the nation mobilized to meet its shelter needs.

Affordability was another problem. The Kaiser Committee estimated that 7.8 million households were paying more than 25 percent of their income for housing, forcing them, it was assumed, to pay too much for standard housing (if they could find it) or else be consigned to the dregs of the substandard housing stock.

What would it take to solve the nation's housing problem? Analysts at HUD and the Kaiser Committee stirred the data on housing deficiencies, low incomes, and projected household formations, and then they came up with a number: 26 million housing units, including 6 million subsidized, to be produced over a ten-year period (1969-78). The White House and Congress adopted the number, and it was written into the 1968 housing act as a quantified national housing goal. The same legislation created two new subsidy programs: Section 235, which provided eligible home purchasers with FHA-insured mortgages subsidized to as low as one percent; and Section 236, which gave apartment developers one percent mortgage financing, also FHA-insured, enabling them to offer below-market rents to low- and moderate-income tenants. The mortgage interest subsidy mechanism of Sections

235 and 236, in contrast to direct federal loans, had the advantage of causing little budget impact in the initial years of production.

President Richard Nixon inherited the 1968 housing goal and programs, and he initially embraced them. His HUD secretary, George Romney, successfully pushed for budgetary support of the new subsidy programs and prodded the HUD bureaucracy into approving record production. Public housing production also went up. The 1970 total of 431,000 subsidized starts was almost seven times greater than in 1965, and the 1970-73 total subsidized production of 1,676,000 units added more federally assisted housing to the stock than had been produced in the entire history of subsidized housing since the Depression era. In addition, the share of total production consisting of subsidized housing rose as high as 29.3 percent in 1970.

The euphoria did not last long. As hundreds of thousands of incremental units were being added to the subsidized stock, the long-term subsidy obligation was building up rapidly—an ominous budgetary "uncontrollable" that worried federal budget managers. There were problems on other fronts as well. Big-city public housing projects were showing the wear and tear, as well as the social pathology, that has plagued them ever since, and federal operating subsidies became necessary for the first time. HUD was also being battered by scandals in its inner-city home mortgage insurance programs (both subsidized and unsubsidized). Nixon, after winning a landslide victory in 1972, abruptly declared a moratorium on new subsidy commitments and said that it was time to look for better ways.

HUD's evaluation of the subsidy programs proceeded on a crash basis in early 1973. The product was *Housing in the Seventies*, a lament over the confusion of objectives in federal housing policy and an indictment of the high cost, inefficiency, and inequities of the subsidy programs (U.S. Department of Housing and Urban Development, 1973). As the Nixon administration was floundering in the Watergate crisis, Congress and housing advocates cast about for a new subsidy vehicle.

The result was Section 8, which was signed into law in the early days of the Ford administration (August 1974). Section 8 was a low-income rental assistance program with separate components for new construction, substantial rehabilitation, and existing housing. Under the new construction and substantial rehabilitation components, private and nonprofit developers secured their own FHA-insured financing, and HUD entered into a long-term (20-30 year) contract to subsidize the difference between "fair market" rents and 25 percent (30% after 1981) of a tenant's income. The Section 8 existing housing component operated quite differently. An eligible tenant got a rental certificate (later generally referred to as a voucher) from the local housing authority and then shopped the private rental market for suitable housing within a fair market rent limit established by HUD. The subsidy was similar; the tenant paid 30 percent of income and HUD paid the balance. Fueled by Section 8 subsidies, housing production and assistance for low-income families picked up speed again during the Ford and Carter administrations, although not on the scale of the early 1970s.

The same 1974 housing act that gave the nation Section 8 also launched the Community Development Block Grant program (CDBG). This program was a product of the Nixon version of "new federalism"; it was an amalgam of previous categorical programs, the largest being urban renewal and model cities, and it provided cities with broad-based, flexible entitlement grants for a variety of purposes. Although CDBG was not specifically a housing program, cities could use the funds for housing rehabilitation, either alone or in combination with other federal, local, and private funds. (New construction was not permitted.) Many cities used one-third or more of their CDBG funds for housing.

Another milestone of housing policy evolution in the 1970s was the Experimental Housing Allowance Program (EHAP), which tested a variety of housing allowance or "voucher" models in twelve sites across the nation at a total cost of about $160 million. EHAP was certainly among the most ambitious and expensive social experiments ever financed by the federal government. Begun in the early 1970s, EHAP was mounted in response to growing problems in public housing projects and other low-income developments that concentrated—and, it was thought, also stigmatized—poor people with multiple problems. Instead of stacking poor people into projects built especially for them, EHAP sought to discover what happens when the federal government gives them an allowance or voucher to seek housing on the open market. How do they spend it? Do they end up in better housing and neighborhoods? How is the housing market affected?

EHAP generated a huge body of housing research literature that remains a basic resource in housing policy analysis (Struyk and Bendick, 1981). In general, EHAP findings indicated that "allowances provide a level of housing service equivalent to other [housing subsidy] programs, but at a lower cost" (Struyk and Bendick, 1981, p. 18). EHAP findings also suggested that an allowance program has little or no inflationary effect on housing prices

(Struyk and Bendick, 1981, p. 15). Although allowances are clearly not a cure-all for all housing problems, EHAP "contributed to the evidence indicating the importance of varying the mix of housing programs in different housing markets" (Struyk and Bendick, 1981, pp. 19-20).

In summary, the 1970s were a period of intense and varied activity in national housing affairs: high production, temporary shutdown, several different subsidy schemes involving both new construction and existing stock, a major new non-housing program (CDBG), and an experimental program of unprecedented scale. By 1980, housing policy analysts were blessed with a surfeit of program data and generated a host of reports under the sponsorship of government agencies, universities and "think tanks," and housing industry and advocacy groups. Nothing approaching unanimity emerged from this rich literature, but the terms of the debate as Ronald Reagan entered the White House in 1981 were far different from those in the 1960s, when the need for high rates of housing production dominated housing policy analysis.

THE REAGAN ERA: THE RISE
OF THE AFFORDABILITY ISSUE

Ronald Reagan came into office determined to bring domestic spending under control. Housing subsidies were a fat target. But many Republican builders, bankers, and lawyers had prospered for at least ten years under the subsidy programs, and they prevailed on the White House to take a time-honored approach to complex issues—appointment of a presidential commission.

The President's Commission on Housing, reporting thirteen months into the Reagan administration, adopted a general theme of "Housing Triumph, Housing Tragedy." The triumph was that the nation had made enormous progress since 1940 in the areas of housing supply and quality; the tragedy was that pockets of substandard housing still existed and that a large and increasing percentage of renters were paying a high proportion of their income for housing. The commission concluded: "The primary national need is not for massive production of new apartments for the poor, but for income supplements that will enable low-income families to live in available decent housing at a cost they can afford" (President's Commission on Housing, 1982, p. xxii)

The President's Commission did not overlook new construction subsidies entirely; however, instead of continuing the old axis between HUD and developers, it recommended that a "housing component" be tacked on to the Community Development Block Grant and that new housing construction be permitted under CDBG itself. "New federalism" would extend to housing.

Although the commission made the obligatory Reaganesque bows to "the genius of the market economy, freed of the distortions forced by government policies and regulations," its recommendations of a "housing payments programs" (vouchers) and a housing block grant attracted considerable support from housing advocates. The Reagan administration, however, only embraced the voucher component, introducing a less generous and more flexible "experimental" version of the Section 8 existing program in 1985 (later made permanent by Congress). New construction programs barely survived, but they continued to provide a handful of units for the elderly, Indians, and local public housing authorities.

The annual wrangle over the mix of subsidy programs was perhaps less important than what was going on elsewhere in housing. Private construction, after scraping bottom at barely one million starts in 1981, came back smartly to the 1.7 million range as interest rates dropped sharply. Apartment construction was particularly strong, as developers and investors took advantage of shorter depreciation schedules written into tax laws in 1981. In fact, a glut of new apartments hit many local markets, and vacancy rates soared. Congress reacted in 1986 by stripping investment incentives out of the tax law, causing a subsequent slowdown in new development. But "without tax reform," as one real estate analyst has commented, "it is hard to know when apartment construction would have slowed down" (Lachman, 1988, p. 5). As it was, overbuilding apartments and other speculative development helped bring on the savings and loan collapse.

When Congress enacted tax reform in 1986, it also threw a bone to housing advocates in the form of a new low-income housing tax credit, a highly lucrative incentive to corporate investors to offset federal income taxes by investing in the construction or rehabilitation of low-income housing. Each state receives a limited amount of credits to be issued annually. Nonprofit housing groups and organizations such as the Chicago Equity Fund can use low-income housing tax credits to attract private capital.

As federal programs faded, local and state governments were rapidly stepping up their housing activities. Local governments often drew on CDBG funds and packaged them with other public and private sources. The result was what Kevin Villani has called an "entrepreneurial frenzy"—hundreds of "creative" programs spawned by cities and some states (Villani, 1987, p. 147). The programs include new housing trust funds established by states and cities using dedicated revenue sources, major investments by foundations in housing and neighborhood improvement, and initiatives by local nonprofit organizations. These initiatives were facilitated and enhanced by the Community Reinvestment Act of 1977, which required lending institutions to report on financing activities in their neighborhoods and gave leverage to community groups in pressing for greater commitment by banks to neighborhood development. The result of all this activity is that local governments and organizations have built up a professional capacity to manage the daunting complexities of getting housing built or rehabilitated for people of lower income.

As the end of the Reagan administration approached, housing advocates gathered their forces under the rubric of the National Housing Task Force, a privately funded group organized to help set a "new national housing agenda." Chaired by developer/philanthropist James Rouse, the task force worked in cooperation with the Senate Committee on Housing and Urban Affairs and the Massachusetts Institute of Technology, which commissioned a series of 20 housing policy papers for review by the task force.

The task force report, *A Decent Place to Live*, issued in March 1988, presented a persuasive case for a national response to the plight of the low-income renter (National Housing Task Force, 1988). Its centerpiece recommendation had a familiar ring: a $3 billion housing block grant program, which would provide wide discretion to states and local governments in using the funds. Also recommended was "an adequate rental assistance program" (vouchers) at the rate of 200,000 incremental units annually. Other recommendations included assistance to first-time homebuyers, and a "complete modernization of the public housing inventory" (National Housing Task Force, 1988). Missing from the list of recommendations was a subsidized rental "production" program in the tradition of Section 236 and Section 8, the favorite and virtually risk-free instruments of well-connected developers. With Reagan out of the White House, Congress pushed ahead with shaping new housing legislation, and the task force report was an important influence in defining the contours of the 1990 housing act. Later in this chapter, I will summarize the main provisions of the 1990 act.

IN SEARCH OF NATIONAL HOUSING POLICY

In this section, I step back from the chronological sketch of housing program evolution and pull out for consideration some of the important housing policy themes and tensions that have run through the national housing debate. As the chronology suggests, housing programs have often not worked out as anticipated. After the fanfare accompanying enactment come the implementation scramble, the analysis of results, the counting of costs in budgetary and social terms, the second thoughts and recriminations, and the search for a new model.

A good part of the reason for this program instability is that housing policy has usually reached beyond the provision of shelter in the narrow sense—the obligation to see that enough roofs exist to shelter a growing population from the elements—and has been freighted with a variety of economic, social, and community development objectives, as different and sometimes competing constituencies seek to leverage the shelter objective for broader purposes.

Housing and Economic Policy

The economic stimulus value of housing construction has long been an accepted lever of national policy. As Sternlieb and Listokin point out in their survey of national housing policy, the Depression-era programs of FHA mortgage insurance and public housing were supported by a political "constituency primarily interested in jobs and economic reinvigoration" (Sternlieb and Listokin, 1987, p. 19).

The positive connection between housing construction and economic benefit persists in the lore of the nation's business press; a jump in monthly housing starts is always good news because it signals jobs and profits across a wide spectrum of the economy, from forest products to rug dealers. Similarly, when housing "slumps," this is invariably bad news for the economy. To the extent that housing is good for the economy, it seems we can never have too much of it. The anxious tracking of ups and downs in housing starts is seldom connected to the nation's need for shelter or the danger to the economy of speculative overbuilding.

Homeownership

Homeownership is another objective of national housing policy that obviously goes beyond providing shelter. The mystique of homeownership has been evoked in American politics at least since Herbert Hoover, who spoke of homeownership as being "so embedded in the American heart that millions of people who dwell in tenements, apartments and rented rows of solid brick have the aspirations for wider opportunity in the ownership of their houses" (U.S. Department of Housing and Urban Development, 1973, p. 1-6).

Since the days of President Hoover, the federal government has promoted ownership with generous tax incentives, mortgage insurance, sheltered sources of mortgage capital, and sometimes direct subsidies to homebuyers. These policies have been successful; the national homeownership rate rose steadily from 43 percent in 1940 to 65.6 percent of all households in 1980 before a small downturn to 64 percent in 1988 (Turner and Reed, 1990, p. 28).

Homeownership is sometimes vested with almost magical power to bring about social as well as financial betterment. "Something happens when people own things," says former HUD Secretary Jack Kemp (Bishop, 1990, p. 2). The flip side is the supposed threat to the nation if fewer people own.

Hodding Carter III, a former State Department official and now head of a television production firm, recently lamented "the shredding of the dream of homeownership as an American entitlement." Only two of his seven children (in their twenties and thirties), all "firmly in the middle class," have been able to afford homeownership so far, Carter wrote in a *Wall Street Journal* column. Carter acknowledged that most American families already own their own homes. "But," he warned ominously, "something dangerous is happening with the change in homeownership patterns in the U.S., dangerous to our collective psychology and social health" (Carter, 1990).

Despite the dominance of homeownership in American housing, the supposed civic and moral superiority of owning versus renting continues as a basis for policy. The plight of the aspiring homebuyer is a well-worn theme of the homebuilding lobby and its political supporters. "The American Dream," as it is invariably referred to, is always fading for countless Americans, even when the homeownership rate is climbing steadily and people are buying bigger houses with more amenities.

The political appeal of homeownership means, at a minimum, that any package of housing proposals is likely to include something for the current or aspiring homeowner. Usually, the benefits of such proposals will flow to people who are not desperately needy—people like Hodding Carter III's children. The issue then becomes whether the homeownership constituency tends to divert attention and resources from the housing needs of the poor.

Housing Quality

National housing policy has played a key role in improving the quality of the housing stock in the United States. The FHA, for example, used its leverage as a mortgage insurer to require homebuilders and subdivision developers to adhere to quality standards that became general industry practice (Weiss, 1987, pp. 141-158). Within central cities, the urban renewal program was aimed at removing slum housing and replacing it with both market-rate and subsidized housing built to high standards. Public housing, with its minimalist "decent, safe, and sanitary" standard, was a notable lapse of federal interest in quality during the period of urban high-rise projects (mainly the 1950s and 1960s); however, construction of such projects was outlawed more than 20 years ago, and construction standards since then provide for a modest, if not luxurious, level of amenity.

The federal government's insistence on high standards of new construction in its housing programs (the same applies to "substantial rehabilitation" programs) means that subsidizing poor people in such dwellings is very expensive. And, unfortunately, subsidized housing is even more costly to build than comparable market-rate housing because the federal government must take the time and trouble to review developers' applications and make sure the project is actually meeting all standards. These steps add to cost and hence to the subsidy burden.

Political leaders and the media sometimes give the impression that housing costs can be cut dramatically by technological innovation, modernized building codes, or land-use deregulation so that housing can be made "affordable." Many proposals in these areas are worth adopting and would save money on the margins, but they are no substitute for the inescapable need to provide deep subsidies for poor people who occupy housing built to today's standards.

Housing Policy and Social Policy

To the extent that federal housing programs are targeted to low-income families, the homeless, the elderly, and other groups that are frequently beset by multiple problems, a persistent issue is how housing assistance should be linked to other services so that beneficiaries achieve more economic independence, better health, and greater social well-being. Whether this is properly a "housing" issue is not very clear. Some would argue that bad housing itself exacts a damaging toll on its occupants, and that a move to good, well-located housing can itself have a transforming effect on a family's health, morale, and economic prospects. Others assert that housing assistance to multi-problem groups should be directly linked to such programs as health clinics, child care, family counseling, job training, drug prevention and treatment, and the like. According to this view, such programs not only will provide needed services close to home, but will also prolong the life of housing structures by fostering more responsible occupants.

A variant of the social policy theme is the notion of "empowerment" as a housing policy objective in settings such as public housing where low-income tenants are concentrated. Former HUD Secretary Jack Kemp embraced empowerment as a policy emphasis. The concept involves giving tenants a direct role in managing their own developments by forming resident management organizations that may also take charge of arranging for social services. The ultimate goal of empowerment is economic independence and homeownership.

Equal opportunity is another dimension of social policy. Initially, the federal government, through the FHA, had an official policy of encouraging housing segregation. FHA believed housing in integrated or "changing" neighborhoods was a bad insurance risk and therefore excluded or "redlined" such neighborhoods from the benefits of FHA mortgage insurance. The federal government was also complicit in establishing racial ghettos in central-city public housing projects by permitting Chicago and other large cities to build public housing clearly intended for low-income minorities. Although FHA reversed its notorious "neighborhood homogeneity" policy in 1949, and a national fair housing act was passed in 1968, the federal government has had little success in changing the basic pattern of housing segregation fostered by continuing discrimination in mortgage lending and a dual real estate market.

Housing and Community Development Policy

Typically, a federal housing program triggers the construction of a house or group of housing units without any particular regard to its relation to transportation, other infrastructure, recreation, job opportunities, commerce, schools, and all the other elements of a community. This has always bothered many national policymakers because it seems self-evident that housing policy should be connected to other national policies that influence community development. Also, at the local and metropolitan level, public officials should be coordinating housing with other kinds of development.

Translating these sensible ideas into operating reality has been largely frustrated. When HUD was created in 1965, the HUD secretary was given "convenor authority" over other domestic cabinet secretaries in order to encourage federal program coordination, but this authority carried no real leverage over other federal program budgets or allocation decisions. In the late 1960s, HUD mounted a sizeable program of grants to metropolitan planning agencies (such as the Northeastern Illinois Planning Commission in Chicago), which were to prepare comprehensive plans including a "housing element." The planning grants were killed in the late 1970s, but the housing element requirement was never effective anyway because of entrenched local opposition to dispersing subsidized housing.

Other planning requirements have been inserted into federal housing legislation—the Housing Assistance Plan (HAP), which was tied to the CDBG program, enacted in 1974, and HAP's recently passed successor, the Comprehensive Housing Affordability Strategy (CHAS), part of the 1990 housing act. Both HAP and CHAS require localities to spell out how housing assistance will, among other things, relate to neighborhood impacts and broader land-use policies; however, if the HAP experience is indicative, CHAS will have no discernible effect on community development patterns (although the CHAS process may indeed have some value in setting specific housing allocation decisions).

In sum, the idea of integrating housing policy with broader community development policy persists in the rhetoric of federal housing legislation. Achieving this integration, however, has proved frustrating and elusive.

Housing and Intergovernmental Policy

Prior to the 1970s, housing built under federal programs was mainly produced either by private developers (both for-profit and nonprofit) who submitted applications directly to HUD or by local housing authorities who also dealt directly with HUD. State governments and general-purpose local governments played little direct role in initiating or approving such proposals. This changed in the 1970s when many state governments, including Illinois, created their own housing development authorities that could apply for HUD subsidy funds, and when cities began receiving Community Development Block Grants that could be used for housing rehabilitation.

As states and cities became more important players in housing programs, national housing policy came to be debated in the broader context of the so-called "new federalism." Should the federal government remain in the business of project-by-project control of programs created by Congress, or should states and cities be given a block of funds that could be used flexibly on homegrown programs tailored to the local situation by local politicians?

This issue raised complex questions ranging from the technical capacity of states and cities to set up and manage their own programs, to the wisdom of entrusting to non-federal governments the responsibility for allocating housing assistance: To put it bluntly, can City Hall be trusted to help the poor and disadvantaged? Other political issues also surfaced. Congress does not readily give up political and direct budgetary control over its own creatures to governors and mayors, nor does the housing lobby—a cocoon of builders, real estate people, mortgage bankers, lawyers, consultants, and others who specialize in and profit from the arcane world of HUD programs—willingly allow its habitual and often too cozy connections with the HUD bureaucracy to be disrupted. These issues were critical as Congress debated new housing legislation over a three-year period in the late 1980s, resulting in a clear but by no means total victory for the "new federalists" in the 1990 housing act.

Housing and Federal Fiscal Policy

Housing policy intersects with federal fiscal policy in several ways. First, there is the general question of how to rank direct housing assistance spending against all the other claims on the federal budget such as defense, space, environment, and health. Each fiscal year the president and Congress must make a judgment about how urgent housing needs are in comparison to other national priorities, and that judgment becomes more difficult as federal fiscal health deteriorates.

What is more, different types of housing programs can have quite different effects on the fiscal bottom line, a fact that can influence program choice as well as lead to confusion about the growth or decline of the federal commitment to housing. For example, front-end capital subsidies for housing construction, or direct federal loans, have an immediate, high per-unit cost impact on spending ("outlays") and therefore on the federal deficit. Other programs commit the federal government to long-term (20 years or more) contracts to subsidize interest payments or rents. For such programs, the entire multi-year obligation is stated in the budget as "budget authority," but the payment of those obligations—outlays—is stretched out far into the future. Outlays do build up steadily over time, however, as incremental units are added to the subsidized stock each year.

Housing advocates frequently state that low-income housing assistance was "slashed" by 70 to 80 percent during the Reagan period. This statement is often linked with the homeless problem, implying that thousands of people were thrown out of subsidized housing onto the streets. But the cutbacks of the 1980s actually refer to budget *authority*—long-term future obligations—not annual outlays, which rose steadily to cover past subsidy commitments and annual increments of additional units. Budget authority did decline sharply because the Reagan administration successfully sought the virtual elimination of long-term, deep subsidy commitments for new construction and substituted a voucher strategy costing much less (about half) per unit and carrying shorter-term contract commitments (usually five years).

But direct housing assistance for low- and moderate-income beneficiaries is only part of the fiscal equation. Generous federal tax benefits tied to homeownership cut into federal revenue on a much larger scale than outright subsidies do on the spending side of the budget. Other tax provisions that permit housing to be financed by tax-free bonds, or that provide tax credits for building low-income housing, also reduce federal revenues.

These "tax expenditures" present low-income housing advocates with a dilemma. On the one hand, the benefits of these tax breaks flow heavily to wealthy homeowners and investors and also swell the federal deficit. On the other hand, they also stimulate some affordable housing construction. Some advocates would like to reduce the tax breaks, particularly for the richest homeowners, and divert the increased federal revenue into housing subsidies for the poor. But this has been a hard sell politically because most homeowners think of their mortgage interest and property tax deductions as a sacred right, not a tax break, and strongly resist any encroachment on ownership benefits.

THE NATIONAL AFFORDABLE HOUSING ACT OF 1990

The National Affordable Housing Act of 1990, signed into law in November 1990, was the culmination of a three-year bargaining process among the many groups seeking to shape housing policy according to their own interests. There was a strong consensus that major housing legislation should happen in 1990, but powerful disagreement on specific provisions.

On the Senate side, the housing bill sponsors pushed for a Housing Opportunity Program (HOP), a new housing block grant to states and cities—the approach recommended by the National Housing Task Force in 1988. The sponsors in the House of Representatives, however, advocated a new subsidized rental production program administered by HUD, as well as a much smaller block grant to cities for funding community housing partnerships—nonprofit organizations engaged in community-based housing construction and rehabilitation. Representing the Bush administration, HUD Secretary Jack Kemp pushed for a bagful of initiatives built around his themes of empowerment and low-income homeownership.

Differences between the House and Senate versions of the housing bill were sorted out in a conference committee. HOP emerged as the HOME Investment Partnerships program, a new block grant—a key victory for the new federalism view that it is time to give states and cities more control of housing program decisions. Advocates of a freestanding rental production program lost out, yet salvaged something: HUD was required to set aside 15 percent of HOME funds for rental construction; these funds are to be allocated to at least 30 percent of all HOME jurisdictions that meet HUD criteria for new construction need.[1]

Another key set-aside in the HOME program underlines the maturity of nonprofit housing organizations as a political force in housing legislation. Under this provision, jurisdictions receiving HOME funds must set aside at least 15 percent for nonprofit Community Development Housing Development Organizations (CHDOs) that have "a history of serving the local community or communities within which housing to be assisted . . . is to be located" (Low Income Housing Information Service, 1991, p. 29).

After the total appropriation for HOME programs is determined by Congress ($1.5 billion in fiscal year 1992), HUD prepares an allocation formula based on relative need for affordable housing, with states receiving 40 percent and local governments 60 percent of the total. In order to get HOME funds, states and cities must submit to HUD a Comprehensive Housing Affordability Strategy (CHAS), a five-year plan—to be updated annually—that includes a statement of housing needs by income group, tenure, and household type; the extent of homelessness and the "near homeless"; characteristics of the housing market; effects of public policies on affordability; plans for leveraging non-federal funds with federal funds; plans for improving the public housing inventory, including resident management and homeownership programs; plans for implementing the CHAS, including coordination of state and local bodies; and standards for monitoring activities under the 1990 act. In preparing the CHAS, jurisdictions must share information and analyses with the general public and provide chances for citizen input through public hearings.

The appeal of the homeownership mystique is also evident in the 1990 housing act. First, there is the new National Homeownership Trust Fund, a demonstration program scheduled to expire in September 1993. The fund will help median-income, first-time

---

[1] In the original HOME legislation, the local matching fund requirement was highest for new construction—50 percent, as opposed to 33 percent for substantial rehabilitation and 25 percent for tenant-based assistance (vouchers) and moderate rehabilitation. However, in the first year of HOME funding (fiscal year 1992), the matching requirements were waived. In the fiscal year 1993, state and local matches were changed to 30 percent for new construction and 25 percent for all other activities.

homebuyers buy an FHA-insured house for as little as one percent down and financed by a mortgage rate of 6 percent or less.

The 1990 housing act also contains other "homeownership" initiatives that require deep subsidies because the targeted beneficiaries are poor. These are the three HOPE programs (the acronym for Homeownership and Opportunity for People Everywhere) advocated by HUD Secretary Kemp, immediately dubbed as HOPE I, HOPE II, and HOPE III. In brief, HOPE I is to help public housing residents or other low-income families buy public housing; HOPE II aims to help tenants in multi-family buildings owned or insured by HUD buy the buildings they live in; and HOPE III would help low-income families buy single-family houses owned or held by HUD, the Resolution Trust Corporation, or the Department of Veterans Affairs.

HOPE funds provide support to nonprofit sponsors for planning and technical assistance to low-income residents and for the cost of rehabilitating units slated for conversion to ownership. When units are ready for occupancy, prices are set so that the new owners pay no more than 30 percent of their income for mortgage, taxes, and insurance. They are also eligible for operating subsidies to pay for repairs and utilities for a period of five years after transfer. By then the owners are expected to have achieved economic self-sufficiency with the help of job training programs paid for or arranged by the HOPE sponsor.

The HOPE version of the American dream does not come cheap—each unit will require public subsidies adding up to $50,000 to $60,000, according to HUD estimates (Sawhill, Struyk, and Sachs, 1991, p. 2). Partly because of the big public investment in HOPE, owners are not permitted to reap a windfall profit from selling their units unless they have lived there more than 20 years. Up to that time, gains are limited by law.

Besides HOPE and HOME, the 1990 housing act includes a number of innovations in programs for special populations, including the elderly, AIDS victims, the homeless, the handicapped, and public-housing residents. Although initial funding is limited, HUD will be extending its reach much more directly into paying for supportive social services for residents who live in subsidized housing. Local housing authorities, for example, may apply for HUD funding to convert vacant dwelling units into space for "Family Investment Centers," to hire staff for the centers, and to pay up to 15 percent of the cost of child care, literacy and job training, and other "appropriate services." Also, by 1993, all local housing authorities are to develop "family self-sufficiency action plans" in cooperation with other local agencies providing job training, education, welfare assistance, and other services. HUD would pay administrative costs of the plans, but not for the actual services (NAHRO and APWA, 1991). For AIDS victims, the homeless, and frail elderly persons in subsidized housing, HUD is funding demonstration programs that will bring supportive services into or near housing for these special populations.

The 1990 housing act is not all innovation. The two voucher programs (Section 8, now called "rental certificates"; and vouchers, now called "rental vouchers") remain in place with some minor tinkering. The public housing program, despite the flurry of initiatives already outlined, rolls on, requiring ever larger subsidies for operating costs and capital improvements as Congress again presses HUD to define what a well-managed housing authority looks like. Congress also acted to deal with private subsidized housing built under HUD programs in the 1960s and 1970s. Much of this housing has been in danger of being lost to the subsidized stock as contracts expired or mortgages were pre-paid by owners wishing to convert it to market-rate housing, forcing current tenants to pay much steeper rents or move out. The act sets up procedural restrictions to such conversions, on the one hand, and, on the other, offers financial incentives to owners to maintain the housing for low- and moderate-income renters.

NATIONAL HOUSING POLICY IMPACTS IN METROPOLITAN CHICAGO

National housing policies since the 1930s have played out in the Chicago region in ways not unlike other major urban centers of the Northeast and Midwest. Strong incentives for homeownership certainly helped fuel rapid suburban growth with the single-family home as the dominant housing type. And as the parade of subsidized housing programs came down the pike in the 1960s and 1970s, private developers (including nonprofit developers) and the Chicago Housing Authority (CHA) employed these programs to build housing for low- and moderate-income families. In the 1980s, as subsidized production programs were phased out, the Community Development Block Grant became a key source of funds, often packaged with other city, corporate, and philanthropic sources. Vouchers also became a relatively more important source of housing assistance.

There is no systematic accounting of the total number of HUD-assisted units in the Chicago area, although the great bulk are located within the city of Chicago. According to figures supplied by the Chicago regional office of HUD, about 93,000 units of subsidized housing are in the city of Chicago, of which about 40,000 units are under CHA management, while the balance consists of apartments subsidized under various programs since the 1960s. In total, these units would make up about 8 percent of the city's stock of occupied housing and 15 percent of its rental stock. This is clearly far short of meeting the housing needs of Chicago's low-income population, but attempting to quantify that need is outside the scope of this chapter.

The 1990 housing act will be no panacea for Chicago's housing problems. The most important and, in my view, the most beneficial impact will be the new money that will come to the city under the HOME block grant. This will be the first major infusion of new housing funds in a long time, and it will come in a way that will do the most good, by providing flexible funds that can be combined with other sources for maximum impact. As shown in Table 1, the City of Chicago has been the main beneficiary of HOME funds in the first two years of the program, with grants totaling $67 million out of $82 million flowing to eligible jurisdictions in the metropolitan area. In addition, the state government was allocated $21.8 million for fiscal year 1992 and $12.9 million for fiscal year 1993, some of which will presumably be spent in the Chicago region.

Chicago and the other HOME grant jurisdictions worked entirely independently of each other to complete the "CHAS" planning documents required by HUD. One reason was that the pressure of time prevented a cooperative effort; however, a more fundamental problem is that no jurisdiction or external body has the responsibility or political leverage to act as a coordinating and planning body for housing in the region. The Metropolitan Planning Council (MPC) has begun preliminary analyses of the first round of CHAS documents and is planning to monitor program implementation of the 1990 act. One can hope that MPC's efforts will eventually lead to a more regionwide approach to housing.

The various low-income homeownership initiatives (HOPE) will not have very widespread benefits. Although they are easy to grasp conceptually and have an appealing symbolism, the actual number of units that lend themselves to low-income homeownership is very low, and the legal and administrative complexities of implementing them require several years of effort.

TABLE 1: Formula Allocations for HOME Investment Partnerships Program to Local Jurisdictions in the Chicago Metropolitan Area, Fiscal Years 1992 and 1993

	FY 1992	FY 1993
City of Chicago	$40,364,000	$26,673,000
Cook County	4,679,000	4,689,000*
DuPage County	1,443,000	1,301,000**
Lake County	1,263,000***	847,000***
Will County	750,000****	388,000
Total	48,499,000	33,898,000

* Consortium including Cook County, Arlington Heights, Berwyn, Chicago Heights, Cicero, Des Plaines, Evanston, Mount Prospect, Oak Park, Schaumburg, and Skokie.

** Consortium including DuPage County, Aurora, and Naperville.

*** Consortium including Lake County, North Chicago, and Waukegan.

**** Includes $159,000 from the State to bring Will County up to $750,000 minimum for HOME participation jurisdiction.

Source: Illinois Housing Development Authority.

Other features of the 1990 act should have positive outcomes in Chicago. The commitment to deal with the problem-laden legacy of public housing is good news, although actual appropriations by Congress remain to be seen. Several provisions will support CHA's efforts to achieve a better income mix in public housing. The continuation of the voucher programs is also welcome, particularly in light of Chicago's rather high rental vacancy rate. Finally, the CHAS process, although off to a rushed and clumsy start in the first year of the HOME program, offers at least the prospect of focused, participatory planning for housing in Chicago in the future.

126   *Charles J. Orlebeke*

REFERENCES

ibliography
ishop, Janet Spector (1990). "A Time for Solutions," *Humphrey Institute News*, June 1991.
Carter, Hodding, III (1990). "Housing Costs Create a New Privileged Class: Home Buyer," *Wall Street Journal*, December 13, 1990, p. A11.
Lachman, M. Leanne (1988). *Decade to Decade.* New York: Shroder Real Estate Associates.
Low Income Housing Information Service (1991). *Overview Summary of the National Affordable Housing Act of 1990.* Washington, D.C.: Low Income Housing Information Service.
NAHRO and APWA (National Association of Housing and Redevelopment Officials and American Public Welfare Association, 1991). *Family Self-Sufficiency: Linking Housing, Public Welfare and Social Services.* Washington, D.C.: NAHRO.
National Housing Task Force (1988). *A Decent Place to Live.* Washington, D.C.: National Housing Task Force.
President's Commission on Housing (1982). *Report of the President's Commission on Housing.* Washington, D.C.: U.S. Government Printing Office.
Sawhill, Isabel V., Raymond J. Struyk, and Steven M. Sachs (1991). "The New Paradigm: Choice and Empowerment as Social Policy Tools," *Policy Bites.* Washington, D.C.: The Urban Institute.
Sternlieb, George, and David Listokin (1987). "A Review of National Housing Policy." In Peter Salins, ed., *Housing America's Poor.* Chapel Hill: University of North Carolina Press.
Struyk, Raymond J., and Marc Bendick, Jr., eds. (1981). *Housing Vouchers for the Poor: Lessons from a National Experiment.* Washington, D.C.: Urban Institute Press.
Turner, Margaret Austin, and Veronica M. Reed (1990). *Housing America: Learning from the Past, Planning for the Future.* Washington, D.C.: The Urban Institute.
U.S. Department of Housing and Urban Development (1973). *Housing in the Seventies.* Washington, D.C.: U.S. Government Printing Office.
Villani, Kevin (1987). "Finding the Money to Finance Low-Cost Housing." In Peter Salins, ed., *Housing America's Poor.* Chapel Hill: University of North Carolina Press.
Weiss, Marc A. (1987). *The Rise of the Community Builders.* New York: Columbia University Press.

COMMENTS

Phillip L. Clay

Charles Orlebeke has presented an excellent menu of issues for discussion. The history he has summarized is rich and deep, and it highlights the many crosscurrents in housing and economic policy over the years.

Housing policy might be viewed as a three-legged stool on which the burden of meeting the nation's housing needs rests. The first leg is subsidies to promote *housing production*. These subsidies are embedded in the production process. In regard to the private sector, various federal programs have provided incentives (e.g., low-interest financing) to producers of low- and moderate-income housing. In the case of public housing, the government has simply built the housing and partially subsidized its operation. During the 1980s, direct federal subsidies for housing production were greatly reduced.

The National Affordable Housing Act of 1990 provides new support for nonprofit organizations, but even for them the production of housing requires a host of costly transactions that only relatively mature community-based developers can perform. These developers do not need incentives, but they do need operating funds and working capital to make the development process work. We have to ask ourselves if Chicago and other cities have in place a development process that can assure that decent, affordable housing can be produced. My fear is that given the incentives and subsidies in place, there is not enough nonprofit development capacity to replace the private sector as the major supplier of housing, nor are there adequate incentives for the private sector to enter this area. Chicago, with its many great community development corporations, may be an exception, but I suspect it is only a partial exception.

With *tenant-based subsidies*, resources are made available to households and landlords to cover the difference between fair market rent (defined by the government) and 30 percent of the household's income. While such assistance does not directly lead to the production of housing, it does make an existing unit available to families that would otherwise be unable to afford it.

We might be willing to accept this as a solution except for the fact that we have not figured out a way to avoid exploitation and segregation in the marketplace. We also have to face the possibility that landlords are not likely, given the disincentives to invest in low-income rental housing, to make improvements in the housing stock. A voucher with a limited term is not the basis on which to de-velop or rehabilitate housing. We face the very real risk that vouchers will simply subsidize the deterioration of the housing stock, rather than supporting its maintenance or expansion or increasing accessibility for the poor, especially minority households that continue to be restricted in where they obtain get decent housing.

The third leg of the stool involves the *tax and regulatory systems* that regulate credit and subsidize housing indirectly. At various times in the past, special provisions have been added to stimulate a particular type of housing or target a population. These systems now work largely in the reverse. Regulations are more likely to add to the cost of housing, and the tax incentives for investment in rental housing have shrunk since the passage of the Tax Reform Act of 1986.

THE NEW HOUSING LEGISLATION

The National Affordable Housing Act of 1990 is the first major piece of housing legislation in more than a decade. The authorizing legislation and potential appropriations suggest several interesting points about implementation.

(1) The new housing act promotes housing *partnerships* among the private sector, nonprofit organizations, and the public sector. This is a more complex set of relationships for developing housing than has historically been the case in most cities. While the federal government is encouraging this approach, local communities must actually implement it. There is no national leadership to give voice to housing goals. Precedents at the local level offer little direction because they mainly involved local governments acting in downtown projects, whereas local governments now find themselves in partnerships in which they are not always the senior or most enthusiastic members.

(2) The housing act specifically encourages the development of local *plans*, empowers state and local discretion with respect to *housing strategies*, and provides additional tools to state and local governments to design affordable housing. Cities have not had to

do this before. They will have to set priorities that operate partly in the market and partly in the policy arena. For example, the legislation provides funds that can be used in a flexible manner by states and localities for rehabilitation, new construction, and tenant-based assistance. Preference is given to rehabilitation and vouchers. The choice between new construction and rehab is one that the federal Department of Housing and Urban Development (HUD) used to make. This consequential choice now must be made by local governments.

(3) The HOPE Program will assist low-income families in buying public housing and other foreclosed property owned by the federal government. The program also authorizes funding for capacity-building for tenant councils and supportive services. Local communities will also have to deal with the issue of capacity-building for people who might want to take advantage of what may be viewed as an opportunity. Cities will also have to address supply implications and target some resources that are needed to match federal funds.

(4) The Public Housing Drug Initiative provides for the expansion of supportive services in public and assisted housing. The 1990 Housing Act also includes programs to help people with special needs—the elderly, persons with disabilities, the homeless, and persons with AIDS—to live in dignity and independence. This also poses challenges for both ingenious programming and complementary local activities that will be critical if these initiatives are to work. All of these programs require the joining of housing development systems with social service systems. In the past, these two systems have been poorly coordinated (and sometimes working at cross-purposes).

(5) The Preservation Title of the 1990 Housing Act addresses the problem of mortgage prepayments in the older, federally subsidized inventory, with primary emphasis on retaining the affordability of this vital piece of the housing stock. The act provides for transition support in housing development and offers protection to tenants who might be displaced when preservation is not achieved. Although Chicago may want to wash its hands of this issue and say that it is a federal problem, the city was the home of early and vigorous attempts on the part of HUD housing tenants to make sure their interests were protected. Because the City has some influence on the preservation process and because some foundations can be helpful, Chicago may take over where HUD regulations leave off and meet the need not addressed in legisla-

tion, namely, how to help the tenant groups do what the law allows.

(6) The legislation places substantial reliance on nonprofit housing developers as major players and underscores the need to expand both the number of organizations capable of taking on the responsibilities anticipated in the legislation and the number of communities and regions covered by networks of nonprofit developers and their supporting intermediary groups. The HUD role is reduced compared to its former pre-eminence in housing and community development. The role of the private, for-profit sector is also reduced.

The points above define a policy that, whatever its other features, requires that responsibility for the future of urban policy rests with local governments and with nonprofit community organizations. They will jointly have to formulate plans, review options, allocate and share costs, and take the political heat for targeting, siting, and other aspects of implementation.

STATE AND LOCAL POLICIES AFFECTING AFFORDABLE HOUSING IN ILLINOIS

Thomas J. Lenz and Barbara A. Shaw

The federal government's involvement in affordable housing began nearly six decades ago with the New Deal. By contrast, most states and cities launched their first housing programs in the 1960s and 1970s, often in direct response to federal policies and funding opportunities. More recently, with the withdrawal of federal support, state and local governments have begun to pursue housing policies independent of federal initiatives. This includes designing and managing local housing policies and programs, providing finance mechanisms, and regulating residential land-use decisions (Terner and Cook, 1990).

The State of Illinois and the City of Chicago fit this pattern. Although zoning and other forms of land-use regulation have been around for decades, only in the 1970s did the State and City become directly involved in the production of low-income housing. And not until the late 1980s did both units of government begin to commit their own, non-federal funds to affordable housing.

This chapter examines the affordable housing activities of state and local governments in Illinois. The local government focus of the chapter is northeastern Illinois and, in particular, the city of Chicago. Although small cities and rural areas in Illinois are not discussed, much of the analysis is relevant to their situation as well. We argue that Illinois and Chicago have lagged behind much of the country in developing housing policy and funding affordable housing production. The 1980s saw the creation of a number of new state and local housing initiatives, but these programs have not been funded at a level that would allow them to meet more than a fraction of the need. In addition, the programs developed over the last decade are not effective in providing housing for the very poor, who need the assistance the most. We conclude with an examination of issues and trends that are likely to affect housing policy in Illinois and Chicago in the 1990s.

OVERALL ASSESSMENT OF ILLINOIS
AND CHICAGO HOUSING EFFORTS

Deep cuts in federal low-income housing assistance, spiraling housing and energy costs, stagnant household incomes, and an aging housing stock have contributed to a severe and growing housing crisis in Illinois. Statistics compiled by the State of Illinois and City of Chicago indicate that 38 percent of Illinois households (1.6 million statewide and 360,000 in Chicago) experienced one or more housing problems, including cost burden, physical defects, and overcrowding (State of Illinois, 1991; City of Chicago, 1991).

Not surprisingly, these housing problems disproportionately affect low- and very low-income households. Forty-one percent of Illinois's low-income households (those with incomes between 50% and 80% of the median) experience housing problems. Over 82 percent of the state's "very low-income" households (which the federal government defines as those with incomes below 50% of the median) experience one or more housing problems. The most serious housing problem is excessive cost burden, with 62 percent of very low-income households spending more than 30 percent of their already limited incomes on housing (State of Illinois, 1991).

Despite these statistics, the State of Illinois and the City of Chicago have responded very slowly to the withdrawal of federal housing assistance. For example, both units of government have continued to rely almost exclusively on the dwindling supply of federal funds to address the affordable housing needs of low- and very low-income households.

In total local dollars per capita spent on affordable housing in 1989, the City of Chicago ranked 25th out of the 25 most populated cities that commit local dollars to housing (Berenyi, 1989). The City depended primarily on shrinking federal Community Development Block Grant (CDBG) dollars for housing programs, yet it spent only 26 percent of its available CDBG budget on housing. In contrast, New York spent 67 percent of its CDBG funding on housing, Philadelphia spent 56 percent, and Milwaukee spent 51 percent (Berenyi, 1989).

On the state level, until the recent establishment of the Illinois Affordable Housing Trust Fund in 1989, Illinois and Texas were the only major states with no state revenue committed to affordable housing (COSCAA, 1990). The trust fund, financed by an increase in the state real estate transfer tax, represents the only state revenue dedicated to housing development. Yet the fund only provided $13 million annually for housing assistance—a drop in the bucket compared to the need in a state as large as Illinois.

Instead of directly appropriating state funds, Illinois has relied primarily on tax-exempt bonds and dwindling federal subsidies for its housing programs, methods that have been increasingly incapable of reaching low- and very low-income households. Most other major states have a wide array of housing programs addressing the needs of low-income citizens (COSCAA, 1990).

In addition to the scarcity of local resources for housing, neither Illinois nor Chicago has developed effective mechanisms for planning and coordinating housing policies and programs. The Illinois Housing Development Authority (IHDA) is the entity with the most responsibility for housing production in Illinois. IHDA is not a "code department," that is, an agency that is part of the executive branch of state government. Instead, it is a quasi-public body overseen by a board of directors appointed by the governor.

In the past, IHDA has functioned primarily as a housing financier, generating capital for affordable housing through the sale of bonds. IHDA has not been responsible for state housing policy development or for program and resource coordination among the various state agencies involved in implementing housing and homeless programs. Nor have these functions been vested in any other state department. This historic lack of centralized policy and program coordination has been a major factor in Illinois's sluggish, reactive, and fragmented response to the affordable housing crisis.

There are indications that Illinois may become more effective in housing policy development in the future. In November 1991, the governor sponsored a conference on housing that brought together housing leaders from across the state. At the conference, the governor announced the creation of an "Office of Housing Coordination Services" (OHCS) to "coordinate housing policy development and housing programs, to initiate and respond to public input on housing programs and to act as a housing information resource for nonprofit organizations, local governments, state agencies and others" (State of Illinois, Office of the Governor, 1991). OHCS, which is housed at IHDA, has since hired staff and organized a 36-person advisory committee.

Locating OHCS at IHDA, together with the governor's decision to make IHDA the lead agency to administer the federal HOME block grant and to write the state's Comprehensive Housing Affordability Strategy (CHAS), suggest a growing role for

IHDA in the area of housing policy. It is less clear whether IHDA will have power to implement coordinated policies and programs, or whether it will simply encourage collaboration among diverse state agencies.

The governmental structure for delivering housing programs and developing housing policies in Chicago is also in transition. Although the City of Chicago has had a Department of Housing for over ten years, its efforts focus primarily on financing low-income, multi-family housing. Other housing-related functions are located in city agencies such as the Department of Buildings (code enforcement, transfer of city-owned properties), the Department of Human Services (homeless services and shelters), and the Law Department (loan underwriting policies).

In the fall of 1991, the administration of Mayor Richard M. Daley announced a reorganization of the City's Planning, Housing, and Economic Development departments. The shake-up brought new leadership to the Department of Housing, which also lost some of its land-assembly and urban-renewal functions to the newly created Department of Planning and Development.

A further internal reorganization of the Department of Housing was announced in May 1991. These changes were intended to enable the department to operate more like a private-sector financial institution. Specifically, new "developer services" and "household services" divisions have been established to bring the agency closer to the two markets it serves (City of Chicago, 1992). Four teams of "relationship managers" have been organized to work with private and nonprofit developers to expedite projects and speed the notoriously slow loan-closing process. As is the case with the recent State moves to coordinate housing policy through the OHCS, the new organizational structure of the City's Department of Housing seems to represent an advance over the previous ways of doing business. Time will tell whether a more market-driven department will be able to boost production and assume the leading role in City housing policy formation.

In many suburbs in the Chicago metropolitan area, particularly those northwest of the city, rapid job growth has created a growing need for housing affordable to working low-income households. Unfortunately, few implementation mechanisms exist for actually addressing this problem. Barriers to the development of lower cost housing in the suburbs are considerable, especially those zoning restrictions that limit multi-family housing and require large lots for single-family development.

It is unclear whether the suburban communities in question will incorporate affordable housing into their growth plans. The Federal Commission on Regulatory Barriers to Affordable Housing recently recommended that states become more aggressive in requiring land-use plans that address the housing needs of all income groups (Advisory Commission, 1991). Political realities suggest that the State of Illinois, which has ceded most land-use regulation powers to "home rule" cities, is unlikely to follow this approach. IHDA has, however, decided to form a committee of homebuilders, suburban officials, and others concerned with the issue to explore ways to reduce or eliminate regulatory barriers to affordable housing.

Why have the City of Chicago and the State of Illinois been so slow to respond to the affordable housing crisis? Several reasons can be posited for this minimalist response. First, because the federal government had been the only game in town for so many years, state and local governments were unprepared to create and administer housing programs, especially for the poor. In addition, state and local government budgets have been and are increasingly financially strapped. Finally, in the absence of clear national, state, or local mandates, there has been no real standard as to the role that state and local governments should assume in meeting the housing needs of their citizens.

That having been said, however, it is important to repeat that other major cities and states have been far more aggressive in filling the vacuum left by the federal retreat from low-income housing. Although it certainly is commendable for state and local officials to urge the federal government to renew its commitment to housing assistance for low-income households, it is also true that more responsibility for addressing the housing crisis is being placed on states and cities. The State of Illinois and the City of Chicago have a substantial way to go, as compared to other major cities and states, to demonstrate that they are willing to accept this responsibility as an important element of their governmental roles.

CHICAGO AND ILLINOIS HOUSING INNOVATIONS

Although Illinois and Chicago housing policies and programs have not been in the forefront, a balanced assessment suggests that there have been some accomplishments that deserve mention. The IHDA Partnership Program was created in 1987 in response to the inability of the agency's tax-exempt bond financing to reach low-income households without federal Section 8 rental assistance. The program uses approximately $14 million of IHDA's administrative reserves to create a revolving fund for low-interest loans to cities and community organizations that leverage other funds for the production of low-income housing. The Partnership Program has contributed to the development of over 5,000 units of low-income housing since its inception.

The Illinois Affordable Housing Trust Fund was enacted into law in 1989, largely through the efforts of a coalition organized by the Statewide Housing Action Coalition, an advocacy group that first proposed the concept in 1987. The trust fund represents the first commitment of state revenue to affordable housing for low-income households in Illinois. A modest increase in the state real estate transfer tax finances the program and generates $13 to $15 million annually. The trust fund is administered by IHDA and makes available low-interest loans and grants that support the production of housing for low- and very low-income households. During 1990, its first year, the trust fund allocated $17 million (in 16 months of funding) and assisted approximately 1,800 units of housing throughout the state. In 1991, the fund is expected to provide $13 to $14 million in assistance to about 1,200 units.

The Affordable Housing Trust Fund represents an important and necessary first step, but in order for the program to have a significant impact on the affordable housing crisis, the State must substantially increase its financial commitment to the trust fund. Its current resources are totally inadequate to address the level of need.

The Chicago Housing Partnership was created in 1985 and brings together the major players involved in the production of affordable housing in Chicago. Participants include the City of Chicago, private lending institutions, the Chicago Equity Fund, the Local Initiatives Support Corporation (LISC), and representatives from the network of community-based and private housing developers.[1] The partnership has served as a vehicle for coordinating, planning, and problem-solving for the Chicago affordable housing industry. For example, in 1991, the partnership per-

---

[1] The Chicago Equity Fund is a nonprofit entity that raises capital from corporations to invest in affordable housing through the federal Low-Income Housing Tax Credit. The Local Initiatives Support Corporation is a nonprofit community development intermediary organization that provides neighborhood-based developers with loans and grants.

suaded the various agencies and banks that invest in low-income housing to simplify and coordinate their loan-closing documents.

Another Chicago innovation is the Cook County Tax Reactivation Program, which was developed in 1983 through the efforts of the Chicago Rehab Network, an association of neighborhood-based housing developers. The program relies on cooperation between the City and Cook County to transfer chronically tax-delinquent multi-family properties to developers, who then agree to rehab the properties and make them available for low- and moderate-income tenants. The program is one of Cook County's most widely used low-cost acquisition strategies for affordable housing developers. Since its inception, the program has processed 237 buildings containing over 4,500 units for transfer to developers to increase the supply of decent housing for low- and moderate-income households.

A recent new twist on the program is the City's budgeting of $2 million of its share of Scavenger Sale revenue for affordable housing activities. The Scavenger Sale is a public auction of chronically tax-delinquent properties. Proceeds from the sale are distributed to various taxing bodies in Cook County, including the City of Chicago. The City's allocation of a portion of this revenue to affordable housing is a promising precedent that could eventually result in the City's entire Scavenger Sale revenue being dedicated to affordable housing programs.

The New Homes for Chicago program, initiated by the Chicago Department of Housing in 1990, makes available city-owned land and direct subsidies to developers who construct single-family housing affordable to low- and moderate-income first-time homebuyers. The program is designed to attract new homebuilders into the city to increase the supply of affordable housing and to take advantage of City-owned land in distressed neighborhoods. New Homes for Chicago provides an array of subsidies to developers, including up to $20,000 per unit in cash subsidy, free City-owned land, fee waivers, and low- or no-cost site improvements. In 1990, $3 million was allocated to the program to subsidize the construction of 180 single-family units. The 1991 commitment of $2 million will assist in the development of up to 120 units. The program is expected to continue at approximately the same funding level ($2 million per year) through 1994.

Finally, the Chicago Low-Income Housing Trust Fund was created by City ordinance in 1989 to provide financial assistance for housing serving Chicago's poorest households. This trust fund was incorporated as a nonprofit organization and is managed by a fifteen-member board of directors appointed by the mayor. The City's trust fund was capitalized from fees paid by developers of the Presidential Towers complex, a middle-income, downtown rental housing development, in exchange for the City's issuance of tax-exempt bonds to finance the complex. The fund distributes approximately $350,000 annually, which subsidizes roughly 120 units for very low-income households. Unless other sources of revenue are identified, however, the fund can only reach a very small number of Chicago's poorest citizens.

WHO IS SERVED BY STATE AND
LOCAL HOUSING PROGRAMS?

As was described above, during a decade of federal retrenchment in low-income housing production, the State and City did manage to create a number of innovative, if relatively modest, programs. The question then arises: Who is served by these new state and local housing efforts?

The issue is relevant to any discussion of housing policy because, unlike public aid and food stamps, housing assistance is not an entitlement; that is, eligible households do not automatically receive housing assistance just because they qualify. Assistance is available up to the limits of annual appropriations on a first-come, first-served basis. It cannot be assumed that those who need housing assistance the most will receive it. In fact, housing assistance over the last decade has shifted away from the very poor as federal funds for new construction of public housing and Section 8 rental assistance have dried up and the number of poverty households has increased.

This shift of housing assistance away from the poor is a serious problem that states and cities must confront as they design their housing programs and allocate scarce public dollars. The dramatic rise in homelessness over the last decade, particularly for families, is clear evidence of the impact of the massive reduction in housing subsidies that serve the very poor.

Yet those state and local housing development programs that have survived or have been created to fill the gap tend to reach households with incomes at or above 50 percent of the median. The deeper subsidies required for very low-income households have not generally been available within the affordable housing delivery system over the last decade. For example, as Section 8 subsidies dried up, IHDA's ability to finance rental housing for low-income households was severely limited. In response to this, low-interest, single-family mortgages became the dominant IHDA housing finance program of the 1980s.

Even the advent of the Illinois Affordable Housing Trust Fund, which targets low- and very low-income households, does not guarantee that resources will reach the very poor. During two 1990 funding cycles of the trust fund, the rental projects funded for Chicago had average rent levels of $425 for one-bedroom units and $518 for two-bedroom units. These rent levels are affordable to households on the upper end of the low-income spectrum but are not affordable to very low-income households, particularly those with incomes below 30 percent of median. Because less than 20 percent of the poverty population receives any form of housing subsidy, the substantial majority are left to fend for themselves in the increasingly expensive private market.

As was stated earlier, the impact of the affordable housing crisis is most severe for these very low-income families. It is true that more and more first-time homebuyers are unable to afford to purchase a home and that too many low- and moderate-income renters pay excessive costs for their housing. However, excessive cost burdens are more than twice as prevalent among very low-income Illinois households (62%) than among low-income households (27%). The burden of housing costs leaves little money left over for poor families to purchase other life essentials such as clothing and health care (State of Illinois, 1991).

THE OUTLOOK FOR HOUSING POLICY IN ILLINOIS AND CHICAGO

After a decade of inaction, the federal government is once again poised to provide leadership and resources for affordable housing. The National Affordable Housing Act (NAHA), passed in late 1990, will result in millions of dollars in new federal funds for housing in Illinois and Chicago. The first year of funding (fiscal year 1992) of the HOME program alone brought $76 million for housing efforts in Illinois, $40.3 million of which was earmarked for Chicago.

Without describing NAHA or HOME in much detail, three points should be made about the impact of these funds on state and local housing policies.[2] The first is the fairly broad leeway given to cities and states to craft local programs to meet housing needs.   Unlike previous national housing finance programs, NAHA and HOME provide general guidelines and targeting requirements but do not mandate how the funds must be spent.

Second, as a condition of receiving funds with such flexibility, state and local governments are required for the first time to develop a multi-year Comprehensive Housing Affordability Strategy (CHAS). As was mentioned earlier, neither the State of Illinois nor the City of Chicago has been able to set more than annual housing objectives; state and local housing funds are usually budgeted and spent with little sense of an overall strategy or priorities. At this writing, it is unclear how useful the first CHAS planning process has been. The rules of the Department of Housing and Urban Development for the CHAS document were new and evolving. For example, most cities and states were unable to provide credible data on local housing needs because information from the 1990 census was not available. Still, the CHAS plan's requirement to identify and analyze the housing needs of special populations (e.g., the elderly, the disabled, the homeless) is likely to stimulate broader discussion of and attention to these groups than has happened in the past.

Finally, NAHA originally mandated that states and cities match the federal HOME funds with local resources. In the face of tight state and local budgets during 1991-92, the matching requirement (which ranged from 25% to 50%, depending on how the funds were used) was temporarily waived. For fiscal year 1993, the matching requirements were restored at 30 percent for new construction and 25 percent for all other uses of HOME funds.

Although the National Affordable Housing Act and the HOME program will exert a strong pull on the formation of state and local housing programs in the foreseeable future, other trends will also shape affordable housing policies in Chicago and Illinois in the next decade. The balance of this chapter examines these trends.

---

[2] For a more thorough discussion of the National Affordable Housing Act and the HOME program, see Charles Orlebeke's chapter in this volume (Orlebeke, 1993).

Resource Targeting

The income-targeting requirements of the federal HOME program suggest that the federal government recognizes the need to reverse the trend of the last decade toward "moderate-income" housing. Under the federal guidelines, the majority of HOME funds are targeted to households with incomes below 60 percent of the area median. However, unless state and local governments establish additional targeting goals, it is likely that these resources will continue to follow recent patterns and will not reach the very poor—those with incomes well below 50 percent of the median. The ongoing CHAS planning process represents a critical opportunity for state and local governments to design balanced housing programs that ensure that a reasonable share of public resources reaches those who need them the most.

Apart from the federal CHAS requirements, states and localities will be under increasing local pressure to target housing resources to very low-income and special-needs households. In 1991, the Illinois General Assembly limited to six months the cash benefits that an "employable" person can receive under the state's General Assistance program; a year later, these benefits were eliminated entirely. These developments are likely to push even more low-income single people onto the streets. As a result, low-income housing and homeless advocates in Illinois are redoubling their efforts to see that housing programs serve the poorest of the poor.

The disabled have also become increasingly vocal and effective in lobbying for accessible housing. Legislation such as Illinois Environmental Barriers Act of 1985, the Federal Fair Housing Amendments of 1987, and Omnibus Budget Reconciliation Act of 1987 (which mandates additional deinstitutionalization of the mentally ill and developmentally disabled) will influence the design of state and local housing programs. It is unclear whether this will result in sweeping new initiatives to allow the disabled to enter the mainstream or, more likely, a plethora of smaller-scale programs to serve the needs of various disabled constituencies.

Community-Based, Nonprofit Sponsors

Even before the HOME program mandated a 15 percent set-aside of funds for community development corporations (CDCs), these nonprofit developers were responsible for 60 percent of all assisted housing developed in Chicago and nearly 40 percent in the rest of Illinois.[3] The HOME requirement follows a national trend that has seen CDCs emerge as a primary vehicle for housing production across the country.

As the above statistic suggests, nonprofit developers in Chicago have fared better than their colleagues elsewhere in the state. In general, the support system for CDCs is better developed in Chicago than in the rest of Illinois. To cite but one example, CDCs in Chicago can access operating funds from the Fund for Community Development (an $11.3 million venture of the John D. and Catherine T. MacArthur Foundation and LISC) and the United Way of Chicago. No companion effort exists in the rural areas and small cities of Illinois.

A key factor in the expansion of CDC capacity in Illinois will be the role played by state and local governments. The State has used some monies from its Affordable Housing Trust Fund to provide technical assistance to CDCs outside Chicago. Direct operating grants to CDCs are needed, however, if nonprofit developers statewide are to emulate the success of the Chicago CDCs.

Antipoverty Housing Strategies

With their emphasis on local participation and leadership development, CDCs have long been recognized as a means to rebuild devastated low-income communities "from the bottom up." In addition to CDCs, there is a renewed interest in pairing housing with intensive social service programs to end the cycle of poverty in poor neighborhoods. Often this linkage of housing and social services occurs in public housing projects. For example, the Ounce of Prevention Fund's "Beethoven Project" is linking children in six buildings in the Robert Taylor Homes with an array of social services. Open to all children in the service area of the Beethoven Public School, the project includes high-quality infant and child care, health services, and parent-children activities, all located on two floors of the housing development.

The "Wells Initiative" is a joint venture of Centers for New Horizons, the Chicago Housing Authority (CHA), the Ounce of

---

[3] Estimates provided by officials of the Chicago Rehab Network and the Illinois Affordable Housing Trust Fund in fall 1992.

Prevention Fund, the Metropolitan Planning Council, and state and local government. Its goal is to create "significant change in a large, seriously distressed public housing development through an integrated set of social, physical and economic development programs which have individually been proven to work in separate communities and among separate populations across the country" (Chicago Housing Authority, 1990). The program will include resident training, human services (e.g., drug and alcohol treatment, child care), job training, tenant safety patrols, and a variety of site improvements over a seven-to-ten-year period.

Beyond existing public housing, the CHA's Mixed Income New Community Strategy (MINCS) is an attempt to create viable multi-income neighborhoods adjacent to public housing developments. All the above efforts recognize in different ways the necessity of providing increased opportunities to low-income housing residents to overcome the effects of isolating poor people in one-dimensional enclaves.

Tapping New Revenue Sources

Both the Illinois and Chicago governments are facing rising costs that are outpacing revenue sources—and an electorate that is perceived as hostile to tax increases. Given this scenario, what are the prospects for new local sources of revenue for housing, like those needed to match federal HOME funds?

The chances for dedication of state income tax revenue for housing—arguably the most simple and direct revenue mechanism—are slim to nonexistent. However, special fees and assessments, such as the tax on real estate transfers, may be politically feasible if the linkage between the revenue source and affordable housing can be made.

Looked at this way, there are a number of potential methods for raising local resources for affordable housing. Among the mechanisms that have been suggested are tax-increment financing and impact fees (especially in high-growth areas) and state housing tax credits. Although a "linked development" tax on all commercial construction in Chicago's Loop appears unlikely given the real estate slump, some version of linkage may be proposed in connection with large-scale public projects (such as the McCormick Place expansion and the proposed casino/entertainment center) and in rapidly gentrifying neighborhoods.

Less controversial for state and local governments are the ways in which existing pools of public-sector capital can be deployed for low-income housing development. State Treasurer Patrick Quinn's linked-deposit program and the City of Chicago's CD Float Loan Program provide below-market financing by depositing or lending government funds for short periods of time. Undoubtedly, ways will continue to be sought to free up government pension funds for low-income housing development. To date, Illinois and Chicago have been unsuccessful in tapping this immense investment source.

Finally, in addition to lending and investing their own funds, states and cities can work to channel private capital into affordable housing production. The federal Community Reinvestment Act has prompted many Chicago-area banks to establish neighborhood lending programs that offer mortgages for affordable rental housing. Regulatory pressure on financial institutions will continue in the 1990s and offers state and local governments numerous opportunities to "partner" with local banks and savings and loans. Like the linked-deposit programs mentioned above, mechanisms can be created to use public-sector guarantees or interest-rate subsidies to access and direct private capital for affordable housing.

Property Transfer Programs

As was noted earlier, Chicago has been particularly creative in using the inventory of tax-delinquent and City-owned buildings to promote housing development. In addition to the Tax Reactivation Program, the Chicago Abandoned Property Program (CAPP) and the Accelerated Real Estate Sales (ACRES) program have recently been used to access property for housing and community development purposes. The CAPP program permits the City to take title to abandoned properties and transfer the title to individuals or organizations that agree to either demolish or rehabilitate the property. ACRES is the disposition/sales program for City-owned vacant lots, which can be acquired for discounted prices if the land is to be used for a public purpose such as affordable housing. Together with the sizeable portfolios of repossessed homes owned by the federal Department of Housing and Urban Development and the Resolution Trust Corporation, these publicly controlled properties are an important resource for affordable housing production.

Simplifying Housing Production Programs

One unintended by-product of the current process of financing
low-income housing is the complex legal arrangements that go
with this "patchwork" of funding sources. It is not uncommon for
a low-income apartment building being rehabbed in Chicago to
have the following elements:

- acquisition through the Cook County Tax Reactivation
Program;
- a predevelopment loan from LISC or a bank;
- a federal tax credit allocated by the City or State;
- corporate equity from the Chicago Equity Fund;
- a loan to bridge the equity pay-ins;
- a first mortgage loan from a bank;
- a second mortgage loan from the Chicago Department of
Housing;
- a third mortgage loan from the Illinois Affordable Housing
Trust Fund; and
- an operating subsidy from the Chicago Low-Income Housing
Trust Fund.

Each agency or institution has its own legal department and
underwriting approach that may or may not "fit" with the other
partners. The resulting closing documents can be over a foot
thick for a 40-unit apartment building. This practice caused one
prominent local housing attorney to quip that "these deals are being consistently over-lawyered. What makes sense for a $200-
million project is not appropriate for a $2-million project."

Efforts are currently underway to simplify or "streamline" the
above process. The range of options includes simply coordinating
and reducing the complexity of the documents, privatizing City
loan underwriting, and creating deeply subsidized bond pools to
eliminate one or more funding sources. Whatever measures are
agreed on, the goal will be the same: To create a predictable and
efficient financing process that reflects the true level of risk borne
by each participating party.

Other Housing Policy Trends

The 1990s will see continued efforts to bolster affordable housing
through a variety of other measures, including the following:

Additional property tax relief for multi-family, low-income buildings: This could include special abatement programs or expansion of the existing Cook County "Class 9" program. The Class 9 program significantly reduces the property tax assessments for rehabbed multi-family buildings that are rented at below-market rates.

Regulatory reforms: Support for further modernization of the Chicago building code exists in a number of places, including business-oriented civic groups such as Chicago United and the Chicago Development Council. There is also growing interest in loosening restrictions on manufactured housing, which can often be fabricated and assembled for much less than traditional stick-built structures, without sacrificing quality.

Suburban housing initiatives: With new federal HOME funds available to them, several suburban "collar counties" (three in 1992) will be grappling with housing programming and allocation issues. Housing advocacy groups will continue to push for more affordable suburban housing and for tough fair-housing enforcement. Noteworthy examples of such efforts include the North West Housing Partnership's plans for moderate-income and elderly housing, the Leadership Council for Metropolitan Open Communities' successful fair-housing monitoring program, and active fair-housing groups in DuPage County and in suburban communities north of Chicago.

CONCLUSION

Overall, the decade of the 1980s was not a good one for proponents of affordable housing in Illinois. Planning and coordination of housing policies and programs received very little attention. Targeting of housing assistance to the very poor was minimal. Despite some innovation at the state and local level, the overall resources available for low-income housing are a fraction of what they were when the decade began. And the need is arguably far greater now than at any time in the last 20 years.

What will be the fate of the state and local housing initiatives described above in the 1990s? Will Illinois and Chicago assume more prominent roles in affordable housing production, or will they continue to lag behind other states and cities in planning and resource allocation? The answer to these questions depends on how the political process in Illinois responds to a growing affordable housing crisis. Experience suggests that three factors will influence the outcome:

The effectiveness of grassroots efforts to organize the constituents of low-income housing programs: Affordable housing advocacy efforts, such as the Chicago Affordable Housing Coalition and the Statewide Housing Action Coalition, will need to continue and expand if politicians are to view low-income housing as a fiscal priority.

The level of public awareness of the causes of and solution for the housing crisis: To date, most local media attention has been focused on homelessness. Lacking has been the kind of in-depth, ongoing coverage of the housing issue that could provide a basis for broader support of new housing initiatives.

The involvement of business and philanthropic leaders in affordable housing efforts: Corporate and foundation officials bring two key things to the housing debate: resources and "clout." Intermediaries such as the Chicago Equity Fund and LISC have helped channel private-sector funds to affordable housing projects. The business leadership of Chicago United has addressed housing issues from time to time. But Illinois's private-sector leaders have not embraced affordable housing on anywhere near the scale needed to trigger a major re-examination of the issue by the state's politicians.

The public school reform movement in Chicago may be both instructive and encouraging for Illinois housing advocates. With a combination of hard work and luck, the 1990s may see a similar constituency trigger substantial affordable housing initiatives in Illinois and Chicago.

REFERENCES

Advisory Commission on Regulatory Barriers to Affordable Housing (1991). *Not In My Back Yard: Removing Barriers to Affordable Housing.* Washington, D.C.: U.S. Department of Housing and Urban Development.

148 *Thomas J. Lenz and Barbara A. Shaw*

Berenyi, Eileen Brettler (1989). *Locally Funded Housing Programs in the United States: A Survey of the 51 Most Populated Cities.* New York: New School for Social Research.

Chicago Housing Authority et al. (1990). "The Ida B. Wells Community Initiative Proposal." Chicago: Chicago Housing Authority.

Chicago Rehab Network (1990). *The Chicago Affordable Housing Fact Book: A Resource for Community Action.* Chicago: Chicago Rehab Network.

City of Chicago (1991). *Comprehensive Housing Affordability Strategy (CHAS), FY 1992 to FY 1996.* Chicago: Chicago Department of Housing.

City of Chicago, Department of Housing (1992). "Overall Functional Organization Chart."

COSCAA (1990). *State Housing Initiatives: The 1990 Compendium.* Washington, D.C.: Council of State Community Affairs Agencies.

Orlebeke, Charles J. (1993). "Federal Housing Policies." In this volume.

State of Illinois (1991). *Comprehensive Housing Affordability Strategy (CHAS), FY 1992 - FY 1996.* Chicago: Illinois Housing Development Authority.

State of Illinois, Office of the Governor (1991). "Governor Acts to Coordinate State's Housing Programs" (press release). Springfield, Ill., November 20, 1991.

Terner, Ian Donald, and Thomas B. Cook (1990). "New Directions for Federal Housing Policy: The Role of the States." In Denise DiPasquale and Langley C. Keyes, eds., *Building Foundations: Housing and Federal Policy.* Philadelphia: University of Pennsylvania Press.

COMMENTS

Robert D. Katz

In order to address the issue of affordable housing in Illinois, it will be helpful to put housing policy in historical context. To a large extent, state and local housing policies in the United States have been developed in response to federal housing legislation and programs. In this regard, Illinois and the Chicago metropolitan area are no exception. State legislation and executive actions leading to the establishment of local public-housing and urban-renewal authorities, as well as the Illinois Housing Development Authority (IHDA), are illustrations from the past; Comprehensive Housing Affordability Strategies (CHAS) are current examples (City of Chicago, 1991; State of Illinois, 1991). The practice of following the federal lead has come about because the preponderance of the funding for publicly assisted housing has come from Washington, and states and localities have been anxious to capture as much of these funds as possible.

Because of this practice of relying on federal direction, housing has not been very high on the list of priorities for candidates for local or state offices, and, as a result, we have seen relatively few affordable housing initiatives in Illinois. If housing had been identified by elected officials as a major issue of public concern, state and/or local legislation would have followed. In addition, the electorate would have expected new programs to be enacted and monies appropriated. However, most housing programs come with high price tags and with a fair degree of uncertainty as to their success. Against this background, and the absence of a well-organized affordable housing constituency, it should come as no surprise that housing has been relegated to the back burner. Why promote public policies for affordable housing when someone else is already doing the job, when the success of these policies is uncertain, and when funding will be needed to pay for the programs?

The situation has now changed, and Congress and the executive branch are more than willing for states and localities to assume a greater share of responsibilities (what I call giving away problems but not adequate funds to deal with them). Thomas

Lenz and Barbara Shaw correctly point to some of the factors that contribute to the "severe and growing housing crisis in Illinois." They imply that most of the public is not aware that a housing crisis exists. What is missing in their otherwise clear analysis and useful suggestions for new housing policies and programs are some ideas on how to make housing an issue that is a higher priority for state and local action.

Lenz and Shaw have provided a useful analogy with their closing reference to public school reform in Chicago. They might also have chosen medical care. What has brought these issues to the front pages—and, more important, kept them there long enough for state and local government to respond—is the fact that they touch the lives of a large proportion of the population. In contrast, housing has been, until recently, something that the majority of Americans could afford, and our housing standards are still among the highest in the world. When enough people came to believe that public education had declined and medical costs were soaring out of control, cries for reform were heard. The same can be expected with respect to affordable housing.

In the case of housing, most of the headlines have dealt with homelessness or crime and drugs at some public housing projects. We are not a society without compassion, and we have tried to address these problems, albeit in a modest way. However, we are rapidly reaching the point where persons of modest incomes can no longer afford a decent home. It has been pointed out that the majority of U.S. homeowners could not afford to purchase the home they currently occupy if it were now on the market. Young married couples, even with two incomes, have a difficult time finding a house they can afford to buy, and rents are equally out of reach for many employed persons and the elderly.

In the face of budget shortfalls at all levels of government, housing is not likely to garner significantly greater resources until we begin to highlight the problems faced by persons of moderate income in addition to those of low income. The CHAS process can already be credited with initiating an important debate, which can be expected to intensify in the future and might well be the vehicle for significant housing reform. There are at least two important policy issues that will dominate the debate: Which segments of the population should be the recipients of housing resources, and where should these resources be distributed? Some housing advocates can be expected to mount a major effort to direct the bulk of the resources to very low-income individuals and households. However, the case will be made that such a strategy will result in helping fewer persons than would a strategy of assisting those with slightly higher incomes with lower subsidies per housing unit. There will also be pressure to distribute affordable housing funds geographically on the basis of need alone. This concern must be balanced against the argument that because resources are so scarce, clustering funds to target neighborhoods and communities would have much greater impact.

As the authors suggest, there is a great need to develop an acceptable political process to respond to the need for more affordable housing once the issue is on the table. Three factors are mentioned as influencing the outcome. I would redirect one and add a fourth.

Public awareness of housing issues can and should receive more media attention. However, as I have stated, this attention is likely to endure if the focus of housing strategies goes beyond those of very low income, the homeless, and others with special housing needs. For years, the greatest housing subsidy has come in the form of tax savings enjoyed by homeowners. Even in the face of the need to generate more revenues, no politician has seriously suggested that we eliminate this subsidy, because it affects so many voters. We need to develop state and local housing programs that have similar widespread appeal to those with modest incomes, along with programs for those with more serious housing needs.

The other key factor influencing the political process is the participation of the homebuilding industry. Past successes in forging housing policies, such as the federal housing programs that were born in the 1930s, had as one of their objectives the employment of workers in the building trades. Likewise, continuing support for a variety of publicly assisted housing programs has come from private builders who have contracted with the public agencies and nonprofit organizations that administer these programs. The homebuilding industry stands to benefit from increased state and local participation in the production of affordable housing, and their support should be enlisted in the process of developing new policies for affordable housing.

REFERENCES

City of Chicago (1991). *Comprehensive Housing Affordability Strategy (CHAS), FY 1992 to FY 1996.* Chicago: Chicago Department of Housing.

State of Illinois (1991). *Comprehensive Housing Affordability Strategy (CHAS), FY 1992 - FY 1996.* Chicago: Illinois Housing Development Authority.

COMMENTS

George S. Tolley

The chapter by Thomas Lenz and Barbara Shaw is an excellent overview of housing programs in Illinois and their effectiveness in meeting the housing needs of the poor. Although the authors have related Illinois programs to broader housing issues to a certain degree, it could be useful to go even further in that direction. How effective are housing programs in combating poverty? Can housing program dollars be spent more effectively elsewhere on non-housing programs, or should more funds be allocated to housing programs? How does housing fit into an overall antipoverty strategy? Within housing policy, what is the magnitude of the target groups? Is re-targeting needed? Is there a role for housing vouchers?

The state and local programs in Illinois appear to be so modest that they can almost be viewed as pilot endeavors. If the programs are viewed as experiments, systematic efforts to learn from the experiences by comparing the effectiveness of the different programs would be warranted. Such efforts would help make a case for more funding, if necessary.

In concentrating on housing assistance programs, the chapter has little to say about other policy considerations that affect housing affordability for the poor—in particular, regulatory considerations. Finding a balance between legitimate needs for regulation and allowing for efficient provision of goods and services has been high on the policy agenda in the era of deregulation of the past decade or so. Currently, the effects of rising housing costs on lower-income people, as well as the increased awareness of homelessness, is leading to more emphasis on regulation as it affects housing. Anthony Downs of the Brookings Institution in Washington, D.C., has estimated that in the United States, "75 percent of the cost of housing is due to requirements in excess of the minimum needed for health and safety" (Chapman, 1989).

National concern with housing conditions goes back at least to 1892, when Congress commissioned an investigation into living conditions in the nation's large cities. New York's lower east side had a density of 1,000 people per acre, exceeding any European or Asian city. The closest rival was one district in Bombay. The study, however, led to no significant federal legislation. The regulation of housing remained, as it does today, at the local level, and it should be an important focus in a discussion of state and local policies affecting affordability of housing.

BUILDING CODES

Although building codes are not the sole cause of high and rising housing costs, their role in restricting the affordability of housing for poorer people needs attention. The City of Chicago's building code is regarded as one of most restrictive and obsolete in the nation. For example, the City's building code requires a "grease trap," which is rarely required in other cities and towns. Also required are separate drainage pipes for the kitchen sink, garbage disposal, and dishwasher. In the suburbs and most other places, a single pipe is considered adequate and acceptable.

The plastic versus metal pipe debate has gone on for quite some time in Chicago. Proponents of plastic pipe state that the polyvinyl chloride (PVC) pipe is lighter, easier to work with, and significantly less expensive than cast iron, copper, or lead pipe. The heavy metal pipes require professional installation at professional rates, whereas plastic pipe can be installed by the homeowner. Opponents of plastic pipe (the plumbers' union and other building trade unions) claim that it may leach toxic materials into the water supply and that it can be a fire hazard, although there is little credible evidence to back either claim. There is, however, considerable evidence that *lead pipe* constitutes a health hazard—and lead pipe was not only permitted but required by Chicago's code until several years ago, when the U.S. Environmental Protection Agency banned its use in water lines. The City of Chicago did recently relax its restrictions on PVC pipe, allowing its use in buildings under three stories. Unfortunately, when one's goal is to house many families or individuals in the most cost-effective manner possible, the price of land almost dictates 10- or 20- or 30-story buildings.

Another restrictive building code in Chicago concerns wiring (and the electricians' union). In any other city, a thermostat can be connected with a simple, low-voltage wire, but in Chicago, it must be encased in conduit. Chicago's code also has a ban on new material. There are new products on the market that could decrease the cost of new or rehab electrical work. These products are included in the National Electrical Codes, are listed by Underwriters Laboratories, but are excluded from the Chicago building code.

The entire basis of Chicago's building code should be examined. The City lists specific materials that must be used and procedures that must be followed in order to comply with the law. The plan must be laid out in detail in order to obtain construction permits. An alternative deserving consideration is adoption of "performance codes," which would regulate in terms of results desired rather than how to achieve those results. For example, the building code would state that a roof must be capable of holding the weight of, say, 24 inches of snow, rather than stating that the roofing material should be of a particular type, the nails must be so long and made of some particular metal, and so forth.

Another alternative that should be considered is the concept of "optimum codes" based on risk-return analysis. This approach is often advocated for general environmental regulation, but, to my knowledge, it has not been applied to building codes. The basic idea is to compare the costs and benefits of differing degrees of stringency and to choose the regulation that comes closest to making the extra health and safety benefits worth the extra cost of stringency. An advantage of the approach is that it provides an objective principle to guide policies and a framework to evaluate various counterclaims, often motivated by self-interest.

ZONING

Zoning is a complex area replete with possibilities for unnecessarily increasing the costs of housing. For example, the extent to which zoning interferes with use of empty and abandoned buildings deserves investigation. Given the affordable housing crisis, empty and abandoned buildings and vacant property are underutilized, but the current zoning of a parcel of land could make it difficult to create more affordable housing. Properties that could support housing may have an archaic industrial or manufacturing zoning, and there might be political obstacles to changing the zoning for residential use.

An issue of importance for homeless and near-homeless people is the availability of single-room living space. Lots zoned for residential development, for example, may have minimum land-area or minimum square-footage restrictions. If a developer were attempting to build low- to middle-income housing, the lot-size limitation would increase the cost per unit.

Zoning restrictions and building-code specifications have contributed to the demise of affordable individual living spaces. Old residence hotels (including rooming houses, boarding houses, lodging houses) were at one time a viable alternative for lower-income individuals. Now called SROs (single-room-occupancy), they are becoming an endangered species nationwide. In Chicago alone, the number of SRO units has dropped from more than 27,000 in 1973 to fewer than 8,800 in 1990 (Chicago Rehab Network, 1990, pp. 84-85).

Another regulatory problem relates to SROs and the Food Stamp program. A Food Stamp recipient receives a higher allowance if his or her dwelling unit contains a cooking area, but a kitchenette in the SRO may violate zone restrictions for the building. The addition of a kitchenette somehow magically converts a single-room living space into a "family unit." Another difficulty for SROs is that they are defined as hotels and are assessed for real estate tax purposes at 38 percent of market value versus the 33 percent for apartment buildings and 16 percent for single-family residences.[1] These "hotels" are also required to use professionally installed, conduit- encased wiring throughout, which adds approximately $85,000 to the cost of rehabbing a typical (60-80 room) SRO residence.

FEDERAL REGULATION

States and localities could take the lead in combating federal policies that raise housing costs for the poor. The Davis-Bacon law, requiring payment of the prevailing union wage in the construction of federally subsidized projects, is a well-known cost-raising hindrance to affordable housing. In one case, the residents of public housing projects were prevented from rehabilitating their own buildings, which would have had the further advantage of offering unemployed tenants work and the opportunity to learn a marketable skill, under guidance of a reputable contractor.

Environmental regulation that goes beyond the need for prudent protection is another area for potential reform. One of sev-

---

[1] Beginning in tax year 1993, SROs in Chicago became eligible for reclassification, with an assessment rate of 16 percent.

eral examples is asbestos abatement, which so far has had a major impact on schools and commercial buildings. There have been proposals to extend these regulations to require asbestos removal from residential buildings as well. In a study we conducted on the potential effects of asbestos abatement on neighborhoods, we found that low-income neighborhoods would be the most seriously affected, leading to higher rents, incentives to abandon buildings, and financing difficulties (Croke et al., 1988, 1989). Meanwhile, the benefits of asbestos removal, as opposed to exposure to workers during manufacture of asbestos, are questionable at best.

CONCLUSION

Although attention to housing assistance programs is warranted, there are less expensive and more effective ways to reduce housing costs for all low-income people, not just those few who are lucky enough to be in special programs. The alternative approach is to reform building codes, zoning procedures, and other regulations that needlessly raise the cost of housing.

REFERENCES

Chapman, Stephen (1989). "Housing the Poor: Chicago Can Get More by Doing Less," *Chicago Tribune*, May 14, 1989, sec. 4, p. 3.

Chicago Rehab Network (1990). *The Chicago Affordable Housing Fact Book*. Chicago: Chicago Rehab Network.

Croke, Kevin, Edward Mensah, Robert Fabian, and George Tolley (1988). "Asbestos Removal and Treatment Impacts on Housing and Urban Neighborhoods," *Journal of Environmental Systems*, vol. 18 (1988-89), pp. 123-131.

_____ (1989). "Asbestos in Buildings: Effects on Residential and Commercial Real Estate Values," *The Environmental Professional*, vol. 11 (1989), pp. 256-263.

COMMUNITY-BASED INITIATIVES TO PROVIDE AFFORDABLE HOUSING IN CHICAGO

Teresa Córdova

The problem of affordable housing is reflected in the gap between the costs of housing and the amount of money that people have available to pay for that housing. A large enough gap can lead to living in overcrowded and often unsafe conditions and even to homelessness. Households that spend more than 30 percent of their income on housing pay more than what federal government standards suggest is reasonable. According to that standard, more than 40 percent of all renter households in the city of Chicago had "excessive" housing costs in 1990 (Northeastern Illinois Planning Commission, 1992). The lower the income of a household, the larger the proportion spent on housing, and the harder it is to stretch the remaining percentage to cover other living costs (Voss, 1990). Moreover, household characteristics such as type and size affect the ability to pay for other necessities once the housing costs are paid. Some households pay what they have to in order to obtain housing but then are unable to meet their non-shelter needs—a situation that has been called "shelter poverty" (Stone, 1989). Furthermore, measures of affordability do not take into account the availability and quality of housing, thus further obscuring an even more severe housing crisis. Utilities and additional costs make it increasingly difficult for the low- and moderate-income household to rent, let alone buy, property.

The housing crisis that emerged during the 1980s was exacerbated by changes in federal housing policies. The federal government cut funds to local governments for homeownership programs for low- and moderate-income households. It also cut assistance to low- and moderate-income tenants eligible for housing aid and decreased the amount of federal loans to low- and moderate-income homeowners for the rehabilitation of substandard units. Housing assistance programs for the elderly, the handicapped, Native peoples, and farmers were also cut. In addition, the federal government cut its support for the construction of new housing by the private sector and reduced the tax incentives to the private sector for the construction of rental housing. The production and rehabilitation of public housing was another target of federal cuts. Indeed, expenditure cuts in housing are greater than cuts in any other federal activity. Budget authority for the Department of Housing and Urban Development (HUD) was reduced from $35.7 billion in 1980 to $15.2 billion in 1987. In 1978, the HUD budget was 7 percent of the total federal budget; by 1987, it was down to 1 percent (Schwartz, Ferlauto, and Hoffman, 1988, pp. 46-52).

The small amount of state and local funds for housing compounded market conditions marked by rising interest rates, increased costs of construction and rehabilitation, and large government subsidies for downtown development. This era of neighborhood neglect by federal, state, and local policies was also an era of neighborhood response, with the rise of nonprofit community-based development corporations and advocacy organizations. The history of nonprofit community development efforts is one of struggle for resources and technical know-how. Although access to both has improved, it is probably still safe to say that community development groups are "saddled with goals and objectives that are far beyond their resources to achieve" (Keyes, 1971).

Despite the limitations, community-based organizations have become key actors in the development of affordable housing for low- and moderate-income households. Indeed, Gale Cincotta, executive director of the National Training and Information Center, says that "nonprofits are the critical mass at the base, the ones really doing the work" (Gerhardstein, 1990). This chapter is a brief examination of affordable housing efforts by community-based organizations in Chicago.

PHILOSOPHICAL ORIENTATION

Community initiatives to develop affordable housing are often founded on principles of neighborhood preservation and service to low- and moderate-income households. A statement from Peoples Housing in Chicago's Rogers Park community illustrates the fervor and orientation of the commitment.

> In the fall of 1979 a group of low-income neighborhood residents dared to dream an impossible dream. Having just completed a successful petition drive in favor of new subsidized

housing, this group hopefully asked, "Why not us? Why can't we develop this housing, rather than an outside developer who doesn't really know our community?" . . . this small band of low-income residents were undaunted in their pursuit of a better life for themselves, and for their neighborhood, through community-controlled development. . . . Today, almost ten years later, Peoples Housing is a strong advocate for social justice in its community (Peoples Housing, n.d.).

The Neighborhood Institute (TNI), a nonprofit affiliate of South Shore Bank in Chicago, describes its commitment as "holistic" and concerns itself with both the human and physical needs of its community: "Our primary role is to stimulate a climate whereby people have options and opportunities to help themselves." Dorris Pickens, president of TNI, says that "communities have to be developed from within" (Pickens, 1989).

A recent call for neighborhood participation from the Kenwood-Oakland Community Organization, located on Chicago's south side, says: "For too long, too many of us have sat back waiting for someone other than ourselves to bring decent, livable housing—which we can afford—to use. Well, it will not happen unless we join in the movement to make it happen. Join the movement for affordable housing" (Kenwood-Oakland Community Organization, 1990).

The president's letter in the annual report of the Bickerdike Redevelopment Corporation reveals the value placed in community control and pride. "To be sure everybody gets a decent place to live, at low cost, and more important that you should be proud of where you live, I want to urge you to continue to be active in controlling the redevelopment of your neighborhood" (Bickerdike Redevelopment, 1985).

These community organizations also understand that their neighborhood conditions are shaped by external factors such as redlining by banks and job dislocation. In many cases, housing development is parallel to economic development. For example, Peoples Housing, in addition to its housing activities, has formulated long-range plans for business ventures.

Community-based initiatives for affordable housing are directed toward promoting homeownership, renovating old or abandoned buildings, and constructing new housing units. The ability to carry out this housing agenda requires sophisticated leadership, start-up funds, technical know-how, and creative financing. Advocacy efforts and public-private partnerships have helped to establish programs to meet those needs. The community approach to housing is oriented toward neighborhood empowerment, as signaled through the organization of block clubs and alternative management structures. Community land trusts, cooperative ownership programs, and tiered financing are examples of key strategies of community-based housing development.

NATIONAL LOBBYING EFFORTS

Community development organizations promote homeownership and multi-family rental housing by facilitating loan packages, directing individuals to government programs, and supplying information. Their ability to provide these services has been enhanced by several national lobbying efforts that resulted in significant federal legislation in 1970s.

Community Reinvestment Act

Housing abandonment, and thus a decrease in the supply of housing, has been directly tied to banking policies, particularly redlining (Meyerson, 1986a). Concern about the impact of redlining practices was the impetus for lobbying efforts that resulted in the Community Reinvestment Act (CRA) of 1977. The National Training and Information Center, located in Chicago, provided the leadership for this lobbying effort, which involved a coalition that crossed racial and regional boundaries. The CRA provides for a procedure whereby banks can be pressured to halt their redlining policies and to reinvest in neighborhoods they had previously left disinvested. For example, under CRA, bank regulators can refuse permission to a bank holding company to acquire another bank or bank holding company if any of the banks involved have not adequately responded to the credit needs of local communities. Under these regulations, an individual or organization can petition the bank regulators to deny permission when compliance is not met. It is precisely this leverage that can put financial pressure on institutions to agree to provide mortgage loans to qualified individuals whose income is below a cut-off point. For example, in 1984, eight community groups, called the Chicago Reinvestment Alliance, entered into an agreement with First Chicago Corporation to establish a $120 million, five-year lending program called the Neighborhood Investment and Revitalization Program (Woodstock Institute, 1984). Shortly thereafter,

Harris Trust and Savings Bank and Northern Trust Company entered into agreements with the alliance to provide $35 million and $18 million, respectively, for loan funds to meet neighborhood credit needs. These agreements, reached because of threats by the alliance to challenge the banks for non-compliance with CRA, comprise the Neighborhood Lending Programs of Chicago.

Each lending program has a review board that includes both community members and bank representatives. The board is the primary mechanism for accountability when loan applications are reviewed, when policies for each program are discussed and defined, and when monitoring is done to ensure correspondence between the loans and community needs. CRA is generally considered a success, particularly in terms of the dollars generated through loan programs that had not been available previously (Bradford, 1990). The agreements are also noteworthy as an example of a partnership between community organizations and banks, replacing a previous relationship that was often hostile. According to Calvin Bradford, the review board is an essential component of the success of the Neighborhood Lending Programs:

> It has been the review board process that has contributed the most to the success of the programs. Where the review board did not become a forum for discussion, the lending programs suffered. Where the forum was fully used, issues were addressed, differences were aired, changes were initiated in the programs, and working compromises were reached, even when it was not possible to reach full agreement (Bradford, 1990, p. 7).

Nonetheless, the Neighborhood Lending Programs face challenges. Bradford notes that the lack of public subsidies limits the ability to make private lending affordable to more residents and businesses. He also indicates that the success of the programs will depend on how federal regulators enforce not only the CRA but also the Equal Credit Opportunity Act and the Fair Housing Act. He argues that regulators "need to develop enforcement standards that reward reinvestment and allow for responsible experimentation and lending products and programs that reflect appropriate costs associated with sound loans and the response to real community needs" (Bradford 1990, p. 10).

164 *Teresa Córdova*

Neighborhood Housing Services

In Pittsburgh, citizen reaction to redlining policies resulted in a program to redirect funds to a deteriorated neighborhood. Successful efforts in 1968 to forge a partnership among lenders, residents, and the city served as the basis for the Urban Reinvestment Task Force recommendation to develop similar efforts in other cities. Congressional support of the recommendation led to the 1978 Neighborhood Reinvestment Corporation Act, which gave rise to Neighborhood Housing Services (NHS) throughout the country.

In Chicago, NHS serves predominantly Black or Latino neighborhoods with histories of redlining and disinvestment. NHS regards the neighborhood as the client and works with the residents to build consensus regarding community improvement. Once this initial organizing is done, NHS helps facilitate access to loans for homeowners, particularly from banks that want to meet their lending requirements under CRA but may not want to deal with residents directly. Beyond this brokerage function, NHS has a $2-4 million revolving loan fund available for acquisition or rehabilitation costs. Sources for this fund include Community Development Block Grant (CDBG) money from the City of Chicago and private money from the Ford Foundation.

NHS also helps property owners work with insurance companies that have traditionally redlined neighborhoods. It provides technical assistance on property assessment, helps select contractors, and even assists in the monitoring of contractors. In some cases, NHS has also become an owner, developer, and manager of property, as exemplified by the 300 units it owns in the Austin and Garfield Park communities of Chicago.

THE IMPORTANCE OF KNOWLEDGE, MONEY, AND VISION

Community-based developers have utilized a number of programs and mechanisms to supply affordable housing. Through resourceful leadership and the development of technical know-how, community initiatives have been made possible by cost-cutting measures, start-up funds, creative financing, and alternative ownership and management structures.

Rise of Leadership and Technical Know-How

Community-based housing initiatives have benefited from the rise of several nationwide nonprofit groups that serve as sources of expertise to local development efforts. The National Housing Law Project, for example, specializes in making housing research available to community-based organizations and housing activitists. The Local Initiatives Support Corporation (LISC), established in 1981, is an intermediary organization that provides technical and financial expertise to community-based organizations. LISC, with offices in several cities, has been instrumental in guiding development projects with complicated financial structures and partnership agreements. This technical assistance and the trial-and-error experience of community nonprofit organizations have resulted in a sophisticated, professional set of community development actors. These individuals from Chicago, Cleveland, Boston, Pittsburgh, New York, and many other cities have carried their agenda through the 1980s and into an era that demands endurance and creativity as community-based initiatives emerge as an even more critical source of affordable housing for low- and moderate-income neighborhoods. The Chicago area can certainly boast of a sophisticated cadre of individuals and organizations that are skilled negotiators, developers, and organizers.

Cost-Cutting Measures

The most serious obstacle to providing low-income housing is matching the cost of developing that housing with the amount that a household is able to pay. Thus, the primary difficulty for a nonprofit developer (or, for that matter, a for-profit developer) is how to keep the cost of housing low enough (while still maintaining high enough quality) so that a low-income household can afford it. The first thing that the community group does, therefore, is to search for ways to cut the costs of acquiring the land or buildings to be developed or renovated. Finding the funds to obtain property is more difficult, and there are no tax incentives. Thus, the nonprofit developer, sometimes in competition with for-profit developers (especially in gentrifying areas) searches for inexpensive ways to obtain property. The Cook County scavenger sale and properties in receivership often provide avenues for property acquisition, especially in disinvested neighborhoods.

The Cook County Tax Reactivation Program, begun in 1983, is a good example of how local municipalities can create a means for qualified nonprofit developers to acquire tax-delinquent properties at a negligible cost. Under this program, Cook County obtains tax-delinquent property at the scavenger sale and, after clearing all liens on the property, makes it available to nonprofit community organizations at a minimal cost. The Woodstock Institute, a not-for-profit agency that provides research and policy analysis, has deemed the project a success despite minor administrative problems. The organization has described the program as "extremely successful in generating savings totaling over $4 million to developers attempting to provide quality affordable housing for low- and moderate-income people" (Woodstock Institute, 1988, p. iii). The County benefits both from the sale and from having property returned to the tax rolls.

The City of Chicago has created programs to facilitate the sale of abandoned buildings and has streamlined the process to purchase vacant lots. The Chicago Abandoned Property Program enables the City to obtain the titles to abandoned property and, in turn, to transfer title to individuals or groups to either improve the property or demolish the buildings. Acquiring vacant lots in the city has been deemed a bureaucratic nightmare, and neighborhood groups have called for streamlining the acquisition process (Siewers, 1990). The Accelerated City Real Estate Sales (ACRES) program is the outcome of this streamlining and provides for special assistance to community organizations and others to purchase lots, sometimes for as little as one dollar. Through the ACRES program, the City uses a sealed bid process to sell surplus real estate specifically for projects that increase the supply of low- or moderate-income housing. Interested applicants are able to obtain a list of city-owned surplus properties from the Chicago Department of General Services. Methods to reduce the acquisition costs for land or buildings to be renovated can be a crucial cost-cutting step in the development process.

Grants for Start-Up Costs

Foundations have been an important source for start-up costs for both community organizations and specific projects. Foundation commitment is illustrated by the creation of the National Community Development Initiative in February 1991 to provide a $62.5 million pool for loans to nonprofit neighborhood groups.

Seven foundations and the Prudential Insurance Company are supplying the funds for pre-construction costs such as acquisition of property. Because it is difficult to obtain financing for this stage of development, a new funding source will enable a community group to move more quickly to acquire a piece of desired property. The John D. and Catherine T. MacArthur Foundation is a contributor to the fund, which adds to their long list of efforts to support community development. Other contributors include the Lilly Endowment, the Rockefeller Foundation, the Hewlett Foundation, the Knight Foundation, the Pew Charitable Trusts, and the Surdna Foundation. Nonprofit groups in Chicago will receive $2 million of these funds. Most of this amount ($1.6 million) will be placed in a working capital fund for easy-access loans (which will hopefully be supplemented by other local funds), with the remainder ($400,000) made available as loans to two development corporations to produce housing (Reardon, 1991).

Creative Financing

During the 1980s, large direct federal subsidies were noticeably absent as a source of funding for low-income housing. Federal tax policy, however, provided incentives for corporations to invest in low-income housing projects by granting tax shelters such as accelerated depreciation and passive-loss allowances. As a result of the Tax Reform Act of 1986, tax shelters were modified. Individual investors obtained fewer incentives, but the Low-Income Housing Tax Credit enabled corporations to gain substantial tax benefits for investing in housing specifically for low-income households. Corporations that might desire the tax credit, but that may not be interested in the development or management of housing, could exchange their financial investment for tax credits obtained in a syndicated partnership. The corporations also benefit from cash-flow distributions and sometimes appreciations in value. An added benefit is the boost in their public image.

A key vehicle for facilitating partnership financial packaging is the Chicago Housing Partnership (CHP), which constitutes a network of resources available to community-based groups and makes particular development projects possible. Members of the CHP include the Chicago Equity Fund, LISC, the Chicago Department of Housing, the Illinois Housing Development Authority, major financial institutions, and community-based organizations. The CHP (together with the Boston Housing Partnership) is a prototype of "a new kind of local institution, which orchestrates the activities of all the key actors in the development process who are needed to make high-volume delivery of low-income housing possible without large federal subsidies" (Stegman and Holden, 1987, p. 103).

The Chicago Equity Fund (CEF), created in 1985 as member of the Chicago Housing Partnership, is designed to attract corporate investment for low-income housing in the city of Chicago and the broader metropolitan area. CEF has a two-tiered structure: As managing partner, it sells general partnership shares to corporate investors; the general partnership then acquires a limited partnership interest in qualified housing projects. The corporate investors earn profits through tax savings from the Low-Income Housing Tax Credit. More than 35 corporations have invested a total of $40 million since the inception of the fund, which often comprises one-third of the needed financing for a given project. A typical project is funded from at least three sources and may include CEF, a subsidized loan from LISC, a below-market-rate loan from the Chicago Department of Housing, and a loan from a commercial bank (Stegman and Holden, 1987, pp. 106-107; Chicago Equity Fund, 1991).

The CEF has been used by a number of nonprofit developers, including Bethel New Life, Bickerdike Redevelopment Corporation, Hispanic Housing Development Corporation, Kenwood-Oakland Community Organization, Lakefront SRO Corporation, Latin United Community Housing Association (LUCHA), Peoples Housing, the Neighborhood Institute, and Voice of the People in Uptown. These and more than fifteen other development corporations have met several criteria for access to CEF money: First, the project must be a multi-family development with at least fifteen units. Second, the developer must be either a nonprofit organization, in association with a nonprofit developer for the project, or a for-profit developer "sanctioned" by the community. Third, the developer must provide affordable housing for households whose incomes do not exceed 60 percent of the Chicago-area median income (accounting for household size). Finally, the project must enhance the revitalization of the community in which the project exists (Chicago Equity Fund, 1991).

The growing need of CDCs for corporate equity investment, combined with the success of CEF, was the impetus for LISC to establish the National Equity Fund (NEF) in 1987. NEF, which is based in Chicago, also involves corporations and businesses buying into a general partnership. LISC is promoting the partnership to companies throughout the country and to businesses in the locales where the projects are to be developed. In its first six years, NEF raised more than $600 million for investment in housing developed by CDCs in 51 different cities across the United States (Laue, 1990; Merrion, 1990; National Equity Fund, 1993).

Another private source of financing for community-based housing development in Chicago is Community Investment Corporation (CIC), which is also a member of the Chicago Housing Partnership. CIC is a mortgage banking firm created by Chicago-area financial institutions. It provides subsidized mortgages, information, and technical assistance and may also serve a broker function in facilitating a loan from a commercial banker or a state agency.

The principal source of financing from state government is the Illinois Housing Development Authority, which administers the Illinois Affordable Housing Trust Fund. At the local level, both nonprofit and for-profit developers that provide and maintain affordable housing can draw on funds made available through the Chicago Low-Income Housing Trust Fund and administered by the City. The fund, intended to supplement other sources of funding, was established as a result of negotiations between local housing groups, the City, and developers of Presidential Towers, a major downtown apartment complex that was subsidized through tax-exempt revenue bonds. The 1989 agreement was a renegotiation of an arrangement made during the Byrne administration and allows for grants, loans, and other non-equity financial assistance. The fund is intended to assist persons whose incomes are at or below 50 percent of Chicago's median income and who are disabled, elderly, homeless, or single-room-occupancy residents.

At a time when most other federal funds for housing were eliminated, Community Development Block Grants (CDBGs) were an important, though insufficient, source of federal funds funneled to local entities. Under the Reagan administration, CDBG funds were cut 19 percent (not accounting for inflation), thus further reducing federal funds for nonprofit or community development corporation activities (Schwartz, Felauto, and Hoffman, 1988, p. 171). The National Affordable Housing Act of 1990 will generate new sources of funding that can be used by nonprofit organizations. The HOME Investment Partnerships program provides block grants to state and local governments for the development of affordable housing by way of rehabilitation, new construction, acquisition, and the establishment of private-public partnerships. At least 15 percent of these funds must be reserved for community

housing development organizations. In order for any state or local
entity to receive any of these HOME funds, it must complete a
Comprehensive Housing Affordability Strategy (CHAS), which the
City of Chicago has done with the help of numerous community
organizations and advocacy groups.

Innovative Management and Ownership Structures

The philosophical orientation of community-based initiatives
results in priority being placed on development projects that
enhance community empowerment. Indeed, many development
projects originate directly from community efforts that began as
strategies for community control, but more immediately as a
means of responding to a housing crisis.

Although it is important to caution against seeing these "self-
help" strategies as a panacea for the urban housing crisis, they
represent a significant outcome of urban protest movements for
better housing conditions and have been an important means for
salvaging deteriorated property, offering better services, and
enhancing autonomy and control of neighborhoods.

As the housing movement has become more sophisticated, it
has also looked for creative ownership models that preserve some
of the values of community-based initiatives. One such model is
the community land trust (CLT). The Institute for Community
Economics (ICE), based in Springfield, Massachusetts, developed
the community land trust model and now helps other organizations
throughout the country to form CLTs. By providing direct technical assistance, disseminating educational materials such as
handbooks and videos, and organizing conferences, ICE has
worked to promote the form of community-controlled development. The community land trust is essentially an organization
established to "hold" property on behalf of a community or individuals within a community. The nonprofit organization is "dem-
ocratically structured," and the membership elects a rotating board
of trustees.

The community land trust acquires land, retains title in perpetuity, and then leases the land to those who are interested in using
the land as determined by a CLT planning process. The lease
may either be long-term or life-time and may be passed on to
heirs. Tenants in the cooperative can earn equity through their
investments in improvements but not as a result of increases in
market value. This equity remains with the community land trust.

One of the apparent benefits of this model is that leaseholders have the opportunity to own property when banks may otherwise declare them ineligible due to insufficient income or down payment. Leaseholders have the same assurances of security as regular property-owners and can still draw on their equity. The community benefits in its ability to maintain control of the land and to resist the impact of gentrification or owner abandonment. The CLT, because of its nonprofit goals, has access to grants, loan funds, and its own equity to create additional land trusts.

The CLT is an interesting approach to providing individuals and communities an opportunity for affordable ownership. The model is constructed as a challenge to the notion of property as a commodity and rests on the principle that the speculative housing markets weaken a community's stability and autonomy. The democratic structure of the land trust is intended to enhance the individual's connection to the community.

In Chicago, Erie Neighborhood House (on the city's near northwest side) and Peoples Housing (in the Rogers Park neighborhood) are two community-based organizations that are attempting to develop community land trusts in their neighborhoods. Recognizing the importance of leadership to ensure success of a community land trust, they are developing their plans in conjunction with leadership training. The intention is for these trainees to assume key roles in the organizing that is necessary to build community awareness of the land trust project.

Erie Neighborhood House has had to contend with the high cost of acquisition in a neighborhood that is rapidly gentrifying and, in fact, sees its efforts as part of a larger strategy to stabilize the neighborhood. The organization is also drawing on existing resources in the neighborhood as they seek partners such as Bickerdike Development Corporation, a not-for-profit developer. In addition to the normal complexities of a development project, the community land trust design requires a complex legal structure that depends on the knowledge of experienced individuals.

Peoples Housing has established an ownership model that is a hybrid of a community land trust, a housing cooperative, and a mutual housing association. The Co-operative Ownership Project (CO-OP), a shared equity cooperative, is conceived as an "empowerment program, bolstering independence and self-confidence, and fulfilling the American dream of homeownership for our participants" (Peoples Housing, 1991). Peoples Housing has purchased buildings and converted them to cooperatively owned and managed units, while retaining title to the land. The buildings are owned by the cooperative corporation; residents purchase shares in the cooperative with a low down-payment. This offers the benefits of homeownership while also requiring management responsibilities (along with other CO-OP members). Peoples Housing is providing management and ownership skills training as part of implementation of the CO-OP Project.

PARTNERSHIPS AND ADVOCACY

There are two important characteristics of community-based efforts to supply affordable housing that merit further discussion. First, the most obvious aspect of community-based efforts in Chicago to provide affordable housing is that they are not strictly "self-help" efforts, but rather require several players acting in partnership. These partners include other community-based organizations and development corporations; advocacy groups such as the Chicago Rehab Network or the Chicago Affordable Housing Coalition; research entities such as university-based centers or policy institutes; technical assistance providers; private foundations; financial institutions and brokers; and local, state, and federal agencies. The seriousness of the housing crisis and the complexities of responding to the crisis warrant this widespread involvement. Financial partnerships have been especially key in housing development.

Second, advocacy and activism have been the necessary ingredients leading to legislation, various government programs, the forming of partnerships, and continued pressure to deal with the housing crisis. While each community-based organization may play an advocacy role, there are other organizations that exist exclusively for the purpose of forging paths to establish programs and policies friendly to the low-income housing development process.

Financial Partnerships

It is important to point out the key role that community-based initiatives have played not only in calling attention to the housing problems in their respective neighborhoods but also in providing leadership in forging partnerships to respond to those problems. Partnerships such as the Chicago Equity Fund and the Chicago Housing Partnership did not always arise easily and, in some instances, required federal mandates to provide the leverage. Yet, the partnerships have apparently become essential vehicles for successful development projects and are thus worthy of examination. The syndicated relationship, which involves tax credits in exchange for investment dollars, is a particularly important partnership to evaluate because of the large portion of layered financing that comes from this relationship.

A report prepared for Peoples Housing suggests that syndicated relationships need to be examined very carefully so that the partnerships maximize affordability and long-term control over the property. The report argues that sufficient time may not have been spent in assessing past agreements and that Peoples Housing "may lose control of two of its buildings, and may not be able to afford to exercise an option on a third building" (Levine, 1988, p. 3). Thus, the report advises that an understanding of revised tax regulations and past experiences should become the basis for careful agreement about the "right, duties, and obligations" of each party and the amount of equity that will be generated.

The Chicago Equity Fund can yield up to 30 percent return on an investment. In an effort to reach that figure, the CEF may agree to a lower equity, thus resulting in higher financing costs and smaller fees for the nonprofit developer. Conflict may, then, characterize the negotiations, particularly as community development organizations develop the sophistication to enhance their position in these agreements. For example, an article in *Crain's Chicago Business* reports that community groups were expressing "disgruntlement" with the Chicago Equity Fund and asserting a need to negotiate better terms. One community developer was quoted as saying: "They are a pain in the ass, to tell you the truth" (Merrion, 1990).

Rachel Bratt, an observer of the community housing development process in Boston, suggests that public-private partnerships are problematic because the profit goals of private developers are in conflict with the public need for low-cost housing (Bratt, 1987). She maintains, for example, that use restrictions for limited time (e.g., 15-20 years) are not in the public interest and that measures need to be created to anticipate the expiration of benefits of a given program. The 1986 Tax Reform Act, for example, allows tax credits for fifteen years and requires low-income occupancy for the same time period—but not necessarily beyond that. Long-term availability of low-income housing is not guaranteed beyond these short time periods.

Bratt argues that partnerships should maximize the public good and that incentives should be built in to encourage investment, cost containment, and adequate maintenance and repairs. An over-reliance on tax incentives as the foundation for subsidized housing, she argues, is not in the public interest and should not be the substitute for funding from state and federal governments for subsidies. Bratt suggests that the conflict between private and public interests, which is often ignored in policy debates and decisions, should be more closely examined in the effort to provide decent affordable housing (Bratt, 1987).[1]

Advocacy and Activism

Urban protest in the 1960s against housing conditions and neighborhood deterioration was the forerunner of community-based efforts to confront the housing crisis. Advocacy and activism continue to play a significant role in community-based initiatives to obtain resources to develop affordable housing. Although the possible examples are extensive, we need only highlight a few to illustrate the importance of community-based advocacy and activism.

The Community Reinvestment Act, as a leverage for loan funds, and the Home Mortgage Disclosure Act are direct results of lobbying efforts led by the National Training and Information Center (NTIC). This Chicago-based organization has worked closely with other groups to develop home lending agreements with banks and mortgage associations that not only create mortgage lending funds but also adjust loan eligibility levels and lower down-payment and housing costs. In 1989, for example, NTIC was the impetus behind the formation of a national partnership to provide over $40 million in funds for affordable housing. The partnership also included the Federal National Mortgage Association (FNMA), General Electric Mortgage Insurance Companies (GEMICO), sixteen financial institutions, and several community groups. This home lending program also included agreements to make it easier for lower-income families to purchase houses. For example, both FNMA and GEMICO agreed to waive or lower certain loan eligibility requirements, including allowing 33 percent of income to be spent on housing rather than the normal 28 percent and allowing sellers or donors to pay the closing costs. Additional activities of NTIC include training, consulting, and tech-

---

[1] See also Bratt's chapter in this volume (Bratt, 1993).

nical assistance, particularly relating to CRA agreements. NTIC's affiliate, National People's Action, has been instrumental in bringing together housing advocacy groups throughout the country. This coalition meets annually and will often lobby groups such as the National Association of Home Builders. In April 1989, National People's Action met with Jack Kemp, secretary of HUD in the Bush administration, and argued for increased involvement of the federal government in the housing crisis. The coalition specifically pushed for a national housing trust fund and for expanded homeownership programs. Gale Cincotta, the group's executive director, also argued for expansion of the Federal Housing Administration, low-income housing tax credits, and funding assistance for tenants to buy out the owner of a property. National People's Action has also led successful moves against redlining.

The Chicago Low-Income Housing Trust Fund was established as a result of the efforts of a coalition that included the Chicago Coalition for the Homeless, the Chicago 1992 Committee, the Statewide Housing Action Coalition, and the Balanced Growth Coalition. The trust fund, a source of financial assistance for the lowest-income residents in Chicago, was enacted by the Chicago City Council in 1989 and was incorporated as a nonprofit organization in 1990. The Illinois Affordable Housing Trust Fund, a source of grants and loans for projects for low- and very low-income individuals and families, is also a direct consequence of community initiation. The Statewide Housing Action Coalition proposed the establishment of this trust fund, which will generate additional dollars from developers' equity, loans, and other special financing programs. Other tools that resulted from housing activism include the Cook County Tax Reactivation Program and the Neighborhood Lending Programs. The Chicago Rehab Network and the Chicago Affordable Housing Coalition are active participants in shaping affordable housing policy in Chicago.

Housing activists and advocates are important actors in the efforts to supply much-needed affordable housing at a time when political and economic factors combine to exacerbate crisis conditions—not only for low-income residents but also for the middle class. Alliances are, therefore, essential among housing advocates (both local and national), community-based development corporations, and those committed to a housing agenda that meets the needs of low- and moderate-income individuals and families.

Despite the successes and contributions of community-based interests, efforts have been made to discredit the work of community development groups and to label them as "anti-development"

(McCarron, 1988). Similarly, the media rarely report the accomplishments of community-based initiatives, despite press releases announcing the projects. Nevertheless, community-based groups have proved themselves to be able developers committed to the ideas of community involvement and empowerment and have come forward as cooperative partners in joint ventures. It is appropriate to recognize these contributions and seek further policies to enhance their capacities to meet the needs of their respective neighborhoods.

CONCLUSION

Throughout the 1980s, community-based development corporations and advocacy organizations were key actors in responding to the affordable housing crisis. During that decade, for example, over 6,400 housing units were created by nonprofit developers in the city of Chicago (Chicago Rehab Network, 1990, p. 20-21). Lobbying efforts by housing advocates were influential in creating several programs by private and public entities that facilitated these developments. Community-based initiatives have been especially important because of their commitment to neighborhood preservation, pro-tenant perspectives, and service to low- and moderate-income households.

Despite the importance of community-based initiatives in Chicago's housing strategies, economic conditions and inadequate government funding have "pushed community groups into a leading role which they lack the resources to fulfill" (Gerhardstein, 1990). Bratt, however, makes the argument that "given sufficient financial and technical supports, community-based groups could be central to a new strategy for producing, rehabilitating, and managing housing" (Bratt, 1989a, p. 286). In addition to the financial and technical supports, obstacles to the development process should be replaced with policies that enhance community-based initiatives for affordable housing.

Although community groups may be able to boast of numerous successful development projects throughout Chicago, the problem of availability of affordable housing to low- and moderate-income households remains at crisis proportions. Community groups continue to express concern for the high cost of housing production and the difficulty in keeping rents low. In fact, much of the housing production is meeting moderate-income needs, while low-income households continue to face "shelter poverty" or the threat of homelessness.

Thus, researchers, commentators, and practitioners continue to argue that, given the current economics of housing, the flow of federal subsidies is essential (Gerhardstein, 1990; Bratt, 1989a; Barry, 1988). Thomas Lenz of LISC has said: "There is no excuse for not having a federal presence. . . . It's folly to think we're going to find solutions to homelessness and the low-income housing crisis without it" (Gerhardstein, 1990, p. 28). Richard Hartnack, corporate senior vice-president at First National Bank of Chicago, has expressed a similar sentiment, noting that "we just can't produce an apartment that low-income people can afford without a subsidy" (Gerhardstein, 1990, p. 28). Bratt argues even further for a federally based support system for community-based housing. "In addition to providing adequate financial resources, it should also include a high-quality technical assistance component, a mechanism to acquire land and buildings, and an evaluation and information-sharing network" (Bratt, 1989b, p. 323). Although the National Affordable Housing Act of 1990 resumes some flow of federal dollars, many are skeptical that it will be sufficient to adequately address the crisis.

The economics of providing affordable housing to *low-income* households remains a fundamental concern. In effect, the costs of housing production continue to rise while the earning power of households declines, suggesting the need for fundamental evaluation of an economic system that does not make it feasible to produce low-cost, decent housing. It is therefore desirable to investigate the recommendations of some who suggest a "decommodification" of housing that values social ownership, public financing, and equitable resource allocation. Those advocating this position argue that producing, owning, and financing housing should be removed from the for-profit sector. In its place, they argue for the primacy of a "principle of socially determined need" (Achtenbert and Marcuse, 1986, p. 477; Stone, 1986; Meyerson, 1986b). Such an emphasis would include programs for public financing and social production and would allow for social control of land, resident control of neighborhoods, housing choice, and equitable resource allocation (Stone, 1986).

Community-based initiatives are faced, therefore, with a set of social goals that promote tenant control and homeownership in a housing system that is inherently based on a speculative market that keeps housing prices climbing while the distribution of income remains unequal. The tensions between the nonprofit orientation of the community-based housing developer and the perspectives of for-profit entities are exemplified in the syndicated relationships in which the nonprofit developer is interested in keeping the rents low and the occupancy stable, while the private investor is interested in maximizing profit in a speculative market that encourages high turnover. The tension plays itself out at the negotiation table when determining the amount of return for the investor. The partnership, in fact, is an interesting one in its coalition of divergent interests, each with an eye toward the development of affordable housing yet for markedly different reasons. Indeed, these partnerships warrant close observation and policy analysis not only because of their importance in Chicago for financing affordable housing but also as a case study of how the private, for-profit sector can merge with the nonprofit sector in meeting the housing needs of low- and moderate-income households. There needs to be a careful examination of these partnerships over time. A housing deal with several layers of financing may actually result in raising the cost of production, given that development fees and financing costs are added on at each level of financing. Furthermore, although the financing that emerges from this syndicated, tiered financing is creative, it should not replace the role of government in ensuring housing as a fundamental right.

Community groups in Chicago have demonstrated their sophistication, resourcefulness, commitment, and ability to forge partnerships. Beyond the formal syndicated relationships, alliances have been formed among community groups. These alliances are facilitated by numerous citywide coalitions such as the Chicago Rehab Network, the Community Workshop for Economic Development (CWED), the Chicago Association of Neighborhood Development Organizations (CANDO), and others. Collaborative efforts are also common between community organizations and research entities such as the Center for Urban Economic Development and the Voorhees Center for Neighborhood and Community Improvement at the University of Illinois at Chicago. These alliances should be nurtured and expanded to avoid duplication of effort and to expand the strength and sophistication of the community housing approach. The alliances are especially important because of the wide range of sophistication, leadership, and technical know-how that exists among community-based developers. These partnerships should be pursued as a means for one community-based organization to work directly with another organization while it puts together a development project.

Some of the most important alliances are those between community development corporations and advocacy organizations, as well as among advocacy organizations. Given the critical role that advocacy has played in establishing the programs that facilitate community development, and given the history of housing policies without that role, the neighborhood movement is an essential feature of affordable housing policies. The role that the community housing developer plays when it negotiates with for-profit developers and bankers is not irreconcilable with the role of advocate for housing policies that promote affordable housing for low- and moderate-income households. Although a division of labor between development and advocacy may exist, many organizations combine the roles. Either way, close connections between development and advocacy are essential for the success of community-based initiatives in housing policy.

Many organizations also combine their development strategies with efforts to enhance community empowerment. Latin United Community Housing Association, for example, organizes block clubs to promote leadership, community involvement, and the notion that the neighborhood belongs to the people who live there. Community development organizations are beginning to pursue more widely a strategy to promote tenant management and ownership projects. Community land trusts and efforts similar to the Co-operative Ownership Project initiated by Peoples Housing are examples of innovative approaches to housing, whereby an organization is created to hold land in trust on behalf of the individuals who buy into the structured nonprofit corporation. These joint-ownership ventures are consistent with the philosophical orientation of community-based initiatives that stress community ownership and empowerment, while allowing an individual household to be the beneficiary of both affordable housing and community involvement. The biggest problem that community land trusts face is access to adequate, affordable financing. In addition, because of the complicated legal structures that must be worked out, technical expertise is critical. Thus, policies should be encouraged that facilitate the financing and technical know-how for establishing community land trusts. Groups such as Peoples Housing that have made the effort to create a community land trust will be important in both sharing technical expertise and recommending policies to implement these land trusts.

Finally, urban restructuring and industrial relocation are resulting in a shift in suburban populations. As many suburban municipalities absorb the labor pool that is moving nearer to the suburban jobs, the crisis in housing will reach beyond the city limits. Up to now, however, very few community organizations have arisen in the suburbs to meet these housing needs. Groups such as New Cities Community Development Corporation in southern Cook County have relied primarily on funds from HUD and from the Federal Home Loan Bank. There are perhaps lessons to be gained from the effectiveness of community groups in Chicago that can be applied in the outlying metropolitan area.

Community-based initiatives to provide affordable housing are a result of a cumulative base of experience and expertise. Despite the creative approaches to layered financing, the main problems continue to be the massiveness of the housing crisis and the economics of housing production, financing, and ownership. Nonetheless, the successes of community-based initiatives warrant respect, but more important, more resources. Leadership training, cost-cutting measures, technical assistance, loan programs, federal subsidies, and equitable syndication relationships are among the resources that, if directed toward community organizations, will improve their ability to bring a neighborhood agenda to solutions to the crisis in housing.

REFERENCES

Achtenbert, Emily Paradise, and Peter Marcuse (1986). "Toward the Decommodification of Housing." In Rachel Bratt, Chester Hartman, and Ann Meyerson, eds., *Critical Perspectives on Housing*. Philadelphia: Temple University Press.

Barry, Patrick (1988). "Gimme Shelter: Housing Crunch Hits City's Middle Class," *Chicago Enterprise*, May 1988, pp. 1-5.

Bickerdike Redevelopment Corporation (1985). *Annual Report, 1985*. Chicago: Bickerdike.

Bradford, Calvin (1990). *Partnerships for Reinvestment: An Evaluation of the Chicago Neighborhood Lending Programs*. Chicago: National Training and Information Center.

Bratt, Rachel G. (1987). "Private Owners of Subsidized Housing vs. Public Goals: Conflicting Interests in Resyndication," *Journal of the American Planning Association*, Summer 1987, pp. 328-336.

_____ (1989a). "Community-Based Housing in Massachusetts: Lessons and Limits of the State's Support System." In Sara

Rosenberry and Chester Hartman, eds. *Housing Issues of the 1990s*. New York: Praeger.

_____ (1989b). *Rebuilding a Low-Income Housing Policy*. Philadelphia: Temple University Press.

_____ (1993). "Nonprofit Housing Development in Boston." In this volume.

Chicago Equity Fund (1991). "Fact Sheet." Chicago: Chicago Equity Fund.

Chicago Rehab Network (1990). *The Chicago Affordable Housing Fact Book: A Resource for Community Action*. Chicago: Chicago Rehab Network.

Gerhardstein, Louis (1990). "Housing: Nonprofits Attempt to Fill Void Created by Federal Cuts," *Chicago Enterprise*, February 1990, pp. 15-17, 28.

Kenwood-Oakland Community Organization (1990). Notice for March for Affordable Housing. Chicago, October 17, 1990.

Keyes, Langley (1971). "The Role of Nonprofit Sponsors in the Production of Housing." In *Papers Submitted to Subcommittee on Housing, Panels on Housing Production, Housing Demand, and Developing a Suitable Living Environment*, Part 1. Washington, D.C.: Committee on Banking and Currency, U.S. House of Representatives, 92nd Congress, 1st session.

Laue, Sue (1990). "Housing Peace Pact," *Chicago Enterprise*, July/August 1990, p. 11.

Leonard, Paul A., Cushing N. Dolbeare, and Edward B. Lazere (1989). *A Place to Call Home: The Crisis in Housing for the Poor*. Washington, D.C.: Center on Budget and Policy Priorities and Low-Income Housing Information Service.

Levine, Peter (1988). "Syndicating the Low-Income Housing Tax Credit: From the Perspective of the Community Development Corporation." Chicago: Peoples Housing, April 12, 1988.

McCarron, John (1988). "Chicago on Hold." Series of seven articles in the *Chicago Tribune*, August 28-September 4, 1988.

Merrion, Paul (1990). "Low-Income Housing Funder Shows Cracks in Foundation: Chicago Equity Fund's Fat Investor Terms Irk Developers," *Crain's Chicago Business*, March 19, 1990.

Meyerson, Ann (1986a). "Housing Abandonment: The Role of Institutional Mortgage Lenders." In Rachel Bratt, Chester Hartman, and Ann Meyerson, eds., *Critical Perspectives on Housing*. Philadelphia: Temple University Press.

_____ (1986b). "Deregulation and the Restructuring of the Housing Finance System." In Rachel Bratt, Chester Hartman,

and Ann Meyerson, eds., *Critical Perspectives on Housing*.
    Philadelphia: Temple University Press.
National Equity Fund (1993). Press release. Chicago, January
    1993.
Northeastern Illinois Planning Commission (1992). "1990 Census
    of Population and Housing, Summary Tape File 3." Profile
    Report, City of Chicago. Chicago: Northeastern Illinois Plan-
    ning Commission.
Peoples Housing (n.d.). "Introduction to Peoples Housing."
    Chicago: Peoples Housing.
_____ (1991). "The Co-operative Ownership Project." Chi-
    cago: Peoples Housing.
Pickens, Dorris (1989). "Communities Have to be Developed
    from Within: A Conversation with Dorris Pickens, President
    of The Neighborhood Institute." Reprint from *Cooperative
    Enterprise*, Summer 1989. Washington, D.C.: NCB Develop-
    ment Corporation.
Reardon, Patrick T. (1991). "Housing Groups Get Shot in Arm,"
    Chicago Tribune, February 28, 1991, sec. 2, p. 3.
Schwartz, David C., Richard C. Ferlauto, and Daniel N. Hoffman
    (1988). *A New Housing Policy for America: Recapturing the
    American Dream*. Philadelphia: Temple University Press.
Siewers, Alf (1990). "Activists Want City's Vacant Lots Put to
    Use," *Chicago Sun-Times*, March 15, 1990, p. 4.
Stegman, Michael A., and J. David Holden (1987). *Nonfederal
    Housing Programs: How States and Localities are Responding
    to Federal Cutbacks in Low-Income Housing*. Washington,
    D.C.: Urban Land Institute.
Stone, Michael (1986). "Housing and the Dynamics of U.S. Cap-
    italism." In Rachel Bratt, Chester Hartman, and Ann Meyer-
    son, eds., *Critical Perspectives on Housing*. Philadelphia:
    Temple University Press.
_____ (1989). "Shelter-Poverty in Boston: Problem and Pro-
    gram." In Sara Rosenberry and Chester Hartman, eds., *Hous-
    ing Issues of the 1990s*. New York: Praeger.
Voss, Ron (1990). "What's Affordable? The True Cost of Hous-
    ing." In *The Chicago Affordable Housing Fact Book*. Chi-
    cago: Chicago Rehab Network.
Woodstock Institute (1984). *Neighborhood Reinvestment Part-
    nership: Community Groups Lead the Way for First Chicago
    Corporation*. Chicago: Woodstock Institute.

_____ (1988). *From Obstacle to Opportunity: An Evaluation of the Multifamily Tax Reactivation Program.* Chicago: Woodstock Institute.

COMMENTS

Douglas C. Gills

Teresa Córdova provides an excellent survey of the contemporary state of community-based housing development practice and policy advocacy efforts in Chicago. She observes that the greatest impediment to the provision of affordable housing has been the rising cost of housing production and the declining earning power of area households. She emphasizes that the "excessive housing cost burden" falls disproportionately on the poor, citing studies by Voss (1990) and Stone (1989). Other studies all confirm the growing gap between the number of appropriately priced, available, standard housing units and the increasing number of households with insufficient incomes to afford these units (Chicago Rehab Network, 1990; Northeastern Illinois Planning Commission, 1986; City of Chicago, 1989, 1991).

Córdova calls for "fundamental evaluation of an economic system that does not make it feasible to produce low-cost, decent housing." She concludes by advocating "decommodification" of housing based on values of collective ownership, enhanced public financing, and more equitable resource allocation. She derives her position from a philosophical orientation that emphasizes neighborhood conservation, service to low- and moderate-income households, and constituent mobilization to determine the direction of community development. This approach would involve subordinating the essentially private character of housing development and financing to community-defined ends.

Córdova's insightful survey raises several critical issues and implications for public policy, community practice, and action-oriented research. First, high shelter-cost burdens have serious consequences for disadvantaged households, particularly those headed by single parents with children, who are impoverished and disproportionately Black and Latino and who constitute a growing share of Chicago's population base (Holleb 1993; Apgar, 1990, pp. 39-40). When high proportions of family expenditures are committed to shelter costs, then other household essentials go wanting (Voss, 1990). These include health care, food, education, and child-development expenditures. Moreover, there is a dramatic reduction in available discretionary resources (both time and money) that might be contributed to institution-building and community-development activities. Hence, the social institutions and support structures of poor communities tend to remain weak and limited.

Second, Córdova's analysis points to another effect of the affordable housing crisis that is rarely discussed—that is, the involuntary dislocation and displacement of resource-poor households from central-city neighborhoods. Such is the case among poor and working-class African-Americans who were "relocated" to the suburbs during the 1980s. Their situation was quite different from that of their middle-class, upwardly mobile predecessors who moved out of central-city neighborhoods as a matter of choice during the 1960s and 1970s. This new trend is a function of limited options for increasing numbers of households. It appears to be the result of deterioration, abandonment, and demolition of a disproportionate number of multi-family housing structures, as well as housing policy initiatives by both public and private actors. The forced destruction of low-income communities, historically Black and Latino, has resulted in the depopulation of neighborhoods, the destabilization of social networks, and the dilution of potential political representation and empowerment of these communities.

Third, community-based organizations (CBOs) during the 1980s attempted to address the affordable housing crisis and the destabilization of Chicago's neighborhoods with increasingly conservative financing instruments. As the federal government became disengaged from deep subsidies for housing production, local governments and community groups encouraged public-private housing development ventures and partnerships involving nonprofit organizations, government agencies, and banking institutions. Far from developing adequate quantities of affordable housing, these ventures have often resulted in mixed-occupancy, mixed-income housing development projects that fail to target the needs of low-income households.

At best, given the marginal involvement of the federal government in the provision of subsidized housing, the creativity and innovation of CBOs in financing the rehabilitation and new construction of housing for low-income families has fallen far short of the level and the scope of need. At worst, the prevailing conditions of housing production have contributed little to stem the tide of dislocation and overcrowding of inner-city households. Moreover, these financing schemes may have contributed to the demobilization of community-based housing constituencies, who become frustrated by their inability to occupy housing that they fought for and desire, but cannot afford once the projects are completed.

Fourth, Córdova's chapter dramatizes the apparent absence of political will on the part of elected public officials to aggressively pursue more progressive policies for affordable housing and to allocate resources corresponding to the level of need. There is no commitment at the federal level to adequate provision of affordable housing for low- and very low-income households. At the local level in Chicago, the current administration's policies have emphasized homeownership strategies, as opposed to the development of multi-family rental housing. Simultaneously, the CBO-directed housing movement has subordinated constituency-based housing advocacy to the production of housing within present legal and financial constraints. As a result, the CBO movement has had an increasingly marginal impact on housing policy implementation and on housing production targeted at the level of greatest need.

Fifth, Córdova appropriately identifies the basic impediment to the provision of affordable housing: the gap between the relatively high costs of housing production and the declining earning power of low-income households. Although this assessment must be viewed in the context of the present political situation (and linked to the fourth point mentioned above), Córdova's assertion does raise serious questions about the policy options available to decision-makers and community activists. In short, either we must press to reduce the costs and increase the accessibility of housing, or we must fight to raise household incomes through employment strategies or through public aid benefits that meet the standard of need. This assumes, of course, that the extant political economy can adequately respond to these demands. Córdova argues that it cannot and cites the need for a fundamental restructuring of the political economy.

Sixth, the central implication of the Córdova scenario is that the contributions of CBOs are at best a limited, if necessary, practice. The scope of the expanding crisis makes the scale of current CBO-directed activity insufficient. It is important to note the historical origins and development of the involvement of Chicago's CBOs in housing over the past 15 to 20 years. Community-based housing initiatives emerged as a result of indigenous activities across the city to exercise more control over the affairs of diverse neighborhoods. A set of related factors mandated increasingly elaborate and sophisticated involvement of community-based actors in the housing development process. Among these factors were:

- capital disinvestment and redlining of neighborhood housing markets and land use;
- public-sector neglect, particularly in low-income, Black-majority communities;
- institutionalized (political) corruption that deterred housing-code enforcement in a climate where "machine" politics prevailed;
- inflated production, maintenance, and repair costs in the housing industry;
- marginalization and decline in the standard of living of working-class families, especially Blacks and Latinos who entered the city during the restructuring of the local economy from industrial manufacturing to service-based exchanges and decentralized, high-tech production centers.

The historic role of CBOs has included fighting against market discrimination in the distribution of housing resources and the allocation of housing maintenance services; pressuring public agencies for adequate housing-code enforcement to prevent abandonment and demolition; community-directed development of housing rehabilitation and new construction, moving progressively to increasingly larger equity shares in the ownership of housing development projects; and, most recently, development projects of scale in joint partnerships and experimentation with various forms of collective ownership models. This evolution has brought the CBO movement to the current crossroads of the contemporary affordable housing crisis. Córdova has appropriately introduced the concept of "housing decommodification" for discussion and debate. Collective ownership forms are logical extensions of the CBO projection into the housing development process. Admittedly, both theory and current practice are embryonic, and given the political climate, attempts to popularize this concept will meet with resistance from both within and outside the housing development movement.

In conclusion, present trends do not bode well for CBOs. Among these developments are the following:

- the increasing need for CBO activity in the housing arena in the face of declining support for nonprofit, community-directed participation in housing production;

• the destabilization of neighborhood housing development organizations through local government policy and housing practice, on one hand, and the inadequate levels of operational support, from either government or private foundations, for maintaining staff capacity and expertise in these organizations, on the other hand;
• the absence of radical, grassroots leadership in the affordable housing movement;
• the relative marginalization of CBOs in the development of housing policy.

The City of Chicago has recently restructured its development agencies in an effort to make government services more efficient and more responsive to development actors. The Department of Planning and the Department of Economic Development have been merged, while the Department of Housing has undergone internal reorganization. It is not clear, however, that these changes will enhance the role of neighborhood housing development groups, nor does it mean that community-directed planning, public accountability, and targeted resources for low-income households will be enhanced. Córdova's call for a fundamental change in our perspective in addressing the current housing crisis is most appropriate in light of current political and economic realities.

REFERENCES

Apgar, William C., Jr. (1990). "The Nation's Housing: A Review of Past Trends and Future Prospects for Housing in America." In Denise DiPasquale and Langley C. Keyes, eds., *Building Foundations: Housing and Federal Policy.* Philadelphia: University of Pennsylvania Press.
Chicago Rehab Network (1990). *The Chicago Affordable Housing Fact Book: A Resource for Community Action.* Chicago: Chicago Rehab Network.
City of Chicago (1989). *Housing Assistance Plan, 1989-1991.* Chicago: Chicago Department of Housing.
_____ (1991). *Comprehensive Housing Affordability Strategy (CHAS), FY 1992 to FY 1996.* Chicago: Chicago Department of Housing.
Holleb, Doris B. (1993). "Disparities and Opportunities in Chicago-Area Housing." In this volume.

Northeastern Illinois Planning Commission (1986). *The Need for Affordable Housing in Northeastern Illinois*. Chicago: Northeastern Illinois Planning Commission.

Stone, Michael (1989). "Shelter-Poverty in Boston: Problem and Program." In Sara Rosenberry and Chester Hartman, eds., *Housing Issues of the 1990s*. New York: Praeger.

Voss, Ron (1990). "What's Affordable? The True Cost of Housing." In *The Chicago Affordable Housing Fact Book: A Resource for Community Action*. Chicago: Chicago Rehab Network.

COMMENTS

Richard P. Taub

Teresa Córdova has provided an admirable summary of some of the central issues in the development of affordable housing, as well as a discussion of the role of community-based initiatives. The production of affordable housing is not only an issue for the poor. On average, housing prices have for many years been rising faster than incomes, although we are now seeing a nationwide readjustment downward in response to that fact. It will be many years, if ever, before prices and incomes return to the balance they had in the late 1950s and early 1960s. Parenthetically, the declining purchasing power of the ordinary middle-class consumer has serious consequences for the way we think about our economy. Both housing starts and new car sales, for example, have been linked to this nation's prosperity. Both are now lagging because of issues of affordability. Yet, economists and other prognosticators keep looking to housing starts and car sales to pull the economy ahead. As those in the middle classes and below continue to suffer declines in real income, this is unlikely to happen.

Having outlined the affordable housing problem, Professor Córdova turns to the role of community groups in providing affordable housing and describes the ingenious ways that subsidies and debt are organized to make this effort possible. The problem she fails to address is whether or not this is the best possible route to provide housing for low-income people.

The truth of the matter is that in a city like Chicago, the plethora of community organizations and the various (underfunded) superstructures (described by Professor Córdova) that connect to them have produced very little housing and have done so at very high cost. Worse yet, some of the best known of these projects (e.g., some of the projects developed by Bethel New Life on the west side of Chicago) have been in serious financial difficulty.

One would think that a concern about a housing scarcity would lead one to consider programs that would produce the most housing at the lowest possible cost. Yet, a close scrutiny of community-based housing projects would show that, even without including all the organizational overhead, the cost per unit is higher than what sophisticated private developers can deliver. And that price is still substantially higher than what competent neighborhood rehabbers can produce by doing the work on their own.

One might justify the high cost of community-based housing if the community organizations provided substantial additional value. If they provided jobs for community residents, or included day-care facilities in the project, or did other things to improve residents' lives or strengthen the community, the efforts might be worth the additional cost. Although there are exceptions, a careful examination of the average housing delivery program by community groups would illustrate that the return is not commensurate with the cost. What we get, then, from most community groups is relatively little housing at high cost.

It is a little bit like being against saintliness to be against those organizations that allegedly stand for community. Nonetheless, one needs to look at this issue dispassionately. There are some things that community groups can really do well. They can organize citizens to demand resources that are rightfully theirs, thereby empowering residents and helping them to feel in more control of their lives. They can deliver social services in ways that are sensitive to the needs of residents. However, there is very little evidence that community groups can run businesses well. Full-time professionals, driven by the profit motive, are somewhat more likely to operate efficiently and economically. The structure and organization of community groups makes that difficult to do. Among other things, a commitment to efficiency is less likely to exist without a profit motive. In addition, housing development activity requires high levels of experience and sophistication. Some community-based groups in Chicago—for example, Voice of the People in Uptown—have these requisites, but most do not.

Furthermore, the structure of funding for these housing development projects almost always pushes up the costs. If there are federal funds in the project, the Davis-Bacon Act requires that construction wages be at union scale. If there are government funds, or if the project has major actors in it, the construction must meet the standards of Chicago's building code, which, although somewhat improved over the past few years, is designed more to guarantee employment to the high-priced building trades than to provide safe or affordable housing.

By contrast, local resident rehabbers work weekends and evenings, or they hire low-wage labor. They often do not get building permits, so they need not follow code standards in their rehab efforts. It is true that they do not do "gut rehab" and do not install completely new systems. But they are in the real-world housing market, and if their apartments are really crummy, they will have trouble getting an adequate return from the rent. Rehabbing one unit will cost anywhere from one-quarter to one-eighth of what it would cost a community group to do the same. However, these rehabbers are not providing new Cadillacs; they are providing used Hyundais.

This is not to argue that more federal funds should not be provided in the housing market. Probably the best federal program is the voucher component of the Section 8 program, which provides rent subsidies to low-income people. It is, however, only "best" in principle because the dollars allotted to it are woefully inadequate. Nonetheless, if one wants to increase in any real way the availability of affordable housing, one must figure out how to mobilize local people to become entrepreneurial in their efforts to produce housing. If housing—and not something else—is the goal, this is the way to go. For despite the fact that many of us value the idea of community and the values inherent in community organization and empowerment, the burden of proof ought to be on community groups to demonstrate that they can both deliver the volume of housing needed and deliver it in a cost-effective fashion. If the costs of their projects are out of line, community organizations will have to show that they are delivering something else of value in addition to housing.

"CHICAGO IS NOT ABOUT TO GIVE UP ON A BAD IDEA": THE FUTURE OF PUBLIC HOUSING HIGH-RISES

Alexander Polikoff[*]

Chicago's first ghetto was a product of the great northward migration of southern Blacks, from 1890 to 1930, that ended with the Great Depression. Its Black population became intensely concentrated, and its borders on Chicago's south and west sides were "sharp and clear" (Hirsch, 1983). Chicago's second and greatly enlarged Black ghetto was formed during the three decades from 1940 to 1970. It too was the product of a great migration, one that began with southern Blacks streaming into the World War II factories of northern cities, and then continued during the quarter century that followed the war's close (Lemann, 1991b). Its borders too are clear; its population homogeneously Black (Massey, 1989).[1]

The second ghetto was, however, subjected to two developments that sharply distinguished it from its predecessor. First, in the 1950s and 1960s, legal and political breakthroughs made it possible for middle-class Blacks to make impressive gains in education and employment and to escape the ghetto's confines, with the result that the second ghetto was shorn of the stabilizing role models and economic activity that the middle class had earlier provided (W. Wilson, 1987). The second development was a dramatic shift of low-skilled jobs to the suburbs, negatively altering the opportunity ladder for those who remained behind (Kasarda, 1990). Both developments contributed to the creation of over-

---

[*] The author gratefully acknowledges the assistance of Patricia M. Logue. The title of this chapter is borrowed from Abramowitz, 1991.

[1] Nicholas Lemann observes that the massive migration of Blacks who left the segregated, circumscribed life of the rural South between 1910 and 1970 for the cities of the North, particularly Chicago, was one of the largest internal movements of people in history, outranking the migration of any other ethnic group—Italians, Irish, Jews, or Poles—to this country (Lemann, 1991b).

whelmingly impoverished urban neighborhoods, not organized around work and housing an "urban underclass" that now seems threatened with permanent severance from the American mainstream (W. Wilson, 1987).[2]

A notable feature of the making of the second ghetto was government sanction and support, including a massive public housing high-rise program. Now, a generation after they were built in the 1950s and 1960s, the public housing high-rises are wearing out. Instead of viewing this circumstance as a golden opportunity to dismantle a particularly pernicious feature of its Black ghetto and to provide high-rise residents with the same escape opportunities that were earlier offered to the middle class, Chicago is beginning to rebuild its public housing high-rise buildings. One is reminded of the adage that those who fail to learn from history are doomed to repeat it. In a less elegant formulation, reportedly Yogi Berra's, it's déjà vu all over again. This chapter contends that we can and should change course and seize the golden opportunity.

SYMBOL OF THE SECOND GHETTO

The Chicago History

Restrictive covenants, the hostility of White neighborhoods, and the pervasive, segregatory "gate-keeping" of the real estate industry helped create Chicago's greatly enlarged second ghetto. In addition, the ghetto was fostered by government public housing and urban renewal policies, home insurance practices of the Federal Housing Administration, and federal highway building and homeowner tax subsidy programs that assisted city Whites to move to the suburbs (Polikoff, 1978; Hirsch, 1983).

Had the public housing been scattered, would it have ameliorated the severity of the second ghetto? Or would the weight of other government policies, as well as private hostility to Blacks, have been too great for scattered public housing to have made a difference? We will never know, for Chicago's postwar public

---

[2] Though, more than anyone else, William Julius Wilson has helped legitimize the term "underclass," Wilson worries that some journalists and conservatives are now using the term pejoratively to contend or imply that the poor have created their own plight. He is considering the alternative, "ghetto poor" (DeParle, 1990). "Underclass" is used here, non-pejoratively, because of the widespread usage it has attained.

housing was deliberately concentrated in Black neighborhoods. Indeed, the first ghetto's symbol, the tenement, was replaced by what came to be the symbol of the second ghetto, the concrete and steel public housing high-rise. A brief recapitulation of this history will provide background for the present discussion.

In the aftermath of World War II, the nation readied itself to address housing needs that had been postponed during the war. In 1949, a new housing law signaled a huge expansion in the fledgling public housing program that had begun in the New Deal years. Before 1950, several aspects of public housing had not been clearly defined: the socioeconomic status of its tenants, the location of its developments, and their scale. These three key factors were now to be definitively addressed; the choices made determined the essential nature of public housing in Chicago.

Public housing had begun as a temporary way station for working families down on their luck because of the Depression. Families receiving public aid or having criminal records or other social problems were simply not accepted. During the war years, public housing served war workers who could not find other housing because of war-induced shortages. In the post-war years, however, the public housing clientele began to change. In Chicago and other large cities, public housing was given a "slum clearance" mission, and most slums were in Black neighborhoods. The obligation to house at least some of the displaced persons meant that public housing tenants would become increasingly Black and poor. By 1950, over a quarter of Chicago Housing Authority (CHA) families were receiving public aid, and a third were one-parent families. The CHA was becoming the landlord for hard-core poverty families (Bowly, 1978).

As to location, of the ten public housing developments built in Chicago before or during World War II, four were for Whites in White areas, four were for Blacks in Black areas, and two were intended for mixed occupancy. The CHA's policy followed the federal government's "neighborhood composition rule"—the racial occupancy of a public housing development should mirror the racial composition of the host area.

By the early 1950s, the location factor was also undergoing change. CHA's first executive director, Elizabeth Wood, made a strong effort to bring about some degree of racial integration in CHA's developments. But she lost her battle to the Chicago political establishment, and it became clear that the great expansion in public housing decreed by the 1949 Housing Act would take place in impoverished Black neighborhoods (Meyerson and Banfield, 1955). Years later, *Gautreaux v. CHA*, a racial discrimination lawsuit against CHA (BPI, 1991), formally established what was generally known during the 1950s and 1960s: "the locations for new projects were selected by CHA, and by the political leadership of Chicago, to contain and segregate the poor, black population" (Bowly, 1978, p. 112).[3]

As to the final factor, scale, the ten developments built in Chicago before or during World War II were all low-rise, mostly two-story, rowhouses, with a few three- and four-story walk-ups thrown in. Although density varied, even the larger developments, such as the Jane Addams Houses, were constructed on a "human scale" (Bowly, 1978, p. 20). In the post-war years, however, the design of public housing buildings came to reflect the ideas of the Swiss architect, Le Corbusier, whose architectural vision was a "vertical garden city" composed of blocks of apartments stacked atop one another. In the early post-war years, a few, relatively small, low-rise projects would still be constructed. But Le Corbusier's influence was about to become dominant.

Chicago's first elevator projects were of modest scale, six- to nine-story buildings. Then the buildings began to rise to fourteen and fifteen stories. In addition, because locations in White neighborhoods were unavailable to it by reason of its increasingly Black tenancy, CHA began the practice of "extensions." New projects were built cheek-by-jowl with existing ones in Black neighborhoods. Though the Jane Addams Houses initially had "only" about 1,000 apartments, two extensions soon doubled its size. In 1955, the Grace Abbott Homes added another 1,200 units, including seven sixteen-story buildings. What had begun on a "human scale" had grown to over 3,000 apartments, encompassing 26 city blocks. The overall feeling was now described as "forbidding, and the human scale is completely lost" (Bowly, 1978, p. 91).

In the dozen years from the mid-1950s to near the end of the 1960s, the great public housing construction years, CHA outdid

---

[3] The *Gautreaux* case was filed in 1966 (with the author as lead counsel) on behalf of all CHA tenants and applicants against both CHA and the U.S. Department of Housing and Urban Development (HUD). After the discriminatory nature of CHA location policies was established in 1969, the case entered a long, still-continuing, remedial phase. Among other things, CHA was ordered to build low-rise, scattered-site public housing throughout Chicago, and HUD agreed to implement a rent subsidy program throughout the six-county Chicago metropolitan area (Polikoff, 1989).

itself in terms of scale. Henry Horner Homes, completed in 1957, had 920 apartments in nine buildings, seven of seven stories and two of fifteen. Four years later, CHA added the Horner Extension, with 736 more apartments in seven more buildings, three of eight stories and four of fourteen. Most of the Henry Horner apartments, and most of those to come, were three-, four-, and five-bedroom apartments; thus, the growing concentration of Black and poor families was also a growing concentration of large families with children.

Horner was followed by Stateway Gardens, Robert Taylor Homes, and others. Taylor Homes, renowned as the world's largest public housing development, added 4,400 apartments in 28 identical sixteen-story buildings right next to Stateway Gardens. At the end of the 1960s, CHA's last big development, Madden Homes, had only 450 apartments in three high-rises but was geographically a part of six other family developments. In its last high-rise gasp, CHA had not lost its ability to produce developments on an inhuman scale. And by that time, there were 20,000 apartments in 168 family high-rise buildings.[4]

The Chicago Consequences

These enormous projects were in disadvantaged Black neighborhoods with predominantly low-income residents and a dearth of community services and facilities. Project tenants were virtually all Black, with incomes and job circumstances that placed them near the bottom of the social and economic ladder. The tenancy, segregated ghetto locations, and scale of the projects were a prescription for disaster.

---

[4] Because of *Gautreaux* case court orders, only low-rise, scattered-site housing was built in the 1970s and 1980s, and—due to continuing litigation, and CHA's intransigence and incompetence—very little of that. Today, CHA public housing comprises about 40,000 apartments. Of these, some 9,500 are in 58 buildings for the elderly. The balance of the family apartments (other than the 20,000 in high rises) are in low-rise buildings, some in large, concentrated, low-rise "projects," some in sites shared with high rises, and others ("scattered sites") in dispersed, individual low-rise buildings. CHA's resident population is about 145,000 persons, just under six percent of the Chicago's total population.

In an oft-reprinted passage, Harrison Salisbury, fresh from years in Russia, described what he saw in New York City's public housing:

> the broken windows, the missing light bulbs, the plaster cracking from the walls, the pilfered hardware, the cold, drafty corridors, the doors on sagging hinges, the acid smell of sweat and cabbage, the ragged children, the plaintive women, the playgrounds that are seas of muddy clay, the bruised and battered trees, the ragged clumps of grass, the planned absence of art, beauty or taste, the gigantic masses of brick, of concrete, of asphalt, the inhuman genius with which our know-how has been perverted to create human cesspools worse than those of yesterday (Salisbury, 1958, p. 75).

Similarly, not long after Chicago's Robert Taylor Homes project opened, an anonymous resident was quoted as saying: "We live stacked on top of one another with no elbow room. Danger is all around. There's little privacy or peace and no quiet. And the world looks on all of us as project rats, living on a reservation like untouchables" (M. Newman, 1965).

The ensuing years did not deal kindly with what Salisbury had seen. First, with the end of legal segregation in the 1950s and 1960s, working and middle-class Blacks fled the inner-city ghettos, weakening institutions and stripping the ghetto of its mainstream role models. In the 1940s, 1950s, and as late as the 1960s, according to William Julius Wilson, the presence of working- and middle-class Blacks in ghetto communities provided stability and reinforced and perpetuated mainstream behavior patterns: "Though they may have lived on different streets, blacks of all classes lived in the same neighborhood. Their kids went to the same schools and played in the same parks. Thus, their neighborhoods at that time were more stable" (W. Wilson, 1991, p. 26).

The departure of working- and middle-class Blacks left behind a much higher concentration of the most disadvantaged segments of the Black population and removed an important "social buffer" that had helped keep alive the perception that education was meaningful, that employment was a viable alternative to welfare, and that family stability was the norm, not the exception (W. Wilson, 1987, pp. 49, 56).

Second, during the 1970s and 1980s, northern cities lost dramatically large numbers of blue-collar and low-skilled jobs. Between 1972 and 1989, Chicago's loss of almost 134,000 jobs included 48 percent of all its manufacturing jobs. During the same period, Chicago's suburbs lost only one percent of their manufacturing jobs while gaining over 700,000 total positions (Leadership Council, 1991). Simultaneously, the northern cities that suffered such job losses were also experiencing large growths in their populations of young Blacks with no education beyond high school, the offspring of those who had migrated to northern cities during the 1950s and 1960s when inner-city jobs that required only limited education and skills were far more plentiful. As the jobs dispersed to the suburbs, large numbers of young, unemployed Blacks were left in job-poor, inner-city locations, notably including public housing developments with heavy concentrations of children and teenagers.

By 1980, the impact of these two developments was of "catastrophic proportions," leading to socially isolated communities characterized by high rates not only of joblessness but also of teenage pregnancies, out-of-wedlock births, single-parent families, welfare dependency, and serious crime (W. Wilson, 1987, pp. 15, 22-26). Whereas in 1960, the overwhelming majority of adults were working even in poor Black neighborhoods, such neighborhoods came to house few middle- or working-class families, and the great majority of their adults were unemployed. Poor neighborhoods not organized around work, Wilson believes, constitute "the most fundamental and most significant change in the black community over the last several decades" (W. Wilson, 1991, p. 26). As Kasarda points out, the underground economy may be the only option for poorly educated youth anchored to such inner-city areas, an option that pushes their neighborhoods further along a downward spiral:

> Large concentrations of those who have become dependent on the urban underground economy pose serious problems (crime, drug abuse, loitering, vandalism) that dissuade businesses from locating nearby and push out more economically stable families and others who eschew such behaviors. As a consequence, not only do local employment opportunities further deteriorate, reinforcing neighborhood economic decline, but also selective out-migration of more mainstream-oriented residents spatially isolates the most disadvantaged (Kasarda, 1990, pp. 82-83).

Calling Kasarda's "spatial isolation" by its rightful name of racial segregation, Massey makes the further point that "bootstraps" have been denied to Blacks who are born and grow up in such ghetto communities. Residential mobility, Massey says, has been the crucial avenue of social mobility in America: "Some neighborhoods have good schools, strong ties to employers, excellent services, low crime rates and a youth culture that stresses educational achievement and delayed parenthood; other neighborhoods do not" (Massey, 1991, p. 33).

Moving to a more advantaged neighborhood is the central mechanism by which families improve socioeconomic prospects for themselves and their children. For most American ethnic groups, socioeconomic mobility is a cumulative process: economic advancement (a better job, a raise) is translated into residential progress (a neighborhood with better schools, peer influences, social contacts, etc.), which in turn leads to additional socioeconomic gains (children receive better education and get better jobs). This avenue for cumulative socioeconomic advancement is largely closed to Blacks because of racial barriers to residential mobility.

Massey supports his assertion with statistics and analyses that point to racial discrimination—not economics, Black locational preferences, or any other factor—as the primary explanation for Black residential segregation. But whatever the causal factors, racial segregation largely denies to Blacks America's normal avenue to socioeconomic advancement, and—because they live in isolated, impoverished neighborhoods—leaves ghetto Blacks uniquely vulnerable to economic downturns. Racial segregation, Massey concludes, is responsible for a "new, concentrated form of urban poverty," and is "a primary structural factor behind the creation of the underclass" (Massey, 1991, p. 33). This argument has special force in Chicago, where the *Gautreaux* case has judicially determined that public housing locations were deliberately selected to segregate the poor, Black population.

Beyond the formidable disadvantages of their segregation in impoverished neighborhoods, high-rise residents face the additional problem that their buildings seem particularly conducive to criminal activity (O. Newman, 1972). Newman tells of a Philadelphia project composed of a mixture of high and low buildings, two-thirds of the units in thirteen-story buildings, one-third in two-story rowhouses. Even though the social profiles of families in both building types were virtually identical, the high-rises experienced seven-and-a-half times the vandalism, robberies, and drug arrests as the rowhouses. Newman concludes that for low-income families with children, the high-rise is to be "strictly avoided" (O. Newman, 1972, pp. 191-193).

William Julius Wilson suggests that James Q. Wilson's critical mass theory may be especially relevant to inner-city neighborhoods with large public housing projects. When a "critical mass" of young persons in a given community is reached, "a self-sustaining chain reaction is set off that creates an explosive increase in the amount of crime, addiction, and welfare dependency" (J. Wilson, 1975, pp. 17-18; W. Wilson, 1987). Similarly, as a research monograph observes, the "high density of many developments . . . has complicated the role of police. Preventive patrolling in cars, for example, does nothing to deter drug dealing that takes place in the stairwells or jammed elevators of high-rise buildings" (Weisel, 1990, p. 12.)

Such observations are punctuated by regular accounts in the daily press. In 1980, about 10 percent of Chicago's murders, rapes, and aggravated assaults were committed in Robert Taylor Homes, although the project housed only a little more than 0.5 percent of the city's population (Sheppard, 1980). In 1990, police beat 211, which is CHA's Stateway Gardens, was Chicago's most violent. None of the city's other 275 police beats had more murders or sexual assaults. Beat 211's 20 homicides were more than those reported in any of ten states. Only two other Chicago beats had more serious assaults, and only one had more robberies (Blau and Recktenwald, 1991). By the close of the 1980s, Chicago's public housing high-rises were largely controlled by gangs dealing drugs, while their residents engaged in bullet-dodging. CHA's vacancies—mostly in its high-rises—exceeded 5,000, although its waiting list numbered in the tens of thousands.[5]

Poignant witness to life in Chicago high-rises came from two books published in 1991. In *The Promised Land*, Nicholas Lemann described the lives of four generations of Mississippians in one of the "better buildings" in Robert Taylor Homes. Though it is now over 30 years later, there is an almost eerie resemblance to what Harrison Salisbury had seen—the broken windows, the missing light bulbs (now regularly shot out by gang members, making coming home after dark a "terrifying experience"), the

---

[5] Vincent Lane, current chairman of the CHA, has been trying valiantly and innovatively to deal with CHA's crime problem, especially with coordinated, surprise "sweeps" of crime-ridden high rises by police and CHA personnel to evict gang members and drug dealers and "secure" the buildings for their legitimate residents. But the difficulties are great, the results uncertain. Despite sweeps of all eight high rises in CHA's Rockwell Gardens complex, serious crime there increased 17 percent in 1990 according to the CHA, more according to the Chicago Police Department (Barry, 1991).

stench, the surroundings barren of greenery. But there is also much that Salisbury had not seen—the drugs, the murders, gang recruitment beginning at eight years of age, 50 of 160 apartments vacant in the "better building," outsiders (firefighters, delivery people, social workers) declining to enter. Connie, one of the survivors in Lemann's chronicle, is, in the end, weary and depressed, "and what she wants more than anything is to get out" (Lemann, 1991b, p. 305).

There Are No Children Here, by Alex Kotlowitz, recounts a tale of two young brothers, Lafeyette and Pharoah, who lived in Henry Horner Homes where, says Kotlowitz, violence is "one constant," where the surrounding neighborhood is a "black hole" with an infant mortality rate higher than in a number of Third World countries, where eleven-year-old Pharoah "sat on his bed one day and cried because he worried that he might never get out of the projects," where a friend of Lafeyette's who *was* able to move out "knelt at his bedside before he went to sleep and prayed that God would not make him move back to Horner" (Kotlowitz, 1991).

It did appear, however, that society had learned its lesson regarding new high-rise public housing projects. In 1969, at the end of CHA's post-war building spree, the *Gautreaux* judge outlawed any more Chicago high-rises for families with children. At about the same time, Congress did likewise for the whole country, unless there was "no practical alternative." The reason, according to a congressional report, was that "high-rise, elevator structures provide an undesirable environment for family living" (U.S. House of Representatives, 1968, p. 2903). Never again, it seemed safe to say, would we build Le Corbusier-type family public housing.[6]

---

[6] It is sometimes argued that because middle- and upper-class families with children live quite satisfactorily in high-rise buildings, it cannot be the high-rise configuration, *per se*, that brings about the consequences Wilson, Massey, Newman, Lemann, Kotlowitz, and others describe. We may agree that if a single public housing high-rise building or two, with secure lobbies, sufficient numbers of elevators, an adequate maintenance staff, and the other familiar characteristics of middle- and upper-class residential buildings, were placed in a neighborhood possessed of good schools and jobs, excellent services, low crime rates, and the like, the public housing residents might fare well. We may also agree that the residents of large concentrations of low-rise public housing buildings in isolated, impoverished communities experi-

REBUILDING THE SYMBOL

Although building anew has been outlawed, what about *rebuilding* the high-rises we already have as they wear out and must be replaced? That is where the "déjà vu" comes in. For fiscal year 1991 (ending September 30, 1991), CHA asked the U.S. Department of Housing and Urban Development (HUD) for $218 million in "modernization" funding. Some of this money was for appropriate repair, maintenance, and other purposes, but nearly half of it was to rebuild high-rise buildings to extend their "useful" lives by 20 to 30 years. For example, three vacant high-rises in the Madden Homes area were proposed to be rebuilt at a cost of over $80,000 per unit (Chicago Housing Authority, 1991). For fiscal years 1992-96, CHA requested nearly a billion dollars, much of it for similar rebuilding purposes (Quadel, 1991).

Why, knowing what we now know about life for families in public housing high-rises, would CHA propose to rebuild those structures? Why, if it is going to seek $80,000 per apartment—enough to build single-family townhomes, rowhouses, or walk-ups, or to subsidize rents for its tenants in the private housing market—would CHA not jump at the chance to replace obsolete high-rises with low-rise construction or rent subsidies? Tracing the complex answer may help us chart a course out of present, nearsighted policies.

Although it was foreseeable that buildings not kept up would deteriorate, HUD's public housing funding formula provided no reserve for capital replacements. In 1968, HUD therefore initiated a public housing "modernization" program, and during the 1970s provided funding to public housing agencies for specific needs such as roof repairs, heating system replacements, and the like (Stegman, 1990, p. 342).

In 1980, Congress sought to rationalize this piecemeal activity by creating a Comprehensive Improvement Assistance Program (CIAP), under which public housing agencies would develop comprehensive plans to maintain and upgrade their public housing

---

ence many of the same problems their high-rise counterparts face, although the evidence, such as comparative vacancy rates in high- and low-rise projects sharing the same site, suggests there are differences of degree, if not of kind. But the high-rises are where they are; as regards architectural configuration they are what they are; and they are generally clustered with many others of their kind. Given these three circumstances, it is pointless to engage in the *per se* argument.

stock. Most recently, beginning with fiscal year 1992, CIAP has been changed to the Comprehensive Grant Program (CGP), under which public housing agencies will plan their modernization needs five years ahead.

Whatever its call letters, modernization has been a big-ticket item, $5 billion between 1980 and 1985 alone. Notwithstanding this outflow of billions of dollars, needs seem to have outpaced expenditures. In 1989, based on detailed surveys by consultants, HUD took a comprehensive look at the public housing system's "backlogged" modernization needs. It concluded that between $7.5 and $9.2 billion in 1986 dollars was required just to meet HUD's mandatory building standards for health, safety, and building integrity. (HUD's consultants thought the figure should be a lot higher.) Of this amount, at least $2 billion, and probably much more, must be attributable to the 20 percent of public housing units that are family high-rises because the backlogged needs of high-rises are likely to be proportionally greater than those of low-rises (U.S. Department of Housing and Urban Development, 1990, p. 1-11). HUD's estimates are exclusive of additional amounts to "improve the quality" or enhance the "long-term viability" of public housing projects (especially needed in family high-rises, which frequently lack such amenities as ground-floor washrooms, sufficient elevators, and lobbies), and of what HUD terms "accrual" needs—funding additional modernization work to avoid future backlogs.

Given this financial picture, we may ask of HUD a question similar to the one asked of CHA. Why would HUD, society's agent in this matter, choose to rebuild obsolete family high-rises? While maintaining those that must be kept in service for a time, one would think that HUD, too, would grasp every opportunity to phase out and replace these mistakes of our past with low-rises and rent subsidies.

HUD does give lip service to some phasing out. It estimates that 73,500 "high-cost or problem" units (not exclusively but probably mostly family high-rise units) will not be modernized. Moreover, an additional 93,500 units that fail to provide "humane environments" for their residents—because, among other reasons, they "concentrate the very poor in isolation from the rest of the community"—may be "scheduled for retirement" (U.S. Department of Housing and Urban Development, 1988, pp. 9-10). And HUD rules are supposed to preclude high-rise modernizations that cost more than 69 percent of HUD's allowable costs for new construction of elevator buildings.

Nevertheless, the reality is that phasing out obsolete family high-rises is a problematic undertaking—witness CHA's current modernization applications to HUD and this statement from HUD's top official in Chicago: "We [HUD] feel, and I personally feel, committed to rehabbing those [CHA high-rise] developments . . . HUD Secretary Jack Kemp has often spoken of the fact that he wants to get those buildings rehabbed and get people back in. He does not want to be known as the secretary of demolition for public housing" (Jordan, 1991, p. 11).

The reasons for HUD's view on this matter are to be found in our public housing demolition and development policy. Congress addressed public housing demolition for the first time in 1974 and returned again to the subject in the 1980s. Although there have been some policy changes, since 1987 it has been the law that HUD may not approve proposed demolitions unless it determines that (1) the public housing agency has a plan to replace the units to be demolished, unit for unit, with new construction or rent subsidies, and (2) the project is "obsolete" (as to "physical condition, location, or other factors"), making it unusable for housing purposes, and no reasonable program of modification can return the housing to useful life, or, when demolition of a portion rather than the whole of a project is proposed, the demolition will "help to assure the useful life of the remaining portion of the project." Some other requirements must be met in addition to these two basic ones—for example, demolition proposals are to be developed in "consultation" with tenants, and displaced residents must be assisted in relocating to affordable housing.

HUD's interpretation, possibly erroneous, of the replacement provision gives an important twist to the application of these rules. HUD says that although funds appropriated for modernization may be used to pay for demolishing public housing buildings once the demolition criteria are met, modernization funds may not be used to pay for the statutorily required replacement housing. For that, HUD says, public housing agencies must turn to separate funds expressly appropriated for the development of new housing or the payment of rent subsidies.

On its face, HUD's interpretation seems questionable. Of two costs that must be borne in the case of demolition—wrecking and replacement housing—why would Congress, which itself imposed the replacement requirement, permit modernization funds to be used for the first but not the second?[7]

HUD's interpretation would be less significant were it not for the fact that there is precious little new development or rent subsidy funding available. Modernization funding, and thus money to pay for wrecking costs, though inadequate in relation to true "modernization" needs, has been relatively abundant in absolute dollar terms. But in the last ten years, appropriations for new public housing have been below the level of 5,000 units per year. (Indeed, for some years HUD has sought *zero* funding for this purpose, and Congress has had to force a reluctant administration to take any new public housing funds at all.) Rent subsidy funding for replacement housing is likewise in short supply. Rent subsidies must be committed for fifteen years to qualify as replacement housing for demolished units, and in recent years Congress has appropriated most rent subsidy funding for shorter periods. Thus, given HUD's view that modernization funds cannot be used to pay for replacement housing, it makes little sense for public housing agencies to propose demolition when, absent replacement housing funding, their applications cannot be approved.

There is one final aspect to the problematic nature of demolition today—the understandable opposition of tenant advocates. Before a replacement housing requirement was imposed, demolition would result in a diminished supply of public housing units at a time when housing needs of lower-income families were growing rapidly. Even after the replacement housing requirement was put in place, HUD's enforcement was lax—paper plans were often not required to be implemented. History provides tenant advocates with ample reason to be skeptical of demolition proposals (National Housing Law Project, 1990). Even ghetto public housing may be viewed as better than no housing at all.

---

[7] One answer is that HUD's interpretation may be mistaken. The same section of the law that establishes the demolition criteria provides, "Notwithstanding any other provision of law, the Secretary [of HUD] is authorized to make available financial assistance for applications approved under this [demolition] section using available contributions authorized under section 1437c of this title" (42 USC sec. 1437p(c)(1)). Section 1437c is the basic section that authorizes all sorts of funding for lower-income housing, including modernization. Thus, the "notwithstanding" clause may be read to say that HUD may use modernization funds to pay for all the required costs, *including replacement housing*, of carrying out approved demolition applications.

Historically, the views of tenant organizations have not been particularly influential with HUD, or even with Congress. But the HUD administration under Secretary Jack Kemp made tenant "empowerment" a key plank in its housing policy (Kemp, 1990). Tenant opposition thus helps to explain why Secretary Kemp wished not to become known as "secretary of demolition."

These several factors lie behind CHA's proposal to rebuild its high-rises. Vincent Lane, CHA's chairman, says: "If I had the dollars to build low-rise, scattered-site housing, I'd be the first one out there with a sledgehammer, knocking [the high-rises] down. It was a horrendous mistake building these buildings, the way they were designed. But I don't have the resources. And therefore I'm looking to how I can begin to at least make these places livable and begin to change the environment for these kids" (Abramowitz, 1991). Lane does have the dollars, or at least has applied for them, but since, under HUD's interpretation, they are "modernization" dollars, which cannot be used for replacement, Lane is constrained to use them to rebuild the "horrendous mistake" to which he would prefer to apply a sledgehammer.

That such a course leads to perpetuation of the public housing part of Chicago's second ghetto seems to be an acceptable, if regrettable, outcome to both CHA and HUD. Lane would like to use a sledgehammer but feels he cannot. HUD would perhaps prefer different arrangements but is committed to its view of the law and only hints at the desirability of change which, however, it does not seek from Congress. In its analysis of modernization needs, HUD speaks of projects that are not "viable" because of "fundamental flaws . . . including extremely high densities and isolation from the services and supporting networks of the surrounding community." The families in such projects, HUD candidly acknowledges, are receiving housing assistance "in inhumane circumstances of severe deterioration, high concentration, isolation or danger," and they should be relocated. But, HUD concludes opaquely: "Implementing this policy would require a change in the current statutory provisions governing the demolition and disposition of public housing" (U.S. Department of Housing and Urban Development, 1988, p. 9).[8] Thus, absent change that no

---

[8] In Chicago, at least, "implementing this policy" may be the only course legally available to HUD and CHA. It having been judicially determined in *Gautreaux* that building the high-rise projects where they were located was deliberate and unlawful segregation, how could it now be legal to rebuild them in their still segregated locations?

one appears to be seeking, the door is open to rebuilding the high-rises.

WHAT TO DO?

There is an alternative course, but before discussing it, we should examine two policies that are sometimes advanced as justifications for rebuilding. First, HUD has developed a sizable program to "empower" public housing residents to manage the developments in which they live. Tenant management is a good idea that deserves to be supported, but it can easily be oversold. It does not eliminate the problem of ghettoized housing that is isolated from jobs and from the services and supporting networks of a viable surrounding community. It does not do away with extremely high densities that concentrate overwhelming numbers of poverty families in a single location. It does not do away with buildings that are fundamentally flawed in design (e.g., lacking adequate elevators). In some instances, particularly where charismatic local leadership can be found, tenant management can significantly improve a troubled public housing project. But its record has been spotty; while more than a Band-Aid, tenant management hardly provides a reason for rebuilding failed high-rises. Moreover, its public-relations appeal risks diverting attention from the opportunities that aged high-rises afford to dismantle the ghettos created by huge public housing developments, while providing their residents with options to escape ghetto conditions.

The second justification advanced for rebuilding high-rises is called MINCS (Mixed-Income New Communities Strategy). MINCS is a new, congressionally authorized experiment to try to bring mixed-income tenancy to public housing and its environs. The complicated mechanism involves private development of market-rate housing in a public housing neighborhood, to which some public housing families can be transferred via leasing arrangements, and then moving lower-income but working families into the vacated public housing apartments, thereby producing mixed-income tenancy in both places.

This experiment, too, is good in concept, for it goes to the heart of the problem of so many large-scale public housing developments—their overwhelming concentration of poverty families isolated from the non-poor. Like tenant management, however, MINCS has serious limitations. For example, it cannot even be attempted in areas that will not sustain market-rate housing;

projects such as Robert Taylor Homes are not candidates for a MINCS experiment. And, like untried experiments generally, it may or may not work even in favorable circumstances. Although MINCS should be given every encouragement, it is not a reason to forego opportunities to replace instead of rebuild our high-rise mistakes of the past.

How then can we shift from a rebuilding policy? The answer is to change fundamentally our attitude toward demolition. In the appropriate circumstances, where rebuilding high-rises is costly and conditions are "inhumane," demolition should be *encouraged* as an opportunity to rid ourselves of past mistakes and do better by residents, not discouraged as a last resort alternative to what is viewed as the preferred course of physical rehabilitation.

There are two aspects to the required attitudinal change. First, justifiable fears that demolished housing will not be replaced must be addressed. Replacement housing *in fact*, not just in a plan, must be required. Congress plainly intended to allay tenant fears that demolished public housing would not be replaced; thus, HUD should interpret the replacement requirement as mandating a workable, assured replacement plan, not just a statement of good intentions. Alternatively, Congress should be more specific. If replacement housing is not actually provided before demolition occurs, sites for new construction must be acquired or rental units secured, funding must be assured, and enforceable arrangements must be entered into. The funding could come either from modernization appropriations (HUD modifying its present interpretation of the law or Congress clarifying its intent), or from separate appropriations. It simply makes no sense to throw good money after bad simply because we choose not to fund replacement housing while choosing to fund the rebuilding of obsolete high-rises.

Second, we need more flexibility in the *form* that replacement housing may take. An example is provided by the rent subsidy program operated under the *Gautreaux* case, which has enabled some 4,300 families to make rent subsidy moves (at a one-time cost, apart from the rent subsidy itself, of only a little more than $1,000 per family). About half the families have left inner-city public housing and its environs for outlying city neighborhoods; the other half have moved to more than 100 suburban communities, predominantly White and middle-class. By and large, the families have "made it"; children are getting better educations, mothers are getting jobs (Rosenbaum, 1993). Lemann has described the program as an example of "successful class integration," one that moves the urban poor "out of the ghetto and into the mainstream" (Lemann, 1991a, p. 35). The *New York Times* editorialized that the program "offers stirring lessons for all cities with isolated underclass communities" (*New York Times*, 1988).

The *Gautreaux* program illustrates the attractiveness of a rent subsidy approach to replacement housing. Properly run, it enables families to *leave* the ghetto. Particularly when the moves are to the suburbs, it gets people to where jobs are more plentiful, schools better, life safer, and mainstream role models present. One of the most poignant findings of *Gautreaux* family surveys is that mothers of families in CHA projects did not work because they feared for the safety of their children in their absence (Rosenbaum, 1993).

Of course, rent subsidies have their limitations too. For example, it requires hard, sustained work to find available apartments in adequate numbers, sensitive counseling for families moving to new communities, and some follow-up services once the moves are made. But as part of a replacement housing approach, a *Gautreaux*-type program holds great promise.

The *Gautreaux* case has also begun to produce scattered-site townhomes and rowhouses in non-ghetto neighborhoods, housing that is architecturally compatible with existing housing and is privately—rather than publicly—managed. Such a program, buttressed by acquisition and rehabilitation of privately owned dwellings, is another means of providing replacement housing that offers an opportunity to escape the ghetto.

These *Gautreaux* initiatives do not exhaust the possibilities. For example, so-called project-based subsidies might be used to encourage private developers to rehabilitate their buildings and rent apartments to the poor. The essential point is to foster techniques that turn our replacement housing policy toward encouraging mobility and reducing isolation. As Bowly says:

> The most basic fault . . . of public housing was that it isolated poor families into enclaves containing only other poor families . . . The ideal of making the extremely poor population upwardly mobile, that was part of the original philosophy of public housing, would have best been achieved by getting them out into the general population where there is some interaction across class lines, some exposure to how the economy and the business world operate, and some exposure to persons with substantial education (Bowly, 1978, p. 224).

By "anchoring those with limited resources to distressed inner-city areas where there are few prospects for permanent or meaningful employment" (Kasarda, 1990, pp. 84-85), our present bias in favor of rebuilding rather than replacing may have the effect of keeping public housing residents away from better employment and educational opportunities in non-ghetto areas.

Finally, for those who prefer to remain in their present neighborhoods, some low-density, low-rise construction could be provided on the very site of demolished high-rises. Oscar Newman notes that, within limits, crime rates correlate not with density but with building height and type (O. Newman, 1972, p. 195). It is testimony to the strength of Le Corbusier's influence that all the Robert Taylor Homes apartments could have been put in three-story buildings, and over 60 percent of the site would still have been left for parking, landscaping, and play areas (Bowly, 1978, pp. 126-27). Substantially the same is true of other Chicago high-rise projects. Newman's work tells us that even where we may be constrained to provide some replacement housing within the ghetto, we can significantly improve on high-rise living conditions. Although they do not provide ghetto escape opportunities, low-rise units are, after all, a step in the right direction, not only because of their greater safety but also because, in some places at least, they may open the door to community linkages that the forbidding high-rises keep closed.

Taking these steps would reverse our present policy of deterring demolition. At no greater cost than rebuilding our high-rise mistakes (though greater cost *would* be warranted), we would begin to provide humane, non-ghetto housing opportunities. In the case of Chicago, we might begin to dismantle, instead of rebuild, the second ghetto.

CONCLUSION

Most of the nation's public housing—1.3 million units managed by over 3,000 public housing agencies—is decent housing. It has played, and should continue to play, an important role in housing many of the nation's poor families (Council of Large Public Housing Authorities, 1988). The segregated, ghettoized, inhumane living environment of the inner-city high-rise is only part of the public housing whole. Indeed, as a matter of sound public policy—not addressed here because it is beyond the scope of this chapter—we should spend more money both on developing new, badly needed public housing (over three-quarters of a million people are on the waiting lists of the country's public housing agencies) and on fixing up and maintaining the existing stock that merits modernization. Such a newly invigorated public housing policy should operate on a metropolitan base that could foster moves from high poverty areas of low job potential to low poverty, relatively job-rich communities.

However, because of the stereotyped image of public housing, the dysfunctional inner-city family high-rises cast a "long shadow" that threatens the entire program (Stegman, 1990, p. 346). Too many Americans think of Robert Taylor Homes when they hear "public housing," not of the hundreds of small, well-working developments that have long since found their useful places across the land. Eliminating the long shadow as rapidly as possible is in the long-term interest of public housing.

"As rapidly as possible" does not mean immediately. Supporters of rebuilding the high-rises frequently pretend that opponents are unrealistically calling for overnight demolition of all elevator buildings or peremptory termination of all spending on them. In fact, any reasonable plan will take time, and buildings not slated for prompt replacement and demolition should be maintained in the meantime. A few years ago, a prestigious Chicago committee, co-chaired by former Secretary of Commerce Philip M. Klutznick, suggested phasing out 800 Chicago high-rise units each year over ten years (Advisory Council, 1988). At the end of a decade, some 8,000 units, or 40 percent of CHA's high-rise inventory, would be phased out—a not insubstantial goal.

Is implementing such a recommendation feasible? The committee estimated modernization costs—not including any structural redesign—at $42,000 to $62,000 per unit. At the midpoint of the committee's range, over $50,000 would be needed to rebuild and maintain a high-rise unit for 15 years. The committee also said that rehabbed family high-rise units would "undoubtedly require a second modernization in approximately 15 years" that would be "excessively costly" (Advisory Council, 1988, pp. 20-21). Bearing in mind that these estimates are several years old, that the estimates are averages and many individual buildings would cost more, that no redesign is involved (e.g., "modernized" high-rises would still lack sufficient elevators), and that density and location issues remain untouched, isn't our course absolutely clear on financial grounds alone?

Dollars are not the only measure of sound policy, however. Lemann calls the urban underclass "the principal problem in American domestic life—a problem that poisons not just race relations but also our attitudes toward education, law enforcement, and city life itself" (Lemann, 1991a, p. 35). A *Newsweek* story, "A Crisis of Shattered Dreams," sounds the same theme. Decades of racial progress, the magazine says, have given way to growing resentments on both sides of the color line that are savaging our politics, our schools, our communities, our lives. First among the Black resentments is: "Much of this [Black] underclass lives all but penned up in projects and deteriorating ghettos . . . without any realistic prospect of escaping" (*Newsweek*, 1991, p. 30).

We will not solve the ghetto or underclass problem by what we do with public housing high-rises. We need new labor market policies, improved schools, comprehensive children and family services, and more. But our public housing high-rises are a part of the problem that we have the opportunity to tackle directly and promptly. They stand as living monuments to a monumental public policy mistake. It cannot make economic and social sense to spend our money (purely because of the label we paste on it) to perpetuate that mistake. It cannot make moral sense to consign the children about whom Lemann and Kotlowitz write, and *their* children if they survive to have them, to living out their lives on a reservation like untouchables. It *does* make good sense to view the aging of our public housing high-rises as a chance to help thousands of families to new life opportunities *off* the reservation, and simultaneously to improve our prospects of restoring to livability neighborhoods that today constitute a blight not only on our cityscapes but on our consciences.

REFERENCES

Abramowitz, Michael (1991). "Chicago Is Not About to Give Up on a Bad Idea," *Washington Post, National Weekly Edition*, August 12-18, 1991, p. 31; reprinting "Rehabbing the Projects," *Washington Post*, August 5, 1991, p. A1.

Advisory Council on the Chicago Housing Authority (1988). *New Strategies, New Standards for New Times in Public Housing: Report of the Advisory Council on the Chicago Housing Authority*. Chicago: Chicago Housing Authority, June 1988.

Barry, Patrick (1991). "Housing: Vince Lane's Mixed-Income Dream," *Chicago Enterprise*, September 1991, pp. 12-14.

Blau, Robert, and William Recktenwald (1991). "211, the Beat Where Violence Rarely Rests," *Chicago Tribune*, August 20, 1991, sec. 2, p. 1.

Bowly, Devereux, Jr. (1978). *The Poorhouse: Subsidized Housing in Chicago, 1895-1976.* Carbondale, Ill.: Southern Illinois University Press.

BPI (1991). "What is Gautreaux?" Chicago: Business and Professional People for the Public Interest.

Chicago Housing Authority (1991). Comprehensive Improvement Assistance Program (IL2-922).

Council of Large Public Housing Authorities (1988). "Public Housing Tomorrow." Boston: Council of Large Public Housing Authorities.

DeParle, Jason (1990). "What to Call the Poorest Poor?" *New York Times*, August 26, 1990.

Hirsch, Arnold R. (1983). *Making the Second Ghetto.* New York: Cambridge University Press.

Jordan, Gertrude (1991). "HUD's Jordan: 'CHA Moving Our Way,'" *One City*, Chicago Council on Urban Affairs, July/August 1991, pp. 11-12.

Kasarda, John D. (1990). "Urban Employment Change and Minority Skills Mismatch." In Lawrence B. Joseph, ed., *Creating Jobs, Creating Workers: Economic Development and Employment in Metropolitan Chicago.* Chicago: Center for Urban Research and Policy Studies, University of Chicago; distributed by University of Illinois Press.

Kemp, Jack (1990). "HUD's Commitment to Resident Empowerment." In *Perspective on Resident Management.* Washington, D.C.: National Association of Resident Management Corporations, 1990.

Kotlowitz, Alex (1991). *There Are No Children Here.* New York: Doubleday.

Leadership Council for Metropolitan Open Communities (1991). *Jobs, Housing, and Race in the Chicago Metropolitan Area: A Geographic Imbalance.* Chicago: Leadership Council, April 1991.

Lemann, Nicholas (1991a). "Chasing the Dream: Deep South, Dark Ghetto, Middle-Class Enclaves," *New Perspectives Quarterly*, vol. 8, no. 3 (Summer 1991), pp. 30-35.

_____ (1991b). *The Promised Land: The Great Black Migration and How It Changed America.* New York: Alfred A. Knopf.

Massey, Douglas S. (1989). "Segregation and the Underclass in Chicago." In Chicago Community Trust Human Relations Task Force, *A Report on Race, Ethnic and Religious Tensions in Chicago.* Chicago: Chicago Community Trust.

_____ (1991). "Blacks Held Back by Racial Isolation," *New Perspectives Quarterly*, vol. 8, no. 3 (Summer 1991), pp. 32-33.

Meyerson, Martin, and Edward C. Banfield (1955). *Politics, Planning, and the Public Interest*. New York: The Free Press of Glencoe.

National Housing Law Project (1990). "Public Housing in Peril." Berkeley, Calif.: National Housing Law Project

New York Times (1988). "Chicago's Housing Pioneers" (editorial), November 1, 1988.

Newman, M. W. (1965). "Chicago's $70 Million Ghetto," *Chicago Daily News*, April 10, 1965.

Newman, Oscar (1972). *Defensible Space*. New York: Macmillan.

Newsweek (1991). "A Crisis of Shattered Dreams," May 6, 1991, pp. 28-31.

Polikoff, Alexander (1978). *Housing the Poor: The Case for Heroism*. Cambridge, Mass.: Ballinger.

_____ (1989). "*Gautreaux* and Institutional Litigation," *Chicago-Kent Law Review*, vol. 64, no. 2, pp. 451-478.

Quadel Consulting Corporation (1991). "Comprehensive Plan for Modernization of Public Housing, Five-Year Funding Request Plan, 1992-96, Chicago Housing Authority," Chicago: Chicago Housing Authority, May 31, 1991.

Rosenbaum, James E. (1993). "Closing the Gap: Does Residential Integration Improve the Employment and Education of Low-Income Blacks?" In this volume.

Salisbury, Harrison E. (1958). *The Shook-up Generation*. New York: Harper & Row.

Sheppard, Nathaniel, Jr. (1980). "Chicago Project Dwellers Live Under Siege," *New York Times*, August 6, 1980, p. A14.

Stegman, Michael A. (1990). "The Role of Public Housing in a Revitalized National Housing Policy." In Denise DiPasquale and Langley C. Keyes, eds., *Building Foundations: Housing and Federal Policy*. Philadelphia: University of Pennsylvania Press.

U.S. Department of Housing and Urban Development (1988). *HUD Perspective on Public Housing Modernization*. Washington, D.C.: U.S. Government Printing Office.

_____ (1990). *Report to Congress on Alternative Methods for Funding Public Housing Modernization*. Washington, D.C.: U.S. Government Printing Office.

U.S. House of Representatives (1968). House Report No. 90-1585. Washington, D.C.: U.S. Government Printing Office.

Weisel, Deborah Lamm (1990). "Tackling Drug Problems in Public Housing: A Guide for Police." Washington, D.C.: Police Executive Research Forum.

Wilson, James Q. (1975). *Thinking About Crime*. New York: Basic Books.

Wilson, William Julius (1987). *The Truly Disadvantaged: The Inner City, the Underclass, and Public Policy*. Chicago: University of Chicago Press.

_____ (1991). "Balkanizing by Caste and Class," *New Perspectives Quarterly*, vol. 8, no. 3 (Summer 1991), pp. 26-29.

COMMENTS

Deborah C. Stone[*]

Anyone who debates whether Chicago Housing Authority (CHA) family high-rises should be rehabbed or torn down finds him- or herself between a rock and a hard place. Old, deteriorated, energy-wasteful high-rises with large concentrations of the very poor are not good for the families living there or for the surrounding neighborhood. Yet over half of CHA's 29,000 family units are in high-rises. This a hard fact that we must deal with. Other hard facts are that the private market does not provide decent, safe, and sanitary housing for all and that public programs do not begin to meet the need for low-income housing.

Yes, the CHA needs to produce a building-by-building strategic plan analyzing costs and benefits of rehabbing existing structures, reconfiguring buildings to reduce the number of units, or replacing high-rises with another kind of housing. If a program of replacement is to work, however, and not just recreate segregated ghettos (or fail to produce new housing at all), we must overcome the difficulties that have plagued the CHA's scattered-site program. Also, as replacement goes ahead, safeguards to protect the rights of public housing tenants are needed. Of critical importance, and the main focus of my commentary, is that all possible should be done to make remaining high-rises liveable.

PROBLEMS WITH THE SCATTERED-SITE PROGRAM

The CHA scattered-site program, which was established as a result of the *Gautreaux* decision, is a valuable part of an overall strategy for public housing, but it has been small compared to the total need. In the program's 20-plus years, fewer than 1,000 units of

---

[*] This commentary is a revised version of an article that originally appeared in *One City* (Stone, 1991); it is published here with permission of the Chicago Council on Urban Affairs. Both versions draw heavily from the background work in Revere, 1989.

housing have been produced, and many of those have been poorly managed. The program has been dogged by problems such as site selection, political and bureaucratic opposition, high costs, and poor management and maintenance. CHA management is improving, however, and the federal court has appointed a new receiver to run the scattered-site program. Production is increasing, and present funding provides for 700 new units per year. The scattered-site funds should, however, be used to *add* units to address the problem of scarcity. If we can learn from the scattered-site program ways to overcome both the financial and political difficulties in locating housing for the poor, we can help make a public housing replacement program work.

Vouchers, or rent certificates, also are used to help low-income families. Here also, the number of families served is small compared to the need. The shortage of large apartments, the relative tightness of the housing market in Chicago compared to other cities, and racial discrimination all make the use of vouchers difficult. Without a strong commitment to produce more housing for the poor, the federal government could, over time, pull back its funding for vouchers.

SAFEGUARDS FOR TENANTS

Responsible replacement of high-rises should include procedural safeguards. Plans should include one-for-one replacement of like-sized family units, to be in place before public housing units are destroyed. If the new units are to be in the same neighborhood, market-rate housing should be produced in tandem to assure the mixed-income character of the new community. Replacement public housing should be integrated into the neighborhood, not isolated or concentrated. Also, the needs of low-income renters in the neighborhood, but not living in CHA housing, should be accommodated.

Most important, the U.S. Department of Housing and Urban Development must continue its operating subsidy to the new units. Replacement of family high-rises must not dilute the federal government's responsibility to maintain housing for the very poor.

MAKE REMAINING HIGH-RISES LIVEABLE

High-rises that are to remain for any significant period of time should be improved. Although building these high-rises was a mistake, they can, under certain conditions, be made more liveable. Successful public housing high-rises have some or all of the following:

- *Competent on-site management.* The number of units under one management team should be 800-1,200, not the 3,500 at Cabrini-Green (on Chicago's north side) or the 2,800 at Ida B. Wells (on the city's south side). Managers should be well trained.
- *Economic mix.* The U.S. Department of Housing and Urban Development requires that, within its definition of low-income, public housing tenants have a diversity of amount and sources of income. Chicago has historically ignored this requirement.
- *Active screening of prospective tenants.* Also needed are enforcement of rules and fair, effective eviction programs.
- *Large families on lower floors.* In St. Louis and Boston, buildings were reconfigured with units for large families on lower floors. Stairs for these units limited wear on the elevators and allowed easier supervision of children.
- *Security improvements.* Most successful high-rises have enclosed lobbies, intercoms, and other security measures.
- *Energy efficiency.* Forty percent of the CHA's budget goes for energy. The Metropolitan Planning Council (MPC) and the Center for Neighborhood Technology have outlined rehab projects for a prototypical high-rise to save almost $1 million per year in energy costs, paying back the cost of the investments in 8.2 years.
- *Support services.* A key success factor is support services through public-private partnerships to residents to increase their self-sufficiency and integration into the larger community.
- *Tenant involvement.* Successful and lasting rehab efforts are aided by tenant involvement in planning and implementation.

Working with CHA tenants and architects, MPC has developed rehab blueprints for family public housing high-rises in Chicago. However, people do not just live in buildings, they live in communities, and public housing developments are communities

to many who live there. Programs such as the Wells Community
Initiative (WCI) are designed to address issues of comprehensive
community revitalization. WCI takes a four-pronged approach:
physical, social, and economic improvements proceed in tandem
with tenant leadership development and direction of the overall
program. Many of the individual program components have
proved successful elsewhere. The marriage of "soft" social services provided centrally through a family development center with
"hard" physical improvements to the buildings and site represents
a new approach.

MPC's work with public housing tenants has revealed the importance of physical improvements. If the heat goes off or the
apartments flood, tenants can hardly be expected to attend a meeting to plan for a jobs program. In addition, building security is
a critical prerequisite to any other work. Also critical is establishing linkages between public housing communities and other
public and private institutions, including community organizations,
social service providers, and relevant state and local government
agencies.

Comprehensive physical and social improvements in CHA
communities will take a long time. The goal of these efforts is
not only to improve public housing in Chicago, but also to achieve
better relations between public housing and the larger community.

REFERENCES

Revere, Elspeth (1989). *Not a World Apart: Increasing the Viability of Chicago's Public Housing High-Rises and Large Developments.* Chicago: Metropolitan Planning Council.
Stone, Deborah C. (1991). "Planning Group States 'Principles'
  for Renovations of High-Rises," *One City*, vol. 4, no. 4
  (July/August 1991), pp. 9-10. Chicago: Chicago Council on
  Urban Affairs.

CLOSING THE GAP: DOES RESIDENTIAL INTEGRATION IMPROVE THE EMPLOYMENT AND EDUCATION OF LOW-INCOME BLACKS?

James E. Rosenbaum[*]

Black employment is usually below that of Whites. For instance, in Chicago in 1989, labor force participation was 60 percent for Black adults and 71 percent for White adults. But this employment gap was not evident everywhere. In the suburbs around Chicago, Blacks were somewhat *more* likely than Whites to participate in the labor market: 75 percent of Black adults and 73 percent of White adults were in the labor force (U.S. Bureau of Labor Statistics, 1990). What do these statistics mean? Does housing opportunity increase access to employment opportunities or are the Blacks who live in suburbs more employable than urban Blacks? Could low-income Blacks improve their employment by moving to the suburbs?

Certainly, Blacks could find a stronger labor market in the suburbs. In recent decades, large numbers of jobs have shifted from the central cities to the suburbs (Kasarda, 1989, 1990). For example, between 1975 and 1978, 2,380 firms in Illinois moved from the city to the suburban ring (Wilson, 1987, p. 135). More recently, Cook County experienced a 1.5 percent decline in jobs between 1980 and 1988, while the surrounding counties gained 7.6 percent to 59.5 percent. Chicago's share of metropolitan employment has been forecast to decline from 38.4 percent in 1986 to 32.8 percent in 1995: "This . . . pattern represents a serious labor market barrier for inner-city residents, especially those with minimal education and work skills" (NCI Research, 1991, p. 5).

* The Charles Stewart Mott Foundation, the Ford Foundation, the Spencer Foundation, and the Center for Urban Affairs and Policy Research, Northwestern University, provided support for the studies reported here. Julie Kaufman, Marilyn Kulieke, Susan J. Popkin, and Len Rubinowitz made major contributions to these studies. Of course, the ideas expressed here are those of the author and do not necessarily represent those of any other individual or organization.

Despite the stronger job market in the suburbs, low-income Blacks have not followed jobs to the suburbs. Because of housing discrimination, housing costs, and personal preferences, low-skilled workers have not left the cities as fast as low-skill jobs (Ellwood, 1986, p. 148). The spatial mismatch hypothesis contends that the distance between home and work impedes employment for low-income Blacks, who are largely constrained to central cities (Kain, 1968; Jencks and Mayer, 1989).

The spatial mismatch hypothesis has striking implications for housing policy. It suggests that urban housing programs are keeping the poor away from the growing employment opportunities in the suburbs. Urban housing programs may also reduce the effectiveness of job training programs, most of which have only modest success at improving employment for low-income people, perhaps because job training cannot help people become employed if jobs have moved to suburbs far from the housing provided to the poor (Bassi and Ashenfelter, 1986; Hahn and Lerman, 1985).

Similarly, urban housing programs may be keeping the poor away from the better public schools in the suburbs. Suburban schools tend to offer more resources and better paid teachers than do city schools, particularly the city schools that serve public housing projects (Coleman et al., 1966; Persell, 1977). In addition, students in suburban schools have much higher achievement than students in city schools.

The spatial mismatch hypothesis, if true, suggests that urban housing programs restrict the opportunities of poor people so that even efforts to improve their capabilities will have little benefit. Closing the gap between low-income Blacks and mainstream society may require more than just training and education opportunities; it may also require housing that improves access to good schools and more jobs.

Housing vouchers have been proposed as a way of helping people escape low-income urban areas. Unlike public housing projects, which are socially homogeneous and socially isolated from the larger society, voucher programs integrate poor people into the same housing market as other people, which may help them become integrated in mainstream society and get jobs. Housing vouchers have gained strong support from some national leaders, and they have become a central component of a new federal poverty program. "Operation Bootstraps" proposes to use housing vouchers (Section 8 certificates) to help poor people move to areas where they can obtain employment.[1] Jack Kemp, secretary of Housing and Urban Development in the Bush administration, has expressed confidence that the program can help low-income people attain economic self-sufficiency.

However, voucher programs for the poor are based on two assumptions: that the poor are willing to move to middle-income areas that offer better opportunities, and that the poor will benefit from such moves. There are reasons to doubt both assumptions. The poor may be reluctant to move to middle-income areas because these areas are often very distant and unknown. Recent housing voucher programs support this doubt. Even if the poor did move, they might not benefit from such moves. This chapter raises three separate questions about whether they benefit. (1) Will residential integration lead to harassment and rejection, thereby undermining morale and preventing low-income Blacks from taking advantage of suburban resources? (2) Will low-income Blacks fail to get jobs because of discrimination, poor skills, or poor motivation? (3) Will early disadvantages prevent low-income Black children from catching up with better prepared and socially advantaged suburban classmates?

This chapter addresses these questions by examining the Gautreaux program, a program that gives low-income Blacks housing vouchers to move to many different kinds of communities, including White, middle-income suburbs and low-income, Black city neighborhoods. Since the United States has few examples of residential integration and few successful housing voucher programs, the present results are important evidence about the potential for low-income Blacks to use housing vouchers to move to, and benefit from, middle-income White suburbs. Moreover, because participants are assigned to city or suburban locations in a quasi-random manner, and because participants are not a "highly creamed" group, inferences can be made about the effects of residential moves and the generalizability of the results to other low-income Blacks. This chapter reports the program's impact on the social integration and employment of adults and on the education and employment of children and youth.

---

[1] The Section 8 program is a federal program that subsidizes rents for low-income people in private-sector apartments, either by giving them a Section 8 certificate, which allows them to rent apartments on the open market, or by moving them into a new or rehabilitated building where the owner has taken a federal loan that requires some units to be set aside for low-income tenants.

WILL LOW-INCOME BLACKS MOVE TO
MIDDLE-INCOME WHITE SUBURBS?

Previous Voucher Programs

Critics have raised several concerns about housing vouchers and residential integration programs generally. The first critique contends that vouchers would make only small changes in the racial composition of suburbs because of the limited number of eligible housing units. However, small changes are not necessarily undesirable; they may be desirable in order to avoid creating fear and flight among White residents. One survey suggests that only 76 percent of Whites would stay in a neighborhood that was 13 percent Black, but 93 percent would stay if the neighborhood was 7 percent Black (Farley, Bianchi, and Cosalanto, 1979). Integration is also more effective if it occurs across a wide area; White residents see that their community is not changing more than others and that there is no reason for flight (Yinger, 1979). Even if vouchers can only make small changes, such changes are a good way to initiate socioeconomic and racial integration in a community.

The other critique raises more serious concerns. Critics argue that low-income Blacks will simply choose not to move to middle-income White suburbs because of the distance from friends and the social isolation low-income Blacks would feel in those communities. Indeed, previous programs indicate that low-income people do not use housing vouchers to move to White, middle-income neighborhoods. Studies of the national Experimental Housing Allowance Program found that "the program had virtually no impact on the degree of economic and racial concentration experienced by participants." Most relevant, in South Bend, Indiana, the only experiment site with a sizable minority population, "moves did not involve households migrating from the central city to the suburban ring" (Cronin and Rasmussen, 1981, p. 123).

Similarly, Project Self-Sufficiency was a national program that gave low-income people both job training and Section 8 certificates. In Cook County, this program strongly encourged participants to move to areas with better job prospects. Even though all participants stated a willingness to move to get jobs, very few moved to such areas (Rosenbaum, 1988). Participants were reluctant to make these moves because of strong personal ties to their neighbors, fear of discrimination, and unfamiliarity with the distant suburbs that could have offered better job prospects.

In both cases, although housing vouchers helped people to move to better housing, they did not help people move to areas with better employment and educational opportunities. Critics' predictions that housing vouchers cannot promote socioeconomic or racial integration were supported in these voucher programs. But is this inevitable?

The Gautreaux Program

The Gautreaux program provides another test of the potential of voucher programs. This program is the result of a 1976 Supreme Court consent decree in a lawsuit against the Chicago Housing Authority (CHA) and the U.S. Department of Housing and Urban Development on behalf of public housing residents. The suit charged "that these agencies had employed racially discriminatory policies in the administration of the Chicago low-rent public housing program" (Peroff, Davis, and Jones, 1979). The Gautreaux program is a unique demonstration program whose purpose was to redress the discriminatory nature of public housing in Chicago. Administered by the nonprofit Leadership Council for Metropolitan Open Communities in Chicago, the Gautreaux program allows public housing residents to receive Section 8 housing certificates and move to private apartments either in mostly White suburbs or in the city of Chicago.

Unlike other housing voucher programs, the Gautreaux program succeeded in helping people move to distant middle-class suburbs. Since 1976, over 4,000 families have participated in the program, and over half moved to middle-income White suburbs. This program provides extensive housing services. Two full-time real-estate staff find landlords willing to participate in the program. Then placement counselors notify families as apartments become available, counsel them about the advantages and disadvantages of these moves, and take them to visit the units and communities.

Voucher critics are correct about the reluctance of low-income Blacks to make these moves. A Detroit survey found that few Blacks would choose all-White neighborhoods as their first choice (Farley, Bianchi, and Cosalanto, 1979). Similarly, Gautreaux participants are reluctant to move to distant suburbs that they have never seen before, and few would move without the encouragement of counselors. But the voucher critics are wrong in predicting that low-income Blacks would not choose to make such moves. In the Detroit survey, 38 percent of Blacks viewed such moves as acceptable on a hypothetical question, and the Gautreaux program shows that if a program locates housing and gives supportive counseling, low-income Blacks will indeed make such moves.

WILL LOW-INCOME BLACKS BENEFIT FROM SUBURBAN MOVES?

Suburban Obstacles

Despite the superior economic and educational opportunities in the suburbs, there may be obstacles to poor people benefiting from these opportunities. Do these low-income Blacks interact with and get support from their middle-income neighbors, or will they face rejection and harassment from neighbors? Can these adults benefit from their new opportunities? Does discrimination prevent them from obtaining work? Virtually all the mothers in Gautreaux have received public aid, most for five years or more, many have never had a job, and half grew up in families on public aid. They may lack the skills, motivation, or work experience necessary to obtain work. Similarly, the children lack the home advantages of their suburban classmates, and their city schools may not have prepared them for the more demanding suburban schools. We must wonder if they will be able to catch up. The following sections consider other social science research that is pertinent to our questions.

Will residential integration lead to harassment and rejection?

Although large numbers of young, affluent Blacks moved out of central cities and into surrounding suburbs during the 1970s, Blacks remained significantly more isolated than either Hispanics or Asians (Massey and Denton, 1987). Research also documents extensive antagonism to racial integration. While the majority of Whites have become increasingly supportive of racial integration *in principle*, the majority remain opposed to any government intervention to promote such integration (Schuman and Bobo, 1988). Blacks moving into predominantly White areas have faced threats, physical attacks, and property damage (Berry, 1979). A small-scale experimental effort to move Black families from Chicago housing projects to Valparaiso, Indiana, in the late 1960s was generally unsuccessful. The families encountered organized resistance from the town government, verbal harassment, and violence. Although some families stayed despite the hardship, most moved back to the city (Gehm, 1984). Throughout the past several decades, Black families that moved into White neighborhoods of Chicago were driven from their homes by racial violence (Squires et al., 1987). Yet incidents of harassment, while dramatic, may not reflect the views of all residents, and other neighbors may willingly interact with Black newcomers.

One of the main research findings is the "equal status hypothesis": Residential integration is most successful when Blacks and Whites are of equal social status. Zeul and Humphrey (1971) surveyed the neighbors of Blacks living in suburban communities. They found that Whites were more positive about Blacks when the Blacks were their "socioeconomic equals." Studying women living in integrated public housing developments in Lexington, Kentucky, Ford (1972) found that those who had the most interracial interaction were those whose previous interracial contacts had been with equal-status Blacks. Similarly, Williams (1964) found that the greatest levels of racial interaction occurred among people of approximately equal social status.

The "equal-status hypothesis" implies that suburban movers will be less socially integrated than city movers. Low-income Blacks in the Gautreaux program have had very different experiences from their White middle-income neighbors, which may limit neighbor support, interaction, and friendships.

Will low-income Blacks get jobs in the suburbs?

There are a number of reasons to expect that low-income Blacks may not get jobs in the suburbs. After living in low-income environments for many years, they may have motivational problems that prevent them from doing well even after their opportunities improve. Some scholars contend that the primary problem of the urban underclass is lack of motivation and social obligation among ghetto residents. In the 1960s, much debate centered around Oscar Lewis's theory of the "culture of poverty." Lewis argued that low-income children are socialized into a value system that reduces their motivation to succeed in the labor market. "By the time slum children are age six or seven, they have usually absorbed the basic values and attitudes of their subculture and are not psychologically geared to take full advantage of changing con-

ditions or increased opportunities which may occur in their life-
time" (Lewis, 1968, p. 188). A variant of this view argues that
current welfare policy encourages low-income people to feel no
obligation to contribute to the larger society (Mead, 1986). The
idea that low-income people cannot benefit from improved circumstances because of "deeply ingrained habits" has been adopted by
many writers (Steinberg, 1981).

Employer discrimination or applicants' lack of skills may also
prevent low-income Blacks from getting jobs. Suburban employers' unfamiliarity with Black employees may contribute to an un-
willingness to hire Black applicants. In addition, Gautreaux adults
were educated in poor urban schools, and many lack job training
or job experience. Their poor skills may prevent them from entering the suburban labor market. Suburban employers, accustomed to hiring the graduates of suburban high schools, may be
unwilling to hire people who lack this level of education.

*Will early disadvantages prevent children from catching up with
suburban classmates?*

Housing moves may have even greater impact on children than on
adults because children are in a more formative stage and are still
acquiring education. At the same time, being less mature, children may have even more difficulty coping with the challenges
posed by the suburban move.

School desegregation has been extensively studied over the last
two decades (Crain and Weisman, 1972; Gerard and Miller, 1975;
St. John, 1975; Hoelter, 1982; Patchen, 1982; Grant, 1984; Holland and Andre, 1987). However, the Gautreaux program is distinctive in creating both residential and educational integration,
and it does so with little visibility, thus reducing backlash and
stigma. Moreover, unlike bused children, these low-income Black
children were suburban residents, so the program provided the
possibility for social interaction after school hours.

The basic question is whether low-income Black youth are permanently disadvantaged in the suburban schools. They may find
it hard to meet suburban standards for various reasons: their
low-income background may leave them less prepared or less motivated than middle-income suburban youth; they may have attitudes and habits deemed "undesirable" by suburban teachers and
employers; or racial discrimination may deny them full access to
suburban resources. For any or all of these reasons, these Black

suburban youth may have lower achievement than their city Gautreaux counterparts who do not face these barriers. School desegregation does not always have positive effects on Black student achievement (Patchen, 1982), and it sometimes has negative effects (Winkler, 1975).

A contradictory expectation is that, instead of facing disadvantages, suburban movers will benefit from better educational resources and greater employment prospects in the suburbs, and their fellow suburban students may serve as role models for achievement. Some research has found that school desegregation has positive effects on Blacks' achievement (St. John, 1975). Of course, we do not know which process will operate or, if both do, which will win out. The presumption that both expectations seem plausible makes the Gautreaux studies particularly fascinating.

Therefore, despite the potential gains from the suburban move, there are many reasons to expect failure. Discrimination, poor skills, educational deficiencies, or low motivation may combine to reduce the benefits from the suburban move, or even to leave the adults or children worse off than they were in the city.

THE STUDIES

Gautreaux as a Quasi-Experiment

The Gautreaux program presents an unusual opportunity to test these issues. The United States does not have much experience with economic and racial integration of neighborhoods. Racial and economic homogeneity is the rule in most neighborhoods, so we generally do not know how low-income Blacks are affected by living in middle-income, White neighborhoods. Moreover, even when exceptions exist, we must suspect that Blacks who break the residential barriers and move into White neighborhoods are themselves exceptional people. Their subsequent attainments may reflect more about them as individuals than about the effects of neighborhoods. Therefore, when researchers study Black employment in suburbs, it is hard to tell whether the suburbs increased Black employment or whether the Blacks who happen to live in suburbs are different, perhaps moving to the suburbs *after* getting a job (Jencks and Mayer, 1989). Similarly, most studies of Black achievement in suburban schools cannot determine whether Black children's achievement is due to the suburbs or to some unmeasured family assets or values that may have drawn these Black families to the suburbs.

Gautreaux participants circumvent the ordinary barriers to living in the suburbs, not by their jobs, personal finances, or values, but by getting into the program. The program gives them rent subsidies that permit them to live in suburban apartments for the same cost as public housing. Moreover, unlike the usual case of Black suburbanization—working-class Blacks living in working-class suburbs—Gautreaux permits low-income Blacks to live in middle-income, White suburbs (Jencks and Mayer, 1989). Participants move to a wide variety of suburbs (over 100) throughout the six counties surrounding Chicago. (Black suburbs were excluded by the consent decree, and very high-rent suburbs were excluded by funding limitations of Section 8 certificates.) Gautreaux presents an unusual opportunity to test the effect of helping low-income people move to better labor markets, better schools, and better neighborhoods.

Applying for the program is largely a matter of luck and persistent telephone dialing on registration day, since many more people try to call than can get through on the telephone lines. The program has three selection criteria. The program tries to avoid overcrowding, late rent payments, and building damage by not admitting families with more than four children, large debts, or unacceptable housekeeping. But none of these criteria was extremely selective, and all three only reduced the eligible pool by less than 30 percent.[2] Although these selection criteria make this an above-average group of housing project residents, they are not a "highly creamed" group. All are very low-income Blacks, are current or former welfare recipients, and have lived most of their lives in impoverished, inner-city neighborhoods.

The program's procedures create a quasi-experimental design. Although all participants come from the same low-income, Black, city neighborhoods (usually public housing projects), some move to middle-income, White suburbs, while others move to low-income, Black, urban neighborhoods. In principle, participants have choices about where they move, but, in actual practice, participants are assigned to city or suburb locations in a quasi-random manner. Apartment availability is determined by housing agents who do not deal with clients, and it is unrelated to client interest. Counselors offer clients units as they become available according

---

[2] For more detail, see Appendix 2.

to their position on the waiting list, regardless of clients' locational preferences. Although clients can refuse an offer, very few do so, since they are unlikely to get another. As a result, participants' preferences for city or suburbs have little to do with where they end up moving.

Studies of Adults and Children: Methods and Sample

The remainder of this chapter summarizes four studies of the Gautreaux program, comparing families moving to White, middle-income suburbs with families moving to low-income, Black, city neighborhoods. The city movers are a good comparison group for judging the effects of the suburban move because both groups meet the same selection criteria and get improved housing. Moreover, city movers are a particularly stringent comparison group because they receive better housing and move to better city neighborhoods than they had in the housing projects. We expect that housing-project residents would fare considerably worse than either of the Gautreaux groups. In effect, the suburban effects (relative to city movers) in these studies may be considered "lower-bound" effects.

To examine employment and social integration, we surveyed 332 adults in 1988 and conducted detailed interviews with another 95 individuals.[3] The first study of children interviewed one randomly selected, school-aged child (aged 8-18) from each of 114 families in 1982, and the second study followed up with the same children in 1989 when they were adolescents and young adults and examined their educational and employment outcomes.[4]

---

[3] For a complete description of the sample, instrument, and other analysis, see Rosenbaum and Popkin, 1990. Our refusal rate on the interviews was less than 7 percent. There are no systematic differences between the interview and survey respondents, but the interview sample is used only for qualitative analysis. Responses to the self-administered questionnaire were consistent with those from the in-person interviews.

[4] See Appendix 1 for further methodological details.

Study of Adult Social Integration

As predicted, in their first year after moving, suburban movers reported experiencing more incidents of harassment than city movers (2.60 vs. 0.79), and about twice the proportion of suburban movers experienced harassment as city movers (52% vs. 23%). However, by 1989, suburban movers reported levels of harassment close to the level in the city (1.29 vs. 0.84). Although 52 percent of suburban movers reported harassment in the first year after they moved, just 25 percent said they had such problems in the year prior to the interview (see Table 1). This decrease in harassment over time suggests that hostile neighbors gradually became accustomed to their new neighbors. Most incidents involved name-calling or avoidance.

> Sometimes they [her kids] go to school and people call them Black niggers. White people in the neighborhood would drive by and holler "Blacks go home!"

> The manager of the apartment complex wouldn't speak to Blacks. She would just stare right through you. If you came to her office, she would just ignore you. She was the only problem here.

> They yell at you, make racial slurs.

Some suburban movers, however, reported more severe problems, for example, fighting, stone-throwing, and police harassment. In the interview sample, of the 27 suburban movers reporting harassment, eight reported physical violence or police harassment. Most of those reporting such incidents believed they were racially motivated:

> A White woman told her son to throw a rock at my kids.

> The first year I was here, they shot into my window twice and we were called all kinds of names . . . It was because I was Black.

> Someone broke my tail-lights at work. My tires have been slashed.

> The police came to my house at 10:30 one night and threatened to kick the door down. They were looking for my son because he missed a traffic court hearing.

TABLE 1: Comparison of City and Suburban Movers on Social Integration

	City (n=112)	Suburbs (n=230)
Individual scale items		
Lend things to a neighbor	1.96	1.84
Let neighbor use my phone	1.81	1.83
Watch neighbor's kids	1.81	1.98
Eat lunch or dinner with neighbor	1.65	1.75
Greet neighbor in street/hallway	3.36	3.32
Talk to neighbor for 10 minutes	2.79	2.80
Interaction scale	2.23	2.26
Neighbor friendliness rating	3.86	3.81
Neighbor help	24.8%	25.0%
Harrassment		
No. of times treated badly first year	0.79	2.60*
No. of times treated badly now	0.84	1.29

* Indicates statistically significant difference between city and suburban movers.

Individual scale items range from 1 (never) to 4 (often).
Interaction scale ranges from 1 (no interaction) to 4 (frequent interaction).
Neighbor friendliness scale ranges from 1 (very unfriendly) to 5 (very friendly).
Harassment data based on interviews (suburban n = 52, city n = 43).

We found no difference between city and suburban movers in terms of help from neighbors. About one-quarter of both groups reported that their neighbors went out of their way to help them settle in when they first moved. Suburban movers reported a variety of friendly behaviors by neighbors.

The neighbors are all White. They offered to help. They made a cake. Brought out coffee and wanted to chat.

The neighbors made me feel comfortable. They told me if I had a problem, I could use their phone. Just made me feel like

"you're not alone." We're in this boat together. Anything you
don't know ask us. We'll help you.

I had one neighbor ask if there was anything she could help me
with. She explained things in the building. She watched children for me.

They welcomed me in, gave me things, showed me where the
school was. They showed you where the grocery stores are,
how to take the paths to them without walking on the streets.
They babysat.

Some landlords were also supportive.

My landlord did everything he could possibly do. He checked
on us all the time, was always looking out for Tina. He found
out my kids had never been in an airplane, so he took them and
let them ride in his plane. Took them to his farm and let them
ride his horses. Talked to me a lot.

The maintenance man's wife brought my kids presents.

We also asked about everyday interaction with neighbors.
Both city and suburban movers report that they frequently talk
with their neighbors for more than ten minutes and greet them in
the street or hallway. The other kinds of interaction we asked
about were less frequent for both groups, and both groups reported equal frequencies of these behaviors: lending things to
neighbors, letting neighbors use their phone, watching a neighbor's children, or eating lunch or dinner with a neighbor. On all
measures, suburban movers interacted with neighbors as much as
city movers do.

Some participants, in both city and suburbs, had no friends in
their new communities (Table 2). However, suburban movers
were slightly *less* likely than city movers to say that they had no
friends (26% vs. 33%).[5] Further, suburban movers did not re-

---

[5] It is noteworthy that many of those with "no friends" felt that their
neighbors were friendly. Among city movers with no friends, 68.8 percent said their neighbors were friendly; among suburban movers with no
friends, 57.4 percent say this (not a statistically significant difference).
This suggests that having "no friends" does not necessarily indicate rejection by neighbors. We suspect that it indicates a higher standard for
what it takes to be a "friend," as opposed to a friendly acquaintence.

strict their friendships only to Blacks. Although they had significantly fewer Black friends than city movers (2.64 vs. 3.33), suburban movers had significantly more White friends (3.02 vs. 1.25). As for total number of friends (including friends of other races), suburban movers report having slightly more friends than city movers (6.69 vs. 5.36), but this difference is not statistically significant.

Thus, although suburban movers experienced more harassment, the number of incidents decreased over time and were insignificant by the time of the study. City and suburban movers were also similar in whether they had friends, their total number of friends, the amount they interacted with neighbors, and the number receiving help from neighbors. These findings suggest that the difficulties that low-income Blacks face in moving to middle-class White communities are less severe than is generally believed. The Gautreaux program does not leave them socially isolated from their middle-income neighbors.

TABLE 2: Comparison of City and Suburban Respondents on Post-Move Numbers of Friends and Interracial Friendships

	City (n=112)	Suburbs (n=230)
Number of Black friends	3.33	2.64*
Number of White friends	1.25	3.02*
Total number of friends	5.36	6.69
No friends in neighborhood	33.0%	25.7%

* Indicates statistically significant difference between city and suburban movers.

Study of Adult Employment

Contrary to the "culture of poverty" prediction that low-income Blacks lack motivation to get jobs, we found that both city movers and suburban movers got jobs. Although both groups started from the same baseline, suburban movers were more likely to have jobs than city movers. As Table 3 indicates, while 51 percent of city movers had a job after moving, 64 percent of suburban movers did. Among respondents who were ever employed prior to moving, 74 percent of suburban movers had jobs, compared to 65 percent of city movers. For those who had never been employed before their move, 46 percent found work after moving to the suburbs, while the figure for the city was only 30 percent. For this group of "hard-core unemployed," suburban movers were much more likely to have a job after moving than city movers.[6]

City and suburban movers did not differ in hourly wages or number of hours worked per week (Table 4). Among those who had a job both before and after moving, both city and suburban movers reported gains in hourly wages and no change in hours worked.[7]

---

[6] The suburban advantage arises because city movers declined in employment. The 15.4 percent decline in employment by the city movers is virtually the same as the 16.3 percent decline found in the Census Bureau's Current Population Surveys (CPS) between 1979 and 1989 among poorly educated, central-city, Black adult males, while their non-central-city counterparts had little or no decline (Danziger and Wood, 1991, Tables 5 and 6). Although selectivity concerns are a threat to city-suburban differences in the CPS data, the quasi-random assignment makes selectivity less of a problem in our study, which finds the same city/suburban differences as the CPS. Apparently, the suburban move permitted low-income Blacks to escape the declining employment rates in central cities over the 1980s. Moreover, multivariate analysis showed that suburban movers were significantly more likely than city movers to have jobs, even after controlling for many other factors. For details, see Rosenbaum and Popkin, 1991.

[7] Multivariate analysis on post-move hourly wages and on hours worked per week (controlling for the same variables, plus months of employment and the pre-move measure of the dependent variable [wages or hours, respectively]) confirm the above findings. Suburbs have no effect on either dependent variable. For details, see Rosenbaum and Popkin (1991).

TABLE 3: Employment Rates of City and Suburban Movers

	Percent Employed Post-Move	
	City	Suburbs
Ever employed pre-move	64.6%	73.6%
(No. of cases)	(65)	(144)
Never employed pre-move	30.2%	46.2%
(No. of cases)	(43)	(80)
Total	50.9%	63.8%*
(No. of cases)	(108)	(224)

* Indicates statistically significant difference between city and suburban movers.

TABLE 4: Comparison of Pre-Move and Post-Move Wages and Hours Worked for City and Suburban Movers

	Pre-Move	Post-Move
City movers, post-move earners (n=55)		
Mean hourly wages	$5.04	$6.20*
Mean hours per week	33.3	31.9
Suburban movers, post-move earners (n=143)		
Mean hourly wages	$4.96	$6.00*
Mean hours per week	33.6	33.4

* Indicates statistically significant difference between pre-move and post-move.

When asked how the suburban move helped them get jobs, all suburban participants mentioned the greater number of jobs in the suburbs. Improved physical safety was the second most mentioned factor. Adults reported that they did not work in the city because they feared being attacked on the way home from work, or they feared that their children would get hurt or get in trouble with gangs. The suburban move eliminated that depressing influence, and mothers felt free to go to work. Many adults also mentioned that positive role models and social norms inspired them to work. These comments support William Julius Wilson's contention about the importance of role models and social norms (Wilson, 1987). Seeing neighbors work, Gautreaux adults reported that they felt that they too could have jobs, and they wanted to try. In the city, few adults saw neighbors working.

In sum, the employment rates of suburban movers surpassed those of city movers, particularly for those who had never had a job before. Whatever made these people unemployed in the past—lack of skills or lack of motivation—was not irreversible, and many took jobs after moving to suburbs. This program helped close the gap between low-income, Black adults and their White, middle-income neighbors.

Study of Young Children

Given the children's initial poor preparation in city schools and their social disadvantage, we wondered how they would do in the suburban schools. In 1982, we studied how the Gautreaux program affected young children, comparing Gautreaux children who moved within the city and those who moved to the suburbs (Rosenbaum, Rubinowitz, and Kulieke, 1986; Rosenbaum, Kulieke, and Rubinowitz, 1988). The two groups were similar in average age, proportion of females, and mothers' education. The families were predominantly single-mother households in both the suburban (86%) and city (88%) groups.[8]

We found that suburban movers initially had difficulties adapting to the higher expectations in the suburban schools, and their grades suffered in the first years in the suburban schools. How-

---

[8] See Appendix 1 for details. For a complete description of the sample, instrument, and other analyses, see Rosenbaum, Kulieke, and Rubinowitz, 1988.

ever, by the time of our study, after one to six years in the suburbs, their grades and relative school performance (judged by
their mothers) were the same as those of city movers. In addition, compared to city movers, suburban movers had smaller
classes, higher satisfaction with teachers and courses, and better
attitudes about school. Although the mothers noted instances of
teacher racial bias, the suburban movers were also more likely
than city movers to say that teachers went out of their way to help
their children, and they mentioned many instances of teachers giving extra help in classes and after school.

It is hard to measure academic standards, and we had no systematic indicator in the first study. Yet the mothers who moved
to the suburbs clearly felt that the suburban schools had higher
academic standards, and they reported many observations that
supported their views. They reported that the city teachers did not
expect children to make up work when they were absent, to do
homework, to know multiplication in third grade, or to write in
cursive in fourth grade. "Passing grades" in the city did not indicate achievement at grade level, and even "honor roll" city students were sometimes two years behind grade level.

These mothers were in a good position to notice these differences when their children moved from the city to suburban
schools:

> He was an honor roll student in Chicago. But when he came
> here . . . the school work is much harder here than it was in the
> city. He's just learning what they have had already. Now that
> he's picking it up, he's doing O.K. They might have had the
> things that he had in 7th grade in 5th grade or 6th. So when he
> got to 7th grade, he really didn't know the basics of what they
> had done already. He was an honor roll student in Chicago.
> But when he came here, he realized that the [Chicago] honor
> roll wasn't the honor roll [in the suburban school].

Another mother commented:

> [The suburban school] said it was like he didn't even go to
> school in Chicago for three years, that's how far behind he was.
> And he was going every day and he was getting report cards
> telling me he was doing fine.

Indeed, one mother reported an empirical test:

> The move affected my child's education for the better. I even
> tested it out . . . [I] let her go to summer school by my moth-

er's house [in Chicago] for about a month . . . she was in
fourth grade at that time . . . Over in the city, they were doing
third grade work; what they were supposed to be doing was
fourth grade.

The city curriculum seemed to be one to three years behind the
suburban schools (Rosenbaum, Kulieke, and Rubinowitz, 1988,
p. 32).

Although many suburban movers seemed to be catching up to
the higher suburban standards by the time of the interviews, most
had only been in the suburbs a few years, and most were still in
elementary school, so it was hard to know how they would do
later. Many of these children were still struggling to catch up,
and it was not clear whether they would succeed.

Study of Youth

To study later outcomes, we interviewed these children and their
mothers in 1989.[9] By this time, their average age was eighteen.
However, before turning to those results, it is useful to describe
the schools that youths attended. In 1990, the Illinois State Board
of Education collected average standardized test scores for all
schools in the state. For the schools attended by our sample, the
suburban schools' average eleventh grade reading test score (259)
was just above the state average (250) but significantly higher than
the city schools' average (198). On the ACT, the college admis-
sions test most often taken in Illinois, suburban schools' scores
(21.5) were close to the state average (20.9), but significantly
higher than the city schools' scores (16.1). Moreover, there was
*almost no overlap between the scores of city and suburban schools
these children attended.* Whereas less than 6 percent of the city
sample attended schools with ACT averages of 20 or better (i.e.,
roughly the national average), over 88 percent of the suburban
sample attended such schools. Just as the 1982 study found higher
standards in suburban elementary schools, these results suggest
that the higher standards in the suburbs continued in high school.

Of course, higher standards create new challenges as well as
new opportunities. The suburban movers must face much higher
expectations than they have been prepared for in the city schools.

---

[9] For a complete description of the sample, instrument, and other
analyses, see Rosenbaum and Kaufman, 1991.

The higher levels of achievement in suburban schools may be a barrier to poorly prepared students and may lead to increased drop-out rates, lower grades, lower tracks for those still in school, and to less college attendance and less employment for those over age eighteen. The results of this study contradict those expectations.

High school performance: Although test scores were not available for individual respondents, grades provide a good indication of students' achievement relative to their schoolmates and whether students' work is judged acceptable by teachers. We found that suburban movers had virtually the same grades as city movers (a C+ average in both city and suburbs). At the same time, more city movers dropped out of high school than did suburban movers (20% in the city vs. less than 5% in the suburbs).

High school tracking: Most high schools offer different curricula to college-bound and non-college-bound youth, and these curricula affect college opportunities (Rosenbaum, 1976, 1980). Since students with weak academic backgrounds are often prevented from entering college tracks, we might expect suburban movers to be less likely than city movers to be in college-track classes. The results showed the opposite. Suburban movers were more often in college tracks than city movers (40.3% vs. 23.5%).

College attendance: What happens to students after high school is important not only in terms of college attendance, but also in terms of type of college. Four-year institutions lead to a bachelor's degree, two-year junior or community colleges lead to an associate's degree, and trade schools lead to a certificate. Moreover, while transfers to four-year colleges are theoretically possible, trade schools seldom actually lead to four-year colleges, and two-year colleges rarely do. In the Chicago area, the transfer rate from two-year to four-year colleges was 12.5 percent in 1982 (Orfield, Mitzell, et al., 1984).

Our study of Gautreaux youth showed that suburban movers had significantly higher college enrollment than city movers (54% vs. 21%). Moreover, among those attending college, almost 50 percent of the suburban movers were in four-year institutions, whereas only 20 percent of the city movers were. Of those not attending four-year institutions, two-thirds of the suburban movers were working toward an associate's degree, while just half of the city movers were.

Clearly, the suburban students have not suffered from the challenging competition in suburban schools. Indeed, they have benefited from the higher academic standards in the suburbs, in terms of both staying in high school and enrolling in college. Finally, as shown in Table 5, for those youth who were not attending college, a significantly higher proportion of the suburban youth had full-time jobs than city youth (75% vs. 41%). Suburban youth also had significantly higher pay than city youth, and the suburban jobs were significantly more likely to offer job benefits than city jobs (55% vs. 23%).

TABLE 5: Education and Job Outcomes for Youth: City-Suburban Comparison

	City	Suburbs
Dropped out of school	20%	5%
College track	24	40 *
Attend college	21	54 *
Attend four-year college	4	27 *
Employed full-time (if not in college)	41	75 *
Pay under $3.50 per hour	43	9 *
Pay over $6.50 per hour	5	21 *
Job benefits	23	55 *

* Indicates statistically significant difference between city and suburban movers.

Factors Contributing to Closing the Educational Gap

Although many education programs have little success in closing the gap between Blacks and Whites, the Gautreaux program had some impressive successes for children. One key to the improved college attendance comes from the finding on tracking in high schools. Tracking is often blamed for perpetuating the disadvantages of Blacks. Researchers have found that Blacks are underrepresented in college tracks in racially integrated schools (Coleman et al., 1966; Oakes, 1985; Rosenbaum and Presser, 1978). Indeed, after being desegregated, the Washington, D.C., public schools initiated a tracking system, which a court ruled to be undercutting integration (*Hobson v. Hansen*, 1967). Given the higher standards and greater competition in suburban schools, we might expect these schools to keep low-income Blacks out of college tracks more than the city schools. In fact, we found the opposite, and suburban movers have a higher rate of college-track placements than city movers. This helps explain their higher college attainment compared to city movers.

Another key to improved college attendance may have come from an apparently minor finding: suburban movers had the same grades as city movers. Yet this is somewhat misleading since the same grades probably indicate greater achievement in the suburbs than in the city.

This can be seen in the experience of a child we'll call "Bob." Bob was on the honor roll in the city, but his grades declined when he moved to the suburbs. In 1982, his mother reported that Bob had to work very hard to catch up with his new suburban classmates, and his teachers spent a lot of extra time helping him. By the time of the 1982 interview, his suburban grades had almost caught up with the A's and B's he had received in Chicago. Apparently, catching up with suburban standards had a payoff. In 1989, Bob was in a four-year college, an unusual outcome few city movers achieved. Obviously, the fact that Bob ended up with the same grades in the suburbs as he had had in the city does not reflect how hard he had to work to regain those grades. Bob's A's and B's in suburban schools probably indicate a level of achievement that is one or two grades ahead of the city schools.

Similarly, when "Alice" moved to the suburbs at age 14, she complained that the school was so huge and all White. She wanted to go back to her old school, and she stayed out of school for most of the first week because she was so distressed by the change. By the time of our first interview, after she'd been in the suburb for almost two years, she still often played alone, and she was still working hard to catch up. Unlike the city, where she didn't have to do any homework to get her A grades, she was struggling two hours a night to get Bs and Cs in the suburban high school. Despite her complaints, she said that she was really learning in this school, and she liked what they were teaching her. She also liked the way teachers and counselors worked one-to-one with students. In the city, she disliked the lack of discipline, and sometimes she did not want to go to school because of gangs and fights. Alice reported that most of her suburban friends made good grades, and all will probably go to college. By 1989, her efforts had paid off. She had earned a bachelor's degree and was pursuing a master's degree in business. She reflected that her suburban high school had prepared her well for college, and she had learned good skills and study habits.

Bob and Alice's difficulties in adjusting to suburban high schools are not unusual. We saw the same pattern in many suburban movers. We can also see it in national survey data. We analyzed a national survey of high school sophomores, "High School and Beyond" (HSB), and found that the same grade is associated with a higher achievement test score in suburban schools than in city schools (National Center for Educational Statistics, 1983). For instance, among students with a B average, those in city schools had an average score of 50.72 on the HSB's standardized achievement test, while those in suburban schools had an average score 2.07 points higher. Similarly, among students with a C average, students had 1.53 points higher achievement in suburban schools than city schools (46.71 vs. 45.18).

Put differently, a student who moves from city to suburban schools must have higher achievement to get the same grade. While a typical city student in the HSB got "B's and C's" and had a score of 46.0, if this student moved to the suburbs, his or her test score would put him or her with students several grade categories lower in suburban schools (C's = 46.7; C's and D's = 45.2). Therefore, the finding that suburban movers have the same grades as city movers suggests that suburban movers probably have higher achievement than city movers.

The higher standards in the suburbs led to initial achievement declines for Gautreaux students and required enormous efforts from students and teachers to overcome children's disadvantages. After much effort, most students' grades gradually returned to the level they had been in the city. But these same grades indicate greater achievement in the suburbs, and many of these youths managed to realize their goals of attending four-year colleges. In contrast, although many of those who stayed in the city aspired to the same goal and had the same grades, few managed to attend four-year colleges.

CONCLUSIONS AND POLICY IMPLICATIONS

The results of the studies of the Gautreaux program show that housing vouchers can close the spatial gap between urban Blacks and suburban Whites, and residential integration can help close other gaps between Blacks and Whites. We found that low-income Blacks will choose to move to middle-income, White suburbs if they are given assistance in finding units and counseling about how to deal with the advantages and disadvantages in these areas. The suburban move reduced the social gap as Blacks and Whites interacted in the suburbs. The suburban move also reduced the employment gap, and many adults got jobs for the first time in their lives. However, the education level of adult participants limited the kinds of jobs they got; therefore, a significant gap remained between the jobs of these adults and the jobs of Whites.

The gap was reduced more for the second generation. We found that compared with city movers, the children who moved to the suburbs were more likely to be in school, in college-track classes, in four-year colleges, in jobs, and in jobs with benefits and better pay. The children who went to college or who got jobs with benefits or better pay are on the way toward parity with Whites. The education and employment gaps between low-income, Black youth and middle-income, White youth were significantly reduced. Of course, the children's gains were not immediate. Indeed, virtually all suburban movers experienced great difficulties and lower grades in the first year or two. However, these difficulties were an unavoidable part of adjusting to the higher suburban standards and gaining from the move.

The results of the Gautreaux program are highly encouraging. They suggest that housing vouchers can succeed in moving low-income families to suburbs with better schools and better labor markets and that adults and children will benefit from such moves. This program was able to overcome the reluctance that low-income families naturally feel about moving far from their friends and relatives and into unfamiliar distant suburbs, feelings that prevent other voucher programs from accomplishing such moves.

The Gautreaux program indicates that success is possible but that it requires extensive additional housing services. Real estate staff are needed to locate landlords willing to participate in the program, and placement counselors are needed to inform families about these suburbs, to address their concerns about such moves, and to take them to visit the units and communities. Like participants in other voucher programs, Gautreaux participants were reluctant to move to distant suburbs that they had never seen before, and few would have moved without encouragement from counselors and visits to the suburban apartments. When contrasted with the failures of previous housing voucher programs, the successes of this program indicate the value of having real estate staff and housing counselors.

The studies also suggest some ways that the Gautreaux program could be improved. Transportation was the greatest difficulty that people faced in the suburbs. The suburbs had little or no public transportation, so travel was extremely difficult. Minibus service is probably not practical because few families move to any one location, and a special mini-bus runs the risk of increasing visibility and labeling of participants. If the program could help people finance the purchase of a car, more people might get jobs, children would have an easier time participating in after-school activities, and participants would face fewer frustrations with daily tasks. Child-care assistance would also have been extremely helpful since suburban movers cannot rely on relatives. Finally, job training and education would be helpful. Although this housing voucher program improved employment more than most education or training programs, these various approaches should probably be combined. Indeed, the fact that most suburban and city movers got low-paying jobs indicates the need for better job skills. If the program provided additional education or training, people might get better jobs.

Of course, voucher programs alone are not sufficient to move large numbers of families because of the limited number of housing units available. But if national policy made a long-term commitment to expanding the Section 8 program and increasing suburban moves, then builders and developers could make long-term investments in building apartments to respond to this program over the next decade. Such a program would not be cheap. However, as Alexander Polikoff notes in his chapter, the alternative is to sink many billions of dollars into current housing projects that keep people in areas of the city that hinder their employment and educational opportunities (Polikoff, 1993). As we have seen, that has great human and societal costs in terms of reducing adults' access to employment and children's access to good education.

These studies do support the basic premise of voucher programs—moving people to better areas can improve their self-sufficiency. This should encourage the federal government to see the value of giving housing voucher programs the resources and services needed to succeed. The Gautreaux program shows that moves to better neighborhoods can improve adults' self-sufficiency and can improve the opportunities for their children. Certainly, these benefits make housing vouchers a promising approach, and it is worthwhile to invest more in programs that can lead to these outcomes.

These studies also have implications for non-voucher programs. The results indicate three key factors that helped Gautreaux adults get jobs in the suburbs: personal safety, role models, and access to jobs. If these factors were improved in the city, they might also help city residents. In fact, the Chicago Housing Authority (CHA), at the initiative of its director, Vincent Lane, has recently made impressive efforts to improve safety, role models, and job access in public housing projects. To improve the safety of the housing projects, the CHA has initiated security measures. To provide positive models, the CHA has initiated a mixed-income housing development, Lake Parc Place, that includes working residents who are positive models to their unemployed neighbors. To improve access to suburban jobs, some housing projects have also provided mini-bus service to the suburbs. These are the same factors that Gautreaux adults noted as helping them. However, it is not certain how thorough and successful these efforts will be or whether they will result in greater employment. Even improved security may not make the projects as safe as suburbs, and one-hour commutes may limit the attractiveness of taking a mini-bus to low-paying jobs. It will be some time before we know the success of such programs.

The Gautreaux studies clearly indicate that it is possible to "close the gap" between low-income Blacks and middle-income Whites. Many policymakers have wondered if this is possible, and deficiency theories (like "culture of poverty" theory) suggest that the gap cannot be closed. The Gautreaux results clearly contradict deficiency theories about the poor. Virtually all Gautreaux participants have been exposed to "culture of poverty" factors like public assistance, negative work attitudes, and the work disincentives of the welfare system, yet many got jobs after moving to suburbs and their children experienced greater educational success than city movers. Our findings clearly indicate that the pessimistic predictions of "culture of poverty" models are not supported. The early experiences of low-income Blacks do not prevent them from benefiting from suburban moves.

The success of the Gautreaux program points to a basic point that is often overlooked: geographic location has large effects on opportunities. When people do not gain from training or education programs, it may be because of *deficiencies in their environment, not in themselves*. Programs that help people escape areas of concentrated poverty may improve employment and educational opportunities.

APPENDIX 1: DESIGN OF THE STUDIES

The adult survey mailed questionnaires to a random sample of Gautreaux heads of households in the fall of 1988. We surveyed only female heads-of-household because few Gautreaux households have adult males present. The survey's response rate was 67 percent, including 108 city movers and 224 suburban movers. The adult interview study conducted in-depth interviews with 95 Gautreaux participants in their homes (52 suburban movers and 43 city movers). These studies were used to examine adults' social integration and employment, with the larger survey being the basis of quantitative results (except where noted) and the interviews being the basis of qualitative findings.

Given the severe constraints on participants' choices, we expected city and suburban movers to be highly comparable, and the survey confirmed that expectation. Both groups were similar in their time in the program (about five years), their number of children (2.5), their marital status (about 7% were married), their education (an average of just under 12 years), and their pre-move employment (60% had worked before moving, and both groups earned about $5.00 per hour). Just over 50 percent of both groups reported that their own mothers had received public aid. Because the two groups were highly similar, the city movers are a good comparison group for the suburban movers.

The first children's study examined the experiences of children from families that entered the Gautreaux program between 1976 and 1981. The initial sample included families that had at least one school-aged child before entering the program. The two groups had similar average ages (11.8 years suburb, 13.1 city) and similar proportions of females (52% suburb, 56% city). Most of the families had female heads-of-household in both the suburban (86%) and city (88%) groups. Virtually none of the mothers in either group had finished college, and similar proportions had twelve or fewer years of school (53% suburb and 57% city).[10]

---

[10] The mothers from the 1982 study of children were less educated than those in the 1988 adult survey because they were older and came from an earlier cohort, for whom dropping out of high school was more

The youth study followed up these same children and was able to locate 66 percent of the original sample. The 1989 study interviewed 68 suburban movers and 39 city movers. As with the adult sample, the suburban and city samples for the youth study were very similar. The two groups of youth had similar average ages (18.8 years suburban, 18.2 years city), with a range of 15-25 in both groups. Gender composition was the only significant difference between suburban and city movers in the 1989 youth study. Males were 61.5 percent of the suburban sample and 42.9 percent of the city sample. To remove the potential confounding influence, we tested all results to see if they were altered after controlling for gender. Gender had no effects on any of the outcomes reported here, and controlling for gender did not affect any of these results (see Rosenbaum and Kaufman, 1991).

We compared the 1982 attributes of the full 1982 sample with the 1982 attributes of the people we located in 1989. All differences were small and statistically insignificant. The re-interviewed mothers had the same 1982 education as the full 1982 group, and the re-interviewed children had the same grades, the same rates of being in special education in 1982, the same rates of moving to the suburbs vs. city, and the same ages. The only difference that approached statistical significance was that the re-interviewed children were more likely than the original full sample to have gotten in trouble with teachers in 1982. If that were statistically significant, we might conclude that we found more troublemakers, but the difference is not significant. In sum, the re-interviewed sample would seem to be very representative of the original 1982 sample.

---

common. Low-income people move often, so they are difficult to locate over a seven-year period. We located 66 percent, a reasonably large percentage for such a sample. Of course, one must wonder what biases arise from this attrition and whether we were more likely to lose the least successful people (because they were harder to find) or the most successful ones (because they got jobs in distant locations). We suspect that both happened, but if one happened more often, then the 1988 sample could be seriously different from the original 1982 sample.

APPENDIX 2: PROGRAM SELECTION PROCEDURES AND
GENERALIZABILITY OF GAUTREAUX PARTICIPANTS

The Gautreaux program had three selection criteria that could
make participants distinctive from other housing project residents,
but none of these was extremely selective. First, because suburbs
rarely have large apartments, the program selects families with
four or fewer children. Yet 95 percent of AFDC families have
four or fewer children and 90 percent have three or fewer, so this
is not a serious restriction (U.S. Department of Health and Human
Services, 1987). Second, as in the Section 8 program, Gautreaux
applicants are screened to ensure that they regularly pay their rent
and that they have some source of income (usually AFDC). The
Leadership Council for Metropolitan Open Communities estimates
that about 12 percent are rejected by the credit check or rental
record. Third, applicants are eliminated if their housekeeping
would make them undesirable tenants. This evaluation has the
most potential for biases, but we saw no evidence of it. Accompanying a counselor on such a visit, we noted that counselors
looked for damage to apartments and general cleanliness (taking
garbage out), but the counselor ignored minor disorder and did not
check closets. In actual practice, only about 13 percent of families are rejected on these grounds (Peroff, Davis, and Jones,
1979).

Gautreaux participants are, therefore, probably not typical of
public housing residents in general; they are in some respects
among the "best" public housing residents. They have smaller
families, they have good rent-paying records, and they meet
housekeeping standards (on the day of the counselor's appointment). However, the requirements of the Gautreaux program are
not so stringent as to make participants totally atypical. Program
experience indicates that the three criteria sequentially eliminated
5 percent, 13 percent, and 12 percent, so together they reduce the
eligible pool by less than 30 percent ($.95 \times .88 \times .87 = .727$).
Self-selection may further reduce generalizability, but if these
factors are correlated with the above three criteria, their additional
impact may be quite small. It seems most likely that Gautreaux
families represent over half of public housing residents, but that
is a very rough guess. With over 100,000 families in Chicago
housing projects, the program participants are likely to represent
a large number of people.

To address this issue further, we compared Gautreaux participants with a random sample of AFDC recipients in Chicago (Pop-

kin, 1988). Gautreaux participants are similar to the Chicago AFDC sample in their length of time on public assistance (about 7 years) and their marital status (about 45% never married, 10% currently married). However, Gautreaux participants are less likely to be high school dropouts (39% vs. 50%), tend to be older (median age of 34 vs. 31), and have fewer children (mean of 2.5 vs. 3.0). However, they are more likely to be second-generation AFDC recipients (44% vs. 32%). In sum, although Gautreaux participants may be slightly higher status than the average public assistance recipient, most differences are not large.

REFERENCES

Bassi, Laurie J., and Orley Ashenfelter (1986). "The Effects of Direct Job Creation and Training Programs on Low-Skilled Workers." In Sheldon H. Danziger and Daniel H. Weinberg, eds., *Fighting Poverty: What Works and What Doesn't*. Cambridge, Mass.: Harvard University Press.

Berry, Brian J. L. (1979). *The Open Housing Question: Race and Housing in Chicago, 1966-76*. Cambridge, Mass.: Ballinger.

Coleman, James S., et al. (1966). *Equality of Educational Opportunity*. Washington, D.C.: U.S. Government Printing Office.

Cronin, Francis J., and David W. Rasmussen (1981). "Mobility." In Raymond J. Struyk and Marc Bendick, Jr., eds., *Housing Vouchers for the Poor: Lessons from a National Experiment*. Washington, D.C.: Urban Institute Press.

Crain, Robert Lee, and Carol Sachs Weisman (1972). *Discrimination, Personality and Achievement: A Survey of Northern Blacks*. New York: Seminar Press.

Danziger, Sheldon, and R. G. Wood (1991). "Black Male Joblessness in the 1980s." Unpublished analyses, University of Michigan.

Ellwood, David T. (1986). "The Spatial Mismatch Hypothesis: Are There Teen-age Jobs Missing in the Ghetto?" In Richard B. Freeman and Harry J. Holzer, eds., *The Black Youth Unemployment Crisis*. Chicago: University of Chicago Press.

Farley, Reynolds, Suzanne Bianchi, and Dianne Colasanto (1979). "Barriers to the Racial Integration of Neighborhoods: The Detroit Case," *Annals of the American Academy of Political and Social Science*, vol. 441 (January 1979), pp. 97-113.

Ford, W. Scott (1972). "Interracial Public Housing in a Border City: Another Look at the Contact Hypothesis," *American*

Journal of Sociology, vol. 78, no. 6 (May 1972), pp. 1426-1447.

Gehm, John (1984). *Bringing It Home*. Chicago: Chicago Review Press.

Gerard, Harold B., and Norman Miller (1975). *School Desegregation: A Long-Term Study*. New York: Plenum Press.

Grant, Linda (1984). "Black Females' 'Place' in Desegregated Classrooms," *Sociology of Education*, vol. 57, no. 2 (April 1984), pp. 98-111.

Hahn, Andrew, and Robert Lerman (1985). *What Works in Youth Employment Policy?* Washington, D.C.: National Planning Association.

Hobson v. Hansen (1967). 269 F. Supp. 401 (D.D.C.).

Hoelter, Jon W. (1982). "Segregation and Rationality in Black Status Aspiration Processes," *Sociology of Education*, vol. 55, no. 1 (January 1982), pp. 31-39.

Holland, Alyce, and Thomas Andre (1987). "Participation in Extracurricular Activities in Secondary School: What Is Known, What Needs to Be Known?" *Review of Educational Research*, vol. 57, no. 4 (Winter 1987), pp. 437-466.

Jencks, Christopher S., and Susan E. Mayer (1989). *Residential Segregation, Job Proximity, and Black Job Opportunities: The Empirical Status of the Spatial Mismatch Hypothesis*. Evanston, Ill.: Center for Urban Affairs and Policy Research, Northwestern University.

Kain, John F. (1968). "Housing Segregation, Negro Employment, and Metropolitan Decentralization," *Quarterly Journal of Economics*, vol. 82, no. 2 (May 1968), pp. 175-197.

Kasarda, John D. (1989). "Urban Industrial Transition and the Underclass," *Annals of the American Academy of Political and Social Science*, vol. 501 (January 1989), pp. 26-47.

_____ (1990). "Urban Employment Change and Minority Skills Mismatch." In Lawrence B. Joseph, ed., *Creating Jobs, Creating Workers: Economic Development and Employment in Metropolitan Chicago*. Chicago: Center for Urban Research and Policy Studies, University of Chicago; distributed by University of Illinois Press.

Lewis, Oscar (1968). "The Culture of Poverty." In Daniel Patrick Moynihan, ed., *On Understanding Poverty: Perspectives for the Social Sciences*. New York: Basic Books.

Massey, Douglas S., and Nancy A. Denton (1987). "Trends in the Residential Segregation of Blacks, Hispanics, and Asians:

1970-1980," *American Sociological Review*, vol. 52, no. 6 (December 1987), pp. 802-825.

Mead, Lawrence M. (1986). *Beyond Entitlement: The Social Obligations of Citizenship.* New York: Free Press.

National Center for Educational Statistics (1983). *High School and Beyond: 1980 Sophomore Cohort First Follow-up (1982): Data File Users Manual.* Chicago: National Opinion Research Center.

NCI Research (1991). *Identifying Employment Opportunities for Chicago Inner City Residents.* Evanston, Ill.: Institute for Urban Economic Development.

Oakes, Jeannie (1985). *Keeping Track.* New Haven: Yale University Press.

Orfield, Gary, Howard Mitzell, et al. (1984). *Chicago Study of Access and Choice in Higher Education.* Chicago: Department of Political Science, University of Chicago.

Patchen, Martin (1982). *Black-White Contact in Schools: Its Social and Academic Effects.* West Lafayette, Ind.: Purdue University Press.

Peroff, Kathleen A., Cloteal L. Davis, and Ronald Jones (1979). *Gautreaux Housing Demonstration: An Evaluation of Its Impact on Participating Households.* Washington, D.C.: Division of Policy Studies, Office of Policy Development and Research, U.S. Department of Housing and Urban Development.

Persell, Caroline H. (1977). *Education and Inequality.* New York: Free Press.

Polikoff, Alexander (1993). "'Chicago Is Not About to Give Up on a Bad Idea': The Future of Public Housing High-Rises." In this volume.

Popkin, Susan J. (1988). *Welfare: A View From the Bottom.* Evanston, Ill.: Unpublished dissertation, Northwestern University.

Rosenbaum, James E. (1976). *Making Inequality: The Hidden Curriculum of High School Tracking.* New York: Wiley.

_____ (1980). "Social Implications of Educational Grouping." In David C. Berliner, ed., *Review of Educational Research.* Washington, D.C.: American Educational Research Association.

_____ (1988). "An Evaluation of Project Self-Sufficiency in Cook County." Evanston, Ill.: Center for Urban Affairs and Policy Research, Northwestern University.

Rosenbaum, James E., and Julie E. Kaufman (1991). "Educational and Occupational Achievements of Low-Income Black

Youth in White Suburbs." Paper presented to the Annual Meeting of the American Sociological Association, Cincinnati, August 1991.

Rosenbaum, James E., Marilyn J. Kulieke, and Leonard S. Rubinowitz (1988). "White Suburban Schools' Responses to Low-Income Black Children: Sources of Successes and Problems, *The Urban Review*, vol. 20, no. 1 (Spring 1988), pp. 28-41.

Rosenbaum, James E., and Susan J. Popkin (1990). "Economic and Social Impacts of Housing Integration." Evanston, Ill.: Center for Urban Affairs and Policy Research, Northwestern University.

_____ (1991). "Employment and Earnings of Low-Income Blacks Who Move to Middle-Class Suburbs." In Christopher Jencks and Paul E. Peterson, eds., *The Urban Underclass.* Washington, D.C.: Brookings Institution.

Rosenbaum, James E., and Stefan Presser (1978). "Voluntary Racial Integration in a Magnet School," *School Review*, vol. 86, no. 2 (February 1978), pp. 156-186.

Rosenbaum, James E., Leonard S. Rubinowitz, and Marilyn J. Kulieke (1986). "Low-Income Black Children in White Suburban Schools." Evanston, Ill.: Center for Urban Affairs and Policy Research, Northwestern University.

Schuman, Howard, and Lawrence Bobo (1988). "Survey-Based Experiments on White Racial Attitudes Toward Residential Integration," *American Journal of Sociology*, vol. 94, no. 2 (September 1988), pp. 273-299.

Squires, Gregory D., Larry Bennett, Kathleen McCourt, and Philip Nyden (1987). *Chicago: Race, Class, and the Response to the Urban Decline.* Philadelphia: Temple University Press.

Steinberg, Stephen (1981). *The Ethnic Myth: Race, Ethnicity and Class in America.* New York: Atheneum.

St. John, Nancy H. (1975). *School Desegregation Outcomes for Children.* New York: John Wiley and Sons.

U.S. Bureau of Labor Statistics (1990). *Geographic Profile of Employment and Unemployment, 1989.* Washington, D.C.: U.S. Government Printing Office.

U.S. Department of Health and Human Services (1987). *Characteristics and Financial Circumstances of AFDC Recipients 1986.* Washington, D.C.: Family Support Administration, Office of Family Assistance, U.S. Department of Health and Human Services.

Williams, Robin M. (1964). *Strangers Next Door: Ethnic Relations in American Communities.* Englewood Cliffs, N.J.: Prentice-Hall.

Wilson, William Julius (1987). *The Truly Disadvantaged: The Inner City, the Underclass, and Public Policy.* Chicago: University of Chicago Press.

Winkler, Donald R. (1975). "Educational Achievement and School Peer Group Composition," *Journal of Human Resources,* vol. 10, no. 2 (Spring 1975), pp. 189-204.

Yinger, John (1979). "Prejudice and Discrimination in the Urban Housing Market." In Peter Mieszkowski and Mahlon Straszheim, eds., *Current Issues in Urban Economics.* Baltimore: Johns Hopkins University Press.

Zeul, Carolyn R., and Craig R. Humphrey (1971). "The Integration of Black Residents in Suburban Neighborhoods: A Re-examination of the Contact Hypothesis," *Social Problems,* vol. 18, no. 4 (Spring 1971), pp. 462-474.

COMMENTS

Paul B. Fischer

In the fall of 1979, as a member of the President's urban policy staff, located at the U.S. Department of Housing and Urban Development (HUD), I was asked by my superior, Bob Embry, then Assistant Secretary for Community Planning and Development, to comment on a report, prepared by HUD's research arm, that critically assessed the early experience of the Gautreaux program. The report concluded that out of an eligible plaintiff class of over 40,000 families, fewer than 400 families had been placed by the program over the previous two to three years, indicating a serious lack of client interest. Why spend scarce HUD resources on a program clients didn't want? Why support a program that violated the dominant ethos that only in-place, community-oriented antipoverty strategies were appropriate for minority groups? The Gautreaux program survived that report in part because of the continued support of Bob Embry, in part because HUD, obligated to allocate Section 8 certificates and administrative funds by court order, had no alternative, and in part because of the increase in client demand as more Gautreaux families successfully moved to White areas.

By the end of the 1970s, desegregation approaches lost much of their momentum and legitimacy, victims of unrealized expectations and Black-power politics. With the change to a more conservative direction, the other subsidized housing desegregation efforts begun in the Nixon and Carter years, such as area-wide housing opportunity plans and regional housing mobility programs, were phased out. Only the Gautreaux program, protected by legal sanction, remained as a prototype mobility program. With over fifteen years of experience and more than 4,000 placements, Gautreaux provides an excellent opportunity to examine the effectiveness of the housing desegregation and mobility approach in dealing with inner-city poverty, as well as contributing to possible new policy initiatives that could duplicate Gautreaux efforts across the country. James Rosenbaum's chapter summarizes the results of nearly ten years of such an

effort conducted by a team of social scientists and graduate
students at Northwestern University.

In many ways, the research findings described in the Rosenbaum chapter fulfill all the most optimistic expectations of
mobility advocates, as well as calling into question many of the
negative stereotypes about the behavior of both the Black poor
and the White suburban middle class.   Black families from the
inner city successfully settled in middle-class White suburbs
with a minimum of problems.   The educational achievement of
the children improved in suburban schools with greater resources and safer environments.   More of the parents were employed in expanding suburban labo markets.   But skepticism
remains, rooted in practical, politica, and ideological considerations.   My comments attempt to address that skepticism by discussing a research agenda that builds on the work of Rosenbaum and his colleagues, with the goal of implementing an effective nationwide antipoverty housing mobility strategy.

The Rosenbaum chapter is a case study of a program confined to one metropolitan area.   Like any case study, it is difficult to generalize to other areas or to the national context.   The
lack of a comparative perspective is particularly limiting for
policy development.   In the last ten years, prompted by litigation, other more modest mobility efforts have begun in a number of cities, including Memphis and Dallas.   My own evaluation research, following along the lines of the Gautreaux study,
focuses on a similar, although smaller, mobility program in
Cincinnati that has been operating under court order for about
five years.

Like Gautreaux, the impact of the program in general was
very favorable, and many of the Gautreaux findings were replicated in Cincinnati, particularly in the area of social integration.
However, the school and job findings differed somewhat.   The
contrast between city and suburban movers was not as great as
with Gautreaux families.   This may be explained, in part, by
the contrasting nature of the Cincinnati metropolitan area.   It is
much smaller than Chicago, with a smaller suburban proportion
of the metropolitan area, smaller and less isolated Black ghettos, and, more important, economic and social boundaries between city and suburbs that are less defined.   The city schools
have implemented an elaborate magnet school desegregation
program, proportionately much larger than in Chicago, so many
of the mobility children did not change schools when they
changed neighborhoods.   In addition, the magnet schools are

not that different racially or qualitatively from the suburban schools. Clearly, the nature of the program service area may affect the findings. Subsequent research should integrate data from these different metropolitan sites in developing a national mobility policy.

Another dimension of comparability that is absent from much of the Rosenbaum research is a control group of public-housing tenants living in the inner city, those who were similar in demographic character and part of the plaintiff class, but did not take advantage of the mobility program. In Cincinnati, such a group was interviewed. In contrast to the findings in the Gautreaux study, there was little significant difference in the job experience of suburban and city movers. In fact, suburban movers were earning 7 percent less money than city movers. But more important, mobility clients earned 20 percent more after the move than those who stayed in public housing, and 57 percent of mobility respondents were employed, compared to 24 percent in public housing. Once again, the "peculiarities" of the Cincinnati job market may explain some of the difference, but using public-housing tenants as a control group illuminates more clearly the effects of mobility programs. In Cincinnati, moves into predominantly White areas, no matter where, were more important for mobility respondents than moves from the city to the suburbs. It might be useful to replicate these studies in other areas with mobility programs, such as Memphis and Dallas.

Another research limitation in both the Chicago and Cincinnati studies is the dependence on respondent interviews for most of the evaluation data. Time and resource constraints, as well as the availability of information and privacy concerns, necessitate such limitations. But follow-up studies are required that focus on other data sources and variables, such as the impact of the program on receiving communities. Information about White resident experiences with the program will improve levels of program acceptance and open up more housing opportunities for mobility clients. It is not clear whether Gautreaux clients who returned to the ghetto or dropped out of the program were interviewed by Rosenbaum, but they represent a source of experiences worth examining to get a total picture of program impact. As Gautreaux and other programs mature, longitudinal evaluations become more possible. Comparisons of the same clients over time add greatly to our knowledge of program effectiveness. The impact of mobility programs on the larger issue of metropolitan racial segregation and Black suburbanization can be delineated by exploring the link between Gautreaux placements and other Black migration to a community. In developing an effective national mobility strategy, research must go beyond impact issues to include management questions involving costs and administrative procedures, as well as potential connections with other antipoverty strategies such as job training and placement.

In conclusion, Rosenbaum and his colleagues have made a major contribution to the poverty policy debate. Through their research, they have given greater credibility to one of the most controversial antipoverty programs in operation. Rosenbaum proves that the Gautreaux program has been a success. The next important question is how to build on that success. Should the program be greatly expanded in the Chicago area? Should its focus be skewed more to the suburbs and linked more directly to areas of job growth? Should it be implemented on a national scale as part of the HUD subsidized housing programs? Should its services be expanded to include job training and placement? A comprehensive research agenda could address these questions. The research described in the Rosenbaum chapter offers an excellent foundation for that effort.

THE HOMELESS IN CHICAGO

Charles Hoch[*]

During the 1980s, the poor in the United States got poorer and homelessness increased. The visibility of destitute people sleeping and begging on city streets evoked public sympathy and concern. Reporters, researchers, and policy analysts of all sorts studied the homeless. Some explored how and why poor people became homeless. Others analyzed how changes in the housing system increased the risk of homelessness. Political and policy conflicts emerged among research analysts, political advocates, and public officials over the reasons for homelessness. Those studying homeless people argued for programs to treat and serve poor households and individuals. Those studying housing proposed changes in the organization and implementation of private and public housing programs that would increase housing affordability for the poor.

Public policies so far tend to reflect the people-centered rather than housing-centered assessment of the problem. Plans for the homeless offer a series of services and shelters organized to help homeless individuals become self-sufficient. Public funding has expanded to support caretaking institutions serving the individual victims of illness and misfortune. In contrast, public programs adopted to redress economic injustice, such as public aid and subsidized housing, have contracted.

This chapter describes the homeless problem in Chicago and argues that research evidence shows little support for a definition of the homeless problem based on individual behavior, illness, or misfortune. Homeless people differ from other poor people in ways that reflect institutionalized social and economic stratification rather than patterns of individual pathology or deviance. Efforts to isolate and emphasize what differences exist as matters of individual choice and capacity foster a misleading conception of homelessness as a problem of individual mobility and integration.

[*] Special thanks to Laura Leli for assisting in the gathering of data.

Government at all levels has used this idea to justify short-term
treatment policies rather than long-term prevention policies.

DIMENSIONS OF THE PROBLEM

The Regional Geography of Homelessness

The long-established practice of municipal incorporation, combined with the suburban decentralization of economic prosperity,
contributes to urban poverty while obscuring regional economic
and social interdependencies. Suburban residents and officials too
easily believe the homeless to be a product of cities and not the
suburbs. Growing evidence of suburban homelessness has not
stimulated much in the way of public response. Nonprofit shelter
providers and other caretakers find themselves fighting the powerful exclusionary practices of local municipalities. In effect, with
a few exceptions, the *de facto* policy of exclusion forces the
homeless to move elsewhere, usually Chicago (Carolin, 1988;
Lewis, 1989).

Counting the Homeless

When sociologist Peter Rossi conducted his count of Chicago's
homeless in 1986, he and his colleagues at the National Opinion
Research Center (NORC) adopted a definition using the common-
sense notion of literal homelessness. A homeless person was a
resident of an emergency shelter or was on the streets, in public
places or in places that could be reached without destroying property between the hours of 1 a.m. and 6 a.m. The analysts estimated that the number of homeless averaged between 2,000 and
2,800 individuals on any given night, while between 4,600 and
7,000 were homeless at least once during the course of a year
(Rossi, Fisher, and Willis, 1986, pp. 22-23, 65).
      The most recent counts of the "literal" homeless on the streets
and in shelters have provided higher estimates than those made in
the Rossi study. The U.S. Census completed a survey of street
people in March 1990 and found 1,500 homeless individuals—a
smaller estimate than that in Rossi's 1986 survey (Butzen, 1991).
Presently, the Chicago Department of Human Services keeps tabs
on the number of clients who use emergency shelters in Chicago.
Avoiding duplicate counting, they estimate that during the nine

months between July 1990 and March 1991, 20,700 people stayed in a shelter (Edens, 1991).

If we relax the cut-off for who counts as homeless just slightly, say from daily to weekly shelter uncertainty, the number of homeless climbs greatly. Rossi wrote about this relationship in his 1986 report in which he claimed "there is a continuum running from the obviously domiciled to the obviously homeless, with many ambiguous cases to be encountered along that continuum" (Rossi, Fisher, and Willis, 1986). Those with the most tenuous and insecure housing status are most vulnerable to the threat of homelessness, and, under adverse conditions, they move ever closer to the end of the continuum. They share their vulnerability to changing conditions and an uncertain housing status with the homeless, although many will remain in the gray area along the continuum.

The weekly tenant of a rooming house or single-room-occupancy (SRO) hotel would not, using the common-sense notion, be considered homeless. But the same tenant, using the cut-off of weekly shelter uncertainty, would. A November 1990 regional household survey found that slightly more than 1 percent (1.3%) of Chicago households reported having "someone live with them for a short time because they had nowhere else to go." That would mean approximately 13,000 households offered short-term shelter for people who might otherwise have gone homeless (Taylor, 1991). The number of people housed through such sharing for longer periods of time would probably be much larger than this. If we included weekly renters in SRO hotels and in rooming and lodging houses, the number would increase even more dramatically.

Describing Composition and Characteristics

Michael Sosin, Paul Colson, and Susan Grossman (1988) conducted a study of Chicago's homeless at about the same time as Rossi and his colleagues. However, they did not count the homeless, but rather explored the relationships between the literally homeless (defined somewhat more broadly than in the Rossi study) and the broader poverty population in the gray area of the continuum. The Sosin report compares the homeless poor with the never-homeless poor, testing not only the association between individual vulnerabilities (e.g., mental illness, alcoholism) and homelessness, but also the relationship between institutional practices (e.g., welfare agency policies) and homelessness.

The studies by Rossi and Sosin, despite their many methodological differences, found relatively similar social and demographic characteristics among the homeless. Table 1 compares data from these two studies. The homeless population in Chicago consists largely of unattached, young, Black males with very little money and poor prospects for future employment. The relative youth of the homeless reflects the success of Social Security and subsidized housing programs for the elderly. The homeless enjoy few social ties to relatives and friends to whom they might turn for help, and thus many of them live alone. In addition, the proportion having been jailed or hospitalized is quite high.

Behavior and Homelessness

Reporters, photographers, and other media producers seek to distill the complex social diversity of the homeless into a vivid and legible image or character of human interest. For instance, several studies of the mental health of shelter residents in the early 1980s found that most (as high as 90%) of the homeless suffer from mental illness or addictions (Arce et al., 1983; Bassuk, 1984). Reporters were quick to claim that such afflictions led to homelessness. However, the findings in both the Rossi and Sosin reports indicate much smaller proportions than had been previously estimated (see Table 1). In addition, these rates are considerably less deviant when the homeless are compared to the rest of the poor population (see Table 2).

The study by Sosin, Colson, and Grossman offers perhaps one of the best studies in the country for answering these questions. The study compared two groups of very poor Chicago people; one group housed and the other (either currently or ever) homeless. The analysts used statistical methods to test for the simultaneous influence of economic conditions (e.g., income, employment, public aid), housing (e.g., rent, type of accommodation), institutional experience (e.g., incarceration, detox, medical clinic, mental health facility), and behavior (e.g., responses to psychological tests, drinking behavior) on the likelihood that a very poor person would be homeless. Sosin and his colleagues found that homelessness in Chicago is not directly tied to mental illness or other behavioral problems (e.g., drug use), but rather to a complex interaction of individual behavior, institutional experience, and economic distress. For example, a poor man is more likely to end up with no place to stay when he has a history of institutional placement in a foster home, has had military experience, lives alone, goes on drinking binges, and suffers a severe economic hardship (e.g., a big rent increase or an eviction). Or taking another case, a mentally ill poor person with the same income as a healthy poor person, but who pays much less of his or her income for rent, usually has less chance of becoming homeless than the healthy person. But, if both have the same rent burden, then the person suffering from mental illness will bear a greater risk of going homeless (Sosin, Colson, and Grossman, 1988).

The evidence in the Sosin report documents the vulnerability of the homeless, but in a way that challenges those who would use evidence of addiction or mental illness to segment and label the homeless population for purposes of treatment. As the slope of economic hardship increases for the poor, those with chronic drinking problems or other particular vulnerabilities are more likely to lose their footing and slip downward into homelessness than are those with more social support and fewer vulnerabilities. Sosin and his colleagues favor employment and public welfare policies that would increase the incomes of the poor and thus reduce the angle of the slope. Programs and policies treating the vulnerabilities of poor individuals should complement rather than compensate for such policies.

Race and Gender

Black men from poor, inner-city households face few opportunities and plenty of obstacles to successful employment and economic security. In 1987, sociologist William Julius Wilson estimated that the unemployment among Black men in Chicago was 42 percent (Wilson, 1987). Unable to obtain even minimal economic autonomy, poor Black men find themselves unable to support a household. Cut off from conventional avenues of gainful employment and forced to endure separation as a condition for helping their families survive, many of these young men pursue unconventional forms of social deviance, resistance, and withdrawal. The proliferation of criminal gangs, the use and sale of drugs, and predatory, even random, violence reflects bad attitudes—but attitudes that reflect a risky and desperate rebellion against the hopeless indignity imposed by the racial exclusion that these men experience.

TABLE 1: Comparing the Findings of Rossi and Sosin Reports on Chicago's
Homeless

	Rossi (1985-86)	Sosin (1986)
Demographic data		
Percent Black	53.0	62.7
Percent male	75.5	63.2
Percent married	6.9	6.2
Average age	36.1	40.3
Source of income		
Percent public transfer	46.2	48.5
Percent employment	34.5	33.0
Average monthly income	$168	$182
Social relations		
Percent seeing no relatives	33.3	34.1
Percent seeing no friends	55.4	49.9
Percent live alone before homeless	48.3	44.7
Institutional experience		
Percent been in jail/prison	47.8	53.1
Percent hospitalized for mental illness	21.5	19.8
Percent not getting medical care	22.3	26.7
Mean months homeless	21.9	35.8
Median months homeless	7.6	6.1
Total (N)	(721)	(177)

Note: Many of the variable values published in the final reports were not directly comparable. Variables were selected on the basis of comparability. The
Sosin report was much broader in scope and analysis than the Rossi report.

Sources: Peter Rossi, Gene Fisher, and Georgianna Willis, *The Condition of
the Homeless in Chicago* (Chicago: National Opinion Research Center, 1986);
Michael Sosin, Paul Colson, and Susan Grossman, *Homelessness in Chicago:
Poverty and Pathology, Social Institutions and Social Change* (Chicago: School
of Social Service Administration, University of Chicago, 1988).

TABLE 2: Comparison of Select Characteristics of Ever- and Never-Homeless
Poor People in Chicago, 1986

	Ever	Never
Demographic data		
Percent Black	67.0	73.4
Percent male	73.1*	64.6
Percent married	5.0	16.4*
Average age	37.8	37.1
Household composition		
Intact family	3.7*	14.1
Childless couple	4.7	4.5
Woman with child, no spouse	15.7	15.3
Man with child, no spouse	1.3	4.3
Household with other relatives	7.7*	37.2
Behavior		
Consumed alcohol in past 30 days	60.6	53.3
Go on drinking binges	21.6*	9.9
Use illegal drugs	15.8	15.4
Institutional experience		
Percent been in jail	65.0*	42.2
Percent been in prison	14.0	10.1
Percent hospitalized for mental illness	20.0*	8.9
Percent with military experience	26.4*	16.1
Percent childhood out of home**	14.5*	7.2
Total (N)	(721)	(177)

* Statistically significant difference between groups.

** Percent who spent time as child outside home of parents (e.g., as a foster child).

Source: Michael Sosin, Paul Colson, and Susan Grossman, *Homelessness in Chicago: Poverty and Pathology, Social Institutions and Social Change* (Chicago: School of Social Service Administration, University of Chicago, 1988).

The separation of young men from family households per-
versely increases housing costs for the poor. Instead of living
with others and pooling incomes to reduce rent burdens, these
poor men are forced to set up their own independent households.
Those who find their own places usually do so in a rooming- or
lodging-house arrangement. Many who no longer can afford a
room and who have exhausted their social ties with family and
friends end up on the streets.

The housing conditions for young Black women with children
are marginally better than those of the men. Basically, public aid,
public housing, and other subsidized housing programs target
women over men because these women remain responsible for the
care of their children. However, public aid levels have been declining (see below), and many young welfare recipients are unable
to make ends meet. Reports by shelter providers in the city of
Chicago have taken notice of the increase in young women and
children who are showing up homeless. Although only about a
quarter of the homeless were women, this still represents an unprecedented proportion compared to virtually any other period of
economic distress in our country's history.

Housing Affordability Squeeze

Many studies have documented how the homeless get trapped in
a housing affordability squeeze (Hoch and Slayton, 1989, pp. 175-
181; Ringheim, 1990; Rossi, 1989, pp. 31-36; Wright, 1989).
Rent burden, the percentage of income spent on shelter, provides
a measure of this squeeze in the private market. Usually, households with very low incomes and unsubsidized housing carry very
high rent burdens. Since they must devote a large share of their
income to the cost of housing, they often sacrifice other necessities.

Throughout the 1960s and 1970s, a rent burden greater than
25 percent was considered excessive. Federal housing administrators in the early 1980s raised the norm to 30 percent, thereby
weakening the federal standard for housing affordability. But
even using much weaker standards (a 35% cut-off), the affordability of housing for renters in Chicago declined dramatically
throughout the 1980s. During the 1970s, only about 30 percent
of renters paid 35 percent or more of their income for rent. However, this proportion shot up to nearly 40 percent by 1983 and to
43 percent by 1987 (see Table 3.)

TABLE 3: Rent Burden for Chicago Renters, 1975-1987

Rent as Pct. of Income	1975	1979	1983	1987
60% or more	13.5%	13.6%	22.2%	22.2%
35-59%	15.8	15.6	17.3	20.9
Less than 35%	67.9	68.9	58.0	55.4
Not available	2.7	1.8	2.5	1.5
Total (N)	(667,000)	(646,000)	(634,200)	(626,300)

Sources: U.S. Bureau of the Census, *Housing Characteristics for Selected Metropolitan Areas: Chicago* (Current Housing Reports, Annual Housing Survey: 1983), U.S. Department of Housing and Urban Development, sponsor (Washington, D.C., 1985); U.S. Bureau of the Census, *Housing Characteristics for Selected Metropolitan Areas: Chicago* (Current Housing Reports, American Housing Survey: 1987), U.S. Department of Housing and Urban Development, sponsor (Washington, D.C., 1990).

The burden does not get spread evenly among renters, but falls heaviest on the shoulders of the poor. In 1979, more than three-fourths of all low-income renter households in Chicago had rent burdens exceeding 30 percent of their gross income. By 1983, this proportion had increased to almost 90 percent, with more than half of these spending over 60 percent of their income for rent. These figures did not diminish with the economic recovery in the latter half of the decade. Evidence of hardship in city-wide surveys indicates that the poor continue to endure the high levels of poverty that developed earlier in the decade (Cook et al., 1986).

Declining incomes for the poor: A recent report on income distribution issued by the Illinois Department of Revenue indicates that the poorest Illinois taxpayers lost ground between 1980 and 1989. Taxpayers with adjusted gross annual incomes less than $10,000 for 1980 accounted for 35 percent of all returns and 8.6 percent of total reported income. By 1989, the same group of low-income taxpayers, then earning less than $15,000 a year

($9,683 in 1980 dollars), accounted for 37.2 percent of all tax filers and only 7.5 percent of total income (Goozner, 1991). The poverty of the poor has increased due to a decline in the value of income both from public assistance programs and lower earnings from unskilled jobs in the service sector. Unlike Social Security pensions, public aid benefits under Aid to Families with Dependent Children (AFDC) and General Assistance (GA) do not have ongoing cost-of-living adjustments. Table 4 shows the declining inflation-adjusted value of AFDC and GA benefits in Illinois between 1968 and 1985. The erosion of public aid benefits continued throughout the second half of the 1980s. A mother with two children who was eligible to receive $341 per month in 1986 could receive only $367 in 1991. This 8 percent increase fell far short of the nearly 28 percent increase in the cost of living for the same five-year period (U.S. Bureau of the Census, 1991). The situation for GA recipients was even worse. A slight increase in benefits from $155 to $165 per month in 1989 was undermined by budget-cutting legislation in 1991 that limited GA recipients to only nine months of benefits. In 1992, the state legislature completely eliminated GA benefits for "employable" adults.

TABLE 4: Average Monthly Public Aid Benefits in Constant (1985) Dollars, State of Illinois, 1968-1985

	1968	1975	1980	1985
Aid to Families with Dependent Children	$644	$568	$362	$342
General Assistance	$322	----	----	$154

Source: Peter Rossi, *Down and Out in America* (Chicago: University of Chicago Press, 1989), p. 191.

In 1987, the median monthly cost of housing for all households below the poverty level in the eight-county Chicago metropolitan area was $321 (U.S. Department of Commerce, 1990, p. 23).[1] Single adults receiving GA benefits of $154 per month could pay several weeks rent in some of the least expensive SRO-type hotels in the mid-1980s or perhaps cover the entire month's rent in a rooming- or lodging-house arrangement. But even among the estimated 3,700 lodgers in Chicago for whom rental data were available, about half paid rent of $200 or more per month in 1987 (U.S. Department of Commerce, 1990, p. 90).

Both the Rossi and Sosin reports found that although most of the Chicago homeless were eligible for public aid, only a fraction got it. General Assistance may not be much, but something proves better than nothing. For example, Sosin found that only 27 percent of the homeless who were eligible for GA got it, while about 76 percent of those who were eligible and had never been homeless got it (Sosin, Colson, and Grossman, 1988, pp. 207-208).

The shifts in the structure of the Chicago labor market have been well documented (Joseph, 1990). In effect, a large portion of the Chicago adult population, disproportionately minority, continues to bear high rates of joblessness. Structural shifts in the economy and regional shifts in the location of jobs, combined with ongoing patterns of racial exclusion, have concentrated the unemployment in the inner-city neighborhoods of Chicago. The result has been increasing poverty and a decline in real incomes.

The latest growth and expansion of suburban development have dramatically tipped the scales from the center to the periphery. The metropolitan region no longer has one dominant economic center, but several competing centers. However, although suburban municipalities have been quick to absorb wealth-producing activity, they have discouraged the location of housing, facilities, and services for the poor, disabled, or otherwise socially marginal members of the regional population. The poor and vulnerable end up concentrated in the inner city (Dear and Wolch, 1987).

Declining supply of low-rent housing: On the supply side, the abandonment, demolition, and conversion of low-rent housing

---

[1] The eight-county Chicago metropolitan area consists of Cook, DuPage, Grundy, Kane, Kendall, Lake, McHenry, and Will counties.

in the United States, especially in cities like Chicago, have disproportionately depleted some of the most affordable stock. The national figures presented in Table 5 tell two stories. First, small, substandard housing rental units in central cities are being removed at a much greater rate than other forms of housing. Second, the least expensive rental units are being removed as well (Sternlieb and Hughes, 1991).

Data for Chicago tell a similar story of removal of low-rent housing units. In both 1979 and 1983, almost 70 percent of the units removed from the housing inventory in Chicago had been occupied by low-income households, with close to half last occupied by a household with an income less than $5,000 (Gunner, Hannan, and Theodore, 1988). Totals that reflect net changes in the housing inventory miss these distributional effects of the decline in the city's housing stock. Approximately a third of these units were inexpensive, single-room dwellings.

TABLE 5:   Characteristics of Housing Units Removed from the Central-City Housing Inventories, 1973-1983

	Total Units 1973	Removals 1973-83	Pct. Loss 1973-83
All units	24,099	2,039	8.5%
Renter-occupied	11,406	1,419	12.4
1 and 2 rooms	1,639	306	18.7
Lack plumbing	370	156	42.2
Less than $80 rent	1,680	359	21.4

Note: Data for entire United States.

Source: George Sternleib and James Hughes, "Private Market Provision of Low Income Housing," *Housing Policy Debate*, vol. 2, no. 2 (1991), p. 132.

The Loss of SROs

The loss of inexpensive SRO hotels in Chicago provides a dramatic example of the perverse impact of a national public policy that promised to improve the housing conditions of the poor. The demolition of the SRO housing stock during the 1960s and 1970s exceeded the provision of public and subsidized housing to the single, poor residents. Even more damaging was the concentrated geographic impact of these policies, which led to the wholesale destruction of the residential community for the single poor, the skid row neighborhoods bordering Chicago's Loop.

During the 20 years following the onset of urban renewal in the early 1960s, most of Chicago's skid row hotels were demolished. The population in group quarters (a measure of cubicle hotel and mission residents) concentrated in the Near West Side dropped more than 90 percent between 1960 and 1970. The number of single-room units also dropped by 80 percent. Most of these were hotels with shared baths and toilets. The loss of rental units displaced the single male population, and with them left the employment agencies, bars, pawn shops, missions, restaurants, barber shops, and other services of skid row. Many in the relatively elderly population died, and others secured subsidized housing, while some moved to rooming houses or SRO hotels in other areas of the city (Hoch and Slayton, 1989).

The destruction of SRO-type units was not limited to skid row. A 1984 survey of the number of SRO hotel units lost citywide estimated that 18,000 SRO hotel units had been converted, abandoned, or destroyed between 1973 and 1984, a loss of more than half the entire stock of SRO units. An update of this report released in 1991 indicated that the loss has continued and that only about 8,800 units of SRO housing remain (Hoch and Slayton, 1989; Lakefront SRO, 1991).

INFORMAL RESPONSES TO THE PROBLEM

Shared Housing

In 1987, about 4.2 million very poor (less than $4,000 annual income), unattached adults between 21 and 59 years of age shared dwellings with parents, relatives, or others in the United States. These figures do not include the poor people living alone on the streets, in shelters, or in SRO accommodations. The number of very poor adults sharing housing in this fashion increased 130 percent between 1969 and 1986, or six times the rate of population growth (Rossi, 1989, pp. 76-81).

Adults with very low incomes are likely candidates for homelessness, a fate prevented by the willingness of an owner or leaseholder to share his or her dwelling. Sharing accommodations still represents the primary, if informal, response to the extreme poverty of poor, single adults in the United States, especially as compared to the formal efforts taken by public and private agencies. Several studies of the homeless show the connection quite clearly. A 1989 study of homelessness among the very poor in New York City found that 71 percent of the homeless had spent the previous night living with others as compared to only 12 percent of the domiciled poor (Knickman and Weitzman, 1989). A 1983 study of GA recipients in Chicago found that half resided with family or friends (Stagner and Richman, 1985). Sosin and his colleagues found a similar proportion (55%) that shared housing in their sample of homeless people (Sosin, Colson, and Grossman, 1988).

However, sharing does not mean that those doubling up stay rent-free. Only 13 percent of the homeless had shared a residence without paying rent. The big difference between the homeless and those never homeless was rent level. Those who were homeless in 1985 had paid an average of $168 a month for their last residence, compared to only $122 a month for the poor who were not homeless (Sosin, Colson, and Grossman, 1988).

Overcrowding

Overcrowding occurs as households retain or take in members who would otherwise have set up their own household in a separate dwelling. When households without surplus dwelling space grow, the result is overcrowding. Overcrowding had declined during the 1970s but increased throughout the 1980s. The increase in Chicago households with more than one person per room has been modest, but it marks a significant turnaround in a long-term downward trend. Worse yet, the increase has been greatest among the most severely overcrowded households, those with 1.5 or more persons per room. In 1990, there were 35,165 overcrowded households. When multiplied by the Chicago average of 2.67 persons per household, this amounts to more than 90,000 people living in overcrowded conditions. In these households, shared housing diminishes the rent burden for everyone involved, but at the expense of an overall decline in the household standard of living (see Table 6).

Rooming and Lodging

Just as overcrowding declined in the 1970s, so too did the number of rental units in Chicago lacking complete kitchen facilities (stove, refrigerator, and sink). In effect, these low-rent, substandard dwellings were being removed from the housing stock. The SRO units mentioned above made up a large portion of this stock. However, between 1983 and 1987, as the number of rental units continued to decline, the number of units lacking complete kitchen facilities actually increased over 100 percent. Because the construction of such substandard rental units is, for the most part, outlawed by City codes, this turnaround does not indicate the construction of new SRO units, but reflects illegal conversion activity within the existing housing stock (see Table 7). Owners (or even tenants) are subdividing apartments or houses into several dwelling units, usually single rooms, and renting these to relatives, friends, or others.

TABLE 6: Changes in Overcrowding, City of Chicago, 1980-1990

Persons Per Room	1980	1990
Fewer than 1.0	92.0%	91.2%
1.01 to 1.5	5.6%	5.4%
More than 1.5	2.4%	3.4%
Total no. of households	1,093,409	1,025,174

Source: U.S. Bureau of the Census, 1990 Census of Population and Housing, Summary Tape 1 (1992). Chicago Department of Planning, Research Division.

TABLE 7: Renter-Occupied Units Lacking Complete Kitchen Facilities, City
of Chicago, 1970-1987 (in 1,000s)

	1970	1975	1979	1983	1987
Total renter-occupied units	740.2	667.1	646.1	634.2	626.3
Units lacking complete kitchens	26.0	12.3	14.1	9.6	19.4
Pct. lacking complete kitchens	3.5%	1.8%	2.2%	1.5%	3.1%

Source: William Peterman and Tingwei Zhang, "Chicago Housing Trends and
Needs Assessment" (Chicago: School of Urban Planning and Policy, University
of Illinois at Chicago, 1991).

In Chicago, the number of conversion violations recorded in
the five years prior to 1989 was slightly more than 12,000. These
mainly represent responses to complaints and not a systematic
survey. But research on a small sample of 30 south-side Chicago
landlords who provided rooms for rent uncovered a kind of privately subsidized (unlicensed) rooming house market for the poor.
Rents averaged about $200. The escalating costs of repairing,
maintaining, and servicing rental units continue to surpass the
incomes of moderate- and low-income renters in the city—and
short-term projections show no signs of relief. Hence, owners
who rent rooms to the poor find themselves in a tight squeeze.
They can raise rents to levels that force tenants into homelessness,
absorb the loss by using up their savings and other assets, or pack
more paying tenants into the same quarters. These options lead
down different paths, but all end up in the same undesirable location—the creation of slum housing (Hoch and Carolin, 1989).

CURRENT POLICIES

Federal

The federal response to the contemporary homeless problem that
emerged in the early 1980s was belated and meager. In 1983, the
Reagan administration supported a congressional appropriation of

bout $140 million for an emergency food and shelter program administered by the Federal Emergency Management Agency. During the same fiscal year, about $77 million in Community Development Block Grant funds were used by local governments to acquire and rehabilitate shelters for the homeless. An Interagency Task Force on the Homeless was also created in 1983 to find ways to use existing federal resources to help the homeless. Despite the small amount involved, these federal dollars provided an important source of funds for the creation of shelters and services for the homeless.

The 1987 McKinney Act marked the first major step by the federal government to address the problem of homelessness, not as a temporary emergency condition, but as a serious social problem. The bill authorized more federal funds ($350 million) for the homeless in fiscal year 1987 than had been allocated in total over the previous four years. McKinney Act funds were appropriated to fund the local provision of food and shelter for the homeless, while targeting services for the mentally ill homeless and those with substance abuse problems. The distribution of funds has shifted slightly over time, with more money appropriated for transitional housing projects compared to emergency shelter projects and services for special populations. For instance, between 1987 and 1990, the share of appropriated funds allocated for transitional housing projects increased from 28.8 percent to 38.5 percent, while the proportion of funds allocated for emergency shelters declined from 38.9 percent to 34.5 percent (Interagency Council on the Homeless, 1991, pp. 94-95; U.S. General Accounting Office, 1987, p. 9).

The program elements of the legislation are based on a mobility model of individual effort and improvement. Proposals for shelters and service programs that target vulnerable population groups such as the elderly, youth, and women get funding priority. Almost a third of total funds go for specialized health projects that offer services and shelter for the physically and mentally handicapped homeless, as well as those with substance abuse problems. The intent is to promote programs that will assist vulnerable and needy homeless individuals to recover their former independence and obtain permanent housing; hence, the increasing emphasis on funding transitional housing projects. But the legislation does little to either prevent homelessness or increase the availability and affordability of housing for the poor.

State of Illinois

The response of the State of Illinois to homelessness has tended to reflect that of the federal government. Because more people became eligible, public aid funds expanded in the recession years of the early 1980s, although state funds for the homeless were not authorized until 1984. State allocations grew slowly at first and then rapidly, helping finance the provision of emergency shelter care. Public aid expenditures peaked in 1986 (see Table 8). New funds for the homeless were relatively insignificant, given the overall erosion in welfare benefit levels.

State employees in the Department of Public Aid and the Department of Mental Health and Developmental Disabilities recognize the presence of unmet needs but administer existing programs in ways that discourage new applicants due to budget constraints and restrictive application processes. Both the Rossi and Sosin studies analyzed numerous obstacles homeless people in Chicago face in obtaining public aid benefits for which they are eligible. Programs exist to provide money and services for the poor, but they are neither adequately funded nor fairly and generously administered. For instance, the Illinois Department of Public Aid could implement and expand the AFDC-Emergency Assistance programs that already exist. However, few caseworkers are familiar with the program, and those who are frequently offer aid only to those people who suffer acute financial need in the face of a natural disaster such as a fire, flood, or tornado (Rossi, Fisher, and Willis, 1986; Sosin, Colson, and Grossman, 1988).

Long-term policies to decentralize the treatment and care of mental patients in Illinois (as elsewhere) have increased the likelihood that poor people receiving psychiatric and psychological treatment will go homeless. Admission, discharge, and referral practices are neither adequately funded nor properly designed to attend to the material needs of the mentally ill who are poor. Community residential centers and mental health clinics have grown to fill the need for outpatient services but prove woefully inadequate in securing permanent housing arrangements for the mentally ill poor (Sosin, Colson, and Grossman, 1988).

TABLE 8:   State of Illinois Expenditures for Selected Public Aid Programs, 1979-1990 (dollar amounts in millions)

	AFDC	General Assistance	Homeless Shelter	Emergency Food and Shelter
1979	$722.0	$113.0	-----	------
1981	758.4	159.3	-----	------
1983	826.1	221.8	-----	------
1985	862.7	233.8	$ 0.8	$ 2.5
1986	891.3	245.2	1.5	3.7
1987	876.9	229.5	3.6	------
1988	830.0	203.6	3.6	------
1989	783.5	182.2	3.6	------
1990	793.7	178.2	7.1	------

Source: Illinois Department of Public Aid, *Annual Reports* (Springfield, Ill., 1979-1990).

Local Response

Federal and state funds have been translated into program responses at the local level. The City of Chicago has relied heavily on federal and state support in its response to the local homeless problem. Table 9 shows the changing distribution of various funding sources for the homeless programs supported by the City of Chicago. Since 1985, the City has generally contributed more than 40 percent of total government support for homeless programs. This figure does not include the private contribution of most sources of private aid from local non-governmental agencies, foundations, and individuals.

The bulk of public funds in Chicago was used for the rehabilitation, improvement, and operating expenses of overnight and transitional shelters. The number of shelter beds skyrocketed in Chicago from approximately 663 in 1980 to nearly 4,500 by 1991 (see Table 10). Local nonprofit organizations ran most of the shelters, using a combination of private contributions and public funds. But despite the increase in the number of shelter beds, many shelters do not have sufficient space to meet growing demand. For instance, in April 1988, ten overnight shelters reported that they were forced to turn away more than 6,000 persons because the facilities lacked the necessary space and resources to house these people (Gunner, Hannan, and Theodore, 1988, p. 8). In fall 1988, 2,366 Chicago women and children were turned away from nineteen transitional shelters. One year later, the number had more than doubled. With only twelve of the nineteen shelters reporting, more than 5,900 women and children had been turned away (Chicago Coalition for the Homeless, 1989).

TABLE 9: Federal, State, and Local Sources of Funds for City of Chicago Homeless Programs, 1982-1989 (Percentage Distribution)

	Federal				State	Local		All
	CDBG (%)	FEMA (%)	CSBG EHP (%)	HUD ESG (%)	IDPA (%)	Chi. (%)	Other (%)	Total ($)*
1982	93	--	7	--	--	--	--	277
1983	43	--	14	--	--	43	--	468
1984	35	--	26	--	9	30	--	661
1985	31	8	--	--	14	45	2	2,684
1986	28	6	--	--	13	48	5	5,275
1987	11	--	--	4	41	44	--	6,867
1988	3	--	11	19	28	39	--	7,665
1989	4	--	6	18	30	42	--	7,127

CDBG = Community Development Block Grant
FEMA = Federal Emergency Assistance Agency
CSBG = Community Services Block Grant
EHP = Emergency Housing Program
HUD = U.S. Department of Housing and Urban Development
ESG = Emergency Shelter Grant
IDPA = Illinois Department of Public Aid
Other = Chicago Community Trust

* Values in $1,000s

Source: Chicago Department of Planning, *Title IV Comprehensive Homeless Assistance Plan* (Chicago, 1989).

TABLE 10: Supply of Shelter Beds, City of Chicago, 1980-1991

	1980	1983	1987	1991
Overnight shelters	----	395	1,456	2,019
Transitional shelters	----	496	1,084	2,457
Total	663	891	2,532	4,476

Note: These figures do not include 600 warming beds in 1987 and 1,000 warming beds in 1991.

Sources: Jean Gunner, Sherrie Hannan, and Nikolas Theodore, *Housing the Homeless of Chicago: A Preliminary Plan* (Chicago: Coalition for the Homeless, 1988); Interview with John Donahue, director of Chicago Coalition for the Homeless, June 1991.

Many differences exist between shelters, and there is little uniformity in the quality or range of services they provide. Many provide little more than a bed or some refuge from the cold, while others provide meals, services, and support in making the transition back into permanent housing. Some are more desirable than others, and they may serve a wide range of clients or be closely focused on one client group (e.g., single mothers with children). Rules and operating procedures in many shelters can be restrictive, and, in some cases, they divide families and create obstacles to finding or keeping jobs and moving into permanent housing.

EVALUATION OF EXISTING POLICIES

Sheltering the Homeless

There are two serious limitations associated with the widespread development of shelters for the homeless. First, the shelters can do little to help restore the autonomy of the homeless and much to make them dependent (Rossi, 1989, pp. 37-43). Second, the locations of most shelters exclude the homeless from social and economic resources that the urban poor have traditionally used to overcome economic adversity—resources such as second-hand stores, labor exchanges, pawn shops, transportation hubs, neighbors, and kin (Hoch and Slayton, 1989; Dear and Wolch, 1987).

The existing shelter system in Chicago sorts the homeless according to vulnerabilities identified by caretakers and shelter providers. The result has been the creation of a dual shelter system. Single men are directed to large (125-bed average) overnight shelters, while single women are referred to much smaller transitional shelters (33-bed average). Transitional shelters provide for much longer stays and more services than the overnight dormitories (Sosin, Colson, and Grossman, 1988). The internal organization of shelters combines social care with social control. For example, Rossi found that although most of the homeless who had used shelters in Chicago agreed that they provided a decent and clean place to sleep, 47 percent complained about a lack of personal security, and another 40 percent resented the lack of personal freedom imposed by shelter regulations. In other words, users overwhelmingly liked the physical facilities but were divided over social issues such as security and privacy (Rossi, Fisher, and Willis, 1986).

Sheltering the poor on an ongoing basis turns them into a special population marked by their peculiar vulnerabilities. This sets them apart from other citizens as inferior, if deserving, dependents. This spatial and institutional concentration of the vulnerable promotes social exclusion. Thus, community activists in most residential neighborhoods treat shelters for the homeless in both Chicago and the suburbs as they would the threat of group homes or public housing projects. Most shelters in Chicago have avoided the political resistance of residential neighbors by locating in areas zoned for commercial or industrial development or residential locales where neighborhood defense is no longer practiced. This approach has enabled the nonprofit providers to successfully establish shelters in decentralized locations in poor neighborhoods. However, it has also tended to remove the homeless from the advantages of a central location.

The spatial breakup of skid row and the demolition of SRO hotels in Chicago have separated the destitute poor from the social and economic means of obtaining cheap shelter and employment. Thus, in the 1980s, the economic difference between the independent and dependent members of the single urban poor has widened and been institutionalized, due to the spatial dispersal of the dependent poor who sleep in public places throughout the city or in emergency shelters organized and funded by public or private caretakers. Shelters are scattered within the poorest residential neighborhoods. About four out of five shelter beds are located in low-income areas on the west and south sides of Chicago. The sheltering of the homeless may represent not simply a temporary response to the homeless problem, but an ongoing permanent solution. After all, compassionate policing has produced a solution to the unseemly appearance of homeless people sleeping or loitering in public places. Forcibly removing the homeless from Chicago's O'Hare Airport and putting them in a special shelter offers an obvious and recent example.

The Mobility Myth

The legitimacy of the existing shelter system rests on two rationales: a state of emergency, and the potential for individual social mobility. We justify shelters as emergency stop-gap facilities that are temporary accommodations to help individuals who have slipped or otherwise fallen out of the competitive housing market. Plans for the homeless invariably mention a three-stage model of treatment from emergency shelter to transitional shelter to placement in affordable, permanent housing.

The mobility model focuses on the individual person climbing up the housing affordability ladder or clambering up the slope of economic security. The federal McKinney Act, for instance, responds well to this model by allocating most funds to emergency shelter at stage one and transitional shelter for stage two. Unfortunately, the model presumes that those moving up through each stage of shelter care will eventually reach a threshold of permanent shelter security. The escalator of care, however, stops well short of this threshold in most places.

The emergency rationale has lost much of its hold as the homeless population has persisted and grown for nearly a decade since the federal administration first admitted it was a serious problem. The mobility model has proved more durable, mainly among those at the highest policy levels. Reports from shelter providers of all sorts at the local level make it clear that few people who leave shelters successfully find affordable market housing. Transitional shelter is a misnomer as most who leave do not find decent affordable housing on their own.

Homeless Prevention

Linking services and housing: Serious public efforts to prevent homelessness have been mixed.   The most significant initiatives have been undertaken by service and caretaking demonstration projects that focus on poor people with mental illness or alcohol and drug addictions.   Funded by the National Institute of
Mental Health and the National Institute on Alcohol Abuse and
Alcoholism, many of these projects combine the provision of permanent housing arrangements with ongoing supportive services.
For instance, the Arlington Hotel in San Francisco converted an
old SRO hotel into a permanent drug- and alcohol-free center for
homeless people.   Similarly, the rehabilitation of the Harold
Washington Hotel in Chicago combined the provision of social
services with the preservation of permanent affordable housing
(Curtiss et al., 1991).   The National Affordable Housing Act of
1990 includes the Shelter Plus Care program, which offers money
and requires the housing provider to come up with an equivalent
match in services.   However, as of May 1991, the fiscal year
1992 request of the Department of Housing and Urban Development (HUD) was only 7,743 units.

The Interagency Council on the Homeless in their 1990 annual
report outlined a national plan to end homelessness that emphasizes prevention rather than treatment.   The goal of the plan is to
"reduce homelessness by improving the coordination and delivery
of assistance designed to (1) help homeless families and individuals obtain appropriate permanent housing and become as self-sufficient as possible, and (2) prevent others from becoming homeless" (Interagency Council on the Homeless, 1991, p. 9).   Although reflecting a hopeful shift in policy, this goal, and objectives that follow, retain the mobility model that presumes the poor
either possess or can achieve self-reliance in the provision of their
own shelter security.

Emergency assistance: The recently reauthorized McKinney
Act will permit expenditures of as much as 30 percent of the
funds under the Emergency Shelter Grant program for prevention
activities such as rent arrears or rent deposit payments.   Unfortunately, this measure also ends up pitting the financially strapped
shelter providers against those seeking ways to fund prevention
programs at the state and local levels.   For instance, several states
and cities have adopted homeless prevention programs designed to
provide cash assistance to low-income renters who are facing the

threat of eviction due to short-term economic distress such as a job layoff or lost entitlement check (U.S. General Accounting Office, 1990). The Illinois legislature passed a homeless prevention bill in 1990 to fund similar programs in the state by tapping the underutilized emergency assistance funds in the Department of Public Aid. However, the authorization of the funds was delayed and implementation postponed.

POLICY RECOMMENDATIONS

Long-Term Prevention

The foundation of any successful and substantial solution to the homeless problem will rest on the expansion of gainful employment opportunities and public welfare benefits for the poor. Surprisingly, recent analysis of media reports and public opinion surveys indicates that a majority of U.S. citizens believe that the roots of the homeless problem are structural and favor structural reforms to solve the problem—even if it means raising their taxes (Lee, Link, and Toro, 1991). In other words, lack of adequate employment opportunities and affordable housing, rather than individual pathology, deviancy, and dependency, was believed to represent the basic causes of homelessness. However, federal and state governments have shown little interest in expanding welfare benefits or funds for subsidized housing. There are plenty of schemes available to put the reforms in place (Rossi, 1989; Dolbeare and Alker, 1990), but little political will. Rossi, Sosin, and many other analysts have proposed an expansion and reorganization of state and federal welfare programs that would increase benefit levels, remove barriers to new applicants, and offer new programs. For instance, one proposal would create a new program to support families that subsidize poor, unattached members who share the same household—"Aid for Dependent Adults" (Rossi, 1989, p. 208).

The preservation of old and construction of new SRO-type housing would provide an important source of affordable housing for the single poor. Locating such new developments near commercial and transportation centers should be a priority. The burdens of high density and small living space can be offset by the benefits of accessibility to employment, services, and friends. Especially noteworthy is recent new construction of SRO hotels in San Diego, California (San Diego Housing Commission, 1985).

Jack Kemp, secretary of HUD in the Bush administration, announced in May 1991 that Federal Housing Administration mortgage insurance would be made available to developers of affordable SRO-type housing.
Especially pressing is the unjust distribution of the burdens of poverty on minorities. The legacy of racism continues to undermine and distort a fair and efficient operation of the labor and housing markets for Blacks and Hispanics, and Chicago is no exception. Local leadership should reject those policies that blame inner-city poverty and misery solely on the minority poor themselves and should take up policies that will severely punish racial bias and generously reward fairness.

Remedial Measures

The provision of short-term shelters for the homeless is an ironic success story. Many homeless individuals now have a place to sleep other than the streets. However, despite the often heroic efforts of the boards, staff, and volunteers of shelters for the homeless, these institutions remain woefully inadequate when compared to conventional housing. Improvements in the design and operation of new transitional shelters have enhanced the quality of these living environments by offering a greater length of stay, greater privacy, more space, and access to social services. But despite such improvements, these shelters still function as conduits in the service of the misleading mobility model of care. Although systematic evidence is lacking, anecdotal reports from shelter providers suggest that successful transitions from the shelter to the housing market are rare. On their own, these poor households lack the economic assets and social supports that the shelters provide. The economic and social costs of successful independence prove too great.
As the quality of the shelter system improves, so too does its attractiveness to those poor people living with others. In New York City, for instance, of the more than 11,000 families that entered shelters in 1990, three-fourths reported having lived with relatives or friends. Public officials there believe that many people are deciding to enter the shelter system to obtain access to services and housing opportunities that are more promising than conditions in their former shared living arrangements (Dugger, 1991). The expansion of the shelter system becomes perverse when not complemented by the expansion of affordable housing

opportunities for the poor. The future design and production of full-service homeless shelters should abandon the mobility model and focus on the provision of permanent shared-housing arrangements for the homeless.

Eviction Prevention

Short-term prevention measures should be directed at the demand side of the market and emphasize interventions that will keep low-income people in their present dwellings. Low-income households frequently require short-term financial assistance to remain in their homes. A well-funded state homeless prevention program could provide this assistance on an emergency basis to low-income renters or homeowners who cannot pay their rent or make their mortgage payments in times of personal crisis, such as job loss, illness, divorce, or death. The State of Illinois has the legislative and administrative process in place to implement such a program.

Shared Housing

Public and nonprofit agencies need to adopt policies that openly acknowledge and promote shared-housing arrangements for all segments of the population. These arrangements include congregate housing, accessory apartments, rooming houses, and SRO hotels. The "American dream" of homeownership promoted by national and state leadership offers misleading propaganda to millions of poor Americans. So long as significant structural reforms are postponed, poor Americans will need to share the housing available to them to keep it affordable. This means that the poor will necessarily live in poorer quality and denser housing than more prosperous citizens.

In order to anticipate and diffuse the stigma associated with shared housing, government and nonprofit agencies need to take the initiative in funding research and demonstration projects that will illustrate the advantages of shared housing not only for poor tenants, but for segments of the entire community. Middle-class Europeans have lived at much higher densities than Americans for decades without stigma, and some middle-class Americans are experimenting with different forms of shared housing (Franck and Ahrentzen, 1989).

Any serious program of physical improvements for shared housing units will need to be accompanied by some sort of regulatory relief measures by the planning and building departments of local municipalities. Although it is crucial that the physical improvement of structures used as shared housing meets basic safety standards, many other rules and standards could be waived, especially in instances in which home-sharing occurs in structures with four or fewer units.

Improving match-up programs, which link prospective tenants with owners, is an important step in promoting home-sharing and tapping the available supply of vacant housing. Existing match-up systems tend to have too few owner participants for all the potential tenants. Match-up programs could be developed at a local or neighborhood scale by churches or neighborhood organizations as part of a homeless prevention campaign. Members of the same church community may be more willing to rent rooms to another church member who was referred by someone they know than to rent a room to a stranger referred by an unknown professional (Howe, 1985).

Instead of expecting homeless individuals and families to eventually leave transitional shelters, the nonprofit sponsors and staff should encourage the residents to form a community of households that would eventually take control of the management and care of their own housing. The mission of transitional housing could shift from an individual-mobility approach to a community-building approach. Sponsors and staff would seek to find, improve, and establish permanent shared-housing arrangements for the homeless or near-homeless, expecting to staff and operate a shared-housing arrangement for a limited time (e.g., three to five years). This approach would enable tenants to pool their strengths while taking advantage of staff resources in the early years of living together. The growth of individual autonomy and responsibility would be tied to the growth and development of the residential community. Residents might lack the privacy and freedom of a rental apartment, but they would also reduce the risk of economic failure and renewed homelessness that confronts poor households on their own.

CONCLUSION

Chicago's homeless, like the homeless nationwide, are likely to remain a permanent feature of the urban policy landscape. A decade of emergency responses, including a variety of shelters and services, has alleviated the suffering of the homeless but institutionalized their plight. Homeless prevention measures requiring a substantial increase in public funds, for instance, substantially increasing public aid levels, face significant opposition, as do proposals for significant amounts of low-income housing subsidy. But even more discouraging is the emphasis on individual self-reliance and mobility at the root of various programs. I mentioned the mobility model that justifies the treatment of homeless shelter inhabitants, but the same belief inspires other programs as well—for instance, homeownership initiatives for public housing residents. Instead of building on the existing patterns of reciprocity and sharing among and between poor households, these programs completely overlook the social importance and economic efficiency of such efforts. Holding out the promise of homeownership for the very poor without a large allocation of public funds fuels false hopes. So long as we foster the belief that homeownership is the American dream, then shared accommodations will appear as the American nightmare.

Presently, the only way to decently house substantial numbers of poor people in the United States without using substantial amounts of public funds is to support and foster various kinds of shared housing. The nearly obsessive attachment to the single-family dwelling and the marketing practices and armory of government regulations that place these units at the top of the housing market hierarchy actively discourage the production and location of various shared housing accommodations. Removing the stigma of shared living will require changing the beliefs and practices that keep the present hierarchy in place. Such changes will be neither easy nor quick.

REFERENCES

Arce, Anthony, et al. (1983). "A Psychiatric Profile of Street People Admitted to an Emergency Shelter," *Hospital and Community Psychiatry*, vol. 34, no. 9 (September 1983), pp. 814-815.

Bassuk, Ellen (1984). "The Homeless Problem," *Scientific American*, vol. 250, no. 7 (July 1984), pp. 39-42.

Butzen, Jean (1991). "SRO Recommendations to the CHAS Advisory Committee." Chicago: Lakefront SRO Corporation.

Carolin, Paulette (1988). "Suburban Homeless Soon to Find Homes," *Planning*, vol. 54, no. 9 (September 1988), pp. 17-19.

Chicago Coalition for the Homeless (1989). Press Release on Homeless Turnaways in Chicago. Chicago, November 1989.

Chicago Department of Planning (1989). *Title IV Comprehensive Homeless Assistance Plan*. Chicago: Chicago Department of Planning.

Cook, Fay L., et al. (1986). *Stability and Change in Economic Hardship: Chicago 1983-1985*. Evanston, Ill.: Center for Urban Affairs and Policy Research, Northwestern University.

Curtiss, Jim, et al. (1991). *A Guide to Housing for Low-Income People Recovering From Alcohol and Other Drug Problems*. Rockford, Md.: National Institute on Alcohol Abuse and Alcoholism.

Dear, Michael, and Jennifer Wolch (1987). *Landscapes of Despair: From Deinstitutionalization to Homelessness*. Princeton, N.J.: Princeton University Press.

Dolbeare, Cushing, and Joan Alker (1990). *The Closing Door: Economic Causes of Homelessness*. Washington D.C.: National Coalition for the Homeless.

Donohue, John (1991). Interview with author. Chicago Coalition for the Homeless, June 1991.

Dugger, Celia W. (1991). "Families Seek Out Shelters as Route to Better Homes," *New York Times*, September 4, 1991, p. A1.

Edens, Jacquie (1991). Telephone interview with author. Chicago Department of Human Services, June 1991.

Franck, Karen, and Sherry Ahrentzen (1989). *New Households, New Housing*. New York: Von Nostrand Reinhold.

Goozner, Merrill (1991). "'80s Gravy Train Left Most Behind," *Chicago Tribune*, May 12, 1991.

Gunner, Jean, Sherrie Hannan, and Nikolas Theodore (1988). *Housing the Homeless of Chicago: A Preliminary Plan*. Chicago: Chicago Coalition for the Homeless.

Hoch, Charles, and Paulette Carolin (1989). *Shared Housing for Low Income Households in the Chicago Region*. Des Plaines, Ill.: Housing and Shelter Program, Inc.

Hoch, Charles, and Robert Slayton (1989). *New Homeless and Old: Community and the Skid Row Hotel*. Philadelphia: Temple University Press.

Howe, Elizabeth (1985). "Homesharing for the Elderly," *Journal of Planning Education and Research*, vol. 4, no. 3 (April 1985), pp. 185-194.

Illinois Department of Public Aid (1979-1990). *Annual Reports*. Springfield, Ill.: Illinois Department of Public Aid.

Interagency Council on the Homeless (1991). *The 1990 Annual Report*. Washington D.C.: Interagency Council on the Homeless, February 1991.

Joseph, Lawrence B., ed. (1990). *Creating Jobs, Creating Workers: Economic Development and Employment in Metropolitan Chicago*. Chicago: Center for Urban Research and Policy, University of Chicago; distributed by University of Illinois Press.

Knickman, James R., and Beth Weitzman (1989). *A Study of Homeless Families in New York City: Risk Assessment Models and Strategies for Prevention*. Report prepared for the Human Services Administration, City of New York. New York: Health Research Program, New York University.

Lakefront SRO (1991). "SRO Loss in Chicago, 1985-1990: The Need for an SRO Protection Plan." Chicago: Lakefront SRO, January 1991.

Lee, Barrett A., Bruce G. Link, and Paul A. Toro (1991). "Images of the Homeless: Public Views and Media Messages," *Housing Policy Debate*, vol. 2, no. 2, pp. 649-682.

Lewis, Sylvia (1989). "Housing: Suburbs Discover Homelessness," *Chicago Enterprise*, October 12, 1989, pp. 12-13.

Peterman, William, and Tingwei Zhang (1991). "Chicago Housing Trends and Needs Assessment." Chicago: School of Urban Planning and Policy, University of Illinois at Chicago.

Ringheim, Karin (1990). *At Risk of Homelessness: The Role of Income and Rent*. New York: Praeger.

Rossi, Peter (1989). *Down and Out in America*. Chicago: University of Chicago Press.

Rossi, Peter, Gene Fisher, and Georgianna Willis (1986). *The Condition of the Homeless in Chicago*. Chicago: National Opinion Research Center.

San Diego Housing Commission (1985). *San Diego's Downtown Hotels: SRO Study*. San Diego: City of San Diego Housing Commission.

Sosin, Michael, Paul Colson, and Susan Grossman (1988). *Homelessness in Chicago: Poverty and Pathology, Social Institutions and Social Change*. Chicago: School of Social Service Administration, University of Chicago.

Stagner, Matthew, and Harold Richman (1985). *General Assistance Families.* Chicago: National Opinion Research Center.
Sternlieb, George, and James Hughes (1991). "Private Market Provision of Low Income Housing," *Housing Policy Debate,* vol. 2, no. 2, pp. 123-156.
Taylor, D. Garth (1991). *1990 Metro Survey Report.* Chicago: Metro Chicago Information Center.
U.S. Bureau of the Census (1985). *Housing Characteristics for Selected Metropolitan Areas: Chicago.* Current Housing Reports, Annual Housing Survey: 1983. U.S. Department of Housing and Urban Development, sponsor. Washington, D.C.: U.S. Department of Commerce, Bureau of the Census.
_____ (1990). *Housing Characteristics for Selected Metropolitan Areas: Chicago.* Current Housing Reports, American Housing Survey: 1987. U.S. Department of Housing and Urban Development, sponsor. Washington, D.C.: U.S. Department of Commerce, Bureau of the Census.
_____ (1991). *Statistical Abstract of the United States: 1991.* Washington D.C.: U.S. Government Printing Office.
U.S. Department of Commerce (1990). *American Housing Survey for the Chicago Metropolitan Area in 1987.* Washington, D.C.: U.S. Department of Commerce, Bureau of the Census, and U.S. Department of Housing and Urban Development, Office of Policy Development and Research.
U.S. General Accounting Office (1987). *Homelessness: Implementation of Food and Shelter Programs Under the McKinney Act.* Washington D.C.: U.S. Government Printing Office.
_____ (1990). *Homelessness: Too Early to Tell What Kinds of Prevention Assistance Work Best.* Washington D.C.: U.S. Government Printing Office.
Wilson, William Julius (1987). *The Truly Disadvantaged: The Inner City, the Underclass, and Public Policy.* Chicago: University of Chicago Press.
Wright, James D. (1989). *Address Unknown: The Homeless in America.* New York: Aldine de Gruyter.

COMMENTS

Susan Grossman

Charles Hoch provides a concise and comprehensive overview of factors that have contributed to homelessness among Chicago's poor during the past decade. In response to these factors, he argues that broader structural changes are necessary. In particular, he calls for the expansion of employment opportunities among the urban poor and increases in public welfare benefit levels. Because, as Hoch points out, simply being poor, apart from other personal characteristics, is likely to increase one's chances of homelessness, such strategies may serve a preventive function. Hoch also places a great deal of emphasis on housing alternatives in his proposed solutions, especially on shared housing. However, while both income supports and housing strategies are essential in the prevention and amelioration of homelessness, social services may also be necessary.

For example, Michael Sosin and his colleagues provide some evidence for problems beyond poverty among those who have been homeless for a long time or repeatedly. Such individuals are more likely to be males who live alone and to be binge drinkers. They have adapted to life on the streets and find street life somewhat easier than those with less extensive homeless histories. They also appear to be more depressed or in some type of psychological crisis (Sosin, Colson, and Grossman, 1986, p. 338). Similarly, my own research (Grossman, 1991) finds some indication that a lack of connection to such social institutions as the family or the larger community may be more prevalent among homeless men compared to women and that such disconnection contributes to homelessness among this group above and beyond the influence of economic factors such as the lack of work or welfare benefits.

Hoch appears to be aware of the necessity of supportive services when he talks about the need for shelters to provide more than simply beds. It is also apparent in his recognition that some individuals may require ongoing assistance and in his debunking of the "mobility myth." Yet he tends to consider such activities in relation to the provision of permanent shared housing. Several

other strategies are also needed, and these do not necessarily emphasize housing. For instance, the studies cited above suggest
that increased substance abuse services are necessary for some
homeless individuals. Programs whose activities are geared toward reintegrating isolated or alienated individuals, especially
when they have been homeless for an extended period of time, are
also important. One option might be to create job training programs specifically for the homeless. Employment is apparently
important to preventing homelessness, especially among men
(Grossman, 1991). Moroever, regular employment might lead to
increased involvement in other mainstream activities and institutions (e.g., unions or even after-work sports teams).

As noted already, the major emphasis of Hoch's recommendations is on alterations in housing policy. He contends that one
solution to the problem of homelessness is to increase shared-
housing opportunities for poor individuals. This proposal is,
however, problematic. Evidence suggests that many individuals
who become homeless are less likely to have family members or
other persons with whom they can live. Partially, this may be
due to the financial drain that these individuals represent. For
example, one author reports that many of the families of the older
homeless women in her study were aware of their relative's plight,
but the families were so overburdened trying to deal with their
own economic or mental instability that they could not provide for
another dependent member (Rousseau, 1981). Others note that the
networks of the poor tend to be overtaxed, which suggests that
poor families may be least able to help relatives who need shelter
(see Garbarino and Sherman, 1980; Camasso and Camasso, 1986).

Hoch addresses this issue by calling for the creation of shared-
housing opportunities through resources other than family members, particularly through programs in the not-for-profit and private sectors. He also suggests that middle-class families be encouraged to engage in shared-housing activities. However, it is
likely that few such families would be willing to live with certain
groups of homeless individuals—for example, substance abusers
or those with severe and persistent mentally illnesses. One alternative in such cases might be to provide financial subsidies and
supportive services to poor families who are willing and able to
aid their relatives, but who are unable to do so because of the
emotional and economic burdens involved.

Domestic violence in adulthood may be an additional barrier
to remaining in some familial situations, particularly for women.
Bassuk and Rosenberg (1988) found that, compared to poor

housed women, homeless women were more likely to have been in battering relationships. Of interest is their additional finding that homeless women were more likely to escape such relationships by going to battered women's shelters, while housed women generally turned to close friends for help. My research reports similar findings. Homeless women, compared to women who were domiciled, were more likely to have no one to whom they could go for shelter after experiencing disruptions in their households (Grossman, 1991).[1]

Such findings imply that assistance to individuals after disruptions occur may be crucial, including temporary housing for those who have no informal resources to which they can turn. Further, if isolation is characteristic of women in battering situations, interventions aimed at bolstering their informal or formal support networks may serve an important preventive function in relation to homelessness.

Apart from the isolation of some women and the apparent relationship between such isolation and homelessness, my work indicates that "pathological" factors such as mental illness or substance abuse are less likely to distinguish homeless women from other poor women who are able to remain domiciled. This apparent lack of "pathologies" among the causes of female homelessness is promising in that it suggests that interventions directed at ameliorating and preventing homelessness among women can focus less on personal characteristics and more on providing concrete resources. My results indicate that for those who are already vulnerable, the maintenance of whatever welfare is being received is critical if homelessness is to be avoided. Rent subsidies, apart from welfare, also seem crucial for those who have a greater rent burden (Grossman, 1991).

As noted, among men, there is more evidence that problems such as alcoholism or alienation contribute to homelessness. For example, men who become homeless have more limited familial support networks compared to men who, although extremely impoverished, manage to remain housed (Grossman, 1991). They are also more likely to have been living alone in their last residence. Perhaps because of their greater sense of disconnection, it may be harder for men who are homeless to reach out to informal networks for assistance. It seems essential, then, to en-

---

[1] Note that not all disruptions involved spouse abuse. Divorce, fights, abandonment, and being "kicked out" were included as well.

sure that such resources are available through formal means. To the extent that formal services can compensate for the benefits that familial networks render, in terms of both emotional and concrete support, they should be geared to do so. For instance, material assistance could be made available through the direct provision of needed resources such as food, clothing, and so on, so that whatever income is available can be stretched further.

As Hoch points out, some individuals are likely to be dependent on society for many years and may never be self-sufficient. Nonetheless, the ongoing provision of housing, whether shared or not, or of income assistance is unlikely to be enough to sustain all individuals who are at risk of homelessness or who have been homeless. Although such strategies may be an essential part of our intervention efforts, we need to be prepared to address ongoing emotional needs as well through the provision of supportive social services.

REFERENCES

Bassuk, Ellen L., and Lynn Rosenberg (1988). "Why Does Family Homelessness Occur? A Case-Control Study," *American Journal of Public Health*, vol. 78 (July 1988), pp. 783-788.

Camasso, Michael J., and Anne E. Camasso (1986). "Social Supports, Undesirable Life Events, and Psychological Distress in a Disadvantaged Population," *Social Service Review*, vol. 60, no. 3 (September 1986), pp. 378-394.

Garbarino, James, and Deborah Sherman (1980). "High-Risk Neighborhoods and High-Risk Families: The Human Ecology of Child Maltreatment, *Child Development*, vol. 51, no. 1 (March 1980) pp. 188-198.

Grossman, Susan (1991). *Gender Differences Among the Homeless*. Unpublished Ph.D. dissertation, School of Social Service Administration, University of Chicago.

Rousseau, Ann Marie (1981). *Shopping Bag Ladies*. New York: Pilgrim Press.

Sosin, Michael R., Paul Colson, and Susan Grossman (1988). *Homelessness in Chicago: Poverty and Pathology, Social Institutions and Social Change*. Chicago: School of Social Service Administration, University of Chicago.

NONPROFIT HOUSING DEVELOPMENT IN BOSTON

Rachel G. Bratt[*]

Nonprofit developers are now widely regarded as serious players on the affordable housing landscape. As the federal government withdrew from directly subsidizing new construction and substantial rehabilitation projects during the 1980s, public housing authorities and private, for-profit developers found it increasingly difficult to produce affordable housing. By 1989, only about 3,000-4,000 units of public housing were being added to the inventory each year, compared to an average of over 28,000 units between 1981 and 1984. Only during World War II, when the public housing program was suspended, had public housing production been lower. Private developers had been active participants in federal housing subsidy programs since the 1960s (under Section 221(d)(3), 235, and 236 programs) and during the 1970s (under Section 8 New Construction and Substantial Rehabilitation programs). During the 1980s, however, the Reagan administration phased out the last of the production programs (Section 8), and developers began to take their investment dollars elsewhere. As an affordable housing void developed, nonprofit organizations became active producers, owners, and managers.

It would be misleading, however, to view the recent activity of nonprofit developers solely as the result of the virtual disappearance of competitor developers. Nonprofits have played a role in affordable housing production through much of the 20th century, and their knowledge and sophistication have grown dramatically. It also would be erroneous to conclude that the reason that

---

[*] This chapter is based on a report prepared by the author under contract to Professor Phillip L. Clay of the Massachusetts Institute of Technology, as part of a Ford Foundation-funded project, "Nonprofit Housing Development: Boston" (March 1989). The overall study (Clay, 1990) includes an analysis of nonprofit housing production in five additional cities.

nonprofits are increasingly alone on the affordable housing scene is because the need has diminished. In fact, the reverse is true.

• As of 1989, of the nearly 4.3 million poor households living in unsubsidized rental housing, 3.3 million (77.2%) paid more than half their incomes for housing (Apgar et al., 1991, p. 17).
• Between 1978 and 1985, the proportion of poor renter households who spent 60 percent or more of their income for housing grew from 44 percent to 55 percent (Leonard et al., 1989, p. 5).
• In 1989, 25.5 percent of unsubsidized poor renters lived in units that were structurally inadequate. Poor Black and Hispanic households lived in marginal quality units at a disproportionately higher rate than the overall population (Apgar et al., 1991, pp. 16-17).
• There has been a decline in the number of low-rent units both in absolute terms and in relation to the number of households requiring such housing. In 1985, there were nearly 3.7 million fewer units renting for no more than $250 per month than there were households with incomes at or below $10,000. (A $250-per-month unit is affordable to a household earning $10,000, paying 30% of income for rent.) (Leonard et al., 1989, p. xiii).

As the federal government has retreated from its traditional support of subsidized housing production, state and local governments have become more actively involved. Much of the focus of this recent generation of state and local housing programs has been on supporting nonprofits. Using Boston as the model, this chapter examines the types of state and local assistance that have been made available to nonprofits and discusses the obstacles that still need to be overcome in order to make nonprofits more effective producers and managers. There are at least three reasons why a study of state and local initiatives in Massachusetts that support nonprofits is valuable in the context of exploring strategies for affordable housing in metropolitan Chicago. First, as a group, nonprofits are committed to long-term affordability. Therefore, it is useful to understand the types of financial and technical assistance that can be assembled to enable nonprofits to do their jobs. Second, this case illustrates the complexity of nonprofit housing development using current tools and programs. In the absence of a comprehensive federal support system for nonprofit housing, some localities have managed to use ingenuity and imagination to produce affordable housing. But this piecemeal approach is far from simple and is more costly than more direct funding mechanisms. Finally, because the City of Boston and the Commonwealth of Massachusetts both have been singled out for their unusual support for affordable housing, it is valuable to understand what one of the best state and local programs manages to provide, as well as to appreciate the obstacles that still exist for the nonprofit housing sector.

The final section of this chapter assesses some current issues facing nonprofits, including various dilemmas and challenges as well as potential roles under recent federal legislation. Before launching into the central issues of this chapter, however, it is important to briefly describe the types of nonprofit housing producers and provide an overview of their recent accomplishments.

TYPES OF NONPROFIT HOUSING DEVELOPERS

The term "nonprofit housing developer" encompasses at least eight separate types of entities. *Community development corporations* (CDCs) are the most prevalent of the nonprofit housing developers in the United States. CDCs are community-based groups whose boards of directors are controlled by local residents, with participation by other public and private actors from the community or city.

There are now over 300 *Neighborhood Housing Services* (NHS) programs operating in over 130 cities. Originally aimed at providing homeownership rehabilitation loans, many recently have become involved in development. The original NHS was started in Pittsburgh in 1968 by a group of homeowners, financial institutions, and city officials. Subsequently, the NHS model was embraced at the national level. Grants and technical assistance are provided by the Neighborhood Reinvestment Corporation, a congressionally chartered agency created in 1978, as well as by other public and private sources.

Social services agencies often operate, as well as develop, single-room-occupancy, emergency, and transitional housing specifically targeted for such groups as the elderly, handicapped, or homeless. Community action agencies, which were created during the War on Poverty in the 1960s, also have been involved as producers, although minimally.

Labor unions have been involved with nonprofit housing development for over 70 years. Over the past few years in Boston, the bricklayers' union has produced several hundred units of affordable housing. The recent achievements of the hotel and restaurant employees' union are also noteworthy. In their December 1988 contract negotiations, they managed to get employers to agree to donate five cents for each hour worked by each employee to a housing trust fund. This fund, which as of late 1991 totaled about $500,000, is being used by the union to help employees gain access to and maintain both rental and owner-occupied housing. For example, the fund is providing loans to help cover some of the costs of renting a unit, such as the first and last month's rent and security deposit. The influence of this union was also clearly demonstrated by its efforts in 1990 to successfully lobby Congress to gain a change in the federal Taft-Hartley Act to allow housing as a benefit.

Religious groups have played an important role in producing affordable housing for several decades. Habitat for Humanity and the original Nehemiah program (in Brooklyn, N.Y.) are two well-known examples of church-supported housing developments.

Tenant groups often become involved in nonprofit housing ventures when their buildings are being converted to condominiums or market-rate rental housing. Rehabilitation is frequently part of the process with safeguards put into place to assure the long-term affordability of the units. Under such situations, tenants may assume ownership through a limited equity cooperative arrangement. This form of ownership provides virtually all the benefits of homeownership, except that equity is capped at a predetermined level, thereby keeping the units affordable to subsequent households.

Mutual housing associations are relative newcomers to the nonprofit housing development scene. Although a variety of organizations have adopted the name, one specific model is advocated by the Neighborhood Reinvestment Corporation. According to their definition, these are nonprofit organizations that are committed to ongoing management and production of affordable housing. Residents in mutual housing have a controlling voice on the association's board but do not own the project as in a cooperative. Ownership is held by the association. Resident security and a sense of ownership are emphasized and, as much as possible, development is achieved with up-front, public or private grants rather than with debt financing.

Land trusts also are a relatively new form of nonprofit housing developer or development partner. Such organizations try to amass as much land as possible, which can then be used for affordable housing. The housing generally is built and owned by other nonprofits, and it is guaranteed to stay affordable over the long term. Ownership of the land is held by the trust in perpetuity.

The number of nonprofit housing developers that operate in a given locale has some important implications. Although it may be positive to have a variety of groups, since that may increase the volume of production, there is also a down side. Because financial resources are scarce, a great many organizations are competing for virtually the same public and private dollars. Similarly, participation on boards stretches local public and private actors quite thinly. The greater the number of groups in a given city, the less likely that each one can have key bankers, corporate leaders, and public officials on its board. In Massachusetts, there are scores of nonprofit housing developers; in Boston, the situation is particularly competitive, with the bulk of the state's nonprofits located in that area.

NONPROFIT HOUSING PRODUCTION: THE NATIONAL RECORD

As nonprofit housing production increased during the 1980s, there was increasing interest in documenting the record of community development corporations. The National Congress for Community Economic Development (NCCED) initiated a survey in 1988 and a follow-up survey in 1991. The latter effort drew responses from 1,160 community-based development organizations. (According to NCCED, this figure was over half of the total number in the country.) All the organizations in the study were private, locally based nonprofits that completed at least one housing or business development. NCCED reported that such organizations operate in every state and in virtually every major city in the nation. In the aggregate, the groups had built nearly 320,000 units of housing, over 90 percent for low-income occupants. In addition, the survey found that these nonprofits had been actively involved in retail and commercial development and were responsible for some 90,000 jobs (NCCED, 1991).

A second study, by Avis C. Vidal at the New School for Social Research, surveyed 130 community development groups.

For 89 percent of these groups, housing development was a significant component of their work; 60 percent cited commercial or industrial real estate development and business enterprise development as major program areas (Vidal, 1989). Both surveys revealed that advocacy work also constituted an important aspect of the agendas of community-based development organizations.

Many of the assumptions concerning the benefits of producing affordable housing by community-based nonprofits, as opposed to for-profit developers or public agencies, are related to individual and community well-being and empowerment. Participating in a community-based housing initiative can produce an enhanced feeling of personal efficacy and can contribute to one's sense of self. In addition, at the community level, community-based development organizations often provide residents with a host of additional services, such as day care, job training, or services for the elderly, that enhance the overall living environment (Bratt, 1989b). However, to date, most findings in this area have been anecdotal (see, e.g., Peirce and Steinbach, 1990). One important exception is my own survey of residents of a development owned by a mutual housing association in Baltimore. The survey was specifically aimed at determining whether empowerment had, in fact, developed among the residents. Although the survey design had some methodological flaws due to budgetary and time constraints, 62 percent of the respondents indicated that their home lives were better since moving into mutual housing, and 77 percent reported that their hopes for the future had improved. In addition, two-thirds indicated that improved self-esteem or more involvement in the community represented the biggest changes in their lives since moving into mutual housing (Bratt, 1990b, 1991). However, the survey did not provide information on the extent to which these feelings were translated into greater resident control over their lives or how this was expressed within the larger community. But as a first effort at measuring empowerment, the survey did produce some provocative information. A current project at the New School for Social Research is surveying residents of community-based developments across the country in an effort to produce a more in-depth assessment of behavioral changes associated with residency in community-based housing.

STATE AND LOCAL SUPPORT SYSTEMS[1]

At the state level, the Massachusetts support system for nonprofit community-based housing is one of the, if not the, most fully developed in the country. At the local level, under Mayor Raymond Flynn, Boston has been extremely supportive of nonprofits as producers of affordable housing. As a result of these efforts, community development corporations (CDCs) in Massachusetts have reportedly produced almost 35 percent of the privately developed subsidized housing in the state over the past 20 years (MACDC, 1991).

The following two sections present an overview of the agencies and programs that operate at the state and local levels and that provide direct funding or support to nonprofits and, in some cases, to other housing developers as well. In addition, each section presents a brief overview of the regulatory initiatives that both the state and city have initiated to help produce and preserve affordable housing. The final component of the state's support system encompasses an impressive group of private umbrella organizations, intermediaries, consultants, and foundations.

The State's Programs

The first two major components of the Massachusetts system—the Community Development Finance Corporation and the Community Economic Development Assistance Corporation—did not start with a focus on housing. In both cases, their early mandate was community economic development. Nevertheless, the evolving agencies and programs now provide impressive financial and technical supports for nonprofit housing organizations.

The Community Development Finance Corporation (CDFC) was created in 1975 with funding raised through general obligation bonds. CDFC's goal was to enhance local economies through business development and job creation. It provided community development corporations with both equity capital and loans. The early years of the agency were difficult; it got off to a slow start, and many of its early loans defaulted. In the early 1980s, the agency reoriented its efforts toward housing, which, it was hoped,

---

[1] Portions of this section are revised from Bratt, 1989a and 1989b. A similar version appears in Bratt, 1992.

would provide opportunities for better investments. Since its creation, CDFC has supported the development of over 2,600 affordable housing units (CDFC, 1990).

The Community Economic Development Assistance Corporation (CEDAC) was created in 1978 to provide technical assistance to CDCs. Like CDFC, CEDAC's early orientation was toward economic development, but virtually all its activities are now directed to housing. Over the past few years, the agency has helped CDCs rehabilitate or build nearly 4,000 units. CEDAC's major support for nonprofit housing development is in the form of interest-free loans, totaling over $1 million per year, which primarily help to cover project planning costs. By advancing small sums of money in the early stages of the development process, and larger sums as the project moves toward closing, CEDAC has effectively managed to limit its risk. Ninety percent of the funds it lends are recovered when the construction financing agreement is executed.

In 1976, the Massachusetts Executive Office of Communities and Development launched a small pilot program for production-oriented projects. This stimulated a great deal of enthusiasm for the state to create an ongoing capital fund to help nonprofit groups finance planning and start-up activities, and in 1978 the Community Enterprise Economic Development (CEED) program was created.[2] From the outset, the CEED program was targeted to housing. By fiscal year (FY) 1989, it was operating on a record high yearly budget of over $2.2 million. Since then, however, funding has dropped precipitously, with an allocation of $753,000 for FY 1991. CEED, as well as other housing programs, is currently in a precarious position because Governor William Weld has been far less supportive of these initiatives than his predecessor, Michael Dukakis. Although CEED finally received an appropriation for FY 1992 of $750,000, only slightly below the FY 1991 level, Governor Weld's first budget, proposed in February 1991, completely omitted new funding for the CEED program.

The Massachusetts Government Land Bank was created in 1975 to assist in the disposition of federally owned land that had been used for military purposes. In 1980, its mandate was broad-

---

[2] In addition to the CEED program, the state's community development agency runs a series of other programs that are partially or wholly targeted to nonprofits. Some are unique to Massachusetts, whereas others, such as the federal Community Development Block Grant and the Neighborhood Housing Services programs, operate on a national level.

ened, with the state legislature enabling the agency to acquire, develop, and sell surplus state property as well as blighted undeveloped or substandard properties. Since its inception, about 70 percent of the Land Bank's loans have gone to nonprofit community-based developers and local governments (Massachusetts Government Land Bank, 1991).

The Massachusetts Housing Partnership (MHP) was created in 1985, with the Boston Housing Partnership (to be discussed below) as the model. The MHP provides state support and coordinates other public and private resources for local housing initiatives undertaken by municipalities, private developers, and nonprofits. The MHP works through local housing partnerships, which consist of representatives of local government agencies as well as private individuals—bankers, builders, business people, consumer and housing advocates, and other citizens (MHP, n.d.). Although nonprofit groups are not the only eligible recipients of MHP funds and assistance, they do comprise a key constituency.

Created in 1966, the Massachusetts Housing Finance Agency (MHFA) was one of the country's first state housing finance agencies. As of June 30, 1990, the MHFA had provided over $4 billion in loans to finance the construction and rehabilitation of more than 68,000 rental units and had provided homeownership opportunities to over 24,000 households (MHFA, 1991). For the vast majority of MHFA's multi-family developments, the typical borrower has been a private for-profit entrepreneur, but as the overall share of affordable housing development by nonprofits began to increase, the MHFA became significantly more involved with nonprofit housing development.

In 1986, the MHFA convened the Inner City Task Force, whose goal is "to make fundamental improvements in the quality of life in the neighborhoods, looking beyond the repair of bricks and mortar and focusing upon problems of crime and drug trafficking" (MHFA, n.d.). Membership on the task force includes a host of representatives from the public and private sectors who have expertise in housing, law enforcement, and social services. According to the MHFA, the task force was the first such initiative launched by a state housing finance agency in this country.

State Regulatory Initiatives

In addition to the many initiatives outlined above that directly support affordable housing production, the state also has adopted several regulatory measures that relate to nonprofit housing development. In 1969, the Massachusetts legislature passed Chapter 774, which authorizes a state Housing Appeals Committee to override local zoning decisions. The committee can issue a developer a comprehensive permit if it finds that the developer's original application was turned down because it involved the production of multi-family housing. This so-called "anti-snob zoning law" provides a good lever for encouraging a dialogue between developers and local officials, and cases often are resolved before they reach the state committee. If, however, Chapter 774 is invoked and a local zoning decision is reversed, the developer must earmark at least 25 percent of the units built for affordable housing. Since the inception of Chapter 774, an average of only fifteen cases per year have been filed, and only about one quarter of the cases filed resulted in "full substantive decisions" on behalf of the developers. Although Chapter 774 is generally viewed as a good tool for underscoring local responsibility to provide affordable housing, and hundreds of units have been produced under this law, it is, nevertheless, a weak regulation.

Partially in response to the weaknesses of Chapter 774, Executive Order 215 (issued by Governor Edward King in 1982) directs all state agencies that administer development-related assistance programs to consider whether the applicant community's housing policies and practices are unreasonably restrictive (Massachusetts Executive Office of Communities and Development, n.d.). The state has indicated that a realistic goal is for each city or town to eventually have at least 10 percent of its housing stock affordable to low- and moderate-income households. However, cities and towns can be in compliance with the executive order by developing a plan and detailing specific actions that will facilitate affordable housing production. As of November 1990, only nineteen cities and towns in Massachusetts had reached the 10 percent goal. Yet, only four were found to be "unreasonably restrictive." Although the rhetoric of the executive order is supportive of affordable housing development, like Chapter 774, it appears to have had only a small impact on patterns of suburban housing development.

The City of Boston's Programs

With the election of Mayor Raymond Flynn in November 1983, affordable housing in general and nonprofit housing in particular became key concerns of the new administration. Similar to the state, Boston has impressive direct as well as regulatory strategies.

Boston has been aggressively pursuing a policy of disposing of city-owned land to nonprofits committed to producing affordable housing. Vacant school buildings, urban renewal parcels, and tax-delinquent properties are all under the jurisdiction of either the Boston Redevelopment Authority or the Public Facilities Department. It is the policy of the Flynn administration that these properties be used for affordable housing whenever feasible. In order to "make the numbers work," housing sponsors must pay little or nothing for the land. Approximately 350 units of low-cost and market-rate housing have been constructed, with over 1,500 additional units in the "pipeline." Units typically sell for $60,000-$100,000, with low-interest mortgages, to households earning between $25,000 and $38,000 per year.

Boston's Management Assistance Program/Technical Assistance Program (MAP/TAP) is similar to the state's CEED program. MAP/TAP provides operating assistance and funding to cover basic organizational costs, overhead, and salaries. A total of about $500,000 per year is provided through the city's Community Development Block Grant to support about ten community organizations. In addition, the Boston Redevelopment Authority, operating on an ad hoc basis, gives away substantial amounts of money from its own budget (which is partially derived from income from leasing parcels that it owns) to nonprofits in order to make specific deals work. Supplementing this type of funding, staff members from both the Public Facilities Department and the Boston Redevelopment Authority often provide aggressive assistance to nonprofits, virtually serving as project directors in some cases. In addition to the MAP/TAP program, nearly half the City's $18 million Community Development Block Grant goes to nonprofit organizations to support their housing development activities.

An extreme case of the Flynn administration's support for community-based development is the Dudley Street Neighborhood Initiative. In late 1988, this organization was given the ability to acquire by eminent domain and to then lease out for development fifteen acres of privately held land located in the community. The land is being used for construction of approximately 500 units of low- and moderate-income housing, as well as for other community purposes. In order to facilitate the assembly of buildable parcels, the City also has expedited foreclosure proceedings on properties in tax arrears and then turned them over to the Dudley Street organization.

City Regulatory Initiatives

Boston has heavily utilized regulatory measures to produce or maintain affordable housing. In addition to rent control and condominium conversion ordinances, the city has a linkage program and an inclusionary zoning policy.

Boston was the second city in the country to adopt a linkage program. Following the lead of San Francisco, housing advocates concluded that the downtown building boom was having a negative effect on the neighborhoods. With a new group of managers and executives locating in Boston, the affordable housing stock was being squeezed. As the more affluent newcomers began competing with long-time residents for available units, linkage was looked to as a way to make the downtown developers responsible for the plight of lower income Bostonians.

Linkage requires a cash payment by a private developer or the direct provision of neighborhood housing, job training, or social services in exchange for the necessary permits for a given downtown development. The current linkage program called for developers of commercial properties to contribute $6 for every square foot in excess of 100,000 square feet of construction to a housing fund over a period of seven years. In lieu of these payments, the developer has the option of building affordable housing directly and creating a job training program for Boston residents who would become permanently employed at the project.

As of October 1989, over $76 million in linkage funds were committed by 41 downtown developers. More than one-third of this was committed to housing development, totaling about 2,900 units. Eighty-four percent of the funds were allocated to nonprofit housing developers (Dreier and Keating, 1990). The linkage program does have problems, however. Since groups awarded linkage funds must wait seven to twelve years for their full allocation, lenders are unwilling to provide financing based on the promise of future payments. In order to obtain the needed debt financing, nonprofits are having to find sources willing to secure the future value of the linkage funds at a present value rate.

Finally, the Flynn administration has pursued a vigorous inclusionary zoning policy. Any developer who builds more than ten units of housing is strongly encouraged to enter into negotiations with the city and guarantee that 10 percent of the units will be affordable to low- or moderate-income households. A ruling by the U.S. Supreme Court in 1987 cast some doubt on the constitutionality of mandatory inclusionary zoning. As a result, the City has continued to request voluntary compliance with the inclusionary zoning guidelines. Although it is not stated that the necessary permits will be withheld if such a "voluntary" agreement is not reached, there is an implicit understanding that doing business with the City requires this type of cooperation. By early 1989, the inclusionary zoning policy was responsible for producing 231 units of housing affordable to low- and moderate-income tenants and amassing over $2 million in developer contributions (Dreier and Keating, 1990).

Umbrella Organizations, Intermediaries, Consultants, and Foundations

In addition to the array of state and local programs that support nonprofit development, the city and state are also fortunate to have several exemplary umbrella organizations, intermediaries, consultants, and foundations that further enhance nonprofit housing development activities. The first two are local offices of national organizations, while the remainder are Boston-based.

The Neighborhood Reinvestment Corporation is a congressionally chartered, public, nonprofit corporation committed to revitalizing declining neighborhoods for the benefit of current residents. The corporation channels funds, which are raised both through private donations and congressional appropriations, to local projects. As mentioned earlier, the best known of the several public-private partnership approaches used by the corporation is the Neighborhood Housing Services program.

Local Initiatives Support Corporation (LISC), created in 1980, is a national intermediary organization that raises money from corporations and foundations and channels these funds into local nonprofit housing and economic development ventures. LISC has designated Boston as one of its areas of concentration, and it has played an active role in supporting nonprofits in the city. Since the Boston LISC office was opened, over $2 million has been raised from private corporations, financial institutions, and foundations. These funds are then matched by the national LISC organization.

The Neighborhood Development Support Collaborative (NDSC), launched in 1987, is an effort spearheaded by LISC to provide multi-year operating grants and technical assistance funding to support Boston-area community development corporations. Each of ten CDCs received about $65,000 annually for five years. NDSC successfully tapped into the enormous resources of the United Way of Massachusetts Bay, receiving a grant of $1.8 million. Other funding (more than $3 million) for NDSC came from a variety of national and local foundations. NDSC served as the model for the United Way of America's Housing Initiatives Program, an effort that provides grants and technical assistance to five local United Way organizations to support partnership approaches to affordable housing development through CDCs.

The Metropolitan Boston Housing Partnership was formed in 1991 as a result of a merger of two agencies concerned with affordable housing, Metropolitan Housing, Inc., and the Boston Housing Partnership (BHP). The BHP, the larger of the two, was a public-private initiative established in 1983 by city government, large banks, and neighborhood organizations. BHP's overriding goal was to convert declining and abandoned housing into decent, affordable units for low- and moderate-income households, with community-based development organizations as major actors in the process. The partnership was a response to a number of events, including the loss of affordable rental housing in Boston's neighborhoods due to abandonment, arson, condominium conversion, and rising rents, as well as the drastic cutbacks in federal housing subsidies during the Reagan administration, particularly in the Section 8 New Construction and Substantial Rehabilitation programs.

The BHP made at least three major improvements over earlier efforts to rehabilitate housing. First, it managed to pull together a financing package sufficient to allow the rehabilitation to take place. The BHP aggregated financial resources from a host of federal, state, and local public sources as well as from private foundations. Second, the BHP put a great deal of emphasis on technical assistance. In addition to outside consultants, the BHP itself has been a major source of support to the participating nonprofits. Third, the BHP addressed how long-term affordability would likely be achieved. As the problem of "expiring use restrictions" was gaining attention, long-term affordability became a particularly important issue. By selecting community-based nonprofit sponsors, by structuring the syndication agreement to require that the units be maintained as affordable, and by making sure that the sponsors are all owed money when the depreciation benefits run out (due to the accrual of interest on loans made to the limited partnerships at the start of the development), it is hoped that long-term affordability will be realized.

The Massachusetts Association of Community Development Corporations was formed in 1980 and has 46 CDC members. The goals of the organization are to promote the CDC industry, generate resources and support services for CDCs, and conduct and disseminate research that can influence public policies pertaining to CDCs. As of June 1990, its members had produced over 8,300 units of housing and had been active in commercial and job development (MACDC, 1990).

The Boston Community Loan Fund is a private, nonprofit corporation that was created in 1984 to help raise private investment capital targeted for community-based affordable housing development. The Institute for Community Economics in western Massachusetts, provided assistance in developing the fund. A total of $5 million has been raised from over 300 investors, who lend the fund as little as $1,000 for one year at interest rates of 5 percent or lower. Borrowers use the fund to assist with project costs such as land acquisition and gap financing. Average loans have been in the range of $50,000 to $80,000, and they carry an interest rate of about 6.8 percent. To date, the fund has assisted in creating or preserving over 1,000 units of affordable housing (BCLF, 1989/1990).

The Community Builders, Inc. (TCB), a key participant in nonprofit housing development in Boston and throughout the state and region, provides technical assistance to community-based sponsors of housing for low- and moderate-income residents. Although in many respects it operates similarly to a private developer, TCB's first priority is to help community-based groups achieve their own housing and community development goals. Since 1964, TCB and its predecessors have helped over 30 nonprofit housing sponsors to develop over 4,000 units of housing.[3] In addition, TCB manages over 1,500 units of housing, some of which it played a role in developing.

One of TCB's most important contributions has been the way in which it has used limited partnerships and, more recently,

---

[3] Until 1990, TCB was known as Greater Boston Community Development, Inc.; in its earliest years, it was called South End Community Development.

low-income housing tax credits to benefit community-based housing sponsors. TCB claims that it has "structured limited partnerships so as to maximize the financial benefits to the sponsor and
the development while protecting the sponsor's tax exempt status
and control over the development" (Greater Boston Community
Development, 1984, p. 12).
    The Massachusetts Housing Investment Corporation was cre-
ated in 1990 by a consortium of Boston banks. The impetus for
this new entity was a series of reports published by the Boston
Federal Reserve Bank and the Boston Redevelopment Authority
that detailed discriminatory investment patterns in low-income and
minority neighborhoods. The corporation's funds will be allocated
for low-income housing, thereby providing another source of financing for Boston's nonprofit housing developers.

CRITICAL RESOURCE NEEDS AND OBSTACLES
FOR NONPROFIT HOUSING DEVELOPMENT

Despite the wealth of city and state resources, nonprofits in
Boston still face a host of serious obstacles to continued and
increased affordable housing production. There are at least five
critical ingredients of nonprofit housing development—financial
resources, land and buildings, experienced staff, technical assistance, and overall level of public support. Each one presents
problems to varying degrees.

Financial Resources

The largest problem facing nonprofit developers in Massachusetts
(and elsewhere) is money. With the federal withdrawal from
housing production programs during the twelve years of the Reagan and Bush administrations, all developers of affordable housing, regardless of where they are located, face the persistent problem of where and how to finance their projects as well as meet
their organizational expenses. This problem is particularly acute
for areas like Massachusetts, which experienced considerable inflation in housing costs through the 1980s. Although prices in the
early 1990s generally fell slightly, the absolute costs were still
among the highest in the country.
    In order for nonprofits to put together their developments,
they typically use a host of public and private funds. Recently,

it has become common to call these deals "patchwork financing." While the phrase may have a cozy connotation, these arrangements are typically laden with complexity and multiple requirements from each funding source. There are several distinct types of financial resources that are required by nonprofit housing developers. It is important to keep in mind, however, that most of these separate funds could be folded into a fairly simple and straightforward funding mechanism for nonprofits if sufficient federal resources were available.

Non-project-based funding for overhead and salaries: Although both the State and the City offer innovative and extremely valuable sources of this type of funding, grants to nonprofits are not large—usually about $25,000 to $30,000—and only partially cover the costs associated with maintaining an organization. In addition, as mentioned earlier, in recent years there have been major cutbacks in the CEED program, and its overall viability is in doubt.

Access to capital: In order for nonprofits to take advantage of land and building deals that come their way, they ideally should be able to operate as quickly and efficiently as their for-profit counterparts. However, for nonprofits it is very difficult to line up funding for a "good deal" quickly and, further, the purchase would be subject to review by the donor or lender of the funds. Although this arrangement makes sense in many situations, and some bad mistakes are likely avoided, the seasoned nonprofit that knows its local market well would possibly end up losing out while the funding and approvals are being sought.

Front money for site clearance, engineering, and architectural expenses: In the pre-construction phase of development, there are a number of costs that a developer encounters. For the nonprofit, these costs can present significant problems and must somehow be covered through a combination of loans or grants, because the capital that is generally accessible to for-profit developers is not available. Despite the social orientation, goodwill, and commitment of many of the lenders in the state, negotiations are often extremely time-consuming. Even the most experienced nonprofit housing developers in the state have encountered long delays, and for groups with lesser track records, raising up-front money can be even more problematic.

Low-Income Housing Tax Credit: The Tax Reform Act of 1986 replaced a highly popular vehicle for raising equity for low-income developments with a Low-Income Housing Tax Credit. Prior to 1986, developers of low-income housing sold shares of their development to limited partners who were attracted to the venture because of their ability to deduct the losses generated from the development, thereby sheltering other taxable income. Under the tax credit program, tax benefits are less generous, and there are greater financial incentives for private corporations, rather than individual high-income investors, to purchase the tax credits. As a result, in comparison to the capital that could be raised under the pre-1986 tax laws, tax credits generally provide less capital to low-income housing developments. Without adequate syndication proceeds, it is very difficult for nonprofits to raise the needed cash to make the overall financing package feasible.

Gap financing: When investors purchase low-income housing tax credits, their payments are phased in over a number of years, thereby leaving the organization short of funds in the early years, when construction and other start-up costs are highest. The Ford Foundation, LISC, and CDFC (as well as some financial institutions) are all sources of gap financing. However, the amount of money that can be raised through gap financing is usually much lower than the actual amount of money that will be received from future tax credit payments. For example, in a large-scale housing development built in Boston during the late 1980s, known as Tent City, the first payment of the committed $10 million in syndication funds was not due for a full year after construction was started. In order to close the financing gap, only one private lender, Shawmut Bank, was willing to provide a bridge loan—but this was for only $875,000—less than 10 percent of the money due to be paid by investors. A similar problem exists for linkage payments that are sometimes paid over an extended number of years. Again, the nonprofit developer needs the money up-front and must locate other sources of funding to cover the short-term gap.

State subsidies: State commitments for subsidies are often the minimum rather than the maximum. For example, under the state's major housing production program, only 25 percent of the units must be affordable to low-income households. Instead, the program's guidelines could be restructured so that a higher percentage of affordable housing be mandated.

Expiring Section 8 contracts: Most of the older nonprofits in the state, those that have been in operation since the 1970s, are beginning to face the reality that Section 8 rental rehab contracts, which were originally for 20-year terms, will be expiring within the next decade. As with all components of the Section 8 program, the federal government provides a rent subsidy on behalf of low-income tenants. From the point of view of the developer or landlord, Section 8 provides a guaranteed rent for a specified period of time. If a Section 8 contract expires and is not renewed, the owner of the housing may find it difficult to find a tenant who can afford the rental price. For example, in a unit for which operating and debt service costs may total $500, the tenant may only be paying $200, with the remainder of the rent covered by the Section 8 program. However, with these commitments expiring, it is unclear whether new Section 8 subsidies or vouchers will be forthcoming or whether other rental subsidies through the state's Chapter 707 program, for example, will be available. However, as mentioned above, with all state housing programs presently being squeezed, it is not certain that sufficient subsidies will be available. Thus, the nonprofits will have to figure out some way to help tenants pay the rent. The "bottom line" for them, as with all landlords, is that they must raise enough from rentals to pay the bills.

Unexpected shortfalls: Any housing developer, whether experienced or inexperienced, whether nonprofit or for-profit, may have to face unexpected shortfalls in funds. Projects can be delayed for unforeseen reasons, staffing problems can arise, and errors in judgment can occur. For the nonprofit housing developer, any such mishap could jeopardize its operation. City and state officials in Massachusetts have been known to provide substantial financial and technical resources to assist a faltering nonprofit if they feel the organization has long-range potential. Ideally, the public sector should be prepared to help troubled organizations as part of its overall support system but, at the very least, it is crucial that emergency assistance be available.

Land and Buildings

It is somewhat ironic that the old federal urban renewal program, which had such a devastating effect on so many urban neighborhoods, also turned out to be a boon to some nonprofit developers. For example, one prominent affordable housing developer in Boston, known as IBA (Inquilinos Boricuas en Accion—Puerto Rican Tenants in Action), was able to gain a foothold in the South End of Boston primarily because it was named the developer of a parcel of urban renewal land. Without this considerable advantage, it is highly unlikely that the developer would have been able to assemble or afford a comparable piece of land. In that case, the 800 units that are now under IBA's ownership or management never would have been built.

IBA's successes have not come easily, however, Under Mayor Flynn's predecessor, Kevin White, nonprofits faced much more of an "uphill battle," and although IBA finally won in the end, its designation as developer came after years of struggle. At times it seemed likely that the Boston Redevelopment Authority would name a for-profit sponsor, not IBA, to develop the land. Elsewhere in the state, nonprofits and local governments do not always have good working relationships, thereby making the choice of a nonprofit developer even less likely.

Despite Boston's current policies to transfer city-owned land to nonprofits wherever feasible, there is concern that available land is quickly disappearing as the city's land-disposition programs are reaching their goals. While in the short run this contributes to affordable housing production, over the long run this depletion of a scarce resource will certainly further constrain low-income housing efforts. Unless a great deal of buildable land and reusable housing is bought quickly by nonprofits or placed into a land trust, the amount of money needed to produce affordable housing remains substantial. Despite a slight decline in prices since the late 1980s, units in multi-family structures suitable for rehabilitation often cost significantly more than in the mid-1980s. Unfortunately, this increased price does not necessarily translate into better quality units, and costs are further pushed upward by the generally higher construction costs.

Experienced Staff

The ability of nonprofits to hire and maintain high-quality staffs is a major problem facing these organizations. Three aspects of this issue are noteworthy. First, and most obviously, nonprofits pay lower salaries than other employers for comparable positions. At both entry and more experienced levels, there is always the lure of doing similar work for a for-profit developer at much higher pay. In addition, in Massachusetts, where there are so many public- and nonprofit-sector jobs relating to nonprofit development, this problem is of particular concern. Second, the nature of nonprofit development work causes difficulties in maintaining skilled personnel. A common complaint is one of "burnout." The long hours, including community meetings, the frustrations of trying to put together deals with limited resources, the never-ending hustle to raise operating budgets, the long time-lags between project inception and completion can cause even the most dedicated worker to choose other employment. Third, most nonprofit housing development organizations are quite small. As a result, the number of professional staff members is usually very limited, and the opportunities for moving up a career ladder within a given group may be nonexistent. The need for long-term capacity building among nonprofit staffs is a real one, and anything that undermines this process will be detrimental to the nonprofit's work. Neil Mayer, in his seminal work on neighborhood development organizations, underscores the importance of a broadly skilled executive director and a key staff member with knowledge about development projects (Mayer, 1984).

Technical Assistance

Availability of quality technical assistance does not appear to be a major problem facing nonprofit housing developers in Massachusetts, particularly in the Boston area. The array of state and local agencies has enabled many young development organizations to flourish, and any legitimate group could likely locate competent help. Nevertheless, there may still be a need for additional technical assistance providers. Some groups are wary of, or intimidated by, the Community Builders, in part because it is thought that the organization tends to take over a project rather than simply serving as the consultant. Further, the other equally competent private development consultants are usually very busy.

Level of Support by City and State Administrations

The overall level of support offered to nonprofits by the City of Boston has been impressive since the start of the Flynn administration. Clearly, this is a critical component of a successful support system for nonprofits, and Boston's nonprofits are fortunate to be spared the enormous problem of "fighting city hall." There are only two relatively minor points of criticism in this regard, which certainly pale in comparison to the hostile political environment facing some nonprofits in other locales. First, the considerable involvement of the City has sometimes meant that certain decisions are made and priorities set that may conflict with those of the nonprofits. While not malicious, the City's strong ideas may sometimes appear to be "too much of a good thing." For example, the City, based on an assessment of overall housing needs, may have a preference for rental housing development, while the community group may favor building units for sale. Second, many for-profits that feel that they could help produce affordable housing in Boston feel squeezed out. Although they may recognize the unique strengths of nonprofits, they also feel that their proven track records should put them in a more preferred position than the City accords them. This feeling has been particularly evident in the minority development community, where for-profit developers often feel that they should have at least an equal opportunity to get projects in their communities.

During most of the 1980s, the Dukakis era in Massachusetts, nonprofits received unprecedented and unparalleled support. However, with the dawn of the 1990s, fiscal realities in Massachusetts and a no-new-taxes governor (Governor Weld) are creating what may become insurmountable obstacles for the housing support system in the state, as well as for the nonprofits themselves. This, then, is the "Achilles' heel" of the Massachusetts story. Although there have been impressive levels of productivity and creativity by the state's public and private institutions and by the nonprofits, this "golden era" may be short-lived.

As the city and state programs in Massachusetts have evolved and matured, it appears that the system now has too many actors and too many programs and is, overall, too cumbersome. Because the programs at both the city and state levels evolved piecemeal, rather than as part of a comprehensive structure, each new agency and each new program has created something of a bureaucratic maze. In short, the nonprofit housing system in Massachusetts is currently facing problems of coordination. While this is a problem that many groups in many parts of the country would love to face, it still makes for a more complex and time-consuming development process than is optimal. Obviously, it would be far simpler for all city programs and all state programs that support nonprofit housing developers to be coordinated through a single office. However, at this point in each agency's development, turf issues are real, and any effort on the part of city or state officials to create a more rational system would certainly be viewed as a threat to the nonprofit movement in general. Although the recent cutbacks in state funding could enhance coordination, this does not appear to be the motive of Governor Weld's administration. Rather, many agencies and programs are withstanding across-the-board budget reductions. Localities that are considering building a support system for nonprofits more or less "from scratch" would be better able to systematically design each necessary component and to ensure coordination. Elsewhere, however, where some pieces of the system exist, problems such as those cropping up in Massachusetts are likely.

CURRENT ISSUES FOR NONPROFITS

Although the accomplishments of community-based housing have been gaining increased recognition, it is also important to acknowledge the shortcomings of this strategy. Limitations include the relatively small number of units produced and the uncertain ability of nonprofits to increase production and management capacity; the long lead-times needed to get groups ready to develop housing; and the difficulty of trying to attack problems at the local level when the roots of those problems are regional, national, or even international (Bratt, 1989b). While the first two of these could be more fully addressed with adequate financial resources and technical assistance for community-based housing developers, the third is potentially the most problematic. Nevertheless, where housing needs are acute and the responses from other actors and institutions are inadequate or nonexistent, we do not have the luxury of bemoaning larger economic trends that may be beyond the reach of the local nonprofits. The only reasonable response is to work at the margins of the economic system and to do whatever is possible to try to meet the need and alleviate human suffering.

Internal Dilemmas Facing Nonprofit Housing Developers

In addition to the difficulties discussed above, community-based housing groups also face a series of dilemmas, the resolution of which are not always readily apparent. An understanding of these dilemmas is important for several reasons.[4] First, as a practical matter, it is helpful for community-based housing developers to be prepared for these dilemmas and to realize that many of their problems are shared by other groups. Whenever possible, it is also important to chronicle how these dilemmas are being resolved so that groups can learn from each other. Second, from a theoretical and policy perspective, exploring dilemmas of community-based housing increases our understanding of this important strategy for providing affordable housing. It makes housing analysts and policymakers more aware of the potential contributions of the approach, as well as enhancing an understanding of how policies could best be created to address problems facing nonprofits.

Maintaining community and tenant orientation while functioning as a developer and landlord: Clearly, any landlord, whether nonprofit or for-profit, must be concerned with the overall economic viability of the development. The tenants' goal—to keep rents as low as possible—may be at odds with that of the owner, who also must cover the expenses even if this necessitates a rent increase. A sensitive community-based group may be caught between economic realities and human needs.

Balancing advocacy and project development work: Many community-based development groups, which were originally organized around advocacy issues, became frustrated with the limited gains they achieved through protest and became involved in development work. Although some groups appear to have combined advocacy and development, many others have found that protest, on the one hand, and cultivating good relationships with city hall and the real estate and banking communities, on the other, are contradictory.

Potential for conflict between the original objectives of the agency and those of newcomers to the community: As a commu-

---

[4] These dilemmas are discussed in greater detail in Bratt, 1989b, 1990a.

nity changes, possibly upgrading in response to the efforts of the development organization, it is possible that a new group of residents will move into the area and attempt to alter the mission of the original group, including converting any housing owned and managed by the organization into market-rate rental units or condominiums. Unless the low-income housing has been safeguarded through long-term use restrictions, the tenants may run the risk of being displaced.

Marketing units to neighborhood residents while conforming to civil rights and equal housing laws: A significant aspect of community-based housing development work involves providing improved housing to the group targeted by the organization. However, this may conflict with various laws that require housing to be marketed on an equal-opportunity basis. Clearly, there is a need for any community organization to develop its base of support within the community, to enhance its position of leadership, and to legitimize itself as a force for community building. But in the quest of building community, preferential treatment for neighborhood residents may be unfair to others who are equally, or even more, needy. This is particularly troubling—and possibly illegal—if those who are excluded are racial or ethnic minorities.

Limiting equity appreciation to owners who have purchased homes from community-based housing developers, as opposed to allowing them to enjoy the same equity appreciation as other owners: The result is that purchasers of property developed by community-based organizations are not able to gain as much of a foothold in the economy as other comparable property owners. By limiting equity appreciation, the units stay permanently affordable and available as a community resource, thereby promoting long-term neighborhood stability. Yet, one could also argue that it is unfair to treat the first group of purchasers differently from others of the same income level who have managed to purchase property from a market seller. In addition, the policy of equity caps could be viewed as unfair because wealthier owners are able to take full advantage of the appreciation of their property while still enjoying the homeowners' deduction.

Future Challenges for Nonprofits

Despite the obstacles facing nonprofits in their efforts to produce affordable housing, as well as the dilemmas that they are encountering, there is little question that nonprofits *can* develop attractive and affordable projects. Two major questions related to the future of nonprofits should be addressed.

First, will nonprofits be able to go beyond production and contribute to neighborhood revitalization by producing other social benefits for the residents and for the community? As mentioned earlier, we do not yet have good data on the non-housing benefits that accrue to residents and neighbors of community-based housing developments. Since much of the rationale for community-based housing rests on assumptions about the likely social benefits that flow from this form of housing, it is essential to understand what the nonprofit approach can deliver besides providing good housing.[5]

A second key question is: What is the capacity of nonprofits to maintain the units they own over the long term? In the end, the success of the nonprofit production programs will be measured more by whether the developments built remain viable and affordable over the long term, rather than by whether community-based nonprofits can produce needed units over the short term. Informal conversations with CDC directors and individuals working for several of the support agencies mentioned in this chapter point to the necessity of concentrating more resources on management issues. In investigating management, future research will need to focus on the quality of the management, the economic viability of the nonprofits' projects (including the existence of adequate operating and replacement reserves), and the mix of services provided to different types of resident populations.

The Federal Agenda

Despite the relative lack of information about some of the key questions facing nonprofits, they have nevertheless recently gained visibility in policy debates and have won some important legislative victories at the national level. The Financial Institutions

---

[5] As noted earlier, research on this question is currently under way at the New School for Social Research in New York City.

Reform, Recovery, and Enforcement Act of 1989 (known as the savings-and-loan bailout legislation) provides nonprofits the first right to purchase distressed savings-and-loan properties from the Resolution Trust Corporation. In addition, the Cranston-Gonzalez National Affordable Housing Act of 1990 requires each jurisdiction receiving funds under Title II, the "HOME" program, to set aside 15 percent of its allocation for nonprofit, community-based housing development organizations. Although this was a major success for the nonprofit community-based housing movement, it falls far short of developing the kind of overall public support system for nonprofit housing that I would advocate. Further, with the passage of this legislation, it appears that further lobbying for programs in support of community-based housing has waned. In short, advocates may have won the battle, but lost the war. Once again, we will have the opportunity to assess whether half a loaf is better than no loaf at all.

Also significant is the provision under Title VI of Cranston-Gonzalez that gives nonprofit organizations and other "priority purchasers" the first right to make a bona fide offer to purchase a federally subsidized development whose owner has announced an interest in prepaying the mortgage. Under the terms of several public-private housing subsidy programs enacted in the 1960s, notably the Section 221(d)(3) and Section 236 programs, private owners of federally subsidized housing were given the option of terminating their agreements with the Department of Housing and Urban Development at the end of 20 years by paying off the outstanding balance owed on the mortgage. This action would then relieve the owner of the requirement to rent the housing to low- and moderate-income households. As the first of these projects reached their twentieth year, tenants in many projects received eviction notices as their landlords made the decision to convert the buildings to high-cost condominiums or to market-rate rental housing. Title VI of the 1990 housing act was an attempt to address this problem and to provide a permanent solution to the problem known as "expiring use restrictions."

The overriding issue surrounding all these new initiatives that provide a significant role for nonprofits is whether the federal government will commit the financial resources to lift its apparent commitment to these organizations to a level beyond rhetoric.

CONCLUDING NOTE

Persistent problems and difficulties notwithstanding, Boston has been blessed with a relative wealth of supports and financial resources for nonprofit, community-based housing. It can serve both as a model for how much a city and state working together can do and as a way of learning about where the gaps still lie. Boston's experiences also underscore a number of points about nonprofit housing in general and about the ways in which the public sector can best support these initiatives. In considering how various levels of government could best devise resources and supports for nonprofit housing, the following broad, but straightforward, observations may be useful.

First, all public and public-private partnership programs that are created should be *clearly* aimed at promoting nonprofit housing development and at removing as many obstacles to this process as possible. The obstacles discussed above should be addressed, and suitable programs, many of which have been pioneered either in Massachusetts or elsewhere, should be launched to overcome them.

Second, the programs should be kept simple. If one were designing a completely new support system for nonprofits, the city and state programs discussed in this chapter would provide a starting point, but not a model to be replicated in full. These support systems are laden with complexity, overlaps, and probably even inconsistencies. Each agency and program uses different forms, has different guidelines, and has goals that are only slightly different from each other. Extreme care should be exercised to maximize the comprehensiveness of any support system while making certain that it is as streamlined as possible. This is important to make the programs "user friendly" for the nonprofits, as well as to minimize overall costs. It is logical that the more complex the program and the more actors involved, the more costly the final product. Thus, the goal of affordable housing is undermined if layers of bureaucracy are part of the housing development process.

Third, as mentioned earlier, the array of state programs created to support nonprofit housing is currently in jeopardy. Given the tight fiscal situation in Massachusetts, housing programs are being cut back or terminated. Despite the state's longstanding commitment to subsidized housing—a commitment that grew considerably during Dukakis's twelve years as governor—the current outlook for state support of housing programs is not positive.

Without a significant and sustained commitment at the federal level, even a well-developed state support system can be quickly and effectively dismantled.

In conclusion, it is important to underscore that, although the City of Boston and the Commonwealth of Massachusetts have done a great deal to support nonprofit, community-based housing development, these efforts go only part of the way toward building a comprehensive program to support nonprofits. Strong federal policies, programs, and financing are critical to a full-blown affordable housing system.

REFERENCES

Apgar, William C., Jr., Denise DiPasquale, Jean Cummings, and Nancy McArdle (1991). *The State of the Nation's Housing, 1991.* Cambridge, Mass.: Joint Center for Housing Studies, Harvard University.

BCLF (1989/1990). "Annual Report." Boston: Boston Community Loan Fund.

Bratt, Rachel G. (1989a). "Community-Based Housing in Massachusetts: Lessons and Limits of the State's Support System." In Sara Rosenberry and Chester Hartman, eds., *Housing Issues of the 1990s.* New York: Praeger.

———— (1989b). *Rebuilding a Low-Income Housing Policy.* Philadelphia: Temple University Press.

———— (1990a). "Community-Based Housing: Strengths of the Strategy Amid Dilemmas That Won't Go Away." In Naomi Carmon, ed., *Neighbourhood Policy and Programmes: Past and Present.* London: Macmillan.

———— (1990b). "Neighborhood Reinvestment Corporation-Sponsored Mutual Housing Associations: Experiences in Baltimore and New York." Washington, D.C.: Neighborhood Reinvestment Corporation.

———— (1991). "Mutual Housing: Community-Based Empowerment," *Journal of Housing*, vol. 48, no. 4 (July/August 1991), pp. 173-180.

———— (1992). "Federal Constraints and Retrenchment in Housing: The Opportunities and Limits of State and Local Governments," *Journal of Law and Politics*, vol. 8, no. 4 (Summer 1992), pp. 651-701.

CDFC (1990). "Annual Report." Boston: Community Development Finance Corporation.

Clay, Phillip L. (1990). "Mainstreaming the Community Builders: The Challenge of Expanding the Capacity of Nonprofit Housing Development Organizations." Cambridge, Mass.: Department of Urban Studies and Planning, Massachusetts Institute of Technology.

Dreier, Peter, and Dennis Keating (1990). "The Limits of Localism: Progressive Housing Policies in Boston, 1984-1989," *Urban Affairs Quarterly*, vol. 26, no. 2 (December 1990), pp. 191-216.

Greater Boston Community Development, Inc. (1984). "Building Communities." Boston: Greater Boston Community Development.

Leonard, Paul A., Cushing N. Dolbeare, and Edward B. Lazere (1989). *A Place to Call Home: The Crisis in Housing for the Poor*. Washington, D.C.: Center on Budget and Policy Priorities and Low-Income Housing Information Service.

MACDC (1990). "Annual Report, July 1989-June 1990." Boston: Massachusetts Association of Community Development Corporations.

_____ (1991). "1991 Report."

Massachusetts Executive Office of Communities and Development (n.d., circa 1985). "Local Housing Policies and State Development Assistance: A Guide to Executive Order 215." Boston: Massachusetts Executive Office of Communities and Development.

Massachusetts Government Land Bank (1991). "Developments." Winter Newsletter.

Mayer, Neil S. (1984). *Neighborhood Organizations and Community Development: Making Revitalization Work*. Washington, D.C.: Urban Institute Press.

MHFA (1991). "Annual Report." Boston: Massachusetts Housing Finance Agency.

_____ (n.d.). Inner City Task Force memorandum. Boston: Massachusetts Housing Finance Agency.

MHP (n.d., circa 1985). "Initiatives for Local Housing Partnerships." Boston: Massachusetts Housing Partnership.

NCCED (1991). "Changing The Odds: The Achievements of Community-Based Development Organizations." Washington, D.C.: National Congress for Community Economic Development.

Peirce, Neal R., and Carol F. Steinbach (1990). "Enterprising Communities: Community-Based Development in America,

1990." Washington, D.C.: Council for Community-Based Development.
Vidal, Avis C. (1989). "Community Economic Development Assessment: A National Study of Urban Community Development Corporations." Preliminary Findings. New York: New School for Social Research.

ACKNOWLEDGMENTS

I am grateful to the following individuals for the time and information that they provided during the preparation of this chapter: Peter Dreier, Boston Redevelopment Authority; Rebecca Black, Boston Public Facilities Department; Jean DuBois, Boston Community Loan Fund; Miriam Colon, Massachusetts Executive Office of Communities and Development; Louise Elving, The Community Builders; Lew Finfer, Massachusetts Affordable Housing Alliance; Mossik Hacobian, Urban Edge; Bill Jones, Codman Square Community Development Corporation; Margo Kelly, Neighborhood Reinvestment Corporation; Robert Kuehn, Keen Development Corporation; Pat Libby, Massachusetts Association of Community Development Corporations; Werner Lohe, Massachusetts Executive Office of Communities and Development; Pat McGuigan, Boston Public Facilities Department; Nancy Nye, Local Initiatives Support Corporation; Joanne Potter, Boston Aging Concerns; Carl Sussman, Community Economic Development Assistance Corporation; Richard Thal, Inquilinos Boricuas en Accion; Bob Whittlesey, Boston Housing Partnership; and Laura Younger, Massachusetts Executive Office of Communities and Development. I am particularly grateful to Peter Dreier of the Boston Redevelopment Authority for his comments on an earlier draft and to Lawrence B. Joseph, Center for Urban Research and Policy Studies, University of Chicago, for his many editorial suggestions.

COMMENTS

Kristin Faust

Rachel Bratt's chapter gives a thorough description of the policy environment in Massachusetts for nonprofit housing developers. In describing this environment, Bratt identifies several obstacles and issues faced by the developers. Each and every one of those obstacles, dilemmas, and challenges faced by the nonprofits in Massachusetts are also faced by nonprofit community development corporations (CDCs) in Chicago.

Like Boston, Chicago has an exciting development environment. Over 30 successful CDCs build or rehabilitate low-income housing in Chicago. Indeed, CDCs have played an important role in the development of low-income housing in Chicago for at least 20 years.

Several trends have led to the increased role that nonprofit, community-based developers have taken in Chicago:

- There has been a growing self-awareness among nonprofits that they could help the renewal of a neighborhood by stepping into local housing markets that conventional lenders and developers shunned. The successes of the nonprofits led to renewed interest by the private sector to reinvest in communities and prevent their continued deterioration.
- Housing costs soared in the 1980s, reducing the supply of affordable housing and thereby exacerbating the housing problem.
- Housing supply was also decreased by large-scale abandonment of multi-family buildings by their owners. Over the past two decades, more housing units in Chicago were destroyed than built. Most of the new housing was built for people with middle to upper incomes. Altogether, the city lost about 34,000 housing units during the 1970s and more than 41,000 during the 1980s (Holleb, 1993, Table 3).
- The drastic cutbacks of federal funds, as well as the difficulty in getting access to the funding still available, reduced the construction of new affordable housing units.

• The number of families with children living in public housing in Chicago has been decreasing since 1970, while the demand for affordable apartments has continued to grow. The
loss of some Chicago Housing Authority (CHA) units and the
decreased desirability of living in CHA housing have led to
the decrease in demand for CHA housing (Kelly, Kelly, and
Marciniak, 1988, p. 12-16).

Housing production by the nonprofits is impressive and growing. Between 1980 and 1990, CDCs in the city of Chicago created 5,209 units of affordable housing. This included 1,237 new
units and 3,972 rehabilitated units. Another 1,186 units were in
the pipeline in 1990, yielding a ten-year total of 6,395 units
(Chicago Rehab Network, 1990, pp. 20-21).

"A new spirit of confidence, a belief in its capacity and potential, pervades the community development field at the start of the
1990s" (Peirce and Steinbach, 1990, p. 7). The great irony is that
at a time when CDCs have more capacity, more experience, and
more demand for their product than ever before and when they
are poised to produce more housing than ever, resources from the
federal government remain far from adequate. Notwithstanding
the new funds resulting from the National Affordable Housing Act
of 1990, lack of federal resources is still a key obstacle in addressing the affordable housing problem. There are, however,
other dilemmas, obstacles, and challenges that CDCs face.

Bratt's chapter identifies five critical resource needs for nonprofit housing developers: financial resources, land and buildings,
experienced staff, technical assistance, and overall level of public
support. David Hunt, executive director of the Chicago Rehab
Network, a citywide, multi-racial coalition of community-based
housing development organizations, identifies a similar set of issues. Hunt states that the top three issues facing CDCs in low-
income housing production are: (1) the need for more resources,
including dollars for running the agencies, financing the deals,
purchasing land and buildings, providing social services, and subsidizing rents; (2) the need for more programs designed to meet
the needs of the truly needy, especially in times of scarce government resources;[1] and (3) the need to have a respectable place at

---

[1] The Chicago Rehab Network defines the truly needy as 50 percent
of median family income for the city of Chicago (about 35% of the median for the metropolitan area), or about $16,000 for a family of four.

the table—to be invited to the table when policies are being decided in a way that allows input and final say in the design, implementation, and evaluation of programs (Hunt, 1991).

Bratt also identifies two overarching challenges relating to the future of nonprofit developers: Will nonprofits be able to go beyond housing production and contribute to neighborhood revitalization and produce other social benefits for the residents and for the community? What is the capacity of nonprofits to maintain the units they own over the long term? Chicago-based CDCs have begun to address the second challenge with the formation of the Property Management Resource Center, a nonprofit organization with the goal of improving management skills for those who manage low-income housing, particularly nonprofit managers. New programs and ownership structures such as community land trusts have been developed to maintain the long-term affordability of housing units.

The first challenge is being met by those CDCs that have developed a holistic approach to their communities. These organizations offer other services such as job training, health care, day care, and legal assistance. More and more developers, even those who will never offer such a broad range of social services, are recognizing the need for more social services for tenants. At the same time that developers are moving toward providing more social services, more traditional social service agencies are moving into housing. The necessity to look at jobs, education, and housing in a continuum becomes more evident.

A final challenge not raised by Professor Bratt, but one that I would like to pose, is: Can nonprofit housing developers alone meet the demand for affordable housing? The answer to that, I believe, is no. CDCs begin from a position of mission and commitment that few private developers will ever share, and some CDCs can offer the additional social services often needed by tenants. However, in a market-based economy such as ours, where most of the production is driven by the private sector, the private, for-profit developer must become an important provider of low-income housing. This is the only way that this country is ever going to come close to meeting its housing demand. Policies and programs to encourage the development of low-income housing need to address not only the nonprofit developer but also the private developer. Policymakers must understand that it is proper, for both the nonprofit and private developer, to generate income from developing low-income housing. Together, the CDCs, the "ma and pa" investors, and full-time, for-profit developers can develop real estate that will allow all people in this country to live in decent housing and not pay a disproportionate share of their income toward that housing.

REFERENCES

Chicago Rehab Network (1990). *The Chicago Affordable Housing Fact Book: A Resource for Community Action.* Chicago: Chicago Rehab Network.

Holleb, Doris (1993). "Disparities and Opportunities in Chicago-Area Housing." In this volume.

Hunt, David (1991). Interview with author. Chicago Rehab Network, October 7, 1991.

Kelly, Christine Kuehn, Donald C. Kelly, and Ed Marciniak (1988). *Non-Profits with Hard Hats: Building Affordable Housing.* Washington, D.C.: National Center for Urban Ethnic Affairs.

Peirce, Neal R., and Carol F. Steinbach (1990). *Enterprising Communities.* Washington, D.C.: Council for Community-Based Development.

SUBVERTING JUSTICE: THE CASE OF AFFORDABLE HOUSING POLICY IN NEW JERSEY

Roland Anglin[*]

Suburban integration, both racial and economic, has long been proposed as a way to help alleviate some of the problems faced by central cities (e.g., poverty, fiscal distress). The argument, while couched in many forms, finds a base in calls for social justice and economic efficiency. Those arguing social justice make the obvious case that racial and economic exclusion is antithetical to standard American codes of fairness and opportunity (Danielson, 1976). The economic argument states that urban areas have lost their comparative advantage in manufacturing and are no longer large employers of unskilled labor (Peterson, 1985). Blacks and other minorities who came to the central cities in their waning days as large-scale employers are now trapped in a linked cycle of unemployment, poor education, poverty, family dissolution, and crime (Wilson, 1985; Orfield, 1985). The way to break this cycle, it is said, rests with free movement of trapped individuals into circumstances (i.e., suburbs) where jobs are plentiful, education is better, and the social mores are conducive to labor force participation (Orfield, 1985).

By themselves, the social justice and the economic efficiency arguments should be compelling statements for racial and economic inclusion. However, when tried through various policy mechanisms (e.g., busing, open housing), there has been massive opposition. Some of this resistance may well be racist or tinged with a subtle class bias.

---

[*] This research was supported by grants from the Schumann Foundation of New Jersey and the Provost's Office at Rutgers University. I wish to thank Alan Rosenthal and Carl Van Horn of the Eagleton Institute of Politics for their support. Norman Glickman, director of the Center for Urban Policy Research, arranged release time to complete the analysis and writing.

The most embattled form of exclusion may be the exclusionary zoning laws practiced by suburban jurisdictions. By zoning for low densities, a suburb can effectively exclude renters and those unable to purchase large lots. Since many low-income individuals can only afford to rent, they are effectively barred from living in communities with growing economies and good schools (Danielson, 1976).

Of all the efforts to promote inclusionary zoning, perhaps none has been so extensively watched as the long effort by the New Jersey Supreme Court to open the suburbs to the urban poor.[1] In a series of rulings stretching back to 1973, the state supreme court ruled in the case of *Southern Burlington County NAACP v. Township of Mount Laurel* that by promulgating exclusionary zoning, the township of Mount Laurel was violating the equal protection clause of the state constitution.[2] This far-reaching ruling essentially said that growing municipalities in the same region as a central city were obligated to make available low-income housing within their boundaries (Erber, 1983; King, 1978). For nearly ten years, municipalities failed to comply with the court's edict. In 1983, the court handed down a second ruling providing more stringent guidelines and remedies for local compliance.

The second court ruling, and the accompanying remedies, forced the legislature to enact a statute that, when implemented, fostered the production of low- and moderate-income housing (Zax and Kayden, 1983). The Fair Housing Act of 1985 provided for the creation of a Council on Affordable Housing and a variety of other tools to help increase the production of low- and moderate-income housing in the suburbs (Zax and Kayden, 1983).

This chapter examines the history of court-ordered inclusionary housing in the state of New Jersey, ending with the legislative enactment of the Fair Housing Act. The conclusion is that instead of clarifying and adding to the court's intent, the Fair Housing Act diluted the court's effort with policy mechanisms that were

---

[1] New Jersey is not the only state whose supreme court has ruled against exclusionary zoning. New Hampshire's court recently ruled that suburbs cannot use zoning laws to prevent the construction of low-income housing, and California, Pennsylvania, and New York courts have all used part of the *Mount Laurel* rulings to strike down exclusionary zoning.

[2] *Southern Burlington County NAACP v. Township of Mount Laurel*, 67 N.J. 151, 336 A.2d 713 (1975), appeal dismissed and certified.

unable to foster low-income housing but were able to stimulate some moderate-income housing. Coupled with external factors, such as private market constraints, the production of low- and moderate-income housing in the state of New Jersey stands woefully inadequate.

The New Jersey experience offers several lessons for other states (and for advocates of affordable housing): First, judicial attempts at fostering inclusionary zoning are necessary but limited as a means of upward mobility for *low-income* urban dwellers. Second, legislative responses can be just as limited as judicial responses, depending on the political environment surrounding enactment and implementation. Finally, states must employ a variety of policy mechanisms in attempts to foster low- and moderate-income housing.

MAKING HISTORY: THE FIRST *MOUNT LAUREL* DECISION

The New Jersey Supreme Court, in its 1975 decision on *Southern Burlington County NAACP v. Township of Mount Laurel*, held that the township's zoning laws violated the state's constitution because they unduly restricted the construction of low- and moderate-income housing.[3] At the time, Mount Laurel's zoning laws allowed only detached, single-family housing along with a minimum lot size. The crux of the 1975 decision stated that "developing" towns had an obligation under the equal protection clause of the state's constitution to provide for a realistic supply of affordable housing. The court recognized that many developing municipalities surrounded stagnant central cities. Zoning, a state-granted police power (which must promote the general welfare) was being used to prevent central-city dwellers from potentially taking advantage of employment opportunities in these growth areas. Accordingly, the court ruled that due process and equal protection were being denied to individuals of various income classes wishing to live in these growth areas.[4]

---

[3] Ibid.

[4] Ibid.

Initial Redress

In its decree, the court maintained that developing municipalities had a constitutional duty to provide a "fair share" of affordable housing in their region. Unfortunately, the court left open the meaning of "fair share." The decree did not suggest an objective method of determining geographic regions, or regional need, nor did the court broach the issue of what constituted affordability (Rose, 1983). It left these issues for the trial courts to decide. The court ruling did not result in a substantial amount of new affordable housing units. Instead, the ruling launched a great deal of litigation in the lower courts initiated by municipalities, civil rights groups, and developers, all aimed at clarifying the initial ruling (Rose, 1983).

In 1977, the state supreme court, faced with many *Mount Laurel* cases in the lower courts, returned to the question of inclusionary zoning. The major issue in the case of *Oakwood at Madison, Inc. v. Township of Madison* was the court's position on municipal fair-share obligations.[5] In what some termed a major retreat, the court lessened the impact of its first ruling by stating that the lower courts did not have to define what constituted a region, nor should they assign numerical guidelines for fair-share obligations by municipalities.[6] Perhaps reacting to the empirical difficulty of defining what constitutes affordable housing, the court directed that municipalities only had to make a good-faith effort to provide "least-cost housing" instead of low-income housing (Rose, 1983; Payne, 1983).[7]

---

[5] *Oakwood at Madison, Inc. v. Township of Madison*, 72 N.J. 481, 371 A.2d 1192 (1977).

[6] The original ruling resulted in an array of "experts" flooding the lower courts with expert testimony on what constituted appropriate regions and fair-share numbers. It reached the point of statistical overload for the lower courts, which then delayed swift decisions in *Mount Laurel* cases.

[7] "Least-cost housing" was a nebulous concept. Basically, the court acknowledged that suburban jurisdictions were experiencing difficulty promoting low-income housing. Thus, the court allowed suburbs to substitute a good-faith effort at promoting housing at the "least cost" relative to prevailing housing and rental prices.

Specifying "least-cost" housing changed the original target population of *Mount Laurel I,* which had been the urban poor. The only logical beneficiaries of a least-cost strategy seemed to be middle-income individuals and families living in both central cities and the suburbs. Essentially, this ruling released growing municipalities from an obligation to provide housing for the urban poor. The court addressed this perception by stating a hope that the new criteria (least cost) would increase the total number of available housing units, thus speeding the filtering of low-income housing to the poor.[8]

The court also established additional safeguards, such as the "builder's remedy," as a way to ensure that its edict would not be ignored. Through this court-stipulated remedial action, any developer could sue a town in which zoning laws prevented construction of a project where some units were set aside as affordable units. The remedy proved to be an effective stimulant in that it flooded the courts with many suits initiated by builders. It did not prove effective, however, in stimulating a significant amount of housing units—either "low-income" or "affordable."[9]

Dissecting the Solution

The fact that *Mount Laurel I,* and the court's subsequent ruling in 1977, produced much consternation and little housing (affordable or least cost) is a matter of historical record. There are two questions here: Why did the court's initial foray produce such limited results, and what might have happened if the ruling had been implemented in the best possible circumstances?

---

[8] There is some question as to the effect of the least-cost strategy. One pernicious effect, if the ruling had been able to make a difference in housing production, would have been to encourage middle-class urban residents to relocate to the suburbs, further depleting cities of these very important individuals.

[9] The difference between "low-income" and "affordable" is crucial here. Low-income housing was central to the original court intention of creating housing opportunities for individuals and families labeled low-income (usually those at some percentage of the poverty line). Affordable housing carries no such stricture. Affordable housing is a relative concept that can mean housing that is affordable for individuals and families that, by income, are traditionally thought to be middle-class.

Judicial policymaking may seem to present an attractive alternative to the fractious push and pull of mutual adjustment between elected officials, bureaucrats, and the public. It seems attractive in the sense that the judiciary can, theoretically, deliver justice and act in the real interest of the polity without the constraints of the extreme compromises that often limit public policy (Lowi, 1979). It is not clear, though, that judicial policymaking can escape standard problems of implementing public policy (Mazmanian and Sabatier, 1989). For example, a major problem in implementation is the construction of clear, directive policy statements that frame the nature of the problem and the solution. *Mount Laurel I*, although bold and seemingly proactive, did not provide a substantive base that addressed most of the contradictory elements of such a broad and sweeping ruling (Mazmanian and Sabatier, 1989). This is why in the years immediately following the first *Mount Laurel* ruling, the lower courts were deluged with cases attempting to clarify issues of affordability and fair-share obligations.

By not articulating clear directives, the court actually exacerbated these conflictual issues, which were bound to undermine the goals of the ruling. To be fair, it is not clear what the court could have done to avoid this situation. The value of judicial intervention is to set a course, not to draft legislation. Although the ruling was a bold and perhaps correct initiative, it should have been a precursor to legislative debate and action. This is clearly what the court had hoped would happen. Open housing did not have much public support; in fact, it had public antipathy. As a result of the perceived public sentiment, elected officials avoided the issue, thus forcing the court to make public policy that may have been outside its jurisdiction.

Since the ruling did not lead to a response from the legislature, external conflict limited the intent of the ruling. Many of the affected parties, specifically suburban municipalities, had no real incentive to encourage the building of affordable housing. Some would argue that they had a strong incentive not to help this process along (Tiebout, 1956; Peterson, 1981; White, 1978). Granted, there may have been recalcitrance on the part of many suburban jurisdictions, but the court did not provide meaningful guidance on how a local political entity could intervene in private housing markets. The court did suggest tax incentives, but it is doubtful that any local jurisdiction could provide the type of incentives needed to spur a significant number of low-income and affordable housing units.

The first round of the *Mount Laurel* rulings did not provide any clear direction for the process of implementing low-income housing for the urban poor. The subsequent 1977 ruling added to the confusion. In rethinking its original ruling, the court may have recognized the difficulty of providing clear directions for implementation. It was evident, though, that the reformulation of low-income housing to "least-cost" housing significantly changed the intent of the first ruling.

Instead of a specific strategy to help cities, the reformulation had the potential to hasten the death of cities (Rose, 1983; Hughes and Vandoren, 1990). Also, by simply making suburbs responsible for a good-faith effort and least-cost housing, the court opened the door for easy circumvention. Least-cost housing was bound to be a relative concept when put into practice.

In addition to maintaining economic segregation, the least-cost strategy had the potential of contributing more to middle-class flight from central cities, thereby increasing suburban sprawl. The least-cost strategy probably redistributed housing to middle-class households irrespective of initial residence (Rose, 1983; Hughes and Vandoren, 1990). The first round of court-inspired low-income housing did not generate many low-income units. The remedies suggested by the New Jersey Supreme Court generated increased fighting in the lower courts without much resolution (Rose, 1983).

MOUNT LAUREL II

After the 1977 ruling, the lower courts interpreted the ruling as a retreat and acted accordingly. In some cases, the lower courts refused to reprimand jurisdictions that were found guilty of blatant exclusionary practices before *Oakwood at Madison*. Even with this lessening attention by the lower courts, the unresolved issues still caused a number of suits. The state supreme court re-entered the fray in 1980 by considering six cases with the similar, and by now, old problem of how to decide what constituted a municipal fair share of least-cost housing—not low-income housing (Payne, 1983).

The court started its deliberation in October 1980 by hearing testimony from interested parties. Acting much as a legislature, the court required concerned parties to form themselves into interest-group blocs (e.g., municipalities, developers, civil rights groups). As one observer put it:

The "argument" itself was as extraordinary as its setting. Because virtually all the lawyers involved were intimately familiar with the actual process of housing development, their arguments had the feel of testimony at a legislative hearing, rather than appellate advocacy. The members of the court in turn slipped readily into the role of legislators, peppering the speakers with well-informed questions to elicit facts (seldom law) about housing economics and the mechanics of land development (Payne, 1983, p. 88).

The court heard arguments and deliberated for 27 months. A decision was reached in June 1983. The court again changed course and returned to many of the principles outlined in the 1973 decision. *Mount Laurel II*, as the decision has come to be called, was direct and decisive. Unlike *Mount Laurel I*, *Mount Laurel II* set specific standards and methods for determining fair-share obligations. In the past, part of the problem was forecasting growth areas of the state that the court could use to assign fair-share obligations. The court ruled that growth areas were to be determined by the State Development Guide Plan (SDGP), which was a product of the Division of State and Regional Planning located in the Department of Community Affairs (Erber, 1983; Rose, 1983).

The SDGP allowed the court to target specific regions as developing areas or areas of conservation. In developing regions, the court separated housing into two parts: present need and prospective need. Present need covered existing housing that was physically dilapidated, crowded, or occupied by low- or moderate-income individuals. Prospective need tried to predict the increase in eligible households for a six-year period.

The court also tried to rationalize the process through which builders could sue localities. These suits had been clogging the lower courts since *Oakwood at Madison*. The court directed *Mount Laurel* litigation to three specific judges. These judges were mandated to guide the revision of local zoning ordinances, suspend construction on projects until local ordinances were deemed satisfactory, invalidate any local municipal restriction governing land use, and approve specific applications for low- and moderate-income housing.

Overall, the court specified a number of strictures and remedial devices. Some of these include the following:

• The court affirmed the right of government intervention to encourage low-income housing through government subsidy (if available) and tax abatements.
• It approved the device of density bonuses to private contractors. Here, localities could award higher densities to contractors who would then set aside a certain number of low-income units in a market-rate housing development.[10]
• It limited mobile-home construction as a mechanism to satisfy municipal fair obligation.
• It precluded the use of *Mount Laurel* decisions as a basis for encouraging middle-income housing. (The court also limited the least-cost doctrine to only extreme cases where low-income housing could not be built.)
• It held that some exclusionary devices, such as large lot zoning, were legal if the municipality could satisfy its *Mount Laurel* obligation.

This stronger thrust by the court caught the attention of the legislature in a way that they could no longer ignore. The governor, Thomas Kean, pronounced the ruling as something akin to communism. The fact is, though, the court's ruling forced elected officials to confront the issue that they had avoided for five years.

The remedial actions by the court had an immediate impact, particularly the density bonuses and the actions of the three-judge tribunal overseeing local land-use decisions. Local governments in rapidly growing areas (much of New Jersey in the 1980s) were besieged by developers seeking density bonuses and suing localities under the builder's remedy. For example, from 1980 to 1985, 70 of the state's 567 municipalities were sued by developers seeking zoning changes. Local government officials pressed the governor and the legislature for help in fending off these suits (Payne, 1983). The Kean administration, in an effort to wrest the regulation of land use back from the courts, introduced legislation that was to eventually become the Fair Housing Act (which was signed into law in June 1985). The legislative history was uneventful in that legislators of both dominant parties wanted a response to *Mount Laurel II*; thus, political wrangling was relatively minimal.

---

[10] Because higher densities increase economies of scale, developers had an incentive to set aside some of their units as low-income.

The Fair Housing Act created the Council on Affordable Housing (COAH). This administrative agency, with a nine-member governing board composed of private citizens, developers, and public officials, was responsible for separating the state into five regions. COAH then established and projected the need for low- and moderate-income housing in these regions. It set limits for municipal fair shares based on the size of existing housing, present and projected employment opportunities, and amount of open land.[11]

After housing need was determined, COAH set time limits for compliance by the municipalities. It was given quasi-judicial power to enforce its regulations. Thus, in the extreme, COAH could deny access to state-generated infrastructure when that infrastructure was necessary for future development.

Participation in the COAH process was voluntary. The incentives to participate, however, were immunity from the builder's remedy, and if the municipality was being sued, it could transfer the case to COAH's arbitration process.[12] If a municipality chose to become part of the COAH process, the Fair Housing Act required the municipality to adopt a housing element in its master plan. This housing element was comprised of a municipal inventory of its housing stock; projection of future housing stock, along with projection of future construction of low- and moderate-income housing six years into the future; determination of the locality's present and future fair-share obligation and the municipality's ability to satisfy the obligations; and specification of land most appropriate for construction of affordable housing. The locality was also responsible for an inventory of existing stock most suitable for conversion or rehabilitation into low- and moderate-income housing.

Once the housing element of a local master plan was approved, the locality was responsible for outlining remedial mea-

---

[11] Fair Housing Act (P.L. 1985).

[12] The Fair Housing Act was conceived as a direct alternative to litigation in the courts. Thus the act stipulated that *Mount Laurel* cases, if they were filed before May 2, 1985, could be transferred to COAH. Any party in the case could request such a transfer. The courts agreed to honor such a request unless the transfer resulted in what was termed "manifest injustice." The act further stated that the builder's remedy could not be granted after July 2, 1985, thus providing relief to the courts.

sures. The remedial options open to localities included residential re-zoning for higher densities, state funds, tax abatements, funds from regional contribution agreements (explained later), and land donated by the municipality. Clearly, the aim of the legislation was to insert or return a measure of control to the localities. Granted, COAH had target figures for fair-share obligations, but allowing the municipalities to construct their own figures provided a sense of control and inclusion for the municipalities.[13]

When filing its housing plan with COAH, the municipality gained the opportunity to seek substantive certification of its plan. Certification gave the locality the legal presumption of having met its fair-share obligation for a period of six years. It must be noted that once the locality had submitted its plan to COAH, anyone could file an objection. COAH then mediated the differences between those objecting and the municipality. Ultimately, COAH granted or denied certification based on the results of the mediation.[14]

Regional Contribution Agreements

Perhaps the most interesting part of the Fair Housing Act was the inclusion of what were called regional contribution agreements (RCAs). Section 12 of the act provided that a municipality may "send" (essentially transferring) 50 percent of its fair-share obligation to a receiving municipality. The sending municipality pays the receiving municipality to build affordable housing units inside the boundaries of the receiving community.[15] In return, the sending municipality receives credit from COAH against its fair-share obligation.

---

[13] Fair Housing Act (P.L. 1985, c. 222). COAH reduced the 277,808 affordable housing units stipulated by the courts to 145,707. Fair-share quotas for many municipalities were reduced either outright or by allowing renovated housing to satisfy fair-housing requirements. COAH even credited basement apartments toward a town's fair-share quota. Municipalities were also excused if they had large tracts of land that were deemed environmentally sensitive.

[14] Ibid.

[15] The minimum a sending municipality could pay was $10,000 per housing unit.

The argument for regional contribution agreements was that some suburban municipalities did not have the capacity (e.g., land, infrastructure) to support new development, nor did they have the employment and educational opportunities that were based in the *Mount Laurel* rulings. Thus, framers of the legislation thought the best way to achieve a just solution in cases like these was to transfer the obligation to another municipality, usually an urban center with existing capacity.

The framers of the legislation saw the potential for some urban revitalization. The city receiving the obligation could use the money to provide affordable housing for urban residents through new construction, housing rehabilitation, or conversion of nonresidential space. The Fair Housing Act ensured the short- and medium-term affordability of RCA units. Owner-occupied, single-family units had to remain within income guidelines for affordability for six years. Rental units and conversions had a minimum of 20 years before they reverted to market rents.

COAH was responsible for determining regulations concerning the amount of contributions to any given RCA and the overall feasibility of the project. Negotiating an RCA was designed to be an arduous process. The receiving municipality had to submit a proposal to the county planning board, which then certified that the proposed RCA fit within state and local goals of sound regional planning (Selig, 1988). In addition, a project plan had to be submitted to the New Jersey Housing Mortgage and Finance Agency (HMFA). This agency determined the feasibility of the city's or developer's plan for obtaining a site for a project, or whether the units targeted for rehabilitation did indeed meet the guidelines for substandard dwellings (Selig, 1988).

State Funding of the Fair Housing Act

The Fair Housing Act apportioned $125,000,000 in total assistance for local governments through the Department of Community Affairs' Neighborhood Preservation Program and the HMFA's mortgage assistance programs. The Neighborhood Preservation Program granted loans for rehabilitation, conversions, acquisition of property, some pre-construction costs, new construction, and infrastructure costs. Funds from this program were made available to local governments whose housing element was certified or who were part of an RCA. Projects using these funds were required to put affordability limits on applicable units for 20 years.

Much of the assistance offered through the HMFA was through its low-interest mortgage loans. The same set of municipalities eligible for assistance under the Neighborhood Preservation Program was eligible for HMFA financing.

THE FAIR HOUSING ACT IN PRACTICE

The substantive aim of the Fair Housing Act was twofold. The first, and maybe the most important from the perspective of elected officials, was to remove the issue of inclusionary affordable housing from the purview of the New Jersey Supreme Court. The second aim, which follows from the first, was to respond programmatically to the ongoing concern of the court. In the time since the act was signed into law, the key questions have been how the act has been implemented and whether analysts can record any effects.

Dislodging Inclusionary Housing from the Courts

If dislodging the issue of inclusionary housing from the courts was partly the intent of the Fair Housing Act, then COAH has only experienced limited success. By April 1990, COAH had processed 90 municipalities and certified their housing elements for a potential 17,659 low- and moderate-income units. An additional 44 municipalities applied for certification with the potential construction of 12,001 low- and moderate-income units.

By most accounts, certification by COAH had reduced time spent in litigation. The process has compressed the average litigation time from nine years to an average time of 1.4 years. With the builder's remedy, attorneys for developers generally followed a strategy of delay through various motions, depositions, and interrogatories. This, of course, was costly to many local governments. Although many municipalities capitulated under heavy legal fees, the outcomes did not necessarily serve the public interest. The builder's remedy did force some low-income units to be included within larger market-rate developments, but this was a scattershot process without much planning. Thus, the builder's remedy may have contributed to unplanned suburban sprawl (Rose, 1983). It is doubtful that this type of development, without public transportation and ready access to schools and shopping, could provide a comfortable atmosphere for the target population under both *Mount Laurel* rulings (Mallach, 1984, pp. 14-15). The combative nature of litigation also lessened with the increased use of COAH. The burden of proof, which used to rest with the municipality, was removed by the certification process. With the presumption of validity, the burden of proof rested with challengers to any given COAH certification. And even then, the next course open to challengers (by statute) was mediation, not automatic reversal to the courts. In practice, though, some municipalities went back to court when faced with an adverse ruling by the COAH process.

The advantages of COAH (less time and money spent in the courts) resulted in the agency becoming a focus of attention in efforts to foster inclusionary housing. Thus, the strident voice and actions of the state supreme court were softened. COAH became a quasi-judicial organization, but with only a 20-person staff, it lacked the organizational capacity to handle increased caseloads and service functions. Without expansion of the agency, the courts may once more become the center of attention simply because they possess the capacity (e.g., personnel) to handle the cases.

Another reason the courts might again become a battleground is COAH itself. There is a solid argument to be made that COAH was constituted as an alternative to the state supreme court, but it has not become a tool for those wishing to avoid inclusionary zoning. In a 1988 ruling against the town of Fanwood, COAH displayed a marked level of independence during the mediation process. Fanwood was assigned a fair share of 87 subsidized low-income units. The township resisted compliance with the target figure, claiming that there was no space available within township boarders for development. Three developers petitioned COAH to force Fanwood to change its zoning laws to accommodate multi-family dwellings if they, the developers, could raze structures on parcels that they already owned. In other words, these developers had purchased parcels with single-family homes with the intent of building 75 condominium units. Fifteen units were reserved for low-income residents.

COAH ruled that because the developers were willing to subsidize the cost of razing, thus providing suitable sites, the township had to accept the offer or present alternative methods of producing their fair share of units. The decision had an intuitive logic, but municipalities saw it as a direct threat to their ability to make local zoning decisions. Fanwood appealed the results of the mediation to the state supreme court. The court upheld COAH's decision, but it was an indication that municipalities, even those who chose to participate in the COAH process, would not summarily accept an adverse judgment. Thus, the hope that COAH would displace the court as the arena of conflict over inclusionary zoning was premature.

Substantive Challenges to COAH

The Fanwood controversy was not the only challenge to COAH. Perhaps the biggest challenge to the COAH process came from those charging that the regional contribution agreements (RCAs) subverted the intent of the *Mount Laurel* decisions. Many observers were concerned that the ability to sell affordable housing obligations by a suburban municipality violated the spirit of the *Mount Laurel* rulings and continued the practice of economic and racial discrimination by suburban areas.

Proponents countered that RCAs were an optimal solution to the quandary of limited building capacity in one locality. The legislature sought to solve this problem by redistributing money to municipalities with the capacity to handle development but without the capital necessary to develop affordable housing. The problem, however, was that the sending municipalities bargained with more than one potential receiving municipality in order to lower the price of the affordable housing units. This was clearly logical in the context of a market economy, but the result was that receiving municipalities bid the price down to a level that could not cover the cost of building the RCA units. Thus, many receiving municipalities, mainly revenue-starved cities, had to cover the difference between the below-market cost of the units and their own resources. In addition, many of these agreements did not cover operating costs in the short and long term. These costs clearly add to overburdened central-city resources.[16]

The question then becomes: Why did cities enter into agreements that caused them to commit money to arrangements that were meant to be redistributive in their favor? The answer is complex and indicates the level of fiscal distress and need for affordable housing by New Jersey's cities. Even though older,

---

[16] By March 1990, 1,388 RCA units were certified by COAH, with only 677 actually completed.

distressed cities like Newark and Elizabeth expended money in order to cover the difference between the real cost of the development and what the sending municipality was willing to pay, the payment was still a sizable portion of the amount necessary to build or redevelop affordable units. This was not revitalization through redistribution of resources (as the legislature hoped), but a situation in which suburbs divested 50 percent of their fair-housing obligation, and cities paid (in part) for the sending suburb's desire to exclude by race and class.

There are situations in which RCAs have worked without the intensive bidding down of unit price of affordable housing. These instances are unique in that there is only one central city in the region. The city of New Brunswick in central New Jersey is a good example. New Brunswick, the only city in the region, has made extensive use of RCA money to build affordable housing units for local residents. Conversely, the cities of Newark and Elizabeth compete with each other for RCAs from suburbs in the region, thus creating a less than optimal bargaining situation for these cities.[17]

External Limits on the Effectiveness of COAH

Although the RCAs did provide some incentive for the production of affordable housing, such incentive must be placed in the broader perspective of the total number of units produced. COAH stipulated that the process as a whole would produce 145,000 units of new and rehabilitated affordable housing over the six-year period from 1987 to 1993. This target figure will not be achieved. In fact, in a survey of local governments conducted by the New Jersey Department of Community Affairs, it was found that there were only approximately 7,000 affordable housing units built or in the process of being built as a direct result the COAH process.[18] How can we account for the great disparity between the targeted figure and the units actually produced?

---

[17] The effect of this competition has been to fund minimal rehabilitation and not new construction.

[18] Much of the housing that has been built was bought by those earning $30,000 or more.

The answer to why the production of affordable units has been limited rests primarily with market forces. State regulations, though, must also shoulder some of the blame. Even with the remedies dictated by the Fair Housing Act, the fact remains that the production of affordable housing is directly tied to the production of market-rate housing. New Jersey's permit process is long. The average time for granting a permit for new development is approximately two years. This has dampened overall building in the state. Add to this the national recession, and the results have been very little production of affordable units (Council on New Jersey Affairs, 1991).

Thus after fifteen years of court-ordered intervention and then legislative action, the number of affordable housing units is negligible relative to the need COAH has established. The original intent of the court, that of allowing for the mobility of low-income minorities, is clearly not part of the current agenda of the court or the legislature. The current effort, with the emphasis on affordable housing and not low-income housing, resembles a face-saving affair for all involved.

CONCLUSION

This chapter has attempted to place the role of the judiciary in using housing as a means to social and economic mobility. Given the slim results in the New Jersey case, one might draw the conclusion that the court cannot be a force in causing social change—at least in the area of housing policy. This would seem to support a constrained view of the judiciary in this and other efforts to promote social justice.

Another view of this case says that the court was very successful if one views the judiciary as an arena in which the aggrieved can state a complaint, receive a fair hearing, and have the decision passed along to the next branch of government. Initially, the state supreme court attempted a statement of justice with the first *Mount Laurel* ruling. The reluctance of elected officials, perceiving little popular support for open housing, to fashion a legislative response presaged a further judicial action and active redress. Legislative movement on inclusionary housing came only after the court allowed builders and developers to sue localities if they refused to grant the zoning of low-income housing. Without this judicial valve, it is doubtful that supporters of inclusionary housing would have had access to an institutional forum that, at one level, promised justice and, at another level, attempted redress.

Although the court was not successful in the direct movement of low-income individuals from the state's urban areas, its deliberation eventually forced the legislature to act. The legislative response (the Fair Housing Act) created an organizational entity, the Council on Affordable Housing, that was supposed to satisfy the intent of the court. There is sparse evidence that COAH has satisfied the original intent of the court. Most of the problem centers on the limitations inherent in the structure and power of the original legislation (Mallach, 1984).

COAH was constructed to remove the issue of inclusionary housing from the judiciary. Thus, the legislation attempted a compromise between the strong concern for justice by the court and the interests of local and state elected officials who perceived strong opposition to inclusionary housing. The result was an entity that did not mandate participation on the part of local governments.

The legislation and the eventual implementation of the act allowed many avenues to circumvent a forceful inclusionary housing policy (Mallach, 1984). A clear example was the use of Regional Contribution Agreements, which allowed localities to transfer 50 percent of their COAH-stipulated low- and moderate-income responsibilities to other localities. Evidence suggests that this mechanism has not provided economic opportunities for low-income urban minorities. The majority of the transferred obligations are to urban areas with large concentrations of the poor and with limited economic opportunities. Thus, affordable housing units are being built in urban areas, but this violates the court's intention, which was to provide economic opportunity in growing areas of the state.

This politically directed diminution of the judiciary's intent, coupled with the organizational limits of COAH, has stymied justice—defined as free movement and choice by urban minorities. Again, this is a political choice by elected officials (Mallach, 1984). The judiciary played a strong role in forcing the other branches of government to protect the rights of minorities granted by the New Jersey constitution. This is, perhaps, all that can be asked of any court.

The lesson here is that at certain points, the court can be an invaluable tool for change. The judiciary, however, is not a panacea. Forceful movement on "fair housing" must be attempted in tandem with a state legislature that is committed to real change and provision of affordable housing. Without such commitment, it is difficult to imagine not only the construction of affordable housing, but the free and open choice in residence that assures the continued health of our metropolitan areas.

REFERENCES

Council on New Jersey Affairs (1991). "Housing Challenges and Opportunities." Princeton, N.J.: Council on New Jersey Affairs, Princeton University.

Danielson, Michael (1976). *The Politics of Exclusion.* New York: Columbia University Press.

Erber, Ernest (1983). "The Road to Mount Laurel," *Planning,* vol. 49, no. 10 (November 4-12, 1983), pp. 94-99.

Hughes, Mark Alan, and Peter M. VanDoren (1990). "Social Policy through Land Reform: New Jersey's Mount Laurel Controversy," *Political Science Quarterly,* vol. 105, no. 1 (Spring 1990), pp. 97-111.

King, Paul E. (1978). "Exclusionary Zoning and Open Housing: A Brief Judicial History," *The Geographical Review,* vol. 68, no. 4 (October 1978), pp. 459-469.

Lowi, Theodore J. (1979). *The End of Liberalism.* 2nd Ed. New York: Norton.

Mallach, Alan (1984). *Inclusionary Housing Programs: Policies and Practices.* New Brunswick, N.J.: Center for Urban Policy Research.

Mazmanian, Daniel A., and Paul A. Sabatier (1989). *Implementation and Public Policy.* Boston: University Press of America.

Orfield, Gary (1985). "Ghettoization and Its Alternatives." In Paul E. Peterson, ed., *The New Urban Reality.* Washington, D.C.: Brookings Institution.

Payne, John M. (1983). "Starting Over—*Mount Laurel II,*" *Real Estate Law Journal,* vol. 12 (Summer 1983), pp. 85-96.

Peterson, Paul E. (1981). *City Limits.* Chicago: University of Chicago Press.

_____ (1985). "Technology, Race, and Urban Policy." In Paul E. Peterson, ed., *The New Urban Reality.* Washington, D.C.: Brookings Institution.

Rose, Jerome G. (1983). "The *Mount Laurel II* Decision: Is It Based on Wishful Thinking?" *Real Estate Law Journal,* vol. 12 (Fall 1983), pp. 115-137.

Selig, John M. (1988). "Implementing Mount Laurel: An Assessment of Regional Contribution Agreements." Working Paper 14. Princeton, N.J.: Council on New Jersey Affairs, Princeton University.
Tiebout, Charles M. (1956). "A Pure Theory of Local Expenditures," *Journal of Political Economy*, vol. 64, no. 5 (October 1956), pp. 416-424.
White, Michelle J. (1978). "Self-Interest in the Suburbs: The Trend toward No-Growth Zoning," *Policy Analysis*, vol. 4, no. 2 (Spring 1978), pp. 185-203.
Wilson, William J. (1985). "The Urban Underclass in Advanced Industrial Society." In Paul E. Peterson, ed., *The New Urban Reality*. Washington D.C.: Brookings Institution.
Zax, Leonard A., and Jerold S. Kayden (1983). "A Landmark in Land Use," *National Law Journal*, March 14, 1983, pp. 11-41.

COMMENTS

William Peterman

If relevant federal legislation were taken seriously, there would be no housing problem in the United States. The Omnibus Housing Act of 1949 articulated a "goal of a decent home and suitable living environment for every American family," and the Fair Housing Act of 1968 outlawed housing discrimination. Yet decades after the passage of these acts, many Americans remain poorly housed, and segregation by class and race remains the rule rather than the exception.

In the Chicago metropolitan area, nearly one-half of all low-income rental households pay excessive amounts (over 35% of their incomes) for housing. Most of these households are concentrated in the central city. The metropolitan area remains highly segregated racially, and although the 1980s saw many Black households moving to the suburbs, most of these moves merely reinforced pre-existing patterns of segregation.

The disparity between Chicago and its suburbs can be seen in data from the 1987 American Housing Survey. Whereas the median household income for the eight-county Chicago metropolitan area was $30,396, it was only $21,608 for the city of Chicago itself.[1] Blacks in Chicago are in even worse shape. Their median household income was a mere $15,560 (U.S. Department of Commerce, 1990, pp. 22, 113). Computations made recently indicate a need in Chicago for a minimum of 50,000 additional low-income housing units. In the suburbs, where many of the jobs now are, low-income housing is nearly nonexistent.

Roland Anglin contends in his chapter that urban revitalization, low-income housing, racial justice, and affordable housing are separable issues. Although from an analytical perspective this may be true, in reality they are so entangled that it seems impossible to address any one issue without simultaneously addressing the others. A review of what we know about the intersection of race,

---

[1] The eight-county Chicago metropolitan area consists of Cook, DuPage, Grundy, Kane, Kendall, Lake, McHenry, and Will counties.

class, and housing may be helpful in exploring what effect court-enforced zoning changes might be expected to produce.

There are three common theories of why American neighborhoods remain racially segregated: racial segregation reflects class, rather than race, discrimination; segregation is voluntary; and segregation is caused by discrimination. A review of the research evidence finds that only the third theory, that of discrimination, explains observed patterns of segregation (Darden, 1987). Research centered on Chicago tends to support this claim. For example, a study using 1980 census data determined that based on economic status, suburban Schaumburg would have been nearly 15 percent Black rather than 1 percent, and Maywood would have been a little less than 20 percent Black rather than 71 percent (Kain, 1984). Another study, this one of Black households that had moved into integrated communities, found that while these households did not see integration as a primary goal, they viewed integrated neighborhoods as more desirable than segregated neighborhoods (Haines, 1981).

The relationship between racial discrimination in housing and community deterioration has been documented in numerous studies of redlining and disinvestment. In the "cycle of decline," proposed by activist Gale Cincotta to explain the process of neighborhood change in Chicago, the presence of minority households is seen by lenders as a reason to disinvest. My own study of racially changing neighborhoods in Chicago and its suburbs shows that integrated neighborhoods receive fewer loan dollars, fewer conventional loans, and more FHA- and VA-insured loans than all-White neighborhoods (Peterman and Qi, 1991). Race, it appears, is tightly intertwined with processes that lead to housing deterioration.

Low-income housing advocates commonly avoid raising issues of race. Anglin himself, after introducing integration and social justice as goals of the New Jersey Supreme Court's action, ignores them, except for brief remarks at the end of his chapter. He, like others, seems reluctant to talk about what to many is a delicate issue.

Neighborhood advocates and proponents of community-based development argue that funds for low-income housing should be provided in poor neighborhoods. They fear that plans to disperse the poor are plots to keep the poor from becoming organized. Yet, in advocating revitalization of these neighborhoods, they run the risk of perpetuating communities populated only by the underclass and play into the hands of suburbanites who want nothing to do with either minorities or low-income housing. Anglin notes that some suburban New Jersey sites proposed for low-income housing lack public transportation and ready access to schools and shopping. Given the dismal future projected for the Chicago Transit Authority, Chicago's continuing school problems, and the lack of commercial activity in many low-income neighborhoods, there seems to be little difference between critical amenities in these "undesirable" suburban sites and the inner city. But there is one big difference between the two: the jobs are in the suburbs.

Constance Perrin has convincingly argued that zoning and other land-use controls reflect our belief about the way society should be structured and thus are imposed in order to enforce the value systems of the middle-class majority population (Perrin, 1977). If so, then the New Jersey Supreme Court in *Mount Laurel I* correctly identified zoning as the culprit in perpetuating a class-segregated and race-segregated housing market. The court failed, however, to offer any workable remedies in *Mount Laurel I*, and when it did in *Mount Laurel II*, the state legislature quickly acted to thwart the court's intent and preserve the social order.

State government, caught between local government's desire to be autonomous and the federal government's inattention to housing issues, is somewhat helpless when it comes to addressing issues of race and class discrimination in housing. The real power to deal with the issue resides at the federal level, and state governments lack the resources needed to be effective. Unfortunately, the absence of any meaningful federal enforcement of the Fair Housing Act in the 20 years since its passage, as well as the failure of the federal government to pay serious attention to its 1949 housing goal, is sure to mean that housing problems will continue. In New Jersey, in Chicago, and elsewhere, we may be able to win a skirmish here and there, successfully integrate a few suburbs, build a few low-income homes. However, without the muscle and the money that only Washington can provide, we will continue to lose the war.

REFERENCES

Darden, Joe T. (1987). "Choosing Neighbors and Neighborhoods: The Role of Race in Housing Preference." In Gary A. Tobin,

358   *William Peterman*

ed., *Divided Neighborhoods: Changing Patterns of Racial Segregation*. Newbury Park, Calif.: Sage Publications.
Haines, Deborah (1981). *Black Homeowners in Transition Areas*. Chicago: Chicago Urban League.
Kain, John E. (1984). "Housing Market Discrimination and Black Suburbanization in the 1980s." In *Civil Rights in the Eighties: A Thirty-Year Perspective*. Chicago: Chicago Urban League.
Perrin, Constance (1977). *Everything in Its Place: Social Order and Land Use in America*. Princeton, N.J.: Princeton University Press.
Peterman, William, and Sanshi Qi (1991). "Lending Discrimination in Metropolitan Chicago: Continuing Connection Between Race, Racial Change, and Mortgage Credit." In *Credit By Color: Mortgage Market Discrimination in Chicagoland*. Chicago: Chicago Area Fair Housing Alliance.
U.S. Department of Commerce (1990). *American Housing Survey for the Chicago Metropolitan Area in 1987*. Washington, D.C.: U.S. Department of Commerce, Bureau of the Census, and U.S. Department of Housing and Urban Development, Office of Policy Development and Research.

NOTES ON CONTRIBUTORS

Roland Anglin is program officer with the Urban Poverty Program at the Ford Foundation. He was formerly on the faculty of the Department of Political Science and the Eagleton Institute of Politics at Rutgers University. He has also served as a special policy advisor to the governor of New Jersey.

Rachel G. Bratt is associate professor in the Department of Urban and Environmental Policy at Tufts University. Her publications include *Rebuilding a Low-Income Housing Policy*. She serves on the Multifamily Advisory Committee of the Massachusetts Housing Finance Agency.

Phillip L. Clay is professor and department head in the Department of Urban Studies and Planning at the Massachusetts Institute of Technology. His publications include *At Risk of Loss: The Endangered Future of Low-Income Rental Housing Resources.*

Teresa Córdova is assistant professor in the Department of Community and Regional Planning at the University of New Mexico. She was formerly a National Research Council post-doctoral fellow with the urban studies program at DePaul University and assistant professor of Latin American studies at the University of Illinois at Chicago.

Kristin Faust is vice president in the community development department at LaSalle National Bank in Chicago.

Paul B. Fischer is associate professor of politics at Lake Forest College.

Douglas C. Gills is assistant professor in the School of Urban Planning and Policy and the Center for Urban Economic Development at the University of Illinois at Chicago.

Susan Grossman received her Ph.D. from the School of Social Service Administration at the University of Chicago. She is co-author of *Homelessness in Chicago: Poverty and Pathology, Social Institutions and Social Change.*

Charles Hoch is associate professor in the School of Urban Planning and Policy at the University of Illinois at Chicago. He is co-author, with Robert Slayton, of *New Homeless and Old*.

Doris B. Holleb is professorial lecturer in social sciences and geographical studies at the University of Chicago. Her publications include *Social and Economic Information for Urban Planning* and *Colleges and the Urban Poor*. She is a member of the Plan Commission of the City of Chicago and a former commissioner and secretary of the Northeastern Illinois Planning Commission.

Lawrence B. Joseph is senior research associate in the School of Social Service Administration and associate director of the Center for Urban Research and Policy Studies at the University of Chicago. He is also program director of the Chicago Assembly.

Robert D. Katz is professor and director of the Housing Research and Development Program at the University of Illinois at Urbana-Champaign.

Thomas J. Lenz is program director of Local Initiatives Support Corporation in Chicago and former executive director of Voice of the People, a community development corporation in Chicago's Uptown neighborhood.

Laurence E. Lynn, Jr., is professor in the School of Social Service Administration and in the Irving B. Harris Graduate School of Public Policy Studies at the University of Chicago. He is also director of the Center for Urban Research and Policy Studies and project director of the Chicago Assembly.

Charles J. Orlebeke is professor and director at the School of Urban Planning and Policy, University of Illinois at Chicago. He served as assistant secretary for policy development and research in the U.S. Department of Housing and Urban Development during the Ford administration.

William Peterman is associate professor in the School of Urban Planning and Policy at the University of Illinois at Chicago.

Alexander Polikoff is executive director of Business and Professional People for the Public Interest (BPI), a public interest law center in Chicago. He served as lead counsel for the plaintiffs in

Gautreaux v. Chicago Housing Authority and U.S. Department of Housing and Urban Development, a lawsuit that successfully challenged racial discrimination in the location policies of Chicago's public housing. He is the author of *Housing the Poor: The Case for Heroism.*

James E. Rosenbaum is professor in the School of Education and Social Policy and in the Department of Sociology at Northwestern University. He is also affiliated with Northwestern's Center for Urban Affairs and Policy Research.

Barbara A. Shaw is coordinator of housing policy initiatives with Community Investment Corporation in Chicago.

Deborah C. Stone is executive director of the Metropolitan Planning Council in Chicago.

Richard P. Taub is professor in the Social Sciences Collegiate Division at the University of Chicago. His publications include *Paths of Neighborhood Change: Race and Crime in Urban America* (with D. Garth Taylor and Jan D. Dunham) and *Community Capitalism.*

George S. Tolley is professor in the Department of Economics at the University of Chicago. His publications include *Housing Dynamics and Neighborhood Change* (co-edited with William B. Shear).

John C. Weicher is currently a visiting economist with the U.S. General Accounting Office. He served as assistant secretary for policy development and research in the U.S. Department of Housing and Urban Development during the Bush administration.

CHICAGO ASSEMBLY PARTICIPANTS
"AFFORDABLE HOUSING IN METROPOLITAN CHICAGO"
NOVEMBER 4-5, 1991

Roland Anglin
Assistant Professor
Department of Political Science
Rutgers University
(New Brunswick, N.J.)

Yasmin T. Bates
Vice President
Harris Trust and Savings Bank
(Chicago)

John J. Betancur
Assistant Professor
Center for Urban Economic
    Development
University of Illinois at Chicago

Rachel G. Bratt
Associate Professor
Department of Urban and
    Environmental Policy
Tufts University
(Medford, Mass.)

Michael Breslan
President
Chicago Building Trades Council

Cranston Byrd
Deputy Director, Community and
    Economic Development
Lake County Planning Department
(Waukegan)

Eduardo Camacho
Manager of Urban Lending
St. Paul Federal Bank
(Chicago)

Lawrence Christmas
Executive Director
Northeastern Illinois Planning
    Commission
(Chicago)

Phillip L. Clay
Associate Professor
Department of Urban Studies
    and Planning
Massachusetts Institute of
    Technology
(Cambridge, Mass.)

Marion Coleman
Executive Director
Covenant Development Corporation
(Chicago)

Teresa Córdova
Assistant Professor
Department of Community
    and Regional Development
University of New Mexico
(Albuquerque, N.M.)

William P. Cowhey
President
The Civic Federation
(Chicago)

Peg Cullen
Executive Director
Resource Center for the Elderly
(Arlington Heights)

Louis Delgado
Program Officer
John D. and Catherine T.
    MacArthur Foundation
(Chicago)

Charla Denton
Housing Counselor
Will County Center for
    Community Concerns
(Joliet)

John Donahue
Executive Director
Chicago Coalition for the Homeless

Pat Dowell-Cerasoli
Deputy Commissioner
Department of Planning
City of Chicago

Kristin Faust
Vice President
Community Development
    Department
LaSalle National Bank
(Chicago)

Barbara Ferman
Associate Professor
Department of Social Sciences
Illinois Institute of Technology
(Chicago)

Salvatore V. Ferrera
President
Metropolitan Housing
    Development Corporation
(Chicago)

Michael Fontana
Chicago Builders, Developers,
    and Contractors Association

Thomas G. Fuechtmann
Associate Vice President
Loyola University of Chicago

Douglas Gills
Center for Urban
    Economic Development
University of Illinois at Chicago

Kathleen A. Gilmer
Director of Corporate Services
William Rainey Harper College
(Prospect Heights)

William L. Goldsmith
Executive Director
New Cities Community
Development Corp.
(Harvey)

Barbara Gordon
Executive Director
Lake County Community
    Action Project
(Waukegan)

Jennifer Gordon
Assistant to the Governor
State of Illinois
(Springfield)

William J. Grimshaw
Associate Professor of
    Political Science
Illinois Institute of Technology
(Chicago)

Frances R. Grossman
Executive Director
Continental Community
    Development Corp.
(Chicago)

Susan Grossman
Project Coordinator,
    NIAAA Project
School of Social Service
    Administration
University of Chicago

Suzanne Hayes
Community Development Director
Cook County Department of Policy,
    Planning, and Development
(Chicago)

Greg Heine
Director, Office of Development
Chicago Housing Authority

Maureen Hellwig
Director of Community Economic
    Development
Erie Neighborhood House
(Chicago)

James D. Hemphill
President
Homebuilders Association
    of Greater Chicago
(Northfield)

Josephine Herrera
Robert R. McCormick Tribune
  Foundation
(Chicago)

William W. Higginson
President
Chicago Equity Fund, Inc.

Rev. Clarence L. Hilliard
President
West Side Isaiah Plan
(Chicago)

Charles Hoch
Associate Professor
School of Urban Planning
  and Policy
University of Illinois at Chicago

Elizabeth C. Hollander
Director, Government Assistance
  Project
Chicago Community Trust

Doris B. Holleb
Professorial Lecturer
Social Sciences Collegiate Division
  and Committee on Geographical
  Studies
University of Chicago

Robert T. Holtz
Director and Treasurer
Bridge Communities, Inc.
(Wheaton)

Fr. Mike Ivers
St. Agatha Catholic Church
(Chicago)

Robert D. Katz
Director and Professor
Housing Research and
  Development Program
University of Illinois at
  Urban-Champaign

Glen A. Kehrein
Executive Director
Circle Urban Ministries
(Chicago)

Harry Kurshenbaum
President, Local 73
General Services Employees Union
(Chicago)

Thomas J. Lenz
Program Director
Local Initiatives Support Corp.
(Chicago)

Harvey Lichterman
Attorney
Lord, Bissell & Brook
(Chicago)

Robert L. Lucas
Executive Director
Kenwood-Oakland Community
  Organization
(Chicago)

Ed Marciniak
President
Institute of Urban Life
(Chicago)

Jack Markowski
Executive Director
North West Housing Partnership
(Elk Grove Village)

Rosanna Marquez
Assistant to the Mayor
City of Chicago

Luz M. Martinez
Executive Director
Voice of the People, Inc.
(Chicago)

Alberta McCain
President
Dearborn Homes Resident
  Management Corp.
(Chicago)

John F. McDonald
Professor
Department of Economics
University of Illinois at Chicago

Judy Meima
Acting Director
Statewide Housing Action Coalition
(Chicago)

Richard Mergener
Director of Resource Development
Habitat for Humanity
(Chicago)

Therese M. Mierswa
Assistant Vice President
First National Bank of Chicago

Jennifer Miller
Manager, Community Development
Illinois Housing Development
   Authority
(Chicago)

Sid L. Mohn
Chief Executive Officer
Travelers and Immigrants Aid
(Chicago)

Lynn Montei
Executive Director
DuPage Mayors and
   Managers Conference
(Carol Stream)

Barbara Moore
Director of Community Relations
Village of Park Forest

William Moorehead
Near North Development Corp.
(Chicago)

Laurence Msall
Associate Director
Civic Committee of the
   Commercial Club
(Chicago)

Janet R. Muchnik
City Manager
City of Country Club Hills

Hugh P. Murphy
Acting Commissioner
Department of Housing
City of Chicago

Philip Nyden
Chairperson and Professor
   of Sociology
Loyola University of Chicago

Charles J. Orlebeke
Professor
School of Urban Planning
   and Policy
University of Illinois at Chicago

Kathleen Osberger
Program Director
National Assembly of
   Religious Women
(Chicago)

William Peterman
Associate Professor
School of Urban Planning
   and Policy
University of Illinois at Chicago

Alexander Polikoff
Executive Director
Business and Professional People
   for the Public Interest
(Chicago)

John Pritscher
President
Community Investment Corporation
(Chicago)

Paul Rasmussen
Planner
Bucher, Willis, and Ratliff
(Aurora)

Elspeth Revere
Program Officer
John D. and Catherine T.
   MacArthur Foundation
(Chicago)

Michael Roche
Executive Director
Housing Coalition of
the Southern Suburbs
(Homewood)

Hipolito (Paul) Roldan
President
Hispanic Housing
Development Corp.
(Chicago)

James E. Rosenbaum
Professor
School of Education and Social
Policy and Department of
Sociology
Northwestern University
(Evanston)

Don Samuelson
Don S. Samuelson Associates
(Lake Villa)

Barbara Shaw
Coordinator of Housing
Policy Initiatives
Community Investment Corporation
(Chicago)

Darren Sloniger
Director, Real Estate Development
Bethel New Life, Inc.
(Chicago)

Philip Smith
Chief Planner
DuPage County Regional
Planning Commission
(Wheaton)

Donna R. Smithey
Executive Director
Peoples Housing
(Chicago)

Nancy A. Stevenson
Member, Board of Trustees
University of Chicago

Betty L. Tenorio
Executive Director
Spanish Coalition for Housing
(Chicago)

Nikolas Theodore
Economic Development Specialist
Chicago Urban League

Carole J. Travis
President, Local 719
United Auto Workers
(LaGrange)

Richard Walsh
President
Illinois State Federation of Labor
(Springfield)

Wim Wiewel
Director
Center for Urban
Economic Development
University of Illinois at Chicago

Kale Williams
Executive Director
Leadership Council for Metropolitan
Open Communities
(Chicago)

Patricia Wright
Associate Director
Voorhees Center for Neighborhood
and Community Improvement
University of Illinois at Chicago

Timothy W. Wright
Attorney
Sachnoff and Weaver, Ltd.
(Chicago)

Julius Y. Yacker
Attorney
Miller, Shakman, Hamilton,
and Kurtzon
(Chicago)

Observers

Jean Allard
President
Metropolitan Planning Council
(Chicago)

John Foster-Bey
Community Initiatives Program
John D. and Catherine T.
    MacArthur Foundation
(Chicago)

Kent Lawrence
President, M. R. Bauer Foundation
(Chicago)

Patrick Reardon
Chicago Tribune

Rebecca Riley
Director, Community
    Initiatives Program
John D. and Catherine T.
    MacArthur Foundation
(Chicago)

James Tickell
Housing Corporation of
    the United Kingdom

****

Associate Director,
    Chicago Assembly

Lawrence B. Joseph
Associate Director
Center for Urban Research
    and Policy Studies
University of Chicago

Project Associate

Deborah C. Stone
Executive Director
Metropolitan Planning Council

Staff

Patrick Barry
Freelance writer

Amy Keller
School of Social Service
    Administration
University of Chicago

Susan Smith
School of Social Service
    Administration
University of Chicago

****

Drafting Committee

Eduardo Camacho**
Pat Dowell-Cerasoli**
Thomas Fuechtmann*
Douglas Gills
Kathleen Gilmer*
Elizabeth Hollander*
Thomas Lenz
Jennifer Miller
Lynn Montei**
Philip Nyden*

Michael Roche**
Paul Roldan
Don Samuelson
Barbara Shaw
Donna Smithey**
Nikolas Theodore**
Wim Wiewel*
Timothy Wright*

Lawrence B. Joseph (Chair)
Patrick Barry (Staff writer)

* Discussion leader
** Recorder

CHICAGO ASSEMBLY PLANNING COMMITTEE "AFFORDABLE HOUSING IN METROPOLITAN CHICAGO"

Anthony Austin
Vice President for Housing
Bethel New Life, Inc.
(Chicago)

*Larry Bennett
Associate Professor
Department of Political Science
DePaul University
(Chicago)

Marion Coleman
Executive Director
Covenant Development Corp.
(Chicago)

Kristin Faust
Vice President
Community Development
    Department
LaSalle National Bank
(Chicago)

Barbara Gordon
Executive Director
Lake County Community
    Action Project
(Waukegan)

Jennifer Gordon
Assistant to the Governor
State of Illinois
(Springfield)

William W. Higginson
President
Chicago Equity Fund

Thomas Lenz
Program Director
Local Initiatives Support Corp.
(Chicago)

Charles Orlebeke
Professor
School of Urban Planning
    and Policy
University of Illinois at Chicago

Michael Roche
Executive Director
Housing Coalition of
    the Southern Suburbs
(Homewood)

Donna Smithey
Executive Director
Peoples Housing
(Chicago)

*Carole J. Travis
President
Local 719
United Auto Workers
(LaGrange)

Laurina Uribe
Vice President and
    Director of Housing
Chicago United, Inc.

*Timothy W. Wright III
Attorney
Sachnoff and Weaver, Ltd.
(Chicago)

* Member of Chicago Assembly Advisory Board

CHICAGO ASSEMBLY ADVISORY BOARD